CHRONIC
HOPE

CHRONIC HOPE

God's Redeeming Presence in the Midst of Pain

PATTI BURNETT

XULON PRESS

Xulon Press
555 Winderley Pl, Suite 225
Maitland, FL 32751
407.339.4217
www.xulonpress.com

© 2024 by Patti Burnett

All rights reserved solely by the author. The author guarantees all contents are original and do not infringe upon the legal rights of any other person or work. No part of this book may be reproduced in any form without the permission of the author.

Due to the changing nature of the Internet, if there are any web addresses, links, or URLs included in this manuscript, these may have been altered and may no longer be accessible. The views and opinions shared in this book belong solely to the author and do not necessarily reflect those of the publisher. The publisher therefore disclaims responsibility for the views or opinions expressed within the work.

Scriptures marked AMP are from THE HOLY BIBLE, AMPLIFIED BIBLE, Copyright © 2015 by The Lockman Foundation, La Habra, CA 90631. All rights reserved. For Permission to Quote information visit http://www.lockman.org/.

Scriptures marked ESV are from The Holy Bible, English Standard Version. ESV® Text Edition: 2016. Copyright © 2001 by Crossway Bibles, a publishing ministry of Good News Publishers.

Scriptures marked PHILLIPS are from The New Testament in Modern English by J.B Phillips copyright © 1960, 1972 J. B. Phillips. Administered by The Archbishops' Council of the Church of England. Used by Permission.

Scriptures marked KJV are from the King James Version of the Bible. (Public domain.)

Scriptures marked MESSAGE are from the Message Bible, Copyright © 1993, 2002, 2018 by Eugene H. Peterson.

Scriptures marked NASB are from the New American Standard Bible®, Copyright © 1960, 1971, 1977, 1995, 2020 by The Lockman Foundation. All rights reserved.

Scriptures marked NET are from the New English Translation, NET Bible® copyright ©1996-2017 by Biblical Studies Press, L.L.C. http://netbible.com All rights reserved.

Scriptures marked NIV are from THE HOLY BIBLE, NEW INTERNATIONAL VERSION®, NIV® Copyright © 1973, 1978, 1984, 2011 by Biblica, Inc.® Used by permission. All rights reserved worldwide.

Scripture marked NKJV are taken from the New King James Version®. Copyright © 1982 by Thomas Nelson. Used by permission. All rights reserved.

Scriptures marked NLT are from the Holy Bible, New Living Translation, copyright © 1996, 2004, 2015 by Tyndale House Foundation. Used by permission of Tyndale House Publishers, Inc., Carol Stream, Illinois 60188. All rights reserved.

Scriptures marked RSV are from the Holy Bible, Revised Standard Version of the Bible, copyright © 1946, 1952, and 1971 the Division of Christian Education of the National Council of the Churches of Christ in the United States of America. Used by permission. All rights reserved.

Scriptures marked TLB are from The Living Bible copyright © 1971 by Tyndale House Foundation. Used by permission of Tyndale House Publishers Inc., Carol Stream, Illinois 60188. All rights reserved.

Scriptures marked WYC are from the Holy Bible, Wycliffe Bible, 2001 by Terence P. Noble.

Paperback ISBN-13: 978-1-66287-944-9
eBook ISBN-13: 978-1-66287-945-6

This book is dedicated to Mom and Dad Toth.
Thank you for the way you faithfully taught and embodied the value and sustainability of the Word of God.
Your actions spoke volumes and caused me to hunger and thirst after God's Word.
It is truly sweeter than honey.

I would also like to thank Bethany, Rachel, Nick, Sage, and my amazing grandchildren – Jaxson, Noah, Maverick, and Emerson.

You've taught me unconditional love, grace, and the faith of a child.

You have brought light during those times when everything around me seemed dark.

You are a beacon of hope and promise for this next generation.

Thank you, Salem, for your wiliness to patiently navigate me through the publishing process. You more than exceeded my expectations.
I appreciate your not giving up on me and my many limitations and weaknesses.

I especially shout out huge love, appreciation, and praise for my husband and hero, Dan.

I never could have finished Chronic Hope or even walked this Parkinson's Road without you and your constant care, support, and encouragement.

And most significantly, without the guidance of the Holy Spirit and His step-by-step leadership through each crisis, "Chronic Hope" would never have made it out of my little laptop. It's my prayer that through each story, bible passage, song, quote, and testimonial the praise is given to the only One deserving of praise, my Lord and Savior, Jesus Christ.

"Sustain me according to Your word, that I may live;

And do not let me be ashamed of my hope.

Uphold me that I may be safe, That I may have regard for Your statutes continually."

Psalm 119:116-117 (NASB)

Table of Contents

Introduction ix

Chapter 1: All Creation Groans 1
Chapter 2: Is Your Cross Too Heavy? 13
Chapter 3: Have You Given Up All Hope? 23
Chapter 4: The Purpose of Your Pain 35
Chapter 5: No Dropped Calls 53
Chapter 6: A Lamp Unto My Feet 67
Chapter 7: When Christ Calls a Man or a Woman,
 He Bids Them Come and Die 99
Chapter 8: From a Cradle to The Cross 111
Chapter 9: He Has Risen, Just as He Said 121
Chapter 10: Even If He Doesn't 133
Chapter 11: It's a Miracle 145
Chapter 12: Ya Gotta Have Faith 161
Chapter 13: Trust and Obey 183
Chapter 14: Don't Allow Your Pain to Eclipse
 God's Blessings 209
Chapter 15: Emptied of All But Him 217
Chapter 16: The Exact Representation .231
Chapter 17: Pain Compounds Fear Exponentially 239
Chapter 18: Rescue Me 255
Chapter 19: He Is My Refuge and Fortress
 In The Storm 273

Chapter 20: P T L 287
Chapter 21: It Takes The Body of Chrsit......................307
Chapter 22: The Greatest of These is Love 325
Chapter 23: My Grace is Sufficient For You 345
Chapter 24: Post Traumatic Growth 351
Chapter 25: Pain – A Conduit For Moving Head Knowledge
  to Heart Knowledge..............................369
Chapter 26: Be a Wise Guy....................................383
Chapter 27: The Master Teacher 397
Chapter 28: Teach Your Children (And Parents) Well 411
Chapter 29: Her Worth is Far Above Jewels...................433
Chapter 30: The Kingdom of Heaven is Like ... .441
Chapter 31: Lead On 453
Chapter 32: And Death Shall Be No More......................461
Chapter 33: It Will Be Worth it All When
  We See Jesus 471
Chapter 34: From Here To Eternity...........................487
Chapter 35: I Will Be Their God and They Will
Be My People..503
Chapter 36: Our God is an Awesome God.......................517

Epilogue 529

Introduction

"Pain insists upon being attended to. God whispers to us in our pleasures, speaks in our consciences, but shouts in our pains. It is His megaphone to rouse a deaf world." C.S. Lewis [1]

DEALING WITH PAIN in our lives, and in that of those we love, opens our hearts and our ears to the reality of God and the question of why He allows these interruptions to our comfortable existence. More than any other time, we become attentive to His message. A myriad of hospitalizations for myself and loved ones, and the deaths of three of our parents over the course of two years provided impetus for **"Chronic Hope: God's Redeeming Presence in the Midst of Pain."**

Many might say "You don't know how much pain I have endured in my life." You're right; I don't. But I might be able to empathize. My injuries and illnesses started out relatively benign, mostly knee issues common for ski patrollers and runners; but to lend some credibility to my expertise in the pain arena, here's my laundry list of most of my injuries and illnesses:

1. Severe allergic reaction to surgical drape
2. Total Knee Replacement and Manipulation Under Anesthesia following multiple reconstructions and arthroscopes
3. Neck fusion from motor vehicle accident
4. Epiretinal Membrane surgery, followed by three cataract surgeries

---

[1] C.S. Lewis, The Problem of Pain (London: The Centenary Press, 1940), 91.

5. Bilateral Inguinal Hernia surgery with mesh intermingled with internal organs complication
6. Surgical cyst removal in lower back
7. Autonomic Dominant Polycystic Kidney Disease
8. Small Intestine Bacterial Overgrowth – two ER visits
9. Collapsed lung from cortisone injection
10. Hemothorax/Pneumothorax and broken ribs sustained in back country injury
11. Pneumonia
12. Nearly fatal infected kidney
13. Broken nose with Deviated Septum surgery
14. Double vision
15. Hiatal Hernia surgery, GERD, and Burning Mouth Syndrome
16. Multiple shoulder injuries including a fractured humeral head
17. Toe fractures
19. Deep Brain Stimulation surgery scheduled this summer
20. Parkinson's Disease, neurodegenerative condition affecting every bodily system

You might be thinking, "Wow girl; you are a mess."

Little did I realize that an incident from nearly 50 years ago would so profoundly impact my life today. In 1973, long before I knew anything about personal pain, I visited a friend in hospice with brain cancer; we'll call him Mike. In my limited experience, I had never seen anyone so close to death; and I expected that my job would be to cheer him up, to help him forget about his troubles.

Well, was I ever wrong! My friend's one question could be summed up in ten simple words – "Where was God in the midst of all this pain?" Staking his life on the reality of the one and only God of this universe, Mike's single focus was to quickly learn as much as possible about his Creator. His shell of a body and this earthly existence no longer held any attraction or promise for the future. His eyes, heart, and mind were fixed on a true north orientation.

Introduction

There was no small talk. He didn't care about the weather unless it meant delaying his teleportation to heaven. His body, shriveled down to a mere 100 pounds, would be changed in the twinkling of an eye. He figured that when he received a new body, he'd probably trade his hospital gown in for the slick heavenly garments he'd wear to his first seating at the Lord's table. My guess is that however he was clad, he'd look amazing, and no one would be able to wipe the grin off his face.

Mike's motivation was pure and simple: an intense session of concentrating on the hope that He had in Jesus Christ and to learn more about what came next. What a privilege to be a messenger of the magnificent Word of Life. I have often thought back to that day, hoping that he would have returned to us just long enough to tell us what it was like. My guess is that once he saw His Savior's face, there'd be no turning back.

Those sacred moments in the hospital with Mike opened my eyes to a profound truth. With the veil between life and death both immanent and thin, a deep longing to communicate with God is pronounced, literally. In this sacred moment, I wished I could have had a resource to turn to with messages from God that would speak to this desire. Such was the origin of **"Chronic Hope."**

It's one thing to attend to the needs of a friend; it's quite another to care for a family member, especially a parent. A guide like **"Chronic Hope"** would have been particularly powerful the last week of my mom's life, as my family and I stood vigil. Her health had been slowly declining. However, at this time, the only doctor she wished to meet was the Chief Surgeon.

Despite Mom's ailments, there was one area of her life that was never compromised. She loved her Savior and Redeemer and never missed an opportunity to let others know of His love for them. During her final week on earth, the nurses would often ask how she was feeling; and inevitably her response would be "Nothing to complain about. How 'bout you Sweety?" That was my mom, always caring more about others than herself and her many aches and pains.

One of Mom's most annoying dementia symptoms was perseverating – asking the same question time after time after time after time after time after time after time – you get it. One of the things they say about Alzheimer's and dementia is that it tends to bring out a person's inherent temperament. That was undoubtedly the case with Mom. From the early days of their marriage, she and Dad had always started each morning's breakfast time studying a favorite devotional that was marked by highlighters, post-its, bookmarks, cards, and written notes; they loved God's Word. In Mom's case, her perseveration was of memorized Bible passages. Following were some of Dorothy H. Toth's favorites:

- Be anxious for nothing, but in everything by prayer and supplication with thanksgiving let your requests be made known to God. And the peace of God, which surpasses all comprehension, will guard your hearts and your minds in Christ Jesus. (Philippians 4:6-7 NASB)
- The steadfast of mind You will keep in perfect peace because he trusts in You. (Isaiah 26:3 NASB)
- So we confidently say, "The Lord is my helper, I will not be afraid. What will man do to me?" (Hebrews 13:6 NASB)

In fact, when I was looking through Mom and Dad's scrapbooks and loose photos recently, I found a sheet protector with these very verses written in Mom's beautiful penmanship.

One of the last days of her life, I was down in the hospital coffee shop buying a round of lattes for siblings. I heard over the PA "Code One Stat in ICU." It was Mom's room. I prayed, running up the stairs. I'd responded to many Code One's in my ski patrol and search and rescue careers, but never for my own Mom. The medical crash team was able to resuscitate her, but she looked so exhausted. Her body had just about given 100%. We all wondered why the Lord was delaying her homecoming.

Introduction

The next morning, driving to the hospital, God orchestrated the sun's approach preceded by an amazing beam that rose on the horizon like a spotlight. When its radiance hit the shelf of clouds, it painted a horizontal line illustrating an iridescent cross, as from the Master Artist's own hand. Yet, my mom, so humble, so self-deprecating, would never have asked for such a grand, red-carpet entrance into heaven. What a beautiful message to my family from the heart of God! He said, "I've got this – she's mine!"

Mom's support group was six children and their six spouses, 20 grandchildren, 36 great grandchildren and counting. That evening most of us gathered at the hospital. The lead nurse moved Mom to a larger room to handle our standing room only crowd. My family loves music and we broke into some acapella, impromptu singing; and I guess it must have sounded okay as I watched the smiles and tears in the eyes of the hospital staff and patients.

The next day Dan and I took Dad into Rochester to have the battery in his pacemaker replaced. Dad was under too much stress to put this off any longer. During his appointment, we received a call that Mom had gone home to heaven.

Driving back to Canandaigua, we told Dad about Mom's homecoming. Amazingly enough, none of us cried - finally no more pain.

My brother, Chip, likes to think of loved ones' deaths and departures as just a temporary separation, "Almost like they are leaving for New Jersey, and we'll be following closely behind and will meet them there." Personally, I have a hard time likening heaven to New Jersey. Hawaii or Switzerland maybe. But New Jersey?

The three of us knew beyond a shadow of a doubt that Mom had arrived safely at her eternal destination. I imagined Mom's jubilation to hear the words "Well done, good and faithful servant … Come and share your Master's joy!"

About a year after my mom's death, we received a call that my husband's mother, Lois, was in intensive care. She had fallen and broken a hip and hand and never regained consciousness following her surgery.

She had probably suffered numerous strokes; and despite her lack of cognitive engagement, I had good opportunities to read to Mom B. the last week of her life.

It is well documented that when people are unconscious or in comas, they are sometimes able to hear voices. There have been numerous studies conducted using electroencephalograms that detect activity in the brain. Some of the studies analyzed differences in the brain's response to tone and pattern changes for healthy patients, conscious hospice patients, and hospice patients who were actively dying and unresponsive. The unresponsive patients all showed neural auditory perception and attention to tone changes, and some even displayed attention to pattern changes. Researchers concluded that, for at least some unresponsive hospice patients, their brains continued to process auditory information, even when they did not respond in a notable way.

It's my prayer that Mom B. was soothed by the comforting Word of God. Who better to minister to her during this time of uncertainty than her Creator and the Lover of her soul?

A year later, as I was working on this book, we received a call that my dad was not doing well; he wouldn't eat or drink and was just holding on by a thread. Dad was just weeks away from turning 95. Since my mom's passing, he had changed, sometimes to the point of appearing catatonic. He rarely responded when spoken to; but I think his mind and heart were in a different time and place. A few years earlier, he had mentioned that he hoped God would keep him alive long enough to care for Mom in her last days.

For his final day, my sister, Nancy, read to Dad from the Psalms and prayed and sang worship songs. All the while Dad was placing all his hope in God's promise to carry him "across the river." My brother, Steve, sent a text to my siblings and me early that Sunday morning. It read "Dad's home."

The final reason for this book is personal. I need to understand where my Heavenly Father is amid my pain. God has been good to me and if "what doesn't kill you makes you stronger," I must be pretty

Introduction

strong. As was alluded to earlier in this introduction, I have helped to pay many hospitals' mortgages and I have probably overstayed my visit numerous times.

Through it all, there has been one clear message indelibly engraved on my heart and in my head. I have learned that medical facilities are one of the best places to better appreciate this **"Chronic Hope"** we have, that our God is right there with us amid our pain.

Some people may ask "If God's Word is so applicable to an injured or ailing person, where do you start reading?" Perhaps Genesis 1:1, that describes creation? But as you get further along in the Old Testament, I know you would rather not read about bulls being slaughtered and having their blood splashed on the temple altar. That is a little too close to home for the hospital bound. And who wants to study how Satan infected Job from the soles of his feet to the crown of his head; and then Job took a piece of broken pottery to scrape himself as he sat among the ashes? Probably not good dermatology protocol.

However, there are many, many Bible verses that can be a source of great comfort to the wounded and ailing. My dream is that you will be able to select chapters from this book that most appropriately address your unique needs, or those of your loved ones. Obviously, this is not a comprehensive list, and it was never intended to replace your Bible. But perhaps, as the occasion presents itself, you will be able to read chapters from **"Chronic Hope: God's Redeeming Presence in the Midst of Pain"** either to yourself or one of your loved ones. I pray that you will be comforted.

I have tried to categorize and separate Bible verses topically. I have also included song lyrics, excerpts from other books, poems, quotes from famous people and some not so famous people, me included. Much of my writing is living well despite the challenges of Parkinson's.

Enjoy and be blessed! Patti

Chapter 1

ALL CREATION GROANS

OH, VISIT THE EARTH, ASK HER TO JOIN THE DANCE! *Deck her out in spring showers, fill the God-River with living water. Paint the wheat fields golden. Creation was made for this! Drench the plowed fields, soak the dirt clods with rainfall as harrow and rake bring her to blossom and fruit. Snow-crown the peaks with splendor, scatter rose petals down your paths, all through the wild meadows, rose petals. Set the hills to dancing, Dress the canyon walls with live sheep, a drape of flax across the valleys. Let them shout, and shout, and shout! Oh, oh, let them sing! (Psalm 65:9-11 Message)*

PATTI BURNETT

WHEN GOD ORCHESTRATED CREATION, He assembled an amazing Masterpiece. However, in no time at all, Adam and Eve made a decision that would impact generations to come – in fact, the entire human race.

Even as we anticipate eternity and a new heaven and a new earth, so does all of creation. We patiently await our redemption; okay, maybe not so patiently.

It is thought that many, if not all, of our diseases today are a result of the toxins we have put into the food, ground water and air; we are literally poisoning ourselves. This is so much not what God had in mind for His original creation. Romans 8 says that all of creation groans, even as a woman groans in the throes of childbirth. This is a direct result of sin.

> Chuck Smith, in his commentary, says that "The picture I get is that we are in the 'quarry of life' and we are being shaped into the image of Christ ... But all that does not look like Him in our lives is going to be chipped off us as God conforms us into His image while we are in this quarry. The tools that God uses are the "trials" and the "pain" and the "suffering" that is in this world. One day when we see His "finished work" we will be amazed and realize it was worth it all."

But, until that day, we have a tenacious hope that the best is yet to come. Come quickly, Lord Jesus.

THEN GOD SAID, "LET US MAKE MAN IN OUR IMAGE, according to our likeness; let them have dominion over the fish of the sea, over the birds of the air, and over the cattle, over all the earth and over every creeping thing that creeps on the earth." So God created man in His own image; in the image of God He created him; male and female

He created them. Then God blessed them, and God said to them, "Be fruitful and multiply; fill the earth and subdue it; have dominion over the fish of the sea, over the birds of the air, and over every living thing that moves on the earth."

And God said, "See, I have given you every herb that yields seed which is on the face of all the earth, and every tree whose fruit yields seed; to you it shall be for food. Also, to every beast of the earth, to every bird of the air, and to everything that creeps on the earth, in which there is life, I have given every green herb for food"; and it was so. Then God saw everything that He had made, and indeed it was very good. So the evening and the morning were the sixth day. (Genesis 1:26-31 NKJV)

R.C. SPROUL

The very word authority has within it the word author. An author is someone who creates and possesses a particular work. Insofar as God is the foundation of all authority, He exercises that foundation because He is the author and the owner of His creation. He is the foundation upon which all other authority stands or falls.[2]

O LORD, OUR LORD, How majestic and glorious and excellent is Your name in all the earth!

> You have displayed Your splendor above the heavens.
> Out of the mouths of infants and nursing babes
> You have established strength
> Because of Your adversaries,
> That You might silence the enemy and make the revengeful cease.

---

[2] R.C. Sproul, The Divine Foundation of Authority (Philadelphia: Tabletalk Magazine, March 2009), 6.

When I see and consider your heavens, the work of Your finger,
The moon and the stars, which You have established,
What is man that You are mindful of Him,
And the son of [earthborn] man that You care for Him?
Yet You have made Him a little lower than God,
And You have crowned Him with glory and honor.
You made Him to have dominion over the works of Your hands;
You have put all things under His feet,
All sheep and oxen,
And also the beasts of the field,
The birds of the air, and the fish of the sea,
Whatever passes through the paths of the seas.
O Lord, our Lord,

How majestic and glorious and excellent is Your name in all the earth. (Psalm 8:1-9 AMP)

> ### *JOHN PIPER*
> If created things are seen and handled as gifts of God and as mirrors of His glory, they need not be occasions of idolatry - if our delight in them is always also a delight in their Maker.[3]

---
[3] John Piper, Desiring God (New York: Crown Publishing Group, 1996), 143.

THE MIGHTY ONE, GOD, THE LORD, HAS SPOKEN,

And summoned the earth from the rising of the sun to its setting [from east to west].
Out of Zion, the perfection of beauty,
God has shone forth.
May our God come and not keep silent;
Fire devours before Him,
And around Him a mighty tempest rages.
He summons the heavens above,
And the earth, to judge His people:
"Gather My godly ones to Me,
Those who have made a covenant with Me by sacrifice."
And the heavens declare His righteousness,
For God Himself is judge. Selah.
"Hear, O My people, and I will speak;
O Israel, I will testify against you:
I am God, your God.
"I do not reprove you for your sacrifices;
Your burnt offerings are continually before Me.
"I will accept no young bull from your house
Nor male goat from your folds.
"For every beast of the forest is Mine,
And the cattle on a thousand hills.
"I know every bird of the mountains,
And everything that moves in the field is Mine.
"If I were hungry, I would not tell you,
For the world and all it contains are Mine.
"Shall I eat the flesh of bulls
Or drink the blood of male goats?
"Offer to God the sacrifice of thanksgiving
And pay your vows to the Most High;
Call on Me in the day of trouble;
I will rescue you, and you shall honor and glorify Me.
(Psalm 50:1-15 AMP)

> ## JEREMY TAYLOR
> What can be more foolish than to think that all this rare fabric of heaven and earth could come by chance, when all the skill of art is not able to make an oyster.[4]

LORD, YOU HAVE BEEN OUR DWELLING PLACE THROUGHOUT ALL GENERATIONS.
Before the mountains were born
or You brought forth the whole world,
From everlasting to everlasting, You are God. (Psalm 90:1-2 NASB)

> ## JOHN MACARTHUR
> God made all of his creation to give. He made the sun, the moon, the stars, the clouds, the earth, the plants to give. He also designed his supreme creation, man, to give. But fallen man is the most reluctant giver in all of God's creation.[5]

WHEN ISRAEL WENT OUT OF EGYPT,
The house of Jacob from a people of strange language,
Judah became His sanctuary,
And Israel His dominion.
The sea saw it and fled;
Jordan turned back.
The mountains skipped like rams,

---

[4] Maturin Murray Ballou quoting Jeremy Taylor, Treasury of Thought: Forming an Encyclopedia of Quotations (Boston: Houghton, Mifflin, 1884), 261.

[5] J. MacArthur, The Biblical View on Abortion – Part 2 Grace to You, August 30, 1992, from www.gty.org/Resources/Sermons/90-68)

The little hills like lambs.
What ails you, O sea, that you fled?
O Jordan, that you turned back?
O mountains, that you skipped like rams?
O little hills, like lambs?
Tremble, O earth, at the presence of the Lord,
At the presence of the God of Jacob,
Who turned the rock into a pool of water,
The flint into a fountain of waters. (Psalm 114:1-8 NKJV)

> ### MAX LUCADO
> You weren't an accident. You weren't mass produced. You aren't an assembly-line product. You were deliberately planned, specifically gifted, and lovingly positioned on the Earth by the Master Craftsman.[6]

LORD, YOU HAVE SEARCHED ME AND KNOWN ME.
You know when I sit down and when I get up;
You understand my thoughts from far away.
You scrutinize my path and my lying down,
And are acquainted with all my ways.
Even before there is a word on my tongue,
Behold, Lord, You know it all.
You have encircled me behind and in front,
And placed Your hand upon me.
Such knowledge is too wonderful for me;
It is too high, I cannot comprehend it.

---

[6] Max Lucado, Let the Journey Begin: God's Roadmap for New Beginnings (Nashville: Thomas Nelson Inc., 2015), 67.

CHRONIC HOPE

Where can I go from Your Spirit?
Or where can I flee from Your presence?
If I ascend to heaven, You are there;
If I make my bed in Sheol, behold, You are there.
If I take up the wings of the dawn,
If I dwell in the remotest part of the sea,
Even there Your hand will lead me,
And Your right hand will lay hold of me.
If I say, "Surely the darkness will overwhelm me,
And the light around me will be night,"
Even darkness is not dark to You,
And the night is as bright as the day.
Darkness and light are alike to You.

For You created my innermost parts;
You wove me in my mother's womb.
I will give thanks to You, because I am awesomely and
wonderfully made;
Wonderful are Your works, and my soul knows it very well.
My frame was not hidden from You, when I was made in secret,
and skillfully formed in the depths of the earth;
Your eyes have seen my formless substance;
And in Your book were written
The days that were ordained for me,
When as yet there was not one of them.

How precious also are Your thoughts for me, God!
How vast is the sum of them!
Were I to count them, they would outnumber the sand.
When I awake, I am still with You.

Search me, God, and know my heart;
Put me to the test and know my anxious thoughts;
And see if there is any hurtful way in me,

and lead me in the everlasting way. (Psalm 139:1-18, 23-24 NASB)

NEW MORNING MERCIES, JANUARY 29th, PAUL DAVID TRIPP

Today your heart will search for satisfaction. Will you look for it in the creation or in relationship to the Creator? It was obvious what was happening, but not to him. What he was trying to do would never work. I was his gardener, and I was at the base of his property, near the entrance, when he drove in with yet another new car. I had seen him do this same thing again and again. In fact, he was quickly running out of room. As he hopped out of his expensive new toy, he asked me what I thought. I said, "I don't think it's working." He said, "I don't know what you're talking about, it's a brand-new car." I said, "I think what you're trying to do will never work." He said, "I have no idea what you're trying to say to me." I asked, "How many cars is it going to take before you realize that an automobile has no capacity whatsoever to satisfy your heart?" Disappointed, he said, "Boy, you're raining on my parade …"

The glories of the created world are meant to be glorious, but they are not meant to be the thing that you look to for life. No, all the glories of the created world together are meant to be one big finger that points you to the God of glory, who made each one of them and is alone able to give you life. Worshiping the creation is never a pathway to life; it leads you in the opposite direction. Today you will give your life to something. Will it be the Creator, whose grace alone can satisfy and transform your heart, or the creation, which was designed to do neither?[7]

"TO WHOM THEN WILL YOU LIKEN ME,
Or to whom shall I be equal?" says the Holy One.
Lift up your eyes on high,
And see who has created these things,

---

[7] Paul David Tripp, New Morning Mercies: A Daily Gospel Devotional (Wheaton: Crossway, 2014), 29.

Who brings out their host by number;
He calls them all by name,
By the greatness of His might
And the strength of His power;
Not one is missing.
Why do you say, O Jacob,
And speak, O Israel:
"My way is hidden from the Lord,
And my just claim is passed over by my God?"
Have you not known?
Have you not heard?
The everlasting God, the Lord,
The Creator of the ends of the earth,
Neither faints nor is weary.
His understanding is unsearchable.
He gives power to the weak,
And to those who have no might He increases strength.
Even the youths shall faint and be weary,
And the young men shall utterly fall,
But those who wait on the Lord
Shall renew their strength;
They shall mount up with wings like eagles,
They shall run and not be weary,
They shall walk and not faint. (Isaiah 40:25-31 NKJV)

A.W. TOZER

God dwells in His creation and is everywhere indivisibly present in all His works. He is transcendent above all His works even while He is immanent within them.[8]

---

[8] A. W. Tozer, The Pursuit of God: The Human Thirst for the Divine (Columbus: Beta Nu Publishing, 1948), 57-58.

LORD, I HAVE HEARD THE REPORT ABOUT YOU AND I FEAR.
O Lord, revive Your work in the midst of the years,
In the midst of the years make it known;
In wrath remember mercy.

God comes from Teman,
And the Holy One from Mount Paran. Selah.
His splendor covers the heavens,
And the earth is full of His praise.
His radiance is like the sunlight;
He has rays flashing from His hand,
And there is the hiding of His power.
Before Him goes pestilence,
And plague comes after Him.
He stood and surveyed the earth;
He looked and startled the nations.
Yes, the perpetual mountains were shattered,
The ancient hills collapsed.
His ways are everlasting.
I saw the tents of Cushan under distress,
The tent curtains of the land of Midian were trembling.

Did the Lord rage against the rivers,
Or was Your anger against the rivers,
Or was Your wrath against the sea,
That You rode on Your horses,
On Your chariots of salvation?
Your bow was made bare,
The rods of chastisement were sworn. Selah.
You cleaved the earth with rivers.
The mountains saw You and quaked;
The downpour of waters swept by.
The deep uttered forth its voice,
It lifted high its hands.
Sun and moon stood in their places;
They went away at the light of Your arrows,
At the radiance of Your gleaming spear. (Habakkuk 3:3-11 NASB)

Chapter 2

IS YOUR CROSS TOO HEAVY?

I HAVE BEEN CRUCIFIED WITH CHRIST; and it is no longer I who live, but Christ lives in me; and the life which I now live in the flesh I live by faith in the Son of God, Who loved me and gave Himself up for me. I do not nullify the grace of God, for if righteousness comes through the Law, then Christ died needlessly." (Galatians 2:20-21 NASB)

__PATTI BURNETT__

I WAS WORKING AT A CHIROPRACTIC OFFICE when I first noticed a tremor in my foot; the diagnosis of Parkinson's was confirmed by one of our doctors. I was not totally surprised. My brother, Dave, had been diagnosed a few years earlier; but I was still scared and anxious about what the future held. I found myself bombarding God with multiple questions? Would I be able to dance at my grandchildren's wedding? Could I stay as active as I had been with marathon running, skiing, and biking? I naturally feared the prospect of cognition issues; there were so many unknowns. Who did I trust with such vulnerable information? How fast would this disease progress? What were my resources?

I was overwhelmed and felt as though my wonderfully ordinary life was collapsing; and I just stood back, as an observer, and helplessly watched from a distance. Where was God in all this? Did He care? Should I keep this from my elderly parents who had many medical challenges themselves? Being somewhat of a control freak, this was a very uncomfortable place for me.

In May of 2013 a general neurologist asked me what I thought I had – I told him – he agreed. His nonchalant attitude was off-putting. He immediately prescribed Sinemet to confirm the PD diagnosis. That seemed odd to me; I had done enough research to know that Parkinson's medications had a lengthy list of side effects. Now, as I look back, I regret not advocating for myself to get a DaTscan instead. These Parkinson's drugs are far more dangerous than the MDS (Movement Disorder Specialist) let on and the side effects can be devastating.

I made an appointment with an MDS at University of Colorado Health. Dr. K. told me that I did not have bad enough symptoms to require Sinemet and a dopamine agonist and an MAO B inhibitor would suffice.

Somehow at the end of this visit, even though it wasn't scheduled, we were able to see Cari, a UCH social worker. What a gift she was to us. She tried to explain that our lives were not over - we were just going to experience a dramatic paradigm shift. With trepidation we asked many questions. Little did we realize that each person's PD is unique—there are different causes, different treatments, different progressions, and different meds.

We left UCH feeling much more confident, but we knew there would be much to learn. I was most appreciative of my husband and care partner, Dan, and the strong support and love he demonstrated during perhaps the hardest time in my life. We had already been through some challenges, but this next hurdle was going to push us nearly to the limit. I'm glad it's Dan I'm stuck with - I know that he will be there no matter what. There's so much comfort in that reassurance, even if at times he is overprotective.

I would learn later that Cari, Dr. K. and Dan would be just the initial members of my amazingly valuable support team. As each new challenge presented itself, I sought out the assistance of yet other specialists, family members or friends. These people proved to be my life blood.

When I am feeling especially sorry for myself, I remember that there are others who do not have this amazing band of friends and family to help them carry the Parkinson's burden. I also try to imagine Jesus' last days on earth, betrayed by some of His best friends, left to die on a cross, and buried in a cold dark cave. His own Father turned His back on Him.

We read in Acts 5, that some of the apostles, after being flogged, went on their way from the presence of the Council, rejoicing that they had been considered worthy to suffer shame for Christ's name. What a revolutionary concept – that I could be completing the suffering of Jesus, as it says in the Bible. It feels inconceivable, but also hopeful, that I could share in Christ's obedience to God the Father by going through trials and challenges in my life. This is all part of the paradigm shift mentioned earlier.

I am not suggesting that God caused my Parkinson's or that it in any way makes Him happy. I believe that our Creator is saddened by the way we have destroyed this world, and that someday it will be replaced with a New Heaven and New Earth - all things will become new. But, until then, who knows how many diseases result from the indiscriminate use of heavy metals, pesticides, herbicides, and chemicals. They are poisoning us daily.

My belief is that even though God did not create or design disease, He chooses to use these pains to mold me more and more into the image of Christ. It does no good to complain. Jesus knew that when He came to earth; His priority was to do the will of the Father — to redeem that which was lost, to reconcile people who were separated from God by their sin and especially by the sin of Adam and Eve's disobedience. Amazing! While we were still enemies of God, He sent His Son to die on a cross. On a historically well documented date in time He reconciled us to our Creator.

Forgive me for my pity parties Father. But, like my Redeemer, who asked that this cup would pass from Him, not my will, but Your will be done.

BUT IT IS NOT THIS WAY AMONG YOU; rather, whoever wants to become prominent among you shall be your servant; and whoever wants to be first among you shall be slave of all. For even the Son of Man did not come to be served, but to serve, and to give His life as a ransom for many." (Mark 10:43-45 NASB)

> ### PHILIP YANCEY
> Christ bears the wounds of the church, His body, just as He bore the wounds of crucifixion. I sometimes wonder which has hurt worse.[9]

---

[9] Philip Yancey What's So Amazing About Grace? (New York: HarperCollins Christian Publishing, 2003), 112.

WHEN THEY WERE NEARING JERUSALEM, at Bethphage and Bethany on Mount Olives, He sent off two of the disciples with instructions: "Go to the village across from you. As soon as you enter, you'll find a colt tethered, one that has never yet been ridden. Untie it and bring it. If anyone asks, 'What are you doing?' say, 'The Master needs him, and will return him right away.'"

They went and found a colt tied to a door at the street corner and untied it. Some of those standing there said, "What are you doing untying that colt?" The disciples replied exactly as Jesus had instructed them, and the people let them alone. They brought the colt to Jesus, spread their coats on it, and He mounted.

The people gave Him a wonderful welcome, some throwing their coats on the street, others spreading out rushes they had cut in the fields. Running ahead and following after, they were calling out,

> Hosanna!
> Blessed is he who comes in God's name!
> Blessed the coming kingdom of our father David!
> Hosanna in highest heaven!

He entered Jerusalem, then entered the Temple. He looked around, taking it all in. But by now it was late, so he went back to Bethany with the Twelve.

Jesus was matter of fact: "Embrace this God-life. Really embrace it, and nothing will be too much for you. This mountain, for instance: Just say, 'Go jump in the lake'—no shuffling or shilly-shallying—and it's as good as done. That's why I urge you to pray for absolutely everything, ranging from small to large. Include everything as you embrace this God-life, and you'll get God's everything. And when you assume the posture of prayer, remember that it's not all asking. If you have anything against someone, forgive—only then will your heavenly Father be inclined to also wipe your slate clean of sins." (Mark 11:1-11, 22-25 Message)

> **AMY CARMICHAEL**
> If I take offense easily; if I am content to continue in cold unfriendliness, though friendship be possible, then I know nothing of Calvary Love.[10]

AND WHEN THEY CAME TO THE PLACE CALLED THE SKULL, there they crucified Him and the criminals, one on the right and the other on the left. But Jesus was saying, "Father, forgive them; for they do not know what they are doing." (Luke 23:33-34 NASB)

> **UPWARD FALL, BRIAN MYERS**
> He owned the evil, all our sin, that we might own the good, to have all of Him, who wants all of us. For we now produce treasures in heaven by our labors on earth, advance to the substance of our gain by embracing the substance of His pain.[11]

BUT FAR BE IT FROM ME TO BOAST, except in the cross of our Lord Jesus Christ, through which the world has been crucified to me, and I to the world. For neither is circumcision anything, nor uncircumcision, but a new creation. And all who will follow this rule, peace and mercy be upon them, and upon the Israel of God.

From now on let no one cause trouble for me, for I bear on my body the marks of Jesus. The grace of our Lord Jesus Christ be with your spirit, brothers and sisters. Amen. (Galatians 6:14-18 NASB)

---

[10] Amy Carmichael, If: What do I Know of Calvary Love (Fort Washington: CLC, 2003), 34.

[11] Brian Myers, The Upward Fall: Our Pilgrim Journey Through Groaning to Glory (Portland: Dawson Media, 2013), 79.

***THE GIVING TREE, SHEL SILVERSTEIN*[12]**

Once, there was a tree...
And she loved a little boy.
And every day the boy would come
And he would gather her leaves
And make them into crowns and play king of the forest.
He would climb up her trunk
And swing from her branches
And eat apples
And they would play hide-and-go-seek.
And when he was tired, he would sleep in her shade.
And the boy loved the tree... very much...
And the tree was happy.

But time went by,
And the boy grew older.
And the tree was often alone.
Then, one day, the boy came to the tree and the tree said:
"Come, Boy, come and climb up my trunk and swing from my branches and eat apples and play in my shade and be happy!"
"I am too big to climb and play," said the boy. "I want to buy things and have fun. I want some money. Can you give me some money?"
"I'm sorry", said the tree, but I have no money. I have only leaves and apples. Take my apples, Boy, and sell them in the city. Then you will have money and you'll be happy."
And so the boy climbed up the tree and gathered her apples and carried them away.
And the tree was happy...

But the boy stayed away for a long time... and the tree was sad. And then one day the boy came back, and the tree shook with joy, and she said:

---

[12] Shel Silverstein, The Giving Tree (New York: Harper and Row Publishers, 1964).

"Come, Boy, come and climb up my trunk and swing from my branches and eat apples and play in my shade and be happy."
"I am too busy to climb trees," said the boy. "I want a house to keep me warm", he said. "and I want a wife and I want children, and so I need a house. Can you give me a house?"
"I have no house", said the tree. "The forest is my house", said the tree. "But you may cut off my branches and build a house. Then you will be happy".
And so the boy cut off her branches and carried them away to build his house. And the tree was happy.
But the boy stayed away for a long time…

And when he came back, the tree was so happy she could hardly speak.
"Come, Boy" she whispered, "Come and play".
"I am too old and sad to play", said the boy. "I want a boat that will take me away from here. Can you give me a boat?"
"Cut down my trunk and make a boat", said the tree. "Then you can sail away… and be happy".
And so the boy cut down her trunk
And made a boat and sailed away.
And the tree was happy…

But not really.
And after a long time, the boy came back again.
"I am sorry, Boy", said the tree, "but I have nothing left to give you – My apples are gone".
"My teeth are too weak for apples", said the boy.
"My branches are gone", said the tree. "You cannot swing on them".
"I am too old to swing on branches", said the boy.
"My trunk is gone", said the tree. "You cannot climb".
"I am too tired to climb", said the boy.
"I am sorry" sighed the tree. "I wish that I could give you something… but I have nothing left. I am just an old stump. I am sorry…"

"I don't need very much now", said the boy. "Just a quiet place to sit and rest. I am very tired".
"Well", said the tree, straightening herself up as much as she could, "well, an old stump is good for sitting and resting. Come, Boy, sit down… sit down and rest".
And the boy did.
And the tree was happy…
The End

Chapter 3

HAVE YOU GIVEN UP ALL HOPE?

BUT THOSE WHO HOPE IN THE LORD will renew their strength. They will soar on wings like eagles; they will run and not grow weary, they will walk and not be faint. (Isaiah 40:31 NIV)

PATTI BURNETT

AS CHRISTIANS, we find hope in the belief that God will keep His promises to us. If such is the case, we would be wise to discover the content of these covenants. Here are a few of the mere 7,147 promises God makes to those who choose to walk with Him:

- "Give thanks to the Lord, for He is good; For His faithfulness is everlasting." (I Chronicles 16:34 NASB)
- "For the Spirit God gave us does not make us timid, but gives us power, love and self-discipline." (II Timothy 1:7 NIV)
- "Let's hold firmly to the confession of our hope without wavering, for He who promised is faithful;" (Hebrews 10:23 NASB)
- "For I know the plans that I have for you, declares the Lord, plans for prosperity and not for disaster, to give you a future and a hope." (Jeremiah 29:11 NASB)
- "But those who hope in the Lord will renew their strength. They will soar on wings like eagles; they will run and not grow weary, they will walk and not be faint." (Isaiah 40:31 NIV)
- "But as for me, I watch in hope for the Lord, I wait for God my Savior, my God will hear me." (Micah 7:7 NIV)
- "May your unfailing love be with us, Lord, even as we put our hope in You." (Psalm 33:22 NIV)

Feeling hopeless is a significant sign of depression. As believers in Jesus Christ, we know that there is more to life than the eight or nine decades we spend here on planet earth. The best is yet to come. In these Covid-19 days where depression, hopelessness, and despair are wide reaching, it is incumbent on us to point others to Jesus, the only source of unbroken promises and hope. We can be confident in the hope that our God promises because, frankly, He is God.

BUT NOW I AM GOING TO HIM WHO SENT ME and none of you asks Me, "Where are You going?' 'But because I have said these things to you, sorrow has filled your heart. Nevertheless, I tell you the truth: it is to your advantage that I go away, for if I do not go away, the Helper will not come to you. But if I go, I will send Him to you. And when He comes, He will convict the world concerning sin and righteousness and judgment: concerning sin, because they do not believe in Me; concerning righteousness, because I go to the Father, and you will see Me no longer; concerning judgment, because the ruler of this world is judged.

"I still have many things to say to you, but you cannot bear them now. When the Spirit of truth comes, He will guide you into all the truth, for He will not speak on His own authority, but whatever He hears He will speak, and He will declare to you the things that are to come. He will glorify Me, for He will take what is Mine and declare it to you. All that the Father has is Mine; therefore I said that He will take what is Mine and declare it to you.

"A little while, and you will see Me no longer; and again a little while, and you will see Me." So some of His disciples said to one another, "What is this that He says to us, 'A little while, and you will not see Me, and again a little while, and you will see Me'; and, 'because I am going to the Father'?" So they were saying, "What does He mean by 'a little while'? We do not know what He is talking about." Jesus knew that they wanted to ask Him, so He said to them, "Is this what you are asking yourselves, what I meant by saying, 'A little while and you will not see Me, and again a little while and you will see Me'? Truly, truly, I say to you, you will weep and lament, but the world will rejoice. You will be sorrowful, but your sorrow will turn into joy. When a woman is giving birth, she has sorrow because her hour has come, but when she has delivered the baby, she no longer remembers the anguish, for joy that a human being has been born into the world. So also you have sorrow now, but I will see you again, and your hearts will rejoice, and no one will take your joy from you. In that day you will ask nothing of Me.

Truly, truly, I say to you, whatever you ask of the Father in My name, He will give it to you. Until now you have asked nothing in My name. Ask, and you will receive, that your joy may be full.

"I have said these things to you in figures of speech. The hour is coming when I will no longer speak to you in figures of speech but will tell you plainly about the Father. In that day you will ask in My name, and I do not say to you that I will ask the Father on your behalf; for the Father Himself loves you, because you have loved Me and have believed that I came from God. I came from the Father and have come into the world, and now I am leaving the world and going to the Father."

His disciples said, "Ah, now You are speaking plainly and not using figurative speech! Now we know that You know all things and do not need anyone to question You; this is why we believe that You came from God." Jesus answered them, "Do you now believe? Behold, the hour is coming, indeed it has come, when you will be scattered, each to his own home, and will leave Me alone. Yet I am not alone, for the Father is with Me. I have said these things to you, that in Me you may have peace. In the world you will have tribulation. But take heart; I have overcome the world." (John 16:5-33 ESV)

> **LESTER ROLOFF**
> I have all that I need here and hereafter!
> How much richer could anybody want to be?[13]

PAUL, AN APOSTLE OF JESUS CHRIST BY THE WILL OF GOD, and Timothy our brother, To the saints and faithful brethren in Christ who are at Colossae: Grace to you and peace from God our Father.

---

[13] Lester Roloff, 1914-1982, American fundamentalist, Independent Baptist preacher, Founder of teen homes access the American south, from https://www.christian-quotes.info/quotes-by-author/lester-roloff-quotes/.

We give thanks to God, the Father of our Lord Jesus Christ, praying always for you, since we heard of your faith in Christ Jesus and the love which you have for all the saints; because of the hope laid up for you in heaven, of which you previously heard in the word of truth, the gospel which has come to you, just as in all the world also it is constantly bearing fruit and increasing, even as it has been doing in you also since the day you heard of it and understood the grace of God in truth; just as you learned it from Epaphras, our beloved fellow bond-servant, who is a faithful servant of Christ on our behalf, and he also informed us of your love in the Spirit.

For this reason also, since the day we heard of it, we have not ceased to pray for you and to ask that you may be filled with the knowledge of His will in all spiritual wisdom and understanding, so that you will walk in a manner worthy of the Lord, to please Him in all respects, bearing fruit in every good work and increasing in the knowledge of God; strengthened with all power, according to His glorious might, for the attaining of all steadfastness and patience; joyously giving thanks to the Father, Who has qualified us to share in the inheritance of the saints in Light.

For He rescued us from the domain of darkness, and transferred us to the kingdom of His beloved Son, in Whom we have redemption, the forgiveness of sins.

And although you were formerly alienated and hostile in mind, engaged in evil deeds, yet He has now reconciled you in His fleshly body through death, in order to present you before Him holy and blameless and beyond reproach—if indeed you continue in the faith firmly established and steadfast, and not moved away from the hope of the gospel that you have heard, which was proclaimed in all creation under heaven, and of which I, Paul, was made a minister.

Now I rejoice in my sufferings for your sake, and in my flesh I do my share on behalf of His body, which is the church, in filling up what is lacking in Christ's afflictions. Of this church I was made a minister according to the stewardship from God bestowed on me for your benefit, so that I might fully carry out the preaching of the word of God, that is, the mystery which has been hidden from the past ages and generations, but has now been manifested to His saints, to whom God willed to make known what is the riches of the glory of this mystery among the Gentiles, which is Christ in you, the hope of glory. We proclaim Him, admonishing every man and teaching every man with all wisdom, so that we may present every man complete in Christ. For this purpose also I labor, striving according to His power, which mightily works within me. (Colossians 1:1-14, 21-29 NASB)

> ### JOHN NEWTON
> Our righteousness is in Him, and our hope depends, not upon the exercise of grace in us, but upon the fullness of grace and love in Him, and upon His obedience unto death.[14]

THEREFORE, HOLY BRETHREN, PARTAKERS OF A HEAVENLY CALLING, consider Jesus, the Apostle and High Priest of our confession; He was faithful to Him who appointed Him, as Moses also was in all his house. For He has been counted worthy of more glory than Moses, by just so much as the builder of the house has more honor than the house. For every house is built by someone, but the builder of all things is God. Now Moses was faithful in all His house as a servant, for a testimony of those things which were to be spoken later; but Christ was faithful as a Son over His house—whose house we are, if we hold fast our confidence and the boast of our hope firm until the end. (Hebrews 3:1-6 NASB)

---

[14] John Newton, The Amazing Works of John Newton (Edinburgh: Banner of Truth, 1839), 336.

> ## JOHN C. BROGER[15]
> The hope that God has provided for you is not merely a wish. Neither is it dependent on other people's possessions, or circumstances for its validity. Instead, biblical hope is an application of your faith that supplies a confident expectation in God's fulfillment of His promises. Coupled with faith and love, hope is part of the abiding characteristics in a believer's life.

IN YOU, O LORD, DO I TAKE REFUGE
let me never be put to shame;
    in Your righteousness deliver me!
Incline Your ear to me;
    rescue me speedily!
Be a rock of refuge for me,
    a strong fortress to save me!

For You are my rock and my fortress;
    and for Your name's sake You lead me and guide me;
You take me out of the net they have hidden for me,
    for You are my refuge.
Into Your hand I commit my spirit;
    You have redeemed me, O LORD, faithful God.

I hate those who pay regard to worthless idols,
    but I trust in the LORD.
I will rejoice and be glad in Your steadfast love,
    because You have seen my affliction;
You have known the distress of my soul,
    and You have not delivered me into the hand
    of the enemy;
You have set my feet in a broad place.

---

[15] John C. Broger, *Self-Confrontation: A Manual for In-Depth Biblical Discipleship* (Indio: Biblical Counseling Foundation, 1991), 101.

Be gracious to me, O Lord, for I am in distress;
>   my eye is wasted from grief;
>   my soul and my body also. (Psalm 31:1-9 ESV)

> ## JONATHAN EDWARDS
> To go to heaven, fully to enjoy God,
> is infinitely better than the most pleasant accommodations here.[16]

BUT I TRUST IN YOU, O LORD;
I say, "You are my God."
My times are in Your hand;
>   rescue me from the hand of my enemies and
>   from my persecutors!
Make Your face shine on your servant;
>   save me in Your steadfast love!
O Lord, let me not be put to shame,
>   for I call upon You;
>   let the wicked be put to shame;
>   let them go silently to Sheol.
Let the lying lips be mute,
>   which speak insolently against the righteous
>   in pride and contempt.

Oh, how abundant is Your goodness,
>   which You have stored up for those who fear You
>   and worked for those who take refuge in You,
>   in the sight of the children of mankind!
>   In the cover of Your presence You hide them
>   from the plots of men;
You store them in Your shelter
>   from the strife of tongues.

---

[16] Jonathan Edwards, The Works of President Edwards (London: Forgotten Books, 2018), 578.

Blessed be the Lord,
> for He has wondrously shown His steadfast love to me
> when I was in a besieged city.
I had said in my alarm,
> "I am cut off from Your sight."
>> But You heard the voice of my pleas for mercy
>> when I cried to You for help.
Love the Lord, all you His saints!
The Lord preserves the faithful
> but abundantly repays the one who acts in pride.

Be strong, and let your heart take courage,
> All you who wait for the lord! (Psalm 31:14-24 ESV)

R.C. SPROUL

Hope is called the anchor of the soul (Hebrews 6:19), because it gives stability to the Christian life. But hope is not simply a "wish" (I wish that such-and-such would take place); rather, it is that which latches on to the certainty of the promises of the future that God has made.[17]

AS A DEER PANTS FOR FLOWING STREAMS,
So pants my soul for You, O God.
My soul thirsts for God,
For the living God.
When shall I come and appear before God?
My tears have been my food
> day and night,
> while they say to me all the day long,

---

[17] Julie Clinton quoting R.C. Sproul, 100 Days of Healing: Daily Devotions (Carol Stream: Tyndale House Publishers, 2019).

"Where is your God?"
These things I remember,
    as I pour out my soul:
    how I would go with the throng
    and lead them in procession to the house of God
    with glad shouts and songs of praise,
    a multitude keeping festival.
Why are you cast down, O my soul,
    and why are you in turmoil within me?
Hope in God; for I shall again praise Him,
    my salvation and my God.
My soul is cast down within me;
    therefore I remember You
    from the land of Jordan and of Hermon,
    from Mount Mizar.
Deep calls to deep
At the roar of your waterfalls;
    all your breakers and your waves
    have gone over me.
By day the Lord commands His steadfast love,
And at night His song is with me,
    a prayer to the God of my life.
I say to God, my rock:
"Why have You forgotten me?
Why do I go mourning
    because of the oppression of the enemy?"
As with a deadly wound in my bones,
    my adversaries taunt me,
    while they say to me all the day long,
"Where is your God?"
Why are you cast down, o my soul,
    and why are you in turmoil within me?
Hope in God; for I shall again praise Him,
    my salvation and my God. (Psalm 42:1-11 ESV)

BROTHER LAWRENCE

Many things are possible for the person who has hope. Even more is possible for the person who has faith. And still more is possible for the person who knows how to love. But everything is possible for the person who practices all three virtues.[18]

OUT OF THE DEPTHS [OF DISTRESS] I HAVE CRIED TO YOU,
O Lord.
Lord, hear my voice!
Let Your ears be attentive
To the voice of my supplications.
If You, LORD, should keep an account of our sins and treat us accordingly,
O Lord, who could stand [before You in judgment and claim innocence]?
But there is forgiveness with You,
That You may be feared and worshiped [with submissive wonder].
I wait [patiently] for the LORD, my soul [expectantly] waits,
And in His word do I hope.
My soul waits for the Lord
More than the watchmen for the morning;
More than the watchmen for the morning.
O Israel, hope in the LORD;
For with the LORD there is lovingkindness,
And with Him is abundant redemption.
And He will redeem Israel
From all his sins. (Psalm 130:1-8 AMP)

---

[18] Jim Burns and Doug Fields, quoting Brother Lawrence, Spiritual Gifts: High School Study (Ventura: Gospel Light, 2008), 44.

> **_CHUCK SMITH_**
> God will allow us to follow self-help, self-improvement programs until we have tried them all, until we finally come to the honest confession, 'I can't do it. I can't be righteous in my own strength!' It is then, when we admit our utter powerlessness, that we find hope. For it is then when the Lord intervenes to do a work that we could not do for ourselves.[19]

---

[19] Chuck Smith, Effective Prayer Life: Gift Journal (Huntington Beach: The Word for Today, 2006).

Chapter 4

THE PURPOSE OF YOUR PAIN

IT'S NEWS I'M MOST PROUD TO PROCLAIM, this extraordinary message of God's powerful plan to rescue everyone who trusts Him, starting with Jews and then right on to everyone else! God's way of putting people right shows up in the acts of faith, confirming what Scripture has said all along: "The person in right standing before God, by trusting Him, really lives." (Romans 1:16-17 Message)

PATTI BURNETT

OVER A VERY SHORT PERIOD OF TIME, as mentioned in the introduction, pain seemed to be my constant companion. I often found myself sitting at my Father God's feet, asking "why?" As I look back on each of these incidents, I now see how each fracture, plate, screw, and diagnosis provided increased credibility and motivation for me to become an ambassador to others who were beginning to live with the challenges of Parkinson's.

Leaving the professional workforce, I found volunteer opportunities that matched my experience, giftings, and passions almost perfectly – I'm sure this was all in God's plan. A few years after I had been diagnosed with Parkinson's Disease (PD), I had an opportunity to meet some of the staff from one of the Parkinson's foundations.

I signed up for a 79-mile biking event with no training, no knowledge of the terrain, just dumb ol' desire to somehow help. Dan asked that I consider biking just half of the course since I did not have the required endurance and skills. I guess 6,500 vertical feet over four mountain passes could be overwhelming – even to a normal person, not to mention one with PD. So, he dropped me off in Minturn. I felt a bit smug, like I was getting away with something – Cheater! Cheater! That feeling didn't last long as the strongest bikers blazed by me; and eventually I ate my humble pie as the not so strong bikers left me in their dust as well.

When I reached the aid station at the top of Vail Pass, having just completed the most strenuous leg of the course, I noticed a group of bikers with Davis Phinney jerseys standing in a circle. I timidly walked up to them and thanked them for everything they do for people with Parkinson's. Davis, THE Davis Phinney, stepped forward and congratulated me for making it all the way to Vail Pass. I explained that I had only biked from Minturn - that was all Dan would let me do. He told me that Connie, his beautiful wife and care partner, had dropped him off at East Vail. I knew immediately that this was a very humble man who had nothing to prove.

Davis had been diagnosed with PD at only 40 years of age and was purposefully living the best he could with the diagnosis he had been served for the remainder of his life. Davis Phinney is to this day the most medaled US biker in the history of cycling. He won more than 328 races between 1978 and 1991, including two Tour de France stages. His wife, Connie Carpenter Phinney, competed in the 1972 Winter Olympics as a 14-year-old speed skating phenom, and in 1984 was the first person to receive a gold medal in a women's Olympic biking event.

Davis says that at first, he was in "blissful denial." He explains that Parkinson's comes at you like a poisonous venom, advancing up a wall just an inch a year. It takes over your system so slowly, and with such subtlety, that you don't notice until it has a grip around your throat.

Their friend, Dan Koeppel, explains Connie and Davis this way – "I think they're simply people who don't know how to lose. It is the key to Phinney's bravery, to Carpenter's strength, and to whatever the future holds. It is an idea that is utterly alien to most of us – those of us who are mortally ungifted, who come apart merely from witnessing the suffering of our heroes. But it is the idea that keeps them going, that makes every day feel like a triumph."

Davis was, after many misdiagnoses, told that he had Early Onset Parkinson's. In a short time, he realized that because of his biking fame, he had a platform from which to help others living with Parkinson's. Since Michael J. Fox had already established his Foundation, with the goal of finding a cure for PD through research and studies, Davis set about to help people with Parkinson's live better now. Recognizing that most of us will probably not live long enough to see a cure, I had already determined that this was also my strategy for living with Parkinson's.

I have been blessed with a slowly progressing disease; some would label me a positive deviant. I know that this is not necessarily the case for many with PD; and who knows how long this will be true for me. It is my desire and privilege to talk to people about how they can proactively slow their neurodegeneration by having a good Movement Disorder Specialist, exercising, eating healthfully perhaps with a Mediterranean diet, fasting intermittently, remaining socially engaged, helping others who are less fortunate, and mentally challenging oneself.

I am grateful for the opportunity to be a Parkinson's ambassador. It has allowed me to meet some of the most amazing people. I have heard it said that you will never meet a person with PD that you don't like; and this has been undeniably true. There is something very humbling (even humiliating) about having a disease that will very possibly cause you to age more rapidly than your peers.

We can't know for sure how each of our PDs will advance, but it's possible we will not be able to walk as well, think as clearly, tie our own shoes, feed ourselves as capably, sleep well, etc. However, none of us knows what the future holds, whether we have PD or not. It's hard to be proud when you've lost nearly everything, and control of your future has been virtually taken out of your hands. I will never look at another disabled person and think "I'm glad I'm not them." Now I am "them"; and being them makes me look at life differently. I am more empathetic toward those with disabilities. I can relate more easily to underdogs and those less privileged. Everything has changed and it's taken a long time for me to say this, but I am grateful that God cares enough to want to shave off some of my rough, self-centered edges, using Parkinson's as His tool. And, He's not done with me yet.

God, I know You are good and that You love me and have good plans for me. This PD has given me purpose and a platform from which to point other people in a direction where they can find lasting joy, hope, faith, and fulfillment.

SEEING THE CROWD HE FELT COMPASSION FOR them because they were distressed and downcast, like sheep without a shepherd. Then He said to His disciples, "The harvest is plentiful, but the workers are few. Therefore, plead with the Lord of the harvest to send out workers into His harvest." (Matthew 9:36-38 NASB)

A GENTLE THUNDER, MAX LUCADO

Long ago, or maybe not so long ago, there was a tribe in a dark, cold cavern. The cave dwellers would huddle together and cry against the chill. Loud and long, they wailed. It was all they did. It was all they knew to do.

The sounds in the cave were mournful, but the people didn't know it, for they had never known joy. The spirit in the cave was death, but the people in the cave didn't know it, for they had never known life.

But then, one day, they heard a different voice. "I have heard your cries," it announced. "I have felt your chill and seen your darkness. I have come to help ..."

The cave people peered through the darkness at the figure of the stranger. He was stacking something, then stooping and stacking more.

"What are you doing?" One cried, nervous...

The visitor stood and spoke in the direction of the voices. "I have what you need." With that he turned to the pile at his feet and lit it. Wood ignited, flames erupted, and light filled the cavern.

The cave people turned away in fear. "Put it out!" They cried. "It hurts to see it."

"Light always hurts before it helps," he answered. "Step closer. The pain will soon pass ..."

"He's right," one from behind him announced. "It's warmer." The stranger turned and saw a figure slowly stepping toward the fire. "I can open my eyes now," she proclaimed. "I can see ..."

She turned to the stranger. "Why won't they come?"

"They choose the chill, for though it's cold, it's what they know. They'd rather be cold than change."

"And live in the dark?"

"And live in the dark ..."

"Will you leave the fire?" He asked.

She paused, then answered, "I cannot. I cannot bear the cold." Then she spoke again. "But nor can I bear the thought of my people in darkness."

"You don't have to," he responded, reaching into the fire and removing a stick. "Carry this to your people. Tell them the light is here, and the light is warm. Tell them the light is for all who desire it."

And so she took the small flame and stepped into the shadows.[20]

AND JESUS CAME UP AND SPOKE TO THEM, saying, "All authority in heaven and on earth has been given to me. Go, therefore, and make disciples of all the nations, baptizing them in the name of the Father and the Son and the Holy Spirit, teaching them to follow all that I commanded you; and behold, I am with you always, to the end of the age." (Matthew 28:18-20 NASB)

FRIENDSHIP EVANGELISM VS. INVITATIONS FROM THE PULPIT, PATTI BURNETT

WE OFTEN HEAR people refer to Christ's style of spreading the Gospel as friendship or one-on-one evangelism. Yet, He also attracted incredibly large crowds everywhere He went. It was hard for unbelievers to turn away from a Man who loved and cared for them unconditionally. Sometimes I have wondered how effective we are when it comes to continuing the work that our Lord began?

I once had a friend tell me that he had found more compassion and caring in a bar than at the local church he had visited.

I think it's true that some pastors and bible teachers try to flaunt their deep theological knowledge by espousing from the pulpit terms like "evidential apologetics, extra calvinisticum, hypothetical universalism, monophysitism, perspicuity of scripture, sandemanianism, and supralapsarianism." I'm worried about the spiritual condition of my computer, even it did not recognize these words. It would be beneficial if Christians could place themselves in the shoes, or the pews, of

---

[20] Max Lucado, A Gentle Thunder: Hearing God Through the Storm (Nashville: Thomas Nelson, 2012), 174.

unbelievers for just one Sunday to experience an empathetic degree of discomfort and anxiety.

Our goal should not be to offend, but to offer the good news of Christ in a way that is contemporary, understandable, and relevant.

I remember a time when God provided the opportunity for me to visit with a very hurting woman. When I asked her how I could help, the emotional floodgates opened wide. She just needed the ears and heart of someone who cared enough to hear her story. Another time, my pastor encouraged me to call an old friend whose six-year-old daughter had recently died from a terminal illness. I told her that I was always available if she ever needed someone to listen; did she ever!

Recently a mental health clinician mentioned that nearly 50% of our population has deep mental health issues resulting from the last three years of COVID-19. That's huge! My prayer is that we, as Christ followers, will strive to be the hands, eyes, mouth, ears, and heart of Christ and become more open and responsive to the suffering that is going on in our own backyards.

> **"BUT YOU WILL RECEIVE POWER WHEN THE HOLY SPIRIT HAS COME UPON YOU;**
> and you shall be My witnesses both in Jerusalem and in all Judea, and Samaria, and as far as the remotest part of the earth."
> (Acts 1:8 NASB)

A GENTLE THUNDER, MAX LUCADO

A beggar came and sat before me. "I want bread," he said.

"How wise you are," I assured him. "Bread is what you need. And you have come to the right bakery." So, I pulled my cookbook down from my shelf and began to tell him all I knew about bread. I spoke of flour and wheat, of grain and barley. My knowledge impressed even me as I cited the measurements and recipe. When I looked up, I was surprised to see he wasn't smiling ...

"I just want bread," he said ...

The beggar didn't speak. I understood his silence. With my arm around his shoulder, I whispered, "It overwhelms me as well." I then leaped to the podium and struck my favorite pose behind the lectern. "People come from miles to hear me speak. Once a week, my workers gather, and I read to them the recipe from the cookbook of life." By now the beggar had taken a seat on the front row. I knew what he wanted. "Would you like to hear me?"

"No," he said, "but I would like some bread."

"How wise you are," I replied. And I led him to the front door of the bakery. "What I have to say next is very important," I told him as we stood outside. "Up and down this street you will find many bakeries. But take heed; they don't serve the true bread. I know of one who adds two spoons of salt rather than one. I know of another whose oven is three degrees too hot. They may call it bread," I warned, "but it's not according to the book."

The beggar turned and began walking away. "Don't you want bread?" I asked him.

He stopped, looked back at me, and shrugged, "I guess I lost my appetite."

I shook my head and returned to my office. "What a shame," I said to myself. "The world just isn't hungry for true bread anymore."[21]

---

[21] Ibid. 41.

> **BUT I DO NOT CONSIDER MY LIFE OF ANY ACCOUNT AS DEAR TO MYSELF,** so that I may finish my course and the ministry which I received from the Lord Jesus, to testify solemnly of the gospel of God's grace. (Acts 20:24 NASB)

OUT OF THE SALTSHAKER, BECKY PIPPERT

If we notice that non-Christians seem embarrassed, apologetic and defensive, it is probably because they are picking up our attitude. If we assume they will be absolutely fascinated to discover the true nature of Christianity, they probably will. If we project enthusiasm, not defensiveness, and if we carefully listen instead of sounding like a recording of "Answers to Questions You Didn't Happen to Ask," non-Christians will probably become intrigued. Learn to delight in all their questions – especially the ones you cannot answer. I often tell people I'm very grateful that God is using them to change me intellectually when I am stumped by a question.[22]

SINCE GOD HAS SO GENEROUSLY LET US IN ON WHAT HE IS DOING, we're not about to throw up our hands and walk off the job just because we run into occasional hard times. We refuse to wear masks and play games. We don't maneuver and manipulate behind the scenes. And we don't twist God's Word to suit ourselves. Rather, we keep everything we do and say out in the open, the whole truth on display, so that those who want to, can see and judge for themselves in the presence of God.

Remember, our Message is not about ourselves; we're proclaiming Jesus Christ, the Master. All we are messengers, errand runners from Jesus for you. It started when God said, "Light up the darkness!" and

---

[22] Tim Dearborn quoting Rebecca Manley Pippert, Short-Term Missions Workbook (Westmont: IVP Books, 2003), 50.

our lives filled up with light as we saw and understood God in the face of Christ, all bright and beautiful. (2 Corinthians 4:1-2, 5-6 Message)

FRIENDSHIP EVANGELISM, A SURE WAY TO WITNESSING – UNREHEARSED, NONPROGRAMMED, AND PERSONAL, MONTE SAHLIN

Members of the Sunnyvale Seventh-day Adventist Church in suburban San Jose, California, report that one of their most effective outreach activities is the Sunday ball game. It may not seem evangelistic—there is no preaching, no call for decisions, no Bible study or literature distribution—yet many new members of this growing church testify that their decision to join started with friendships developed during ball games ...

Friendship evangelism consists of three elements. Each can be seen as a "layer" of solid foundation in Christ, and each build upon the other.

First, the Christian demonstrates caring and compassion through a genuine friendship that is unconditional—not allied with any expectation of the nonbeliever ...

Second, the Christian seeks to understand the needs of unchurched friends. I do not make a theological judgment or a Christian analysis of their need, but accept their feelings as they understand them ...

Third, the Christian finds opportunities to share the possibility of faith meeting the felt needs of unchurched friends. Such openings are often brief and fragile, and they are always highly personal moments ...

Consider a beautiful example of these skills modeled by Christ in John 4. He encounters a Samaritan woman at a well about a mile outside of town. The conversation begins with the problem of thirst, which Christ quickly identifies with a deep, inner thirst for love and affection desired by a woman who has experienced five failed marriages. He uses "living water" as a metaphorical expression. It carries the deep meaning of the gospel to this lonely woman, who accepts Christ as her Messiah and becomes an active witness in her town … [23]

THEREFORE, BEING ALWAYS OF GOOD COURAGE, and knowing that while we are at home in the body, we are absent from the Lord—for we walk by faith, not by sight—we are of good courage, I say, and prefer rather to be absent from the body and to be at home with the Lord. Therefore, we also have as our ambition, whether at home or absent, to be pleasing to Him. For we must all appear before the judgment seat of Christ, so that each one may be recompensed for his deeds in the body, according to what he has done, whether good or bad.

Therefore, knowing the fear of the Lord, we persuade men, but we are made manifest to God; and I hope that we are made manifest also in your consciences. We are not again commending ourselves to you but are giving you an occasion to be proud of us, so that you will have an answer for those who take pride in appearance and not in heart. For if we are beside ourselves, it is for God; if we are of sound mind, it is for you. For the love of Christ controls us, having concluded this, that one died for all, therefore all died; and He died for all, so that they who live might no longer live for themselves, but for Him who died and rose again on their behalf.

Therefore, from now on we recognize no one according to the flesh; even though we have known Christ according to the flesh, yet now we know Him in this way no longer. Therefore, if anyone is in Christ, he is a new creature; the old things passed away; behold, new things have come.

Now all these things are from God, who reconciled us to Himself through Christ and gave us the ministry of reconciliation, namely, that God was in Christ reconciling the world to Himself, not counting

---

[23] Monte Sahlin, Sharing Our Faith with Friends Without Losing Either (Hagerstown: Review and Herald Pub, 1990), from https://www.ministrymagazine.org/archive/1993/09/friendship-evangelism.

their trespasses against them, and He has committed to us the word of reconciliation.

Therefore, we are ambassadors for Christ, as though God were making an appeal through us; we beg you on behalf of Christ, be reconciled to God. He made Him who knew no sin to be sin on our behalf, so that we might become the righteousness of God in Him. (2 Corinthians 5:6-21 NASB)

> ### *OUT OF THE SALTSHAKER, BECKY PIPPERT*
> If you live by the same priorities and values that He (Jesus) had, you will find evangelism happening naturally. It becomes a lifestyle and not a project.[24]

I CAN'T IMPRESS THIS ON YOU TOO STRONGLY. God is looking over your shoulder. Christ Himself is the Judge, with the final say on everyone, living and dead. He is about to break into the open with His rule, so proclaim the Message with intensity; keep on your watch. Challenge, warn, and urge your people. Don't ever quit. Just keep it simple.

You're going to find that there will be times when people will have no stomach for solid teaching, but will fill up on spiritual junk food—catchy opinions that tickle their fancy. They'll turn their backs on truth and chase mirages. But you—keep your eye on what you're doing; accept the hard times along with the good; keep the Message alive; do a thorough job as God's servant.

You take over. I'm about to die, my life an offering on God's altar. This is the only race worth running. I've run hard right to the finish, believed all the way. All that's left now is the shouting—God's applause!

---

[24] Rebecca Pippert, Out of the Saltshaker and Into the World (Westmont: IVP Books, 1999), 49.

Depend on it, He's an honest judge. He'll do right not only by me, but by everyone eager for His coming.

At my preliminary hearing no one stood by me. They all ran like scared rabbits. But it doesn't matter—the Master stood by me and helped me spread the Message loud and clear to those who had never heard it. I was snatched from the jaws of the lion! God's looking after me, keeping me safe in the kingdom of heaven. All praise to Him, praise forever! Oh, yes! (I Timothy 4:1-18 Message)

THE DIVINE EMBRACE, KEN GIRE

"And I have met Mother Teresa," he said. My eyes lit up. "Really? Tell me about her."

He told us he had met her several years ago. As part of her daily routine, she received visitors between ten and eleven o'clock each morning, and the visitors were allowed to follow her as she made her rounds. The day he met her, she was trailing behind the doctors who were treating the bedridden patients that she cared for. The doctors touched the patients they examined, some of whom had serious and communicable diseases, but their hands were protected by latex gloves. Mother Teresa, he told us, wore no gloves.

With her bare, wrinkled hands, she affectionately touched the hands and arms and faces of these most desperately ill people. As she talked with them or prayed with them, she tenderly rubbed her hands over their withered skin.

What was it like, being there with her?" I asked.

He paused for a moment and smiled. "It was like being in the presence of Christ."[25]

GIVE THANKS TO THE LORD, CALL UPON HIS NAME;
Make His deeds known among the peoples.
Sing to Him, sing praises to Him;
Tell of all His wonders.

---

[25] Ken Gire, The Divine Embrace (Carol Stream: Tyndale House Publishers, 2004), 49.

Boast in His holy name;
May the heart of those who seek the Lord be joyful.
Seek the Lord and His strength;
Seek His face continually.
Remember His wonders which He has done,
His marvels and the judgments spoken by His mouth,
You descendants of Abraham, His servant,
You sons of Jacob, His chosen ones!

He is the Lord our God;
His judgments are in all the earth.
He has remembered His covenant forever,
The word which He commanded to a thousand generations,
The covenant which He made with Abraham,
And His oath to Isaac.
Then He confirmed it to Jacob as a statute,
To Israel as an everlasting covenant,
Saying, "To you I will give the land of Canaan
As the portion of your inheritance,"
When they were only a few people in number,
Very few, and strangers in it.
And they wandered from nation to nation,
From one kingdom to another people,
He allowed no one to oppress them,
And He rebuked kings for their sakes, saying,
"Do not touch My anointed ones,
And do not harm My prophets." (Psalm 105:1-15 NASB)

KEEP YOUR EYE ON THE TARGET, PATTI BURNETT

MANY OF US HAVE BEEN INVOLVED IN A DISCIPLINE in which we were instructed to keep our eye on the target. In ski racing the idea is to focus on the space just outside the gate. In soccer and hockey, the attacker is told to not look at the goalie, but instead concentrate on the area inside the goal where he intends the ball or puck to land. In skiing, soccer, hockey, and the church, hitting the target is a matter of focus and concentration.

Pastor and Author of The Purpose Driven Church, Rick Warren (1995) spent a great deal of time and energy researching the target for Saddleback Community Church. I agree with his conviction that churches that attempt to reach every segment of the population, consequently fail to reach anyone adequately. If neighboring churches would cooperate rather than compete, they could agree that one would target Generation Xers for instance. Another church might be more proficient in serving senior citizens or charismatics. I can envision pastors referring newcomers to other congregations that are better equipped to meet their unique needs.

When a church is searching to fill the pulpit, it rarely gives the candidate time to get out in the neighborhood to determine whether he is qualified to minister to the designated target, if a target has even been designated. Performing a survey would certainly fulfill that need.

As a child, archery was one of the highlights of my summer vacations. Uncle Stubby patiently helped us to position the miniature bow and arrows in our tiny hands and reminded us to never take our eyes off the target. I can picture our Heavenly Father in a similar posture as He directs our attention to His most prized creation. What a privilege it is to be strategically used by Him.

> **"I TELL YOU, OPEN YOUR EYES AND LOOK AT THE FIELDS.**
> They are ripe for harvest. Even now the reaper draws his wages, even now he harvests the crop for eternal life, so that the sower and the reaper may be glad together." (John 4:35b-36 NIV)

THE SPIRIT OF THE LORD GOD IS UPON ME,
Because the Lord anointed me
To bring good news to the humble;
He has sent me to bind up the brokenhearted,
To proclaim release to captives
And freedom to prisoners;
To proclaim the favorable year of the Lord
And the day of vengeance of our God;
To comfort all who mourn,
To grant those who mourn in Zion,
Giving them a garland instead of ashes,
The oil of gladness instead of mourning,
The cloak of praise instead of a disheartened spirit.
So they will be called oaks of righteousness,
The planting of the Lord, that He may be glorified.
Then they will rebuild the ancient ruins,
They will raise up the former devastations;
And they will repair the ruined cities,
The desolations of many generations.
Strangers will stand and pasture your flocks,
And foreigners will be your farmers and your vinedressers.
But you will be called the priests of the Lord;
You will be spoken of as ministers of our God.
You will eat the wealth of nations,
And you will boast in their riches.
Instead of your shame you will have a double portion,
And instead of humiliation they will shout for joy over
their portion.
Therefore, they will possess a double portion in their land,
Everlasting joy will be theirs.
For I, the Lord, love justice,
I hate robbery in the burnt offering.
And I will faithfully give them their reward,
And make an everlasting covenant with them.
Then their offspring will be known among the nations,
And their descendants in the midst of the peoples.

All who see them will recognize them
Because they are the offspring whom the Lord has blessed.

I will rejoice greatly in the Lord,
My soul will be joyful in my God;
For He has clothed me with garments of salvation,
For He has wrapped me with a robe of righteousness,
As a groom puts on a turban,
And as a bride adorns herself with her jewels.

For as the earth produces its sprouts,
And as a garden causes the things sown in it to spring up,
So the Lord God will cause righteousness and praise
To spring up before all the nations. (Isaiah 61:1-8 NASB)

OUT OF THE SALTSHAKER, BECKY PIPPERT

What an insidious reversal of the Biblical Command to be salt and light to the world. The rabbit-hole Christian remains insulated and isolated from the world when he is commanded to penetrate it. How can we be the salt of the earth if we never get out of the saltshaker?[26]

---

[26] Rebecca Pippert, Out of the Saltshaker and Into the World (Westmont: IVP Books, 1999), 114.

Chapter 5

NO DROPPED CALLS

NOW THERE WAS A MAN IN CAESAREA NAMED CORNELIUS, a centurion of what was called the Italian cohort, a devout man and one who feared God with all his household, and made many charitable contributions to the Jewish people and prayed to God continually. About the ninth hour of the day he clearly saw in a vision an angel of God who had just come in and said to him, "Cornelius!" And he looked at him intently and became terrified, and said, "What is it, lord?" And he said to him, "Your prayers and charitable gifts have ascended as a memorial offering before God. (Acts 10:1-4 NASB)

PATTI BURNETT

IT'S HARD NOT TO NOTICE how addicted nearly all of us have become to the fine art of texting. And lest the youth of our country feel picked on, I think this is as much an issue for senior citizens as it is our middle and late adolescents. Psychologists now believe that our cell phones trigger a "dopamine loop." My ears pricked up when I learned this new term, since those with Parkinson's have a reduced level of dopamine.

So, you ask, what is a dopamine loop? Dopamine is a chemical in our bodies that affects thinking, moving, sleeping, mood, and motivation – basically, everything that we do. It affects our motivation to seek pleasure. When we attempt to get or do something and subsequently are rewarded, our desire for it increases exponentially. When we send a text, we initiate this dopamine loop, and we can become obsessed with receiving a response. The beeping and flashing of our phones just add to the addictive nature of this behavior. It used to be, in an earlier time and place, that these dopamine responses were elicited by laughing faces, positive recognition by peers, and messages from loved ones. Those were in the days when we actually met socially with people, face to face, with no masks. Excuse me but I'm feeling the urge to check my phone; it might be something important. Or not – just more spam.

When we misplace our phones, we realize the truth behind the dopamine loop. We spend an average of two to four hours a day using them – that's somewhere between 2000 and 2600 daily touches. I'm not sure who did the math, probably a Harvard professor.

Can you imagine what it would be like if we were addicted to listening for God's still small voice rather than our devices' tiny ding? Our prayer lives would be revolutionized. The slightest whispered message from our Lord would solicit dopamine responses that would be obvious to all those around us.

I want that — to be 100% addicted to listening for my God. I'll take any notifications you want to send my way Lord.

ONE DAY JESUS TOLD HIS DISCIPLES A STORY to show that they should always pray and never give up. "There was a judge in a certain city," he said, "who neither feared God nor cared about people. A widow of that city came to him repeatedly, saying, 'Give me justice in this dispute with my enemy.' The judge ignored her for a while, but finally he said to himself, 'I don't fear God or care about people, but this woman is driving me crazy. I'm going to see that she gets justice, because she is wearing me out with her constant requests!'"

Then the Lord said, "Learn a lesson from this unjust judge. Even he rendered a just decision in the end. So don't you think God will surely give justice to His chosen people who cry out to Him day and night? Will He keep putting them off? I tell you, He will grant justice to them quickly! But when the Son of Man returns, how many will He find on the earth who have faith? (Luke 18:1-8 NLT)

<u>MRS. BEAVER AND THE WOLF AT THE DOOR, CHRISTOPHER A. LANE AND SHARON DAHL</u>

There was once a beaver named Barney who lived with his wife Beatrice on a pond at the edge of the forest. Their beautiful home was made out of fine logs which Barney had selected himself, diligently chewed to fit, and carefully set into place. Beatrice had taken charge of the inside of the house, pasting up wallpaper in the kitchen, painting the rooms pleasant shades, and hanging curtains. Together, Mr. and Mrs. Beaver had built a warm, cozy home in which to live.

It came about one day that tragedy struck. Barney fell off the roof. A doctor was summoned, but the poor beaver didn't live through the night.

That next day animals from across the land gathered at the Beaver home. Sir Humphrey, the wealthy business bear, addressed the crowd with a few words about Mr. Beaver.

"Those who knew Barney," the bear growled, "loved Barney. A kinder, more faithful animal you wouldn't hope to meet. We will all miss him dearly."

When her friends and family had returned to their own homes, Beatrice sat inside her house and cried for a whole week straight. She was so sad and lonely that she cried until she felt she could cry no longer, and then she cried some more.

One day, after her sniffles had finally passed, there came a knock at the door. After checking her face and fur in the hall mirror, Beatrice opened the door to find two animals outside.

"After we get rid of this old house," a weasel was saying to a large wolf in a top hat "your hotel will fit neatly here next to the pond. I can see it now – 'The Wolf's Den Hotel.'"

"Ahem." Beatrice cleared her throat to gain their attention. "Is there something I can help you with?"

"Good day, Madame," the weasel said with a smile. "This will explain everything." And he handed her a sheet of paper.

The note said: "Your home is now the property of the J.B. Wolf Company. You and all of your possessions must be off the premises by tomorrow, or else!"

"What!" Beatrice was shocked. "You can't do this. This is my home!"

"Was your home," the weasel said, shuffling through a file of papers. "Says right here that after your husband died, the title deed was transferred to our company."

"I insist on speaking with your superior!" Beatrice demanded.

"Let me introduce myself," the wolf smiled, stepping forward.

"Mr. J.B. Wolf, robber baron extraordinaire. My good Mrs. Beaver, I am afraid that your house is now my property."

"We'll see about that," Beatrice said, trying to sound brave. But after closing the door, she felt like crying.

"Sir Humphrey" she suddenly thought. "If anyone can help me, he can."

Beatrice scurried off through the forest to Sir Humphrey's mansion. But when she arrived, she was disappointed to find that he was not at home.

She was about to give up hope when Reginald, Sir Humphrey's butler, suggested that she see Judge Kensington. The butler explained that the judge was a wise elk who settled various arguments between woodland creatures.

Beatrice thanked Reginald and set out to find the judge.

When she arrived at the courthouse, Beatrice introduced herself to the receptionist.

"My name is Mrs. Beatrice Beaver, and I must see Judge Kensington," she told the young crow.

"Do you have an appointment?" the bird cawed sleepily.

"No, but it is a matter of some urgency," Beatrice explained. The crow leafed lazily through a calendar on her desk. "How's two weeks from next Thursday sound?"

"That's much too late," Beatrice objected.

The crow ignored this and began primping her feathers.

Beatrice didn't know what to do. But she knew that she needed to see the judge.

When the crow wasn't looking, Beatrice slipped out of the courthouse and went around to the back. There she found a service entrance used by the maids and cooks. She tiptoed through it and found herself in a long hallway with many doors. Walking quietly down the hall, she eventually came to a door which had a plaque on it. The plaque read: "Behind this door sits a fair judge committed to what is right and just."

Beatrice tapped on the door lightly. When no one answered, she gave it a sharp rap.

Then she spotted a window above the door.

"If only I had a ladder," she thought. But there was nothing in the hall except a serving cart filled with dirty dishes.

Removing the dishes from the cart, she wheeled it in front of the door. Climbing up onto it, she steadied herself with her tail and strained to look through the high widow. What she saw was a gray-haired elk wearing a pair of round spectacles. Squinting to get a better look, she noticed that his eyes were closed. The judge was dozing!

Suddenly the cart began to roll and Beatrice lost her balance. Gripping the edge of the windowsill, she hung on with all her might.

"Help!" she screamed.

This startled the judge, who jumped out of his chair and came running out of his office at a gallop – only to have Beatrice fall into his arms as he passed through the doorway.

"What? Who are you?" the surprised elk asked as he put her down.

By this time, the crow from the entryway had arrived on the scene along with a collection of servants and cooks.

"My name is Mrs. Beatrice Beaver and I have an urgent request, your Honor," she blurted out.

"Make an appointment like everyone else," the judge grumbled. "Now, where was I?" he asked himself as he returned to his office and slammed the door.

Sitting on the steps of the courthouse, Beatrice wondered what to do. She was about to head for home when she heard a door close behind her. Turning around, she saw the judge leaving the courthouse.

Beatrice followed him down the path. "Judge Kensington, I must see you!" she pled.

"Oh, not you again," the elk shook his head.

"It's urgent! I must talk with you today!"

"I'm going home," he snorted. I suggest you do the same." And he walked away at a brisk pace.

Beatrice had to run just to keep the elk in sight.

When the judge reached his home, he hurried inside, leaving Beatrice standing in the street. He gave a sigh of relief, thinking he was rid of the pesky beaver. But he was mistaken.

First there was a knock at the door. The judge didn't answer it. Then there came a tapping at the window. So, the judge drew the curtains. Next a rock with a note attached to it came bouncing down the chimney. But he refused to read it. Then he heard a noise outside.

"Judge Kensington!" Beatrice hollered at the top of her voice. "Please hear my request!"

Beatrice was making such a racket that the judge threw open the door.

"Stop it!" the judge begged. "I'll do anything you ask, Mrs. Beaver! I'll see to it that your request is granted, if only you will promise to leave me alone."

Beatrice nodded her head in agreement and then explained her problem to the grumpy elk. When she finished, she showed him the note she had been given by the weasel and the wolf.

"Here," the elk said, scribbling a message on the bottom of the notice. "This will take care of the problem. Now I insist that you leave me alone!" And he trotted back inside and slammed the door.

By the time Beatrice reached her home it was very late, and she was quite tired. So, she went directly to bed.

But early the next morning she heard a knock at the door. Hopping up, she checked her face and fur in the hall mirror and answered the door.

It was the weasel and the wolf.

"You've got an hour to gather your things and get out!" the weasel said, pointing to a crew of animals waiting outside to demolish her home. "As soon as Mr. Wolf gives them the signal ..."

"Well, perhaps Mr. Wolf should read this," Beatrice smiled, handing him the notice.

The weasel's jaw dropped as he read it: "This notice is deemed illegal. The J.B. Wolf Company has no right to claim the home of Mrs. Beaver. By order of Judge Kensington, you are hereby required to leave her alone."

With his tail drooping between his legs, the weasel turned and gave the notice to his boss.

The wolf read it quickly and then bared his fangs.

"I should have known not to trust a weasel with a wolf's job," the wolf growled. "You have upset me for the last time."

Just as the wolf lunged, the weasel bolted for the road. The wolf took up chase, snapping at his heels.

Won't you stay for breakfast Beatrice called after them, as a peaceful smile spread across her face. But they were already too far away to hear.[27]

FINALLY, BE STRONG IN THE LORD AND IN THE STRENGTH OF HIS MIGHT. Put on the full armor of God, so that you will be able to stand firm against the schemes of the devil. For our struggle is not against flesh and blood, but against the rulers, against the powers, against the world forces of this darkness, against the spiritual forces of wickedness in the heavenly places. Therefore, take up the full armor of God, so that you will be able to resist on the evil day, and having done everything, to stand firm. Stand firm therefore, having belted your waist with truth, and having put on the breastplate of righteousness, and having strapped on your feet the preparation of the gospel of peace; in addition to all, taking up the shield of faith with which you will be able to extinguish all the flaming arrows of the evil one. And take the helmet of salvation and the sword of the Spirit, which is the word of God.

With every prayer and request, pray at all times in the Spirit, and with this in view, be alert with all perseverance and every request for all the saints, and pray in my behalf, that speech may be given to me in the opening of my mouth, to make known with boldness the mystery of the gospel, for which I am an ambassador in chains; that in proclaiming it I may speak boldly, as I ought to speak. (Ephesians 6:10-20 NASB)

> **MOTHER TERESA**
> Prayer is not asking. Prayer is putting oneself in the hands of God, at His disposition, and listening to His voice in the depth of our hearts.[28]

---

[27] Christopher A. Lane and Sharon Dahl, Mrs. Beaver and the Wolf at the Door (Wheaton: Victor Books, 1994), 129.

[28] Boyd Bailey quoting Mother Teresa, The Spiritual Life of a Leader: A God-Centered Leadership Style (Eugene: Harvest House Publishers, 2021),140.

FINALLY, BROTHERS AND SISTERS, pray for us that the word of the Lord will spread rapidly and be glorified, just as it was also with you; and that we will be rescued from troublesome and evil people; for not all have the faith. But the Lord is faithful, and He will strengthen and protect you from the evil one. We have confidence in the Lord concerning you, that you are doing, and will do, what we command. May the Lord direct your hearts to the love of God and to the perseverance of Christ. (2 Thessalonians 3:1-5 NASB)

MAX LUCADO
Our prayers may be awkward. Our attempts may be feeble. But since the power of prayer is in the one who hears it and not in the one who says it, our prayers do make a difference.[29]

DEAR BROTHERS AND SISTERS, be patient as you wait for the Lord's return. Consider the farmers who patiently wait for the rains in the fall and in the spring. They eagerly look for the valuable harvest to ripen. You, too, must be patient. Take courage, for the coming of the Lord is near.

Don't grumble about each other, brothers and sisters, or you will be judged. For look—the Judge is standing at the door!

For examples of patience in suffering, dear brothers and sisters, look at the prophets who spoke in the name of the Lord. We give great honor to those who endure under suffering. For instance, you know about Job, a man of great endurance. You can see how the Lord was kind to him at the end, for the Lord is full of tenderness and mercy.

But most of all, my brothers and sisters, never take an oath, by heaven or earth or anything else. Just say a simple yes or no, so that you will not sin and be condemned.

---

[29] Max Lucado, NCV, Grace for the Moment Bible Study (Nashville: Thomas Nelson, 2006), 511.

Are any of you suffering hardships? You should pray. Are any of you happy? You should sing praises. Are any of you sick? You should call for the elders of the church to come and pray over you, anointing you with oil in the name of the Lord. Such a prayer offered in faith will heal the sick, and the Lord will make you well. And if you have committed any sins, you will be forgiven.

Confess your sins to each other and pray for each other so that you may be healed. The earnest prayer of a righteous person has great power and produces wonderful results. Elijah was as human as we are, and yet when he prayed earnestly that no rain would fall, none fell for three and a half years! Then, when he prayed again, the sky sent down rain and the earth began to yield its crops.

My dear brothers and sisters, if someone among you wanders away from the truth and is brought back, you can be sure that whoever brings the sinner back from wandering will save that person from death and bring about the forgiveness of many sins. (James 5:7-20 NLT)

ANDREW MURRAY
Beware in your prayers, above everything else, of limiting God, not only by unbelief, but by fancying that you know what He can do. Expect unexpected things 'above all that we ask or think.'[30]

AS JACOB STARTED ON HIS WAY AGAIN, angels of God came to meet him. When Jacob saw them, he exclaimed, "This is God's camp!" So he named the place Mahanaim.

Then Jacob sent messengers ahead to his brother, Esau, who was living in the region of Seir in the land of Edom. He told them, "Give this message to my master Esau: 'Humble greetings from your servant Jacob.

---

[30] Carol Kent quotes Andrew Murray, He Holds My Hand (Carol Stream: Tyndale House Publishing, 2017), 9.

Until now I have been living with Uncle Laban, and now I own cattle, donkeys, flocks of sheep and goats, and many servants, both men and women. I have sent these messengers to inform my lord of my coming, hoping that you will be friendly to me.'"

After delivering the message, the messengers returned to Jacob and reported, "We met your brother, Esau, and he is already on his way to meet you—with an army of 400 men!" Jacob was terrified at the news. He divided his household, along with the flocks and herds and camels, into two groups. He thought, "If Esau meets one group and attacks it, perhaps the other group can escape."

Then Jacob prayed, "O God of my grandfather Abraham, and God of my father, Isaac—O LORD, You told me, 'Return to your own land and to your relatives.' And You promised me, 'I will treat you kindly.' I am not worthy of all the unfailing love and faithfulness you have shown to me, your servant. When I left home and crossed the Jordan River, I owned nothing except a walking stick. Now my household fills two large camps! O LORD, please rescue me from the hand of my brother, Esau. I am afraid that he is coming to attack me, along with my wives and children. But You promised me, 'I will surely treat you kindly, and I will multiply your descendants until they become as numerous as the sands along the seashore—too many to count.'"

Jacob stayed where he was for the night. Then he selected these gifts from his possessions to present to his brother, Esau: 200 female goats, 20 male goats, 200 ewes, 20 rams, 30 female camels with their young, 40 cows, 10 bulls, 20 female donkeys, and 10 male donkeys. He divided these animals into herds and assigned each to different servants. Then he told his servants, "Go ahead of me with the animals, but keep some distance between the herds."

He gave these instructions to the men leading the first group: "When my brother, Esau, meets you, he will ask, 'Whose servants are you? Where are you going? Who owns these animals?' You must reply, 'They belong to your servant Jacob, but they are a gift for his master Esau. Look, he is coming right behind us.'"

Jacob gave the same instructions to the second and third herdsmen and to all who followed behind the herds: "You must say the same thing to Esau when you meet him. And be sure to say, 'Look, your servant Jacob is right behind us.'"

Jacob thought, "I will try to appease him by sending gifts ahead of me. When I see him in person, perhaps he will be friendly to me." So the gifts were sent on ahead, while Jacob himself spent that night in the camp.

During the night Jacob got up and took his two wives, his two servant wives, and his eleven sons and crossed the Jabbok River with them. After taking them to the other side, he sent over all his possessions. (Genesis 32:1-23 KJV)

WHAT A FRIEND WE HAVE IN JESUS, IAN RANDALL

What a Friend we have in Jesus,
All our sins and griefs to bear!
What a privilege to carry,
Everything to God in prayer!
Oh, what peace we often forfeit,
Oh, what needless pain we bear.
All because we do not carry
Everything to God in prayer![31]

"FOR THIS IS WHAT THE LORD SAYS: "When seventy years have been completed in Babylon, I will visit you and fulfill My good word to you, to bring you back to this place. For I know the plans that I have for you,' declares the Lord, 'plans for prosperity and not for disaster, to give you a future and a hope. Then you will call upon Me and come and pray to Me, and I will listen to you. And you will seek Me and find Me when you search for Me with all your heart. I will let Myself be found by you,' declares the Lord, 'and I will restore your fortunes and gather you from all the nations and all the places where I have driven you,'

---

[31] Joseph Scriven and Charles Converse, What A Friend We Have in Jesus, Originally written in 1855 as a poem, (H.L. Hastings, 1865.)

declares the Lord, 'and I will bring you back to the place from where I sent you into exile.' (Jeremiah 29:10-14 NASB)

DRAW THE CIRCLE, MARK BATTERSON

My grandfather had a prayer ritual that involved kneeling next to his bed at night, taking out his hearing aid, and praying for his family. He couldn't hear himself without his hearing aid, but everyone else in the house could. Few things leave a more lasting impression than hearing someone intercede for you by name…

Grandpa Johnson died when I was six years old, but his prayers did not, … Our prayers have no space or time limitations because the God who answers them exists outside of the four dimensions He created. You never know when His timeless answer will reenter the atmosphere of our lives, and that should fill us with holy anticipation. Never underestimate His ability to answer anytime, anyplace, anyhow … He can answer them more than once. And He answers them forever.

Acts 10:4 declares that our prayers are memorial offerings. I cannot promise that God will answer your prayers how you want or when you want, but I can promise that God will answer … At critical points in my life, the Spirit of God has whispered to my spirit: Mark, the prayers of your grandfather are being answered in your life right now. Those sacred moments rank as the most humbling and exhilarating moments of my life. Like a parent who collects their children's elementary artwork and displays it prominently on a refrigerator door, the heavenly Father loves our prayers … Each one functions like a memorial that jogs the memory of the Almighty.

If our prayers are that precious to God, shouldn't they be more significant to us? Aren't they worth collecting like snapshots in a family photo album? Shouldn't they be treated with respect and dignity, like the monuments that grace the nation's capital? Every prayer we utter is like the marble stones used in the building of the Washington Monument or Lincoln Memorial.

When we pray, we are building a monument to God, a memorial to Him. And those prayers are not perishable ... they are a foundation of gold, silver, and costly stones. They will not be forgotten. They will not go unanswered.[32]

> ### *JOHN PIPER*
> God has given us prayer as a wartime walkie-talkie so that we can call headquarters for everything we need as the kingdom of Christ advances in the world. Prayer gives us the significance of front-line forces, and gives God the glory of a limitless Provider. The one who gives the power gets the glory. Thus prayer safeguards the supremacy of God in missions while linking us with endless grace for every need.[33]

---

[32] Mark Batterson, The Circle Maker Devotions for Kids: 100 Daily Readings (Grand Rapids: Zonderkidz, 2018), 4.

[33] Gailyn Van Rheenen quoting John Piper, Missions: Biblical Foundations and Contemporary Strategies (Grand Rapids: Zondervan, 1996), 10.

Chapter 6
A LAMP UNTO MY FEET

AS FOR GOD, HIS WAY IS PERFECT;
The Lord's word is flawless;
He shields all who take refuge in Him.
For who is God besides the Lord?
And who is the Rock except our God?
It is God who arms me with strength
and keeps my way secure.
He makes my feet like the feet of a deer;
He causes me to stand on the heights. (Psalm 18:30-33 NIV)

THE WORD BECAME FLESH, PATTI BURNETT

"*IN THE BEGINNING WAS THE WORD*, and the Word was with God, and the Word was God. He was with God in the beginning" (John 1:1-2 NIV). Over the years, God has communicated with mankind in a myriad of ways. As the Israelites wandered through the wilderness, God guided them with a pillar of cloud by day and a pillar of fire at night (Exodus 13:21). God dialogued with Moses through a thick cloud so the Children of Israel could perceive His presence (Exodus 19:9). God carved His commandments on stone tablets so that the people would understand the truth (Exodus 24:12). God distinctly commissioned Moses and Paul through a burning bush and a light from heaven, respectively. When the Israelites became stubborn and rebellious, God spoke through the prophets, who proclaimed "Come here and listen to the words of the Lord your God" (Joshua 3:9 NIV).

God created humans for fellowship. "The Lord God said, 'It is not good for the man to be alone. I will make a helper suitable for him'" (Genesis 2:18 NIV). In the Garden of Eden, Adam and Eve had a level of interpersonal communication and sweet fellowship with each other that people only dream about today, not to mention access to unencumbered conversation with the Lord. I have heard it said that the average 21st century couple, after six years of marriage, only communicates about ten minutes a day. I hope that's not the case for Dan and me.

Unfortunately for Adam and Eve, the honeymoon ended when they chose to place more confidence in the deceiver's words than those of the Creator. We have been paying for that one fatal error ever since. Eve's bite into the apple initiated a vicious cycle of shame and fear with fig leaves and masks that has continued for thousands of years. Broken fellowship with God produced broken fellowship between people. Few of us are willing to expose our raw and fragile feelings.

Human beings expend a great deal of energy searching for the message behind the message, only to discover that there are still more layers of metamessages. How do we escape this exasperating conundrum?

"The days are coming, declares the Sovereign Lord, when I will send a famine through the land – not a famine of food or a thirst for water, but a famine of hearing the words of the Lord. Men will stagger from sea to sea and wander from north to east, searching for the Word of the Lord, but they will not find it" (Amos 8:11-12 NIV). I wonder whether this prophecy is being fulfilled each time the Bible or prayer are removed from another school or courtroom. Now, more than ever, we need a word from the Lord. Without intimacy with God, our lives are deficient. As it is said, "… man does not live on bread alone but on every word that proceeds from the mouth of the Lord" (Deuteronomy 8:3b NIV).

"In the past God spoke to our forefathers through the prophets at many times and in various ways, but in these last days He has spoken to us by His Son … The Son is the radiance of God's glory and the exact representation of His being, sustaining all things by His powerful Word" (Hebrews 1:1-2a, 3a NIV). An enormous chasm exists between sinful man and holy God. Picture that chasm as a wall. God designed a bridge or a ladder to reconcile us to Himself. He was so determined to communicate with us that He dispatched His only Son to become a man. "The Word became flesh and made His dwelling among us. We have seen His glory, the glory of the One and Only, who came from the Father, full of grace and truth" (John 1:14 NIV). God made the ultimate sacrifice to get our attention – to help us appreciate that our reception of the gospel, the good news, was worth the very life of Jesus Christ. If God incarnate could not get our focus, then no one and nothing else could.

It is intriguing to me that God created such a unique way to communicate with us. In addition to becoming a man, He then provided us with the opportunity to have His Word reside within us, through the Holy Spirit. The Bible explains that we are to remain in the Word, and, conversely, God desires to make His home in us. He wants us to share fellowship with Him at the deepest level; that's what abiding in Him, and He in us, is all about. Finally, we are thoroughly seen, and the masks must be removed.

As two believers grow in their relationship with the Lord and become more sensitive to His influence in their lives, their interpersonal communication will improve significantly. Conversely, should one decide to walk out of fellowship with God, that person's ability to relate effectively with the fellow believer will suffer. Effective communication is dependent upon honest and sincere motivation. Whether in joyful or disheartening times, believers should be examples to the world of how God intended communication to look. "Let the message of Christ dwell among you richly as you teach and admonish one another with all wisdom through psalms, hymns, and songs from the Spirit, singing to God with gratitude in your hearts. And whatever you do, whether in word or deed, do it all in the name of the Lord Jesus, giving thanks to God the Father through Him" (Colossians 3:16-17 NIV).

What does the world observe when they witness Christians in fellowship? Do they recognize us by our love or our disagreements? Pride can cause us to battle over unnecessary issues that not only detract from meaningful conversation, but also destroy our witness. Even conflict resolution can bring glory to the Father if, with Spirit-filled hearts, our motivation is to build up the other person.

The good news is that God's Word is powerful. "By the word of the Lord the heavens were made, their starry host by the breath of His mouth. For He spoke, and it came to be; He commanded, and it stood firm" (Psalm 33:6, 9 NIV). At Jesus' word, evil spirits fled, storms were calmed, sins were forgiven, and the dead were raised. Never has there been one Who spoke with such authority (Matthew 7:29). That same authority has been granted to believers who obediently carry on the Great Commission (Matthew 28:18-19). God has promised us that His Word will not return void, but will accomplish that which He has purposed (Isaiah 55:11).

One of the beautiful ways that the Word is embodied comes through the sharing of stories and teachings from generation to generation. "These commandments that I give you today are to be upon your hearts. Impress them on your children. Talk about them when you sit at home and when you walk along the road, when you lie down and when you get up" (Deuteronomy 6:6-7 NIV). God has been faithful to preserve a remnant to bear His Word through the ages. Today, Christian homes all over the world have carried on the tradition with family altars and devotionals.

Regarding a Christian's prayer life, much of a believer's communication with God is one-sided. We read His Word and we experience the beauty of creation, but we often fail to reciprocate. It must please Abba's heart when He hears the earnest prayers of Christians intent upon knowing the Almighty God. A believer is absolutely transformed as a result of communing with God. If we are not changed, it is because we are not listening. On the other hand, maybe it's a case of listening, but not doing (James 1:22-25).

Though we are continually being conformed to the image of Christ Jesus, God is unchanging. This is one of the benefits of interacting with God. Each time we approach His throne, we can count on His immutable nature. While friends may come and go, God is the same yesterday, today, and tomorrow.

The quality of my life and spiritual maturity increases proportionally with the contact quotient that exists between God and myself. I know that the richness and quality of my relationship with God is especially low during those times when it feels as though my prayers are bouncing off the ceiling. The other end of the spectrum is when I sense God's continual guidance through the most mundane times of life, even when I do not think to pray.

It is my plea to know God and His will for my life. Like the Psalmist, I want to live according to God's Word – to hide it in my heart and to meditate on it day and night (Psalm 119:9, 11, 15). What might this look like? For me, I choose to daily guard the things that enter my mind through my eyes and ears. I want my heart to be good soil that joyfully receives His Word and in which He multiplies the results exponentially. "But the seed falling on good soil refers to one who hears the Word and understands it. This is the one who produces a crop, yielding a hundred, sixty or thirty times what was sown" (Matthew 13:23 NIV).

Father, please do not allow me to become desensitized to Your Word. Show me how I can more fully experience and practice Your love and presence. Thank You for the assurance that when I grow old and my eyes grow dim, my hearing fails, and my brain is dulled, You will continue to speak to me. This is especially true as I contemplate the prospect of living with Parkinson's. May I always listen to Your still small voice.

FOR THE WORD OF GOD IS LIVING AND POWERFUL, and sharper than any two-edged sword, piercing even to the division of soul and spirit, and of joints and marrow, and is a discerner of the thoughts and intents of the heart. (Hebrews 4:12 NKJV)

CORRIE TEN BOOM
I've experienced His presence in the deepest darkest hell that men can create. I have tested the promises of the Bible, and believe me, you can count on them. I know that Jesus Christ can live in you, in me through His Holy Spirit. You can talk with Him; you can talk with Him out loud or in your heart when you are alone, as I was alone in solitary confinement. The joy is that He hears each word.[34]

THEN SOLOMON SPOKE:
"The Lord said He would dwell in the dark cloud.
I have surely built You an exalted house,
And a place for You to dwell in forever."

---

[34] Corrie ten Boom, He sets the captive free (Grand Rapids: Revell, 1977), (1892-1983) Dutch Watchmaker, Author, from https://quozio.com/quote/f29b3095/1025/ive-experienced-his-presence-in-the-deepest-darkest-hell.

Then the king turned around and blessed the whole assembly of Israel, while all the assembly of Israel was standing. And he said: "Blessed be the Lord God of Israel, who has fulfilled with His hands what He spoke with His mouth to my father David, saying, 'Since the day that I brought My people out of the land of Egypt, I have chosen no city from any tribe of Israel in which to build a house, that My name might be there, nor did I choose any man to be a ruler over My people Israel. Yet I have chosen Jerusalem, that My name may be there, and I have chosen David to be over My people Israel.' Now it was in the heart of my father David to build a temple for the name of the Lord God of Israel. But the Lord said to my father David, 'Whereas it was in your heart to build a temple for My name, you did well in that it was in your heart. Nevertheless you shall not build the temple, but your son who will come from your body, he shall build the temple for My name.' So the Lord has fulfilled His word which He spoke, and I have filled the position of my father David, and sit on the throne of Israel, as the Lord promised; and I have built the temple for the name of the Lord God of Israel. And there I have put the ark, in which is the covenant of the Lord which He made with the children of Israel."

Then Solomon stood before the altar of the Lord in the presence of all the assembly of Israel, and spread out his hands (for Solomon had made a bronze platform five cubits long, five cubits wide, and three cubits high, and had set it in the midst of the court; and he stood on it, knelt down on his knees before all the assembly of Israel, and spread out his hands toward heaven); and he said: "Lord God of Israel, there is no God in heaven or on earth like You, who keep Your covenant and mercy with Your servants who walk before You with all their hearts. You have kept what You promised Your servant David my father; You have both spoken with Your mouth and fulfilled it with Your hand, as it is this day. Therefore, Lord God of Israel, now keep what You promised Your servant David my father, saying, 'You shall not fail to have a man sit before Me on the throne of Israel, only if your sons take heed to their way, that they walk in My law as you have walked before Me.' And now,

O Lord God of Israel, let Your word come true, which You have spoken to Your servant David. (II Chronicles 6:1-17 NKJV)

> **MARTIN LUTHER**
> The Bible is the cradle wherein Christ is laid.[35]

YOUR WORD IS LIFE TO ME, TRAVIS COTTRELL

I am a stranger in this place;
This world is not my home.
I want more than it can give.
I am a desert needing rain;
I'm thirsty for your voice.
The very reason that I live –
You are the Word, my one desire,
An all-consuming holy fire,
The very breath that I am longing for.
My heart is desperate for Your ways,
Refine me in your holy blaze,
If that is what it takes to know you more.
You are the Truth that sets me free;
Your Word is life to me.
Only the power of Your Word
Can melt away these chains
That have held me far too long.

So light the fire and let it burn
these shackles and restraints,
And I will sing this freedom song.
You are the word, my one desire …

---

[35] Greg Cootsna Quoting Martin Luther, Mere Science and Christian Faith (Westmont: IVP Books, 2018), 96.

You are the truth that sets me free.
Your word is life to me.[36]

THEN ALL THE PEOPLE GATHERED TOGETHER as one man at the open square in front of the water gate; and they asked Ezra the scribe to bring the Book of the Law of Moses which the Lord had given to Israel. So Ezra the priest brought the Law before the assembly of men, women and all who could listen with understanding, on the first day of the seventh month. Then he read from it, in front of the open square which was in front of the WaterGate, from early morning until midday, in the presence of the men and women, those who could understand; and all the people listened carefully to the Book of the Law. Ezra the scribe stood on a [large] wooden platform which they had constructed for this purpose. And beside him [on the platform] stood Mattithiah, Shema, Anaiah, Uriah, Hilkiah, and Maaseiah on his right; and Pedaiah, Mishael, Malchijah, Hashum, Hashbaddanah, Zechariah, and Meshullam on his left. Ezra opened the book in the sight of all the people, for he was standing above them; and when he opened it, all the people stood up. Then Ezra blessed the Lord, the great God. And all the people answered, "Amen, Amen!" while lifting up their hands; and they knelt down and worshiped the Lord with their faces toward the ground. Also Jeshua, Bani, Sherebiah, Jamin, Akkub, Shabbethai, Hodiah, Maaseiah, Kelita, Azariah, Jozabad, Hanan, Pelaiah, and the Levites, explained the Law to the people, and the people remained in their places. So they read from the Book of the Law of God, translating and explaining it so that the people understood the reading.

Then Nehemiah, who was the governor, and Ezra the priest and scribe, and the Levites who taught the people said to all the people, "This day is holy to the Lord your God; do not mourn or weep." For all the people were weeping when they heard the words of the Law.

---

[36] Travis Cottrell, Your Word is Life to Me, released 2006, Kent Hooper (producer), Chris Thomason (executive producer), distributed by Word Entertainment, track 8 on Found, 2006, album.

Then Ezra said to them, "Go [your way], eat the rich festival food, drink the sweet drink, and send portions to him for whom nothing is prepared; for this day is holy to our Lord. And do not be worried, for the joy of the Lord is your strength and your stronghold."

So the Levites quieted all the people, saying, "Be still, for the day is holy; do not be worried." Then all the people went on their way to eat, to drink, to send portions [of food to others] and to celebrate a great festival, because they understood the words which had been communicated to them.

On the second day, all of the heads of fathers' households of all the people, the priests, and the Levites, were gathered before Ezra the scribe to gain insight into the words of the Law (divine instruction). They found written in the Law how the Lord had commanded through Moses that the Israelites should live in booths (huts) during the feast of the seventh month. So they proclaimed and published an announcement in all their cities and in Jerusalem, saying, "Go out to the hills and bring olive branches, wild olive, myrtle, palm, and other leafy branches to make booths, as it is written." So the people went out and brought them and made booths for themselves, each on the roof of his house, and in their courtyards and the courtyards of God's house, and in the open square of the Water Gate and in the square of the Gate of Ephraim. The entire assembly of those who had returned from the captivity made booths and lived in them. Indeed since the days of Joshua the son of Nun until that very day, the Israelites had not done so. And there was great rejoicing and celebration. Every day, from the first day to the last, Ezra read from the Book of the Law of God. They celebrated the feast for seven days; on the eighth day there was a [closing] solemn assembly in accordance with the ordinance. (Nehemiah 8:1-18 AMP)

PATTI BURNETT
I want to know God's Word so well
that when I hear His voice, there is no doubt.

THEODORE ROOSEVELT
A thorough knowledge of the Bible is worth more than a college education.[37]

HOW BLESSED AND FAVORED BY GOD ARE THOSE whose way is blameless [those with personal integrity, the upright, the guileless],
Who walk in the law [and who are guided by the precepts and revealed will] of the LORD.

Blessed and favored by God are those who keep His testimonies,
And who [consistently] seek Him and long for Him with all their heart.

They do no unrighteousness;
They walk in His ways.

You have ordained Your precepts,
That we should follow them with [careful] diligence.

Oh, that my ways may be established
To observe and keep Your statutes [obediently accepting and honoring them]!

---

[37] Michael McAfee and Lauren Green McAfee quoting Theodore Roosevelt, Not What You Think (Nathville: Thomas Nelson, 2019), 119.

Then I will not be ashamed
When I look [with respect] to all Your commandments [as
my guide].

I will give thanks to You with an upright heart,
When I learn [through discipline] Your righteous judgments [for
my transgressions].

I shall keep Your statutes;
Do not utterly abandon me [when I fail].

How can a young man keep his way pure?
By keeping watch [on himself] according to Your word [conforming
his life to Your precepts].

With all my heart I have sought You, [inquiring of You and
longing for You];
Do not let me wander from Your commandments [neither through
ignorance nor by willful disobedience].

Your word I have treasured and stored in my heart,
That I may not sin against you.

Blessed and reverently praised are You, O Lord;
Teach me Your statutes.

With my lips I have told of
All the ordinances of Your mouth.

I have rejoiced in the way of Your testimonies,
As much as in all riches.

I will meditate on Your precepts
And [thoughtfully] regard Your ways [the path of life established
by Your precepts].

I will delight in Your statutes;
I will not forget Your word.

Deal bountifully with your servant,
That I may live and keep Your word [treasuring it and being guided by it day by day].

Open my eyes [to spiritual truth] so that I may behold
Wonderful things from Your law.

I am a stranger on the earth;
Do not hide Your commandments from me.

My soul is crushed with longing
For Your ordinances at all times.

You rebuke the presumptuous and arrogant, the cursed ones,
Who wander from Your commandments.

Take reproach and contempt away from me,
For I observe Your testimonies.

Even though princes sit and talk to one another against me,
Your servant meditates on Your statutes.

Your testimonies also are my delight
And my counselors.

My earthly life clings to the dust;
Revive and refresh me according to Your word.

I have told of my ways, and You have answered me;
Teach me Your statutes.

Make me understand the way of Your precepts,
So that I will meditate (focus my thoughts) on Your wonderful works.

CHRONIC HOPE

My soul dissolves because of grief;
Renew and strengthen me according to [the promises of] Your word.

Remove from me the way of falsehood and unfaithfulness,
And graciously grant me Your law.

I have chosen the faithful way;
I have placed Your ordinances before me.

I cling tightly to Your testimonies;
O Lord, do not put me to shame!

I will run the way of Your commandments [with purpose],
For You will give me a heart that is willing.

Teach me, O Lord, the way of Your statutes,
And I will [steadfastly] observe it to the end.

Give me understanding [a teachable heart and the ability to learn], that I may keep Your law;
And observe it with all my heart.

Make me walk in the path of Your commandments,
For I delight in it.

Incline my heart to Your testimonies
And not to dishonest gain and envy.

Turn my eyes away from vanity [all those worldly, meaningless things that distract—let Your priorities be mine],
And restore me [with renewed energy] in Your ways.

Establish Your word and confirm Your promise to Your servant,
As that which produces [awe-inspired] reverence for You.

A Lamp Unto My Feet

Turn away my reproach which I dread,
For Your ordinances are good.

I long for Your precepts;
Renew me through Your righteousness.

May Your lovingkindness also come to me, O Lord,
Your salvation according to Your promise;

So I will have an answer for the one who taunts me,
For I trust [completely] in Your word [and its reliability].

And do not take the word of truth utterly out of my mouth,
For I wait for Your ordinances.

I will keep Your law continually,
Forever and ever [writing Your precepts on my heart].

And I will walk at liberty,
For I seek and deeply long for Your precepts.

I will also speak of Your testimonies before kings
And shall not be ashamed.

For I shall delight in your commandments,
Which I love.

And I shall lift up my hands to Your commandments,
Which I love;

And I will meditate on Your statutes.
Remember [always] the word and promise to Your servant,

In which You have made me hope.

CHRONIC HOPE

This is my comfort in my affliction,
That Your word has revived me and given me life.

The arrogant utterly ridicule me,
Yet I do not turn away from Your law.

I have remembered [carefully] Your ancient ordinances, O Lord
And I have taken comfort.

Burning indignation has seized me because of the wicked,
Who reject Your law.

Your statutes are my songs
In the house of my pilgrimage.

O Lord, I remember Your name in the night,
And keep Your law.

This has become mine [as the gift of Your grace],
That I observe Your precepts [accepting them with loving obedience].

The Lord is my portion;
I have promised to keep Your words.

I sought Your favor with all my heart;
Be merciful and gracious to me according to Your promise.

I considered my ways
And turned my feet to [follow and obey] Your testimonies.

I hurried and did not delay
To keep Your commandments.

The cords of the wicked have encircled and ensnared me,
But I have not forgotten Your law.

At midnight I will rise to give thanks to You
Because of Your righteous ordinances.

I am a companion of all who [reverently] fear You,
And of those who keep and honor Your precepts.

The earth, O Lord, is full of Your loving kindness and goodness;
Teach me Your statutes.

You have dealt well with Your servant,
O Lord, according to Your promise.

Teach me good judgment (discernment) and knowledge,
For I have believed and trusted and relied on Your commandments.

Before I was afflicted I went astray,
But now I keep and honor Your word [with loving obedience].

You are good and do good;
Teach me Your statutes.

The arrogant have forged a lie against me,
But I will keep Your precepts with all my heart.

Their heart is insensitive like fat [their minds are dull and brutal],
But I delight in Your law.

It is good for me that I have been afflicted,
That I may learn Your statutes.

The law from Your mouth is better to me
Than thousands of gold and silver pieces.

Your hands have made me and established me;
Give me understanding and a teachable heart, that I may learn Your commandments.

May those who [reverently] fear You see me and be glad,
Because I wait for Your word.

I know, O LORD, that Your judgments are fair,
And that in faithfulness You have disciplined me.

O may Your loving kindness and graciousness comfort me,
According to Your word (promise) to Your servant.

Let Your compassion come to me that I may live,
For Your law is my delight.

Let the arrogant be ashamed and humiliated, for they sabotage me with a lie;
But I will meditate on Your precepts.

May those who fear You [with submissive wonder] turn to me,
Even those who have known Your testimonies.

May my heart be blameless in Your statutes,
So that I will not be ashamed.

My soul languishes and grows weak for Your salvation;
I wait for Your word.

My eyes fail [with longing, watching] for [the fulfillment of] Your promise,
Saying, "When will You comfort me?"

For I have become like a wineskin [blackened and shriveled] in the smoke [in which it hangs],
Yet I do not forget Your statutes.

How many are the days of Your servant [which he must endure]?
When will You execute judgment on those who persecute me?

The arrogant (godless) have dug pits for me,
Men who do not conform to Your law.

All Your commandments are faithful and trustworthy.
They have persecuted me with a lie; help me [Lord]!

They had almost destroyed me on earth,
But as for me, I did not turn away from Your precepts.

According to Your steadfast love refresh me and give me life,
So that I may keep and obey the testimony of Your mouth.

Forever, O Lord,
Your word is settled in heaven [standing firm and unchangeable].

Your faithfulness continues from generation to generation;
You have established the earth, and it stands [securely].

They continue this day according to Your ordinances,
For all things [all parts of the universe] are Your servants.

I will never forget Your precepts,
For by them You have revived me and given me life.

I am Yours, save me [as Your own];

For I have [diligently] sought Your precepts and required them [as my greatest need].

The wicked wait for me to destroy me,
But I will consider Your testimonies.

I have seen that all [human] perfection has its limits [no matter how grand and perfect and noble];
Your commandment is exceedingly broad and extends without limits [into eternity].

Oh, how I love Your law!
It is my meditation all the day.

Your commandments make me wiser than my enemies,
For Your words are always with me.

I have better understanding and deeper insight than all my teachers [because of Your word],
For Your testimonies are my meditation.

I understand more than the aged [who have not observed Your precepts],
Because I have observed and kept Your precepts.

I have restrained my feet from every evil way,
That I may keep Your word.

I have not turned aside from Your ordinances,
For You Yourself have taught me.

How sweet are Your words to my taste,
Sweeter than honey to my mouth!

From Your precepts I get understanding;
Therefore I hate every false way.

Your word is a lamp to my feet
And a light to my path.

I have sworn [an oath] and have confirmed it,
That I will keep Your righteous ordinances.

I am greatly afflicted;
Renew and revive me [giving me life], O Lord, according to Your word.

Accept and take pleasure in the freewill offerings of my mouth, O Lord,
And teach me Your ordinances.

My life is continually in my hand,
Yet I do not forget Your law.

The wicked have laid a snare for me,
Yet I do not wander from Your precepts.

I have taken Your testimonies as a heritage forever,
For they are the joy of my heart.

I have inclined my heart to perform Your statutes
Forever, even to the end.

I hate those who are double-minded,
But I love and treasure Your law.

You are my hiding place and my shield;
I wait for Your word.

Leave me, you evildoers,
That I may keep the commandments of my God [honoring and obeying them].

Uphold me according to Your word [of promise], so that
I may live;
And do not let me be ashamed of my hope [in Your great goodness].

Uphold me that I may be safe,
That I may have regard for Your statutes continually.

You have turned Your back on all those who wander from
Your statutes,
For their deceitfulness is useless.

You have removed all the wicked of the earth like dross [for they have no value];
Therefore I love Your testimonies.

My flesh trembles in [reverent] fear of You,
And I am afraid and in awe of Your judgments.

I have done justice and righteousness;
Do not leave me to those who oppress me.

Be the guarantee for Your servant for good [as Judah was the guarantee for Benjamin];
Do not let the arrogant oppress me.

My eyes fail [with longing, watching] for [the fulfillment of] Your salvation,
And for [the fulfillment of] Your righteous word.

Deal with Your servant according to Your [gracious] lovingkindness,
And teach me Your statutes.

I am Your servant; give me understanding [the ability to learn and a teachable heart] that I may know Your testimonies.

It is time for the LORD to act;
They have broken Your law.

Therefore I love Your commandments more than gold,
Yes, more than refined gold.

Therefore I esteem as right all Your precepts concerning everything;
I hate every false way.

Your testimonies are wonderful;
Therefore my soul keeps them.

The unfolding of Your [glorious] words give light;
Their unfolding gives understanding to the simple (childlike).

A Lamp Unto My Feet

I opened my mouth and panted [with anticipation],
Because I longed for Your commandments.

Turn to me and be gracious to me and show me favor,
As is Your way to those who love Your name.

Establish my footsteps in [the way of] Your word;
Do not let any human weakness have power over me [causing me to be separated from You].

Redeem me from the oppression of man;
That I may keep Your precepts.

Make Your face shine [with pleasure] upon Your servant, and teach me Your Statutes.

My eyes weep streams of water
Because people do not keep Your law.

Righteous are You, O Lord,
And upright are Your judgments.

You have commanded Your testimonies in righteousness
And in great faithfulness.

My zeal has [completely] consumed me,
Because my enemies have forgotten Your words.

Your word is very pure (refined);
Therefore Your servant loves it.

I am small and despised,
But I do not forget Your precepts.

Your righteousness is an everlasting righteousness,
And Your law is truth.

Trouble and anguish have found me,
Yet Your commandments are my delight and my joy.

CHRONIC HOPE

Your righteous testimonies are everlasting;
Give me understanding [the ability to learn and a teachable heart]
that I may live.

I cried with all my heart; answer me, O LORD!
I will observe Your statutes.

I cried to You; save me
And I will keep Your testimonies.

I rise before dawn and cry [in prayer] for help;
I wait for Your word.

My eyes anticipate the night watches and I awake before the call of the watchman,
That I may meditate on Your word.

Hear my voice according to Your [steadfast] lovingkindness;
O LORD, renew and refresh me according to Your ordinances.

Those who follow after wickedness approach;
They are far from Your law.

You are near, O LORD,
And all Your commandments are truth.

Of old I have known from Your testimonies
That You have founded them forever.

Look upon my agony and rescue me,
For I do not forget Your law.

Plead my cause and redeem me;
Revive me and give me life according to [the promise of]
Your word.

Salvation is far from the wicked,
For they do not seek Your statutes.

Great are Your tender mercies and steadfast love, O LORD;
Revive me and give me life according to Your ordinances.

Many are my persecutors and my adversaries,
Yet I do not turn away from Your testimonies.

I see the treacherous and loathe them,
Because they do not respect Your law.

Consider how I love Your precepts;
Revive me and give me life, O Lord, according to Your lovingkindness.

The sum of Your word is truth [the full meaning of all Your precepts],
And every one of Your righteous ordinances endures forever.

Princes persecute me without cause,
But my heart stands in [reverent] awe of Your words [so I can expect You to help me].

I rejoice at Your word,
As one who finds great treasure.

I hate and detest falsehood,
But I love Your law.

Seven times a day I praise You,
Because of Your righteous ordinances.

Those who love Your law have great peace;
Nothing makes them stumble.

I hope and wait [with complete confidence] for Your salvation, O Lord,
And I do Your commandments.

My soul keeps Your testimonies [hearing and accepting and obeying them];
I love them greatly.

I keep Your precepts and Your testimonies,
For all my ways are [fully known] before You.

Let my [mournful] cry come before You, O Lord;
Give me understanding [the ability to learn and a teachable heart]
according to Your word [of promise].

Let my supplication come before You;
Deliver me according to Your word.

Let my lips speak praise [with thanksgiving],
For You teach me Your statutes.

Let my tongue sing [praise for the fulfillment] of Your word,
For all Your commandments are righteous.

Let Your hand be ready to help me,
For I have chosen Your precepts.

I long for Your salvation, O Lord,
And Your law is my delight.

Let my soul live that it may praise You,
And let Your ordinances help me.

I have gone astray like a lost sheep; seek Your servant, for I do not forget Your commandments. (Psalm 119:1-176 AMP)

JOHN WYCLIFFE, PATTI BURNETT

IT WAS BY THE BLOOD OF THE BROTHERS AND SISTERS who preceded us that believers today enjoy freedom to view the heart of God through the window of His Word. In 1330, an Englishman by the name of John Wycliffe was one of those men who paid dearly with his health. This great spiritual leader was so committed to the truth that no obstacle could deter him from his mission of translating the Bible into the English vernacular. He inspired others with his passion to such a degree that they are continuing his work even today.

John Wycliffe lived during the Pre-Reformation period. There was great economic, political, militaristic, and spiritual turmoil amongst the common people. Much animosity was directed toward the Pope, who received a large percentage of the increasing wealth in Europe. His influence also extended into governmental circles since kings and emperors were threatened with excommunication if they spoke against the Church's directives. King Edward III placed loyal men in respected church offices who were strong in government and administrative skills, while often lacking in the spiritual gifts required for such appointments. Some of the friars and local priests were even illiterate, except to recite Latin during the celebration of Mass. Such was the vacuum that existed when Wycliffe entered the scene.

This respected man obtained a Bachelor of Divinity from Oxford and was one of the foremost philosophers, teachers, and political writers in that area. "Master" Wycliffe enjoyed the favor, protection, and high standing of many government officials, especially the King, and reached the zenith of his political career in 1378. He wisely determined that by aligning himself with the government authorities rather than the Church he would have a strategic advantage in advancing the Gospel.

At this time, the hierarchical Roman Church taught many tenets that were contrary to scripture and based merely on tradition. For example, it held that people could only come to God through the clergy. This priestly authority created a dependence upon the Church that God never intended. Wycliffe believed that man was able to enter God's presence through Jesus Christ, the great High Priest. "Therefore He (Jesus) is able to save completely those who come to God through Him, because He always lives to intercede for them" (Hebrews 7:25 NIV).

Wycliffe taught that the Church was in error in its requirement that individuals perform certain indulgences, sacraments, and works to earn a way into heaven. The Bible promises that God grants grace and forgiveness as a gift to those who humbly come to Him through the blood of Jesus Christ. Wycliffe also attacked the teaching of the Church, that in communion, the bread and the wine are literally transformed into the body and blood of Jesus, a doctrine known as transubstantiation. He argued that the elements of communion were meant to be a symbolic reminder of Christ's sacrificial death for us. "And when He (Jesus) had given thanks, He broke it and said, 'This is my body, which is for you; do this in remembrance of Me.' In the same way, after supper He took the cup, saying, 'This cup is the new covenant in my blood; do this, whenever you drink it, in remembrance of me'" (I Corinthians 11:24-25 NIV).

Western Europeans' only source of Biblical knowledge came through the Roman Church since they had no translation of God's Word in their own language. The Church prohibited the common person from reading scripture for fear of misinterpretation and subsequent misunderstanding. For this reason, literature that opposed the Church's edicts was considered heretical and was destroyed.

In the later years of his life, Wycliffe translated the New Testament for members of the clergy. However, he decided that there still needed to be a translation in the vernacular, "the people's language;" and he inspired his followers to carry on the work even after his death. The driving force in Wycliffe's second translation (the Lollard Bible) was Purvey, his secretary, and one of his most scholarly disciples. The Lollards were followers of Wycliffe, and they challenged the Roman Catholic church's authority and departure from the authority of God's Word. They held strongly to the belief that a Christian could come directly to the Lord and did not need the intercession of a priest. The name Lollard came to be synonymous with "heretic" and the title was applied to Wycliffites.

Wycliffe was convinced that for man to know his Creator, he had to know scripture. He believed that each person, given the gift of scripture, could be empowered to personally receive God's truth and His salvation. "To the Jews who had believed Him, Jesus said, 'If you hold to My teaching, you are really My disciples. Then you will know the truth, and the truth will set you free'" (John 8:31-32 NIV).

Wycliffe defended scriptural authority with his whole heart, and neither government nor Church opposition could deter him. He was asked to step down from his professorship at Oxford and exiled to Lutterworth, England. Wycliffe used this banishment as an opportunity to lead his followers in completing the Old and New Testaments into the English vernacular without distraction. This translation work led to Wycliffe's martyrdom and even after his burial, Church officials dug up his bones and burned them.

> However, the spreading of the Word could not be contained. "And as rain and snow cometh down from (the) heaven(s), and turneth no more again thither, but it filleth, or maketh moist, the earth, and be sheddeth it, and maketh it to burgeon, and giveth seed to him that soweth, and bread to him that eateth, so shall be My word, that shall go out of My mouth. It shall not turn again void to Me, but it shall do whatever things I would (It shall not return to me void, or empty, but it shall do whatever I desired of it), and it shall have prosperity in these things to which I (have) sent it" (Isaiah 55:10-11 Wycliffe Bible Translation).

Great spiritual leaders do not draw people to themselves; they redirect them to God. Like John the Baptist, John Wycliffe did not accept the praise and glory of his followers. The Word of God was the standard for Wycliffe's life, and he imparted this conviction to his followers, who evangelized during the later days of his life, continuing to this day. This is best illustrated by the spiritual leaders who followed in His footprints.

After Wycliffe's death, these men carried on his work amid even greater persecution, heralding in the Reformation. One of these men was Jan (John) Hus, a Bohemian priest accused of being a disciple of the "Arch Heretic," John Wycliffe. This "Rebel of God" was excommunicated from the Catholic Church because of his stand that Christ was head of the Church, not the Pope. He was promised safe conduct if he came before the Council of Constance and give an account of his doctrine. When he arrived, he was arrested and told to recant his views. His answer was, "I appeal to Jesus Christ, the only judge who is almighty and completely just. In His hands I plead my cause, not on the basis of false witnesses and erring councils, but on truth and justice." He was dressed in his priestly garments and then stripped of them one by one as he again refused to recant his beliefs.

Hus' final prayer was "Lord Jesus, it is for Thee that I patiently endure this cruel death. I pray Thee to have mercy on my enemies." He recited Psalms as the flames surrounded him; and even then, he sang until he breathed his last breath of praise to his Lord. It is written that his executioners scooped up his ashes and threw them into a lake so that nothing remained of him. That was how much they feared him and his teachings.

Today:

- One in five people still have no translated Bible, but 2,731 languages have active translation work going on.
- 1,551 different languages have the entire New Testament which potentially reaches 815 million people.
- 704 languages have a full Bible (New and Old Testaments) that is understandable and accessible to 5.7 billion people.

- There are 7,360 languages spoken in the world, and 1,160 languages have some portions of the Bible, potentially reaching 458 million people.

Wycliffe Bible Translators, founded in 1933, teaches missionaries how to live in jungle boot camps, and then make their homes among the people they are commissioned to serve. These "revolutionaries through literature" learn an unwritten language by analyzing the spoken dialect and constructing its written form. Translation work is extremely labor intensive, sometimes requiring up to two hours for the interpretation of a single verse.

Wycliffe Bible Translators' brochure reads, "Wycliffe believes every man, woman, and child should have the Bible in his or her language. Our commitment is to:

1. Provide God's Word in the language of the world's peoples,
2. Enable them to read it themselves,
3. And encourage them in personal spiritual growth and growth as a body of believers.

John Wycliffe and many other fathers of the pre-Reformation Christian Church gave their lives so that I could have the Bible and enter into a personal relationship with its Author. Studying Mr. Wycliffe's life has given me a fresh appreciation for God's Word and the One who made the ultimate sacrifice so that I might spend the rest of my life and through eternity getting to know Him. "The Word became flesh and made His dwelling among us. We have seen His glory, the glory of the One and Only Who came from the Father, full of grace and truth" (John 1:14 NIV).

Before becoming a Christian, the believers that I held in the highest esteem were some close friends of ours who were life-long Wycliffe missionaries in Papua, New Guinea. They were so influential in the lives of their daughter that she and her husband moved more than 40 years ago to Brazil to pursue mission work with people on the Amazon who had never heard the gospel. When their nine children were quite young, each led a small group of locals who were just slightly younger than themselves. I am sure that Scott and Michelle have lost track of the number of churches they have planted, each eventually pastored by Brazilian nationals. They have become so immersed in Brazilian culture, that many of their children have married local South Americans, and they, in turn, are carrying on the mission of their parents and grandparents.

John Wycliffe was a man courageous enough to initiate a tremendous paradigm shift. In the Middle Ages, he stood apart as a leader with spiritual insight and commitment to the truth. Spiritual leadership does not come without its cost.

In the short life span of 54 years, John Wycliffe ignited a fire in the hearts of men and women to spread the knowledge of the word of God to the ends of the earth. He was considered by many "the Morning Star of the Reformation."

He inspires me to want to passionately carry on God's Great Commission.

Chapter 7

WHEN CHRIST CALLS A MAN OR A WOMAN, HE BIDS THEM COME AND DIE

"LET ME GIVE YOU A NEW COMMAND: love one another. In the same way I loved you, you love one another. This is how everyone will recognize that you are My disciples – when they see the love you have for each other. (John 13:34-35 Message)

THIS IS GOING TO HURT ME MORE THAN IT HURTS YOU, PATTI BURNETT

THE AUTHOR OF PROVERBS 3 EXHORTS THE BELIEVER, "My son, do not despise the Lord's discipline and do not resent His rebuke, because the Lord disciplines those He loves, as a father the son he delights in" (Proverbs 3:11-12 NIV). I always hated it when my dad would tell me "This is going to hurt me more than it hurts you." For some reason I never believed him. My parents both subscribed to the admonition, "He who spares the rod hates his son" (Proverbs 13:24a NKJV). Or, as Dr. Spock taught, "Spare the rod, spoil the child." It did not go well for me when I explained to my dad that I was not a son, and that I had four brothers who were more qualified. "But he who loves him is careful to discipline him" (Proverbs 13:24b NIV). Is there supporting evidence for the author's principles? What are the purposes and implications of discipline? Is discipline one of God's principles I should expect continually throughout my life?

Job is the perfect person to consult on the topic of discipline, in fact, he considered discipline a good thing. "Blessed is the man whom God corrects; so do not despise the discipline of the Almighty. For He wounds, but He also binds up; He injures, but His hands also heal" (Job 5:17-18 NIV). Deuteronomy 8:5 and Revelation 3:19 are two of many passages that reinforce the reality that God's discipline is evidence of two things: 1) our sonship and daughter ship, and 2) His love for us.

The Bible uses the word "discipline" nearly 50 times. Hebrews 12:4-13 gives us insight into God's reason for discipline. "Our fathers disciplined us for a little while as they thought best; but God disciplines us for our good, that we may share in His holiness" (Hebrews 12:10 NIV). God's purpose in discipline is to conform us to the image of Jesus Christ. It is no coincidence that a disciple is one who has placed himself under another's discipline. The question is whether I will wriggle away from His transforming hand or allow Him to do His work. AM I WILLING?

When Christ Calls A Man Or A Woman, He Bids Them Come And Die

I often ask myself what the life of a disciple looks like and how I measure up. The early believers underwent severe suffering and received support from fellow believers as well as God's Word. Dietrich Bonhoeffer says, "When Christ calls a man, He bids him come and die." Bonhoeffer was martyred when the Nazis discovered that he was plotting to kill Adolf Hitler. He identified suffering as a badge of true discipleship. I would be lying if I claimed to embrace suffering and discipline; I am much too narrow-minded, selfish, and pampered. Am I preventing God's perfect work in my life when I reject His discipline? Is my problem that I do not recognize God's hand and just assume it to be some "random act of meanness?" Discipline is the process a believer experiences from the time he surrenders his life to Jesus. God's design and goal is to complete what He started in each one of His children (Philippians 1:6).

After training search and rescue dogs for 30 years I became a student of dog behavior. In the wild, before wolf cubs are four months old, the mother grabs them around the neck and gently, but firmly, pins them to the ground. I found that with my new pups we had to establish canine submission to master/handler dominance. We did this by placing them on their sides and holding the scruff at the back of their necks. In fact, if done correctly, this seemingly insignificant step caused the puppy's heart rate to slow and became the foundation of all other disciplinary training for the developing search dog. This discipline was for their good so that they understood the difference between right and wrong. The intent of this behavior was to instill respect in the pup, not harm or fear. This is also true of God's discipline for us.

> God develops character in us when He places us under fire. "So be truly glad! There is wonderful joy ahead, even though the going is rough for a while down here. These trials are only to test your faith, to see whether or not it is strong and pure. It is being tested in much the same way that fire tests gold and purifies it – and your faith is far more precious to God than mere gold; so

if your faith remains strong after being tried in the test tube of fiery trials, it will bring much praise and glory and honor on the day of His return" (1 Peter 1:6-7 TLB).

JESUS NOW CALLED THE TWELVE, and gave them authority and power to deal with all the demons and cure diseases. He commissioned them to preach the news of God's kingdom and heal the sick. He said, "Don't load yourselves up with equipment. Keep it simple; you are the equipment. And no luxury inns—get a modest place and be content there until you leave. If you're not welcomed, leave town. Don't make a scene. Shrug your shoulders and move on."

Commissioned, they left. They traveled from town to town telling the latest news of God, the Message, and curing people everywhere they went.

Herod, the ruler, heard of these goings on and didn't know what to think. There were people saying John had come back from the dead, others that Elijah had appeared, still others that some prophet of long ago had shown up. Herod said, "But I killed John—took off his head. So who is this that I keep hearing about?" Curious, he looked for a chance to see Him in action.

The apostles returned and reported on what they had done. Jesus took them away, off by themselves, near the town called Bethsaida. But the crowds got wind of it and followed. Jesus graciously welcomed them and talked to them about the kingdom of God. Those who needed healing, He healed.

As the day declined, the Twelve said, "Dismiss the crowd so they can go to the farms or villages around here and get a room for the night and a bite to eat. We're out in the middle of nowhere."

"You feed them," Jesus said.

They said, "We couldn't scrape up more than five loaves of bread and a couple of fish—unless, of course, you want us to go to town ourselves and buy food for everybody." (There were more than five thousand people in the crowd.)

When Christ Calls A Man Or A Woman, He Bids Them Come And Die

But He went ahead and directed His disciples, "Sit them down in groups of about fifty." They did what He said, and soon had everyone seated. He took the five loaves and two fish, lifted His face to heaven in prayer, blessed, broke, and gave the bread and fish to the disciples to hand out to the crowd. After the people had all eaten their fill, twelve baskets of leftovers were gathered up.

One time when Jesus was off praying by Himself, His disciples nearby, He asked them, "What are the crowds saying about Me, about who I am?"

They said, "John the Baptizer. Others say Elijah. Still others say that one of the prophets from long ago has come back."

He then asked, "And you—what are you saying about Me? Who am I?"

Peter answered, "The Messiah of God." Jesus then warned them to keep it quiet. They were to tell no one what Peter had said.

He went on, "It is necessary that the Son of Man proceed to an ordeal of suffering, be tried and found guilty by the religious leaders, high priests, and religion scholars, be killed, and on the third day be raised up alive." Then He told them what they could expect for themselves: "Anyone who intends to come with me has to let me lead. You're not in the driver's seat—I am. Don't run from suffering; embrace it. Follow Me and I'll show you how. Self-help is no help at all. Self-sacrifice is the way, my way, to finding yourself, your true self. What good would it do to get everything you want and lose you, the real you? If any of you is embarrassed with me and the way I'm leading you, know that the Son of Man will be far more embarrassed with you when He arrives in all His splendor in company with the Father and the holy angels. This isn't, you realize, pie in the sky by and by. Some who have taken their stand right here are going to see it happen, see with their own eyes the kingdom of God."

About eight days after saying this, he climbed the mountain to pray, taking Peter, John, and James along. While He was in prayer, the appearance of His face changed, and His clothes became blinding white. At once two men were there talking with Him. They turned out to be Moses and Elijah—and what a glorious appearance they made! They talked over His exodus; the one Jesus was about to complete in Jerusalem.

Meanwhile, Peter and those with Him were slumped over in sleep. When they came to, rubbing their eyes, they saw Jesus in His glory and the two men standing with Him. When Moses and Elijah had left, Peter said to Jesus, "Master, this is a great moment! Let's build three memorials: one for You, one for Moses, and one for Elijah." He blurted this out without thinking.

While he was babbling on like this, a light-radiant cloud enveloped them. As they found themselves buried in the cloud, they became deeply aware of God. Then there was a voice out of the cloud: "This is my Son, the Chosen! Listen to Him."

When the sound of the voice died away, they saw Jesus there alone. They were speechless. And they continued speechless, said not one thing to anyone during those days of what they had seen.

When they came down off the mountain the next day, a big crowd was there to meet them. A man called from out of the crowd, "Please, please, Teacher, take a look at my son. He's my only child. Often a spirit seizes him. Suddenly he's screaming, thrown into convulsions, his mouth foaming. And then it beats him black-and-blue before it leaves. I asked Your disciples to deliver him, but they couldn't.

Jesus said, "What a generation! No sense of God! No focus to your lives! How many times do I have to go over these things? How much longer do I have to put up with this? Bring your son here."

While he was coming, the demon slammed him to the ground and threw him into convulsions. Jesus stepped in, ordered the vile spirit gone, healed the boy, and handed him back to his father. They all shook their heads in wonder, astonished at God's greatness, God's majestic greatness.

While they continued to stand around exclaiming over all the things He was doing, Jesus said to His disciples, "Treasure and ponder each of these next words: The Son of Man is about to be betrayed into human hands."

They didn't get what He was saying. It was like He was speaking a foreign language and they couldn't make heads or tails of it. But they were embarrassed to ask Him what he meant.

They started arguing over which of them would be most famous. When Jesus realized how much this mattered to them, he brought a child to his side. "Whoever accepts this child as if the child were me, accepts me," he said. "And whoever accepts me, accepts the One who sent me. You become great by accepting, not asserting. Your spirit, not your size, makes the difference."

John spoke up, "Master, we saw a man using Your name to expel demons and we stopped him because he wasn't of our group."

Jesus said, "Don't stop him. If he's not an enemy, he's an ally."

When it came close to the time for His Ascension, He gathered up His courage and steeled Himself for the journey to Jerusalem. He sent messengers on ahead. They came to a Samaritan village to make arrangements for His hospitality. But when the Samaritans learned that His destination was Jerusalem, they refused hospitality. When the disciples James and John learned of it, they said, "Master, do you want us to call a bolt of lightning down out of the sky and incinerate them?"

Jesus turned on them: "Of course not!" And they traveled on to another village.

On the road someone asked if he could go along. "I'll go with You, wherever," he said.

Jesus was curt: "Are you ready to rough it? We're not staying in the best inns, you know."

Jesus said to another, "Follow me."

He said, "Certainly, but first excuse me for a couple of days, please. I have to make arrangements for my father's funeral."

Jesus refused. "First things first. Your business is life, not death. And life is urgent: Announce God's kingdom!"

Then another said, "I'm ready to follow You, Master, but first excuse me while I get things straightened out at home."

Jesus said, "No procrastination. No backward looks. You can't put God's kingdom off till tomorrow. Seize the day" (Luke 9:1-62 Message).

PURSUIT OF GOD, A.W. TOZER
Jesus calls us to His rest, and meekness is His method.
The meek man cares not at all who is greater than he,
for he has long ago decided that the esteem of the world
is not worth the effort.[38]

WHOEVER DOES NOT CARRY HIS OWN CROSS and come after Me cannot be My disciple. For which one of you, when he wants to build a tower, does not first sit down and calculate the cost, to see if he has enough to complete it? Otherwise, when he has laid a foundation and is not able to finish, all who are watching it will begin to ridicule him, saying, 'This person began to build, and was not able to finish!' Or what king, when he sets out to meet another king in battle, will not first sit down and consider whether he is strong enough with ten thousand men to face the one coming against him with twenty thousand? Otherwise, while the other is still far away, he sends a delegation and requests terms of peace. So then, none of you can be My disciple who does not give up all his own possessions. (Luke 14:27-33 NASB)

ALAN REDPATH
When God wants to do an impossible task
He takes an impossible man and crushes him.[39]

---

[38] A. W. Tozer, Renewed Day by Day Volume 1: Daily Devotional Readings (Camp Hills: WingSpread Publishers, 1980), 14.

[39] Gavin Anthony quoting Alan Redpath, The Refiner's Fire: In All Things, God Works for Good (Hagerstown: Review and Herald Pub Assoc, 2007), 51.

MAX LUCADO

In our faith we follow in someone's steps. In our faith we leave footprints to guide others. It's the principle of discipleship[40]

AS IRON SHARPENS IRON, so one person sharpens another. (Proverbs 27:17 NASB)

OSWALD CHAMBERS

Our Lord's conception of discipleship is not that we work for God, but that God works through us.[41]

ELISABETH ELLIOT

Our vision is so limited we can hardly imagine a love that does not show itself in protection from suffering ... the love of God did not protect his own Son ... He will not necessarily protect us – not from anything it takes to make us like his son. A lot of hammering and chiseling and purifying by fire will have to go into the process.[42]

THE LORD GOD HAS GIVEN ME THE TONGUE OF DISCIPLES, so that I may know how to sustain the weary one with a word. He awakens Me morning by morning, He awakens My ear to listen as a disciple. (Isaiah 50:4 NASB)

---

[40] Max Lucado, NKJV, The Lucado Life Lessons Study Bible (Nashville: Thomas Nelson, 2010), 1665.

[41] Oswald Chambers, He Shall Glorify Me: Talks on the Holy Spirit and Other Themes (Whitefish: Kessinger, 2015).

[42] Jack Lenza quoting Elisabeth Elliot, God is in the Business of Restoration: You Are His Business (Spring Hill: Holy Fire Publishing LLC, 2012), 236.

DRAW THE CIRCLE, MARK BATTERSON

In ancient Jewish culture, formal education began at six years of age. Jewish boys enrolled in their local synagogue school called bet sefer (house of the book). On the first day of class, according to tradition, the rabbis would cover their slates with honey. Honey was the symbol of God's favor. Then the rabbis would instruct the students to lick the honey off their slates while reciting from Psalm 119. "How sweet are Your words to my taste? Yes, sweeter than honey to my mouth."

The students learned that the Word of God was the sweetest thing of all. When the students graduated from bet sefer, they had memorized the entire Torah. The following four years they memorized the rest of the Old Testament. If they successfully completed their program, the students applied to local rabbis to be their disciples. The rabbi would then invite the student to "Come, follow me," which meant a relationship of total surrender and devotion.[43]

SAMUEL "CHIP" TOTH, LEADERS INSPIRE

"And He appointed twelve, that they might be with Him" (Mark 3:14a NIV). And He said to them, "Follow Me, and I will make you fishers of men" (Matthew 4:19 NASB).

Discipleship primarily operates within the parameters of a teacher/student relationship. The student admires and desires to emulate certain character traits of the teacher. He may even begin to take on various behavioral patterns that he sees in the teacher.

Such is certainly the case for disciples of Jesus. We are highly attracted to Him. He is like no teacher we have ever had before. We experience personal transformation the more diligently we follow Him. Almost magically, subconsciously, our thoughts and desires and behavior show a striking resemblance to those of our Lord.

In mindset, we become lifelong learners. We humbly learn from others with an intense curiosity and nonjudgmental openness. We

---

[43] Mark Batterson, Draw the Circle: The 40 Day Prayer Challenge (Grand Rapids: Zondervan, 2012), 165.

carefully consider our questions with the express purpose of drawing the best out of people. We recognize and admit that we have not even come close to mastering the scriptures and that we are still disciples of Jesus, harvesting new insights from our Teacher each new day.

"Master of Divinity" degree?! Really? The two temptations we most war against are pride and arrogance, which threaten our standing and progress as disciples.

In behaviors and practices, we learn to approach prayer with a stronger need to listen than to hear ourselves talk. We hunger and thirst for Christ's wisdom, guidance, and commands. We establish a mutual confidence that we will obey Him. We approach the scriptures with fresh curiosity, excitement, and humility. We even admit an element of fear, understanding WHO has spoken these words (Isaiah 66:2.) We pattern our lives after others who show us what it looks like to be a disciple wholly devoted to Jesus (1 Corinthians 11:1, Hebrews 13:7).

The ultimate mission and reward of effective discipleship is to become like Jesus. This should be our primary driver and vision. We and those we disciple partner with the Holy Spirit in being transformed into Jesus-like beings. "And we all, who with unveiled faces contemplate the Lord's glory, are being transformed into His image with ever-increasing glory, which comes from the Lord, who is the Spirit" (2 Corinthians 3:18 NIV).[44]

---

[44] Samuel "Chip" Toth, pastor, speaker, and home group leader, Leaders Inspire Founder and Coach, author's brother.

Chapter 8

FROM A CRADLE TO THE CROSS

AND THE WORD BECAME FLESH, and dwelt among us and we saw His glory, glory as of the only Son from the Father, full of grace and truth. (John 1:14 NASB)

PATTI BURNETT

WHAT DOES IT MEAN THAT JESUS CAME TO DIE?

To fully appreciate Christmas, we need to keep at the forefront of our minds and hearts the reason Jesus became flesh and dwelt amongst us. No one else could possibly pay the penalty for our sins – God's only begotten, perfect Son was the only qualified warrior.

John MacArthur in the Covenant Blog teaches, "Here's a side to the Christmas story that isn't often told: Those soft little hands, fashioned by the Holy Spirit in Mary's womb, were made so that nails might be driven through them. Those baby feet, pink and unable to walk, would one day stagger up a dusty hill to be nailed to a cross. That sweet infant's head with sparkling eyes and eager mouth was formed so that someday men might force a crown of thorns onto it. That tender body, warm and soft, wrapped in swaddling clothes, would one day be ripped open by a spear."

MacArthur explains that Jesus' horribly painful and gruesome death "was in no sense a tragedy." It was the greatest victory ever achieved in the history of mankind. This Jesus, the faultless Godman achieved victory over death for whosoever … whosoever believes in Him will not perish but have eternal life. Will you?

NOW THE BIRTH OF JESUS THE MESSIAH WAS AS FOLLOWS:
When His mother Mary had been betrothed to Joseph, before they came together she was found to be pregnant by the Holy Spirit. And her husband Joseph, since he was a righteous man and did not want to disgrace her, planned to send her away secretly. But when he had thought this over, behold, an angel of the Lord appeared to him in a dream, saying, "Joseph, son of David, do not be afraid to take Mary as your wife; for the Child who has been conceived in her is of the Holy Spirit. She will give birth to a Son; and you shall name Him Jesus, for He will save His people from their sins." Now all this took place so that what was spoken by the Lord through the prophet would be fulfilled: "Behold, the virgin will conceive and give birth to a Son, and they shall

name Him Immanuel," which translated means, "God with us." And Joseph awoke from his sleep and did as the angel of the Lord commanded him, and took Mary as his wife, but kept her a virgin until she gave birth to a Son; and he named Him Jesus (Matthew 1:18-25 NASB).

> **CHRISTMAS IN HEAVEN, SCOTTY MCCREERY**
> Are you kneeling with shepherds before Him now
> Can you reach out and touch His face
> Are you part of that glorious holy night
> I wonder what Christmas in Heaven is like
> Is the snow falling down on the streets of gold?
> Are the mansions all covered in white?
> Are you singing with angels "Silent Night?"
> I wonder what Christmas in Heaven is like[45]

JESUS WAS BORN IN BETHLEHEM IN JUDEA, during the reign of King Herod. About that time some wise men from eastern lands arrived in Jerusalem, asking, "Where is the newborn king of the Jews? We saw His star as it rose, and we have come to worship Him."

King Herod was deeply disturbed when he heard this, as was everyone in Jerusalem. He called a meeting of the leading priests and teachers of religious law and asked, "Where is the Messiah supposed to be born?"

> "In Bethlehem in Judea," they said, "for this is what the prophet wrote:
> 'And you, O Bethlehem in the land of Judah,
> are not least among the ruling cities of Judah,
> for a ruler will come from you
> who will be the shepherd for my people Israel.'"

---

[45] Scotty McCreery, Christmas in Heaven, Mark Bright (producer), distributed by Interscope Records, track 6 on Christmas with Scotty McCreery, 2012, album.

Then Herod called for a private meeting with the wise men, and he learned from them the time when the star first appeared. Then he told them, "Go to Bethlehem and search carefully for the child. And when you find Him, come back and tell me so that I can go and worship Him, too!"

After this interview the wise men went their way. And the star they had seen in the east guided them to Bethlehem. It went ahead of them and stopped over the place where the child was.

When they saw the star, they were filled with joy! They entered the house and saw the child with His mother, Mary, and they bowed down and worshiped Him. Then they opened their treasure chests and gave Him gifts of gold, frankincense, and myrrh.

When it was time to leave, they returned to their own country by another route, for God had warned them in a dream not to return to Herod.

After the wise men were gone, an angel of the Lord appeared to Joseph in a dream. "Get up! Flee to Egypt with the child and his mother," the angel said. "Stay there until I tell you to return, because Herod is going to search for the child to kill Him."

That night Joseph left for Egypt with the child and Mary, his mother, and they stayed there until Herod's death. This fulfilled what the Lord had spoken through the prophet: "I called my Son out of Egypt."

Herod was furious when he realized that the wise men had outwitted him. He sent soldiers to kill all the boys in and around Bethlehem who were two years old and under, based on the wise men's report of the star's first appearance. Herod's brutal action fulfilled what God had spoken through the prophet Jeremiah:

> "A cry was heard in Ramah—
> weeping and great mourning.
> Rachel weeps for her children,
> refusing to be comforted,
> for they are dead."

When Herod died, an angel of the Lord appeared in a dream to Joseph in Egypt. "Get up!" the angel said. "Take the child and His mother back to the land of Israel, because those who were trying to kill the child are dead."

So Joseph got up and returned to the land of Israel with Jesus and His mother. But when he learned that the new ruler of Judea was Herod's son Archelaus, he was afraid to go there. Then, after being warned in a dream, he left for the region of Galilee. So the family went and lived in a town called Nazareth. This fulfilled what the prophets had said: "He will be called a Nazarene" (Matthew 2:1-23 NLT).

MOMENTS WITH THE SAVIOR, KEN GIRE

The shepherds lived in a gypsy encampment outside Bethlehem. They were a shunned minority. Because of their profession, they were unable to observe the orthodox ritual of washings. Consequently, they were considered unclean. Because they were untutored in the Law, they were considered ignorant. Because they were without roots in the community, they were considered suspect.

This knot of shepherds on the fringe of Jewish society spent the night atop a stone tower, a couple of them watching the flocks while the others huddled around a fire, catching what sleep they could…

The fire is almost out when suddenly the curtain of night is parted by an angel, spilling the glory of heaven everywhere. The incandescent light wakens the men who fall on their faces, trembling, covering themselves with their coats…

The curtain of heaven opens wider, revealing a company of angels, their voices joining together in a chorus of praise: Glory to God in the highest and on earth peace to men on whom his favor rests. …

And the choir steps back to heaven, drawing the curtain behind them…

On these earthiest of men, the favor of heaven has come to rest…

A Savior has been born…. He lies there so meekly. Cradled in the most unexpected of places. Coming to us in the weakest of ways.

Waiting for us to come, yet willing for us not to. Waiting for us to see, yet willing for us to turn away. Waiting for us to worship Him, yet willing for us to renounce Him.

He is Christ the Lord. Yet He has placed Himself at the mercy of His creation. At the mercy of a census to determine where He would be born. At the mercy of strangers to take Him in. At the mercy of animals to warm Him. At the mercy of mortals to feed Him, to protect Him, to raise Him. Forever at our mercy. To betray Him, if we are willing. And if we are willing, to deny Him, mock Him, beat Him with our fists, impale Him on a cross.

Yet even there He comes to us. Cradled in the most unexpected of places. Coming to us in the weakest of ways. His body against the wood. Lying there. Waiting.[46]

IN THOSE DAYS CAESAR AUGUSTUS ISSUED A DECREE that a census should be taken of the entire Roman World. (This was the first census that took place while Quirinius was governor of Syria.) And everyone went to their own town to register.

So Joseph also went up from the town of Nazareth in Galilee to Judea, to Bethlehem the town of David, because he belonged to the house and line of David. He went there to register with Mary, who was pledged to be married to him and was expecting a child. While they were there, the time came for the baby to be born, and she gave birth to her firstborn, a son. She wrapped Him in cloths and placed Him in a manger, because there was no guest room available for them.

And there were shepherds living out in the fields nearby, keeping watch over their flocks at night. An angel of the Lord appeared to them, and the glory of the Lord shone around them, and they were terrified. But the angel said to them, "Do not be afraid. I bring you good news that will cause great joy for all the people. Today in the town of David a Savior has been born to you; He is the Messiah, the Lord. This will

---

[46] Ken Gire, Moments with the Savior (Grand Rapids: Zondervan, 1998), 32.

be a sign to you: You will find a baby wrapped in cloths and lying in a manger."

Suddenly a great company of the heavenly host appeared with the angel, praising God and saying,

"Glory to God in the highest heaven, and on earth peace to those on whom His favor rests."

When the angels had left them and gone into heaven, the shepherds said to one another, "Let's go to Bethlehem and see this thing that has happened, which the Lord has told us about."

So they hurried off and found Mary and Joseph, and the baby, who was lying in the manger. When they had seen Him, they spread the word concerning what had been told them about this child, and all who heard it were amazed at what the shepherds said to them.

But Mary treasured up all these things and pondered them in her heart. The shepherds returned, glorifying and praising God for all the things they had heard and seen, which were just as they had been told (Luke 2:1-20 NIV).

THE GIFT, GARTH BROOKS
A poor orphan girl named Maria
Was walking to market one day
She stopped for a rest by the roadside
Where a bird with a broken wing lay
A few moments passed till she saw it
For its feathers were covered with sand
But soon, clean and wrapped, was traveling
In the warmth of Maria's small hand
She happily gave her last peso
On a cage made of rushes and twine
She fed it loose corn from the market

And watched it grow stronger with time
Now the Christmas Eve service was coming
And the church shone with tinsel and light
And all of the town folks brought presents
To lay by the manger that night
There were diamonds and incense
And perfumes
In packages fit for a king
But for one ragged bird in a small cage
Maria had nothing to bring
She waited till just before midnight
So no one would see her go in
And crying she knelt by the manger
For her gift was unworthy of Him
Then a voice spoke to her through the darkness
Maria, what brings you to me
If the bird in the cage is your offering
Open the door and let me see
Though she trembled, she did as He asked her
And out of the cage the bird flew
Soaring up into the rafters
On a wing that had healed good as new
Just then the midnight bells rang out
And the little bird started to sing
A song that no words could recapture
Whose beauty was fit for a king
Now Maria felt blessed just to listen
To that cascade of notes sweet and long
As her offering was lifted to heaven
By the very first nightingale's song[47]

---

[47] Garth Brooks, The Gift, Stephanie Davis (written by), distributed by Alfred Music, track 4 on Beyond the Season, 1992, album.

FOR A CHILD WILL BE BORN TO US, a Son will be given to us;
And the government will rest on His shoulders;
And His name will be called Wonderful Counselor, Mighty God,
Eternal Father, Prince of Peace.
There will be no end to the increase of His government
or of peace
On the throne of David and over His kingdom,
To establish it and to uphold it with justice and righteousness
From then on and forevermore.
The zeal of the Lord of armies will accomplish this. (Isaiah 9:6-7 NASB)

MOMENTS WITH THE SAVIOR, KEN GIRE

As the morning washes over His cheeks, the sleepy Savior wakes and yawns. The first thing He sees is His mother's eyes, brimming with tears.

He smiles.

She smiles back. He smiles bigger.

And she blinks away the tears.

Unable to understand anything but the language of his mother's face, and already Jesus is an enemy of the state. Unable to talk, and already he is targeted for assassination. Unable to run, and already a fugitive, fleeing for His life.

What secret was God keeping with this child?

A secret so terrifying it could scarcely be uttered without causing the heavens to tremble and the stars to fall from the sky.

The secret??

On that starlit night in Bethlehem, God came to earth to do the one thing He could not do in heaven.

Die.[48]

BREATH OF HEAVEN, AMY GRANT
I am waiting in a silent prayer
I am frightened by the load I bear
In a world as cold as stone,
Must I walk this path alone?
Be with me now

Breath of heaven
Hold me together
Be forever near me
Breath of heaven

Breath of heaven
Light up my darkness
Pour over me Your holiness
For You are holy
Breath of heaven[49]

---

[48] Ken Gire, Moments with the Savior, 44.

[49] Amy Grant, Chris Eaton, Breath of Heaven (Mary's Song,) Arranged by Lloyd Larson, Hope Publishing

Chapter 9

HE HAS RISEN, JUST AS HE SAID

JESUS SAID TO HER, "I AM THE RESURRECTION AND THE LIFE; the one who believes in Me will live, even if he dies, and everyone who lives and believes in Me will never die. Do you believe this?" She said to Him, "Yes, Lord; I have come to believe that You are the Christ, the Son of God, and He who comes into the world." (John 11:25-27 NASB)

PATTI BURNETT

I HAD ALWAYS THOUGHT I WOULD AGE GRACEFULLY. All those years of figure skating and skiing had to count for something. However, more than ten years of living with Parkinson's has taught me that a graceful person with Parkinson's is usually an oxymoron.

We all age; it's a part of the human condition, and the alternative is not all that appealing. Once again, thank you Adam and Eve – VERY LITTLE!

While there are people who get Young Onset Parkinson's, most are diagnosed around the age of 60. Researchers acknowledge that people with Parkinson's (PPD) can live well, far beyond the 10-20 years reflected in obsolete data. I know of many living examples of this truth, myself included, although I certainly have some bad days. The Davis Phinney Foundation has done an excellent job of reinforcing this mantra.

While at one time doctors restricted intense exercise for their patients, today all MDS's agree that exercise (all types and at all levels) is the most important medicine they prescribe. It has been found to significantly reduce the progression of PD. Exercise, eating well, social engagement, and Deep Brain Stimulation Surgery are just a few of the therapies that PPD can utilize to live a healthier and fuller life.

For whatever reason, when I compare myself to those with whom I share this disease, my digression seems to be moving slower. Wishful thinking? Maybe. However, I believe that it's more a case of God giving me the strength, discipline, and motivation to get up and move my body when I don't always feel like it. Has He healed me?

That I don't know, but I do know that my dream of aging gracefully is changing to a dream of aging gratefully and faithfully.

Let's move on to a much more exciting body – our resurrected bodies.

Our new suits will be imperishable according to I Corinthians 15:39-42. They will last forever, never decay or age. That's good news for a person whose body is aging faster than the norm.

We will bear the image of the heavenly Man (I Corinthians 15:48-49, Philippians 3:20-21, I John 3:2). We will have a body like Christ's – no disease, injury, or illness. For the person with Parkinson's – no more tremors, dystonia, falls, nightmares, hallucinations – all the symptoms gone.

There will be no more pain and tears (Revelation 21:4). I'm not much of a crier, but there have been moments in my last ten years when my pain and frustration have reduced me to tears, even as recently as yesterday. The rigidity of my body reminds me almost constantly that a better day is coming.

We will recognize each other (Luke 24:30-43). This was something I wondered about for a long time. When Jesus came back to earth after His resurrection, in the garden of Gethsemane, Mary recognized that it was her Lord after He spoke her name. He showed his disciples the scars on His hands and feet. I think the first thing I'd like to do in heaven, after worshipping and expressing my gratitude to the Lord, is to hold a dance party for all my Parkinson's buddies.

I've always wondered whether heavenly citizens will all be the same age. There are theologians who opine that we will be around 33 because that was Christ's age when He was resurrected, in His prime of life. That was probably about Adam and Eve's ages as well. That would be okay with me.

Bring it Father. Maranatha – Come quickly, Lord Jesus.

AS JESUS WAS ABOUT TO GO UP TO JERUSALEM, He took the twelve disciples aside by themselves, and on the road He said to them, "Behold, we are going up to Jerusalem, and the Son of Man will be handed over to the chief priests and scribes, and they will condemn Him to death, and they will hand Him over to the Gentiles to mock and flog and crucify, and on the third day He will be raised up." (Matthew 20:17-19 NASB)

> **J.R.R. TOLKIEN**
> The birth, death, and resurrection of Jesus means that one day everything sad will come untrue.[50]

SATURDAY EVENING, WHEN THE SABBATH ENDED, Mary Magdalene, Mary the mother of James, and Salome went out and purchased burial spices so they could anoint Jesus' body. Very early on Sunday morning, just at sunrise, they went to the tomb. On the way they were asking each other, "Who will roll away the stone for us from the entrance to the tomb?" But as they arrived, they looked up and saw that the stone, which was very large, had already been rolled aside.

When they entered the tomb, they saw a young man clothed in a white robe sitting on the right side. The women were shocked, but the angel said, "Don't be alarmed. You are looking for Jesus of Nazareth, who was crucified. He isn't here! He is risen from the dead! Look, this is where they laid His body. Now go and tell His disciples, including Peter, that Jesus is going ahead of you to Galilee. You will see Him there, just as He told you before He died."

The women fled from the tomb, trembling and bewildered, and they said nothing to anyone because they were too frightened.

[The most ancient manuscripts of Mark conclude with verse 16:8. Later manuscripts add one or both of the following endings.]

[Shorter Ending of Mark]

---

[50] J.R.R. Tolkien, The Lord of the Rings (New York: Houghton Mifflin, 1954), 951-952.

Then they briefly reported all this to Peter and his companions. Afterward Jesus Himself sent them out from east to west with the sacred and unfailing message of salvation that gives eternal life. Amen.

[Longer Ending of Mark]

After Jesus rose from the dead early on Sunday morning, the first person who saw Him was Mary Magdalene, the woman from whom He had cast out seven demons. She went to the disciples, who were grieving and weeping, and told them what had happened. But when she told them that Jesus was alive and she had seen Him, they didn't believe her.

Afterward He appeared in a different form to two of His followers who were walking from Jerusalem into the country. They rushed back to tell the others, but no one believed them.

Still later he appeared to the eleven disciples as they were eating together. He rebuked them for their stubborn unbelief because they refused to believe those who had seen Him after He had been raised from the dead.

And then He told them, "Go into all the world and preach the Good News to everyone. Anyone who believes and is baptized will be saved. But anyone who refuses to believe will be condemned. These miraculous signs will accompany those who believe: They will cast out demons in My name, and they will speak in new languages. They will be able to handle snakes with safety, and if they drink anything poisonous, it won't hurt them. They will be able to place their hands on the sick, and they will be healed."

When the Lord Jesus had finished talking with them, He was taken up into heaven and sat down in the place of honor at God's right hand. And the disciples went everywhere and preached, and the Lord worked through them, confirming what they said by many miraculous signs. (Mark 16:1-20 NLT)

> **WATCHMAN NEE**
> The greatest negative in the universe is the Cross, for with it God wiped out everything that was not of Himself:
> The greatest positive in the universe is the resurrection, for through it God brought into being all.[51]

EARLY ON SUNDAY MORNING, WHILE IT WAS STILL DARK, Mary Magdalene came to the tomb and found that the stone had been rolled away from the entrance. She ran and found Simon Peter and the other disciple, the one whom Jesus loved. She said, "They have taken the Lord's body out of the tomb, and we don't know where they have put Him!"

Peter and the other disciple started out for the tomb. They were both running, but the other disciple outran Peter and reached the tomb first. He stooped and looked in and saw the linen wrappings lying there, but he didn't go in. Then Simon Peter arrived and went inside. He also noticed the linen wrappings lying there, while the cloth that had covered Jesus' head was folded up and lying apart from the other wrappings. Then the disciple who had reached the tomb first also went in, and he saw and believed—for until then they still hadn't understood the Scriptures that said Jesus must rise from the dead. Then they went home.

Mary was standing outside the tomb crying, and as she wept, she stooped and looked in. She saw two white-robed angels, one sitting at the head and the other at the foot of the place where the body of Jesus had been lying. "Dear woman, why are you crying?" the angels asked her.

"Because they have taken away my Lord," she replied, "and I don't know where they have put Him."

---

[51] Watchman Nee, The Finest of the Wheat, Volume 2 (Richmond: Christian Fellowship Publisher, 1993), 197.

He Has Risen, Just As He Said

She turned to leave and saw someone standing there. It was Jesus, but she didn't recognize Him. "Dear woman, why are you crying?" Jesus asked her. "Who are you looking for?"

She thought He was the gardener. "Sir," she said, "if you have taken Him away, tell me where you have put Him, and I will go and get Him. "Mary!" Jesus said.

She turned to him and cried out, "Rabboni!" (which is Hebrew for "teacher").

Don't cling to me, Jesus said, for I haven't yet ascended to the Father. But go find my brothers and tell them, I am ascending to my Father and your Father, to my God and your God.

Mary Magalene found the disciples and told them, "I have seen the Lord!" Then she gave them His message.

That Sunday evening the disciples were meeting behind locked doors because they were afraid of the Jewish leaders. Suddenly, Jesus was standing there among them! "Peace be with you," He said. As He spoke, He showed them the wounds in His hands and His side. They were filled with joy when they saw the Lord! Again He said, "Peace be with you. As the Father has sent Me, so I am sending you." Then He breathed on them and said, "Receive the Holy Spirit. If you forgive anyone's sins, they are forgiven. If you do not forgive them, they are not forgiven."

One of the twelve disciples, Thomas (nicknamed the Twin), was not with the others when Jesus came. They told him, "We have seen the Lord!"

But he replied, "I won't believe it unless I see the nail wounds in His hands, put my fingers into them, and place my hand into the wound in His side."

Eight days later the disciples were together again, and this time Thomas was with them. The doors were locked; but suddenly, as before, Jesus was standing among them. "Peace be with you," He said. Then he said to Thomas, "Put your finger here, and look at My hands. Put your hand into the wound in my side. Don't be faithless any longer. Believe!"

"My Lord and my God!" Thomas exclaimed.

Then Jesus told him, "You believe because you have seen Me. Blessed are those who believe without seeing Me."

The disciples saw Jesus do many other miraculous signs in addition to the ones recorded in this book. But these are written so that you may continue to believe that Jesus is the Messiah, the Son of God, and that by believing in Him you will have life by the power of His name. (John 20:1-31 NLT)

> ### *DIAMOND IN THE DUST*, JONI EARECKSON TADA
>
> The apostle Paul wrote wistfully about the resurrection body, and my sentiments are his. I, too, groan over my earthly tent. Age, disease, or disability has a way of making us long for a trade-in ...
>
> Perhaps Charles Spurgeon explained it best: 'at present we wear our bodies on the outside and our souls on the inside. But in heaven, we shall wear our bodies on the inside, and our souls on the outside" ...
>
> We will wear our right-standing with God on the outside as though it were a beautiful garment. Our bright-shining raiment will be all glorious, reflecting on the outside the life of Christ cultivated on the inside.
>
> Joni prayed: "Prepare me for heaven. Fit me for eternity. Fashion me into the person You want me to be so that I will be ready for my eternal clothes of righteousness."[52]

---

[52] Joni Eareckson Tada, Diamonds in the Dust (Grand Rapids: Zondervan, 1993), May 24 Devotional.

LET ME NOW REMIND YOU, DEAR BROTHERS AND SISTERS, of the good news I preached to you before. You welcomed it then, and you still stand firm in it. It is this Good News that saves you if you continue to believe the message I told you—unless, of course, you believed something that was never true in the first place.

I passed on to you what was most important and what had also been passed on to me. Christ died for our sins, just as the Scriptures said. He was buried, and He was raised from the dead on the third day, just as the Scriptures said. He was seen by Peter and then by the Twelve. After that, He was seen by more than 500 of His followers at one time, most of whom are still alive, though some have died. Then He was seen by James and later by all the apostles. Last of all, as though I had been born at the wrong time, I also saw Him. For I am the least of all the apostles. In fact, I'm not even worthy to be called an apostle after the way I persecuted God's church.

But whatever I am now, it is all because God poured out His special favor on me—and not without results. For I have worked harder than any of the other apostles; yet it was not I but God who was working through me by His grace. So it makes no difference whether I preach or they preach, for we all preach the same message you have already believed.

But tell me this—since we preach that Christ rose from the dead, why are some of you saying there will be no resurrection of the dead? For if there is no resurrection of the dead, then Christ has not been raised either. And if Christ has not been raised, then all our preaching is useless, and your faith is useless. And we apostles would all be lying about God—for we have said that God raised Christ from the grave. But that can't be true if there is no resurrection of the dead. And if there is no resurrection of the dead, then Christ has not been raised. And if Christ has not been raised, then your faith is useless and you are still guilty of your sins. In that case, all who have died believing in Christ are lost! And if our hope in Christ is only for this life, we are more to be pitied than anyone in the world.

But in fact, Christ has been raised from the dead. He is the first of a great harvest of all who have died.

So you see, just as death came into the world through a man, now the resurrection from the dead has begun through another man. Just as everyone dies because we all belong to Adam, everyone who belongs to Christ will be given new life. But there is an order to this resurrection: Christ was raised as the first of the harvest; then all who belong to Christ will be raised when He comes back.

After that the end will come, when He will turn the Kingdom over to God the Father, having destroyed every ruler and authority and power. For Christ must reign until He humbles all His enemies beneath His feet. And the last enemy to be destroyed is death. For the Scriptures say, "God has put all things under His authority." (Of course, when it says "all things are under His authority," that does not include God Himself, who gave Christ His authority.) Then, when all things are under His authority, the Son will put Himself under God's authority, so that God, who gave His Son authority over all things, will be utterly supreme over everything everywhere.

If the dead will not be raised, what point is there in people being baptized for those who are dead? Why do it unless the dead will someday rise again?

And why should we ourselves risk our lives hour by hour? For I swear, dear brothers and sisters, that I face death daily. This is as certain as my pride in what Christ Jesus our Lord has done in you. And what value was there in fighting wild beasts—those people of Ephesus—if there will be no resurrection from the dead? And if there is no resurrection, "Let's feast and drink, for tomorrow we die!" Don't be fooled by those who say such things, for "bad company corrupts good character." Think carefully about what is right, and stop sinning. For to your shame I say that some of you don't know God at all.

But someone may ask, "How will the dead be raised? What kind of bodies will they have?" What a foolish question! When you put a seed into the ground, it doesn't grow into a plant unless it dies first. And what you put in the ground is not the plant that will grow, but only a bare seed of wheat or whatever you are planting. Then God gives it the new body He wants it to have. A different plant grows from each kind of seed. Similarly there are different kinds of flesh—one kind for humans, another for animals, another for birds, and another for fish.

There are also bodies in the heavens and bodies on the earth. The glory of the heavenly bodies is different from the glory of the earthly bodies. The sun has one kind of glory, while the moon and stars each have another kind. And even the stars differ from each other in their glory.

It is the same way with the resurrection of the dead. Our earthly bodies are planted in the ground when we die, but they will be raised to live forever. Our bodies are buried in brokenness, but they will be raised in glory. They are buried in weakness, but they will be raised in strength. They are buried as natural human bodies, but they will be raised as spiritual bodies. For just as there are natural bodies, there are also spiritual bodies.

The Scriptures tell us, "The first man, Adam, became a living person." But the last Adam—that is, Christ—is a life-giving Spirit. What comes first is the natural body, then the spiritual body comes later. Adam, the first man, was made from the dust of the earth, while Christ, the second man, came from heaven. Earthly people are like the earthly man, and heavenly people are like the heavenly man. Just as we are now like the earthly man, we will someday be like the heavenly man.

What I am saying, dear brothers and sisters, is that our physical bodies cannot inherit the Kingdom of God. These dying bodies cannot inherit what will last forever.

But let me reveal to you a wonderful secret. We will not all die, but we will all be transformed! It will happen in a moment, in the blink of an eye, when the last trumpet is blown. For when the trumpet sounds, those who have died will be raised to live forever. And we who are living will also be transformed. For our dying bodies must be transformed into bodies that will never die; our mortal bodies must be transformed into immortal bodies.

Then, when our dying bodies have been transformed into bodies that will never die, this Scripture will be fulfilled:

"Death is swallowed up in victory.

O death, where is your victory?

O death, where is your sting?"

For sin is the sting that results in death, and the law gives sin its power. But thank God! He gives us victory over sin and death through our Lord Jesus Christ.

So, my dear brothers and sisters, be strong and immovable. Always work enthusiastically for the Lord, for you know that nothing you do for the Lord is ever useless. (1 Corinthians 15:1-58 NLT)

T.D. JAKES
Here is the amazing thing about Easter,
the Resurrection Sunday for Christians is this,
that Christ in the dying moments on the cross gives us
the greatest illustration of forgiveness possible.[53]

---

[53] T.D. Jakes, Lessons on Forgiveness from T.D. Jakes, Easter Sermon 2022, from https://www.azquotes.com/quote/144284.

Chapter 10

EVEN IF HE DOESN'T

***THOUGH THE CHERRY TREES DON'T BLOSSOM** and the strawberries don't ripen, Though the apples are worm-eaten and the wheat fields stunted, Though the sheep pens are sheepless and the cattle barns empty, I'm singing joyful praise to God. I'm turning cartwheels of joy to my Savior God. Counting on God's Rule to prevail, I take heart and gain strength. I run like a deer. I feel like I'm king of the mountain! (For congregational use, with a full orchestra.) Habakkuk 3:17-19 (Message)*

PATTI BURNETT

EVERY HUMAN BEING HAS DREAMS AND HOPES FOR THE FUTURE, i.e., to marry that wonderful guy, to become a millionaire by a certain age, to find the profession that absolutely fits their passions, to live in a beautiful home with 1.94 perfectly well-behaved children, and the list goes on and on. One thing on my bucket list was to do the Haute Route. When you "do" this amazing route in its entirety, you ski the Alps from Chamonix, France to Zermatt, Switzerland.

Dan and I had intended to ski the Haute Route when we were first married; however, I injured my leg and had to cancel. Some consider it the most famous and coveted ski tour in the world. Participants use alpine touring gear with skins in order to stay at a higher elevation on the Alps, spending nights (including breakfasts and dinners) in rugged huts. It is very difficult and about half of those who begin the Route never complete it. Such was the case for Dan and me.

I didn't want Parkinson's to rule my life and I certainly did not want it to crush all our dreams and hopes for the future; we figured that if we didn't begin working on our bucket list, it wasn't going to happen. With three of our best friends, we meticulously planned every detail, down to the ounces of weight we were willing to carry in our backpacks. Too heavy a pack could end a trip in no time at all.

Our first few days went well; I felt as though I could do this. The weather was great, and the skiing was amazing. However, about halfway through the Route, my Parkinson's started to misbehave. Unfortunately, that's the way it is with this strange disease. You can't always predict the next bad day – stiffness and rigidity were compounding my already poor adaptation to the cold temperatures.

The straw that broke my back dropped as we crested the pass above Verbier. Over the course of that day, we had been using ski crampons for the more dangerous terrain; and, standing at the top of the steep, wind-scoured pass, I didn't believe I could go any further. My frozen fingers lacked the dexterity needed to remove ski crampons and reattach my bindings; and I knew that my slowness was holding the rest of our group back. If Dan and I were going to turn around, this was the perfect place. Our guide advised us that we could ski down to the top of the ski area, where we could spend the night at a backcountry hut.

Just so you know how God cared for us at a time when we were especially downtrodden (physically, emotionally, and spiritually) as we entered the hut, we were greeted by an angel. Turns out he was the only English-speaking person there at the time. He welcomed us and listened to our story. He patiently told us where we could stay down in town the next night if we wanted; and then he very explicitly detailed the best route back to Chamonix, which involved trains, buses, and taxis. Trying to figure out transportation in Europe was quite a challenge for us. I was so grateful for our angel.

Dan and I skied at the ski area for two days (on and off-piste) and then traveled back to Chamonix to await our friends' completion of the Haute Route. During our wait I was terribly ill with intestinal issues that often accompanied my Parkinson's symptoms. I cannot even imagine what it would have been like to use the hole in the ground outhouses all the way to Zermatt.

Disappointed? You bet. Seems like I've always been able to meet every challenge and I wondered whether this new failure foretold future frustrations and sadness. I wondered where God was during all this. Did He feel my pain? Did He understand my fears and doubts? Did He really think that this fiery trial was necessary in my life? What was the lesson, the takeaway?

Segueing from a glacial exploit into a thermal adventure, the book of Daniel may answer that question.

I love Beth Moore's Bible study about the prophet, Daniel. His Israeli friends, Shadrach, Meshach and Abednego, were thrown into a furnace after they refused to bow down and worship the image of King Nebuchadnezzar. I guess in those days, incineration was a common form of execution.

The three young men were brought before the King and told that they would have one more chance to fall down and worship the King's image. Shadrach, Meshach, and Abednego answered King Nebuchadnezzar, "Your threat means nothing to us. If you throw us in the fire, the God we serve can rescue us from your roaring furnace and anything else you might cook up, O King. But even if He doesn't, it wouldn't make a bit of difference, O King. We still wouldn't serve your gods or worship the gold statue you set up" (Daniel 3:16-18 Message).

Beth explains that in most situations of trouble and oppression, and in this case, fire, there are three different ways that God can deliver us. I would like to relate these examples to Parkinson's.

- The first is delivery from the fire. Perhaps a person has all the risk factors for Parkinson's and even has relatives who are living with it. If that person does not get PD, they will have been delivered from the fire. As a result, their faith will have been built stronger.
- On the other hand, God may choose to deliver us through the fire, as was the case for Shadrach, Meshach and Abednego. If the Lord heals a person, even after perhaps nine years of living with Parkinson's, they will have been delivered through the fire; and their faith will have been refined.
- The last method of deliverance is by the fire; and we get to meet our Master and Deliverer and our faith is perfected. If our three friends had realized that they were going to die in the furnace, they still would have refused to worship the King. Certainly, death is a form of healing that our Lord sometimes selects for His children. No method of healing could surpass meeting our Savior, receiving a new body, and getting keys to our heavenly mansion.

I love that when the King looked into the furnace, there were four men standing there, but only three had been thrown in. How like our

Lord that He would come alongside Shadrach, Meshach, and Abednego to see them safely through the fire. Had I been one of the three men, I'm sure I would have begged Christ to carry me back to Father God's side. I can imagine the young Israelites' disappointment when the Lord explained that their work in Babylon was not yet completed. As they were escorted from the furnace, the King worshiped the God of Daniel and his three cohorts, and he advanced their careers.

I hesitate to guess what my future will look like; it sometimes scares me to go there. Last fall, I was mentoring a woman who was very depressed and anxious about what Parkinson's would do to her body over the next 20 to 30 years. I am too, but I am learning that my Deliverer is standing by my side in the fire. His presence in my pain is overwhelming and I want to bring glory to Him, Even as Daniel and his friends did – no matter how Christ Jesus chooses to deliver me.

PRAISE THE LORD!
Blessed is a person who fears the Lord,
Who greatly delights in His commandments.
His descendants will be mighty on the earth;
The generation of the upright will be blessed.
Wealth and riches are in his house,
And his righteousness endures forever.
Light shines in the darkness for the upright;
He is gracious, compassionate, and righteous.
It goes well for a person who is gracious and lends;
He will maintain his cause in judgment.
For he will never be shaken;
The righteous will be remembered forever.
He will not fear bad news;
His heart is steadfast, trusting in the Lord.
His heart is firm, he will not fear,
But will look with satisfaction on his enemies.
He has given freely to the poor,

His righteousness endures forever;
His horn will be exalted in honor. (Psalm 112:1-9 NASB)

> ## PHILIP YANCEY
> I have learned that faith means trusting in advance what will only make sense in reverse.[54]

THEN YOU WILL SAY ON THAT DAY,
"I will give thanks to You, Lord;
For although You were angry with me,
Your anger is turned away,
And You comfort me.
Behold, God is my salvation,
I will trust and not be afraid;
For the Lord God is my strength and song,
And He has become my salvation."
Therefore you will joyously draw water
From the springs of salvation.
And on that day you will say,
"Give thanks to the Lord, call on His name.
Make known His deeds among the peoples;
Make them remember that His name is exalted."
Praise the Lord in song, for He has done glorious things;
Let this be known throughout the earth.
(Isaiah 12:1-5 NASB)

---

[54] Philip Yancey, *Disappointment with God: Three Questions No One Asks Aloud* (Grand Rapids: Zondervan, 1988) 201.

RICK WARREN

The more you believe and trust God, the more limitless your possibilities become for your family, your career – for your life![55]

BLESSED IS THE MAN WHO TRUSTS IN THE LORD,
And whose trust is the Lord.
For he will be like a tree planted by the water
That extends its roots by a stream,
And does not fear when the heat comes;
But its leaves will be green,
And it will not be anxious in a year of drought,
Nor cease to yield fruit. (Jeremiah 17:7-8 NASB)

WAITING ON GOD, CHERIE HILL
Every difficulty you face, in every waiting place, you're being given the chance to trust in the things unseen and to be abundantly blessed.[56]

NEBUCHADNESSAR THE KING MADE A GOLD [PLATED] IMAGE, whose height [including the pedestal] was sixty cubits (ninety feet) and its width six cubits (nine feet). He set it up on the plain of Dura in the province of Babylon. Then Nebuchadnezzar the king sent word to assemble the satraps, the prefects and the governors, the counselors, the treasurers, the judges, the magistrates and lawyers and all the chief officials of the provinces to come to the dedication of the image that King Nebuchadnezzar had set up. Then the satraps, the prefects, the

---

[55] Rick Warren, born 1954, Christian pastor of Saddleback Church, author of The Purpose Driven Life, from https://www.wow4u.com/49-trust-god-quotes/.

[56] Cherie Hill, Waiting On God (Christian Art Publishers, 2012), Author, Founder of www.ScriptureNow.com, BA in Psychology, from https://www.wow4u.com/trust-quotes6/

governors, the counselors, the treasurers, the judges, the magistrates and lawyers, and all the chief officials of the provinces gathered together for the dedication of the image that King Nebuchadnezzar had set up; and they stood before it. Then the herald loudly proclaimed, "You are commanded, O peoples, nations, and speakers of every language, that at the moment you hear the sound of the horn, pipe, lyre, trigon (four-stringed harp), dulcimer, bagpipe, and all kinds of music, you are to fall down and worship the golden image that King Nebuchadnezzar has set up. Whoever does not fall down and worship shall immediately be thrown into the midst of a furnace of blazing fire." So when the people heard the sound of the horn, pipe, lyre, trigon, dulcimer, bagpipe and all kinds of music, all the peoples, nations, and speakers of every language fell down and worshiped the golden image that Nebuchadnezzar the king had set up.

At that time certain Chaldeans came forward and brought [malicious] accusations against the Jews. They said to King Nebuchadnezzar, "O king, live forever! You, O king, have made a decree that everyone who hears the sound of the horn, pipe, lyre, trigon, harp, dulcimer, bagpipe, and all kinds of music is to fall down and worship the golden image. Whoever does not fall down and worship shall be thrown into the midst of a furnace of blazing fire. There are certain Jews whom you have appointed over the administration of the province of Babylon, namely Shadrach, Meshach, and Abednego. These men, O king, pay no attention to you; they do not serve your gods or worship the golden image which you have set up."

Then Nebuchadnezzar in a furious rage gave a command to bring Shadrach, Meshach, and Abednego; and these men were brought before the king. Nebuchadnezzar said to them, "Is it true, Shadrach, Meshach, and Abednego, that you do not serve my gods or worship the golden image which I have set up? Now if you are ready, when you hear the sound of the horn, pipe, lyre, trigon, harp, dulcimer, and all kinds of music, to fall down and worship the image which I have made, very good. But if you do not worship, you shall be thrown at once into the midst of a furnace of blazing fire; and what god is there who can rescue you out of my hands?"

Shadrach, Meshach, and Abednego answered the king, "O Nebuchadnezzar, we do not need to answer you on this point. If it be so, our God whom we serve is able to rescue us from the furnace of blazing fire, and He will rescue us from your hand, O king. But even if He does not, let it be known to you, O king, that we are not going to serve your gods or worship the golden image that you have set up!"

Then Nebuchadnezzar was filled with fury, and his facial expression changed toward Shadrach, Meshach, and Abednego. Then he gave a command that the furnace was to be heated seven times hotter than usual. He commanded certain strong men in his army to tie up Shadrach, Meshach, and Abednego and to throw them into the furnace of blazing fire. Then these [three] men were tied up in their trousers, their coats, their turbans, and their other clothes, and were thrown into the midst of the furnace of blazing fire. Because the king's command was urgent and the furnace was extremely hot, the flame of the fire killed the men who carried up Shadrach, Meshach, and Abednego. But these three men, Shadrach, Meshach, and Abednego, fell into the midst of the furnace of blazing fire still tied up.

Then Nebuchadnezzar the king [looked and] was astounded, and he jumped up and said to his counselors, "Did we not throw three men who were tied up into the midst of the fire?" They replied to the king, "Certainly, O king." He answered, "Look! I see four men untied, walking around in the midst of the fire, and they are not hurt! And the appearance of the fourth is like a son of the gods!" Then Nebuchadnezzar approached the door of the blazing furnace and said, "Shadrach, Meshach, and Abednego, servants of the Most High God, come out [of there]! Come here!" Then Shadrach, Meshach, and Abednego came out of the midst of the fire. The satraps, the perfects, the governors and the king's counselors gathered around them and saw that in regards to these men the fire had no effect on their bodies – their hair was not singed their clothes were not scorched or damaged, even the smell of smoke was not on them.

Nebuchadnezzar responded and said, "Blessed be the God of Shadrach, Meshack and Abednego, who has sent His angel and rescued His servants who believed in, trusted in, and relied on Him! They violated the king's command and surrendered their bodies rather than serve or worship any god except their own God. Therefore I make a decree that any people, nation, or language that speaks anything offensive against the God of Shadrach, Meshach, and Abednego shall be cut into pieces and their houses be made a heap of rubbish, for there is no other god who is able to save in this way!" Then the king caused Shadrach, Meshach, and Abednego to prosper in the province of Babylon. (Daniel 3:1-30 AMP)

THE DIVINE EMBRACE, KEN GIRE

The Colosseum stands as a monument to our baser nature. During the time of the Roman Empire, crowds gathered early to get the best seats, where they watched and cheered as wild animals tore prisoners of the empire to shreds, where combatants fought to the death, and where great battles were staged to replicate victories on the frontier. Vanquished gladiators, slaves, prisoners, and Christians were among the victims.

Ignatius, a disciple of John and later bishop of Antioch, was one of the many Christians who was taken prisoner. He was sent to Rome in A.D. 107 and condemned to death for promoting Christianity. After his sentencing, one of the emperor's representatives offered him freedom if he would recant and make sacrifices to other Roman gods. Ignatius replied, "By your bland words you wish to deceive and destroy me. Know that this mortal life has no attraction for me; I wish to go to Jesus, who is the bread of immortality and the drink of eternal life. I live entirely for Him, and my soul yearns for Him. I despise all your torments, and I cast at your feet your proffered liberty."

Enraged, the official pronounced his verdict: "Let him be bound, and let loose two lions to devour him."

How did Ignatius overcome the intimidation of the Roman government and the fear of a horrible death before an arena full of bloodthirsty onlookers? He had experienced something that they never had. The love of Jesus. And he had experienced it so deeply that it created in him such a yearning that nothing on earth attracted him.

Not the enticements of a career.
Not the acceptance of a crowd.
And not the approval of a critic.

If Ignatius teaches us anything, it is this: the fear of criticism is silenced by falling in love. If we fall in love with Jesus, not only will nothing on this earth attract us, but nothing on this earth will intimidate us.[57]

THE LORD IS GOOD, a stronghold in the day of trouble, and He knows those who take refuge in Him. (Nahum 1:7 NASB)

> ### CHARLES SPURGEON
> To trust God in the light is nothing,
> but trust Him in the dark – that is faith.[58]

THOUGH HE SLAY ME,
I will hope in Him.
Nevertheless I will argue my ways before Him. (Job 13:15 NASB)

---

[57] Gire, The Divine Embrace, 176.

[58] Charles Spurgeon, The Complete Works of C.H. Spurgeon, Volume 13: Sermons 728-787 (Morrisville Delmarva Publications, 2015), 91.

Chapter 11

IT'S A MIRACLE

SO THEY TOOK AWAY THE STONE. And Jesus lifted up His eyes and said, "Father, I thank Thee that Thou hast heard Me. I knew that Thou hearest Me always, but I have said this on account of the people standing by, that they may believe that Thou didst send Me." When He had said this, He cried with a loud voice, "Lazarus, come out." The dead man came out, his hands and feet bound with bandages, and his face wrapped with a cloth. Jesus said to them, "Unbind him, and let him go." (John 11:41-44 RSV)

PATTI BURNETT

PEOPLE WHO ARE ILL OR INJURED CAN'T HELP BUT OBSESS OVER THE IDEA OF MIRACLES.

I remember reading in the Gospel of Mark that there was a man who had symptoms similar to mine, and then thinking that certainly Jesus could heal me if he could heal that guy. That guy may have even been possessed by a demon. Surely it would be easier to heal me … if He wanted to.

But on second thought, it matters not how bad my symptoms are. If Jesus is truly God, He can heal anything, big or small. He healed the blind. He calmed the storm. He raised the dead. He exorcized demons. He walked on water. He was born of a virgin. He multiplied food. He caused the lame to walk. He healed lepers. He stopped bleeding. He rose from the dead. Parkinson's seems relatively insignificant and benign.

I was once told by a man sitting near me in church that Jesus wants everyone to be healthy and that if I had enough faith, I would be healed. After all, in the days when Jesus walked on the earth, He healed everyone who came to Him, this man told me. This is certainly a topic of much debate within the Body of Christ and definitely not one for which I have any authority.

I am continually trying to find ways to live better and to feel better. I sometimes think that if I eat healthfully, consistently exercise, faithfully meditate, read the Bible, reduce my anxiety, take the right medications – if I do all of that, then I will get better. In the back of my mind, I think I will help God out, in case He plans to bless me that way. As if God really needs my help. "Yes, I believe, Lord. Help my unbelief." I need all the help I can get.

I also sometimes wonder what would happen with my role as an advocate for people with Parkinson's. If I am healed, will I still be able to help people who are newly diagnosed? Will they still be able to relate to me if I don't have their symptoms? Or could my improvement encourage them?

I know that God has changed me since being diagnosed with Parkinson's. I am a more patient and compassionate person. I don't tend to be as domineering and controlling with others; I think I might be a better listener. I try to empathize and see things from others' points of view more often. And most of all, I realize that life is short and there is no time to complain, criticize, and worry. In some ways I guess you could say I'm healed. When we all get to heaven, the Lord may have to explain to us that our idea of healing was off base. Could it be that inner healing is far more important than the kind of healing that people can see from the outside?

JESUS WAS GOING ABOUT IN ALL GALILEE, teaching in their synagogues and proclaiming the gospel of the kingdom, and healing every disease and every sickness among the people.

And the news about Him spread throughout Syria; and they brought to Him all who were ill, those suffering with various diseases and severe pain, demon-possessed, people with epilepsy, and people who were paralyzed; and He healed them. Large crowds followed Him from Galilee and the Decapolis, and Jerusalem, and Judea, and from beyond the Jordan (Matthew 4:23-25 NASB).

MOMENTS WITH THE SAVIOR, AN INCREDIBLE MOMENT AT A WEDDING, KEN GIRE

When the Son of God stepped down from His throne to become a man, the finest of heaven's wines funneled itself into the common earthen vessel of a Palestinian Jew.

For thirty years this vintage from heaven was cellared away in a carpenter's shop in Nazareth. But now the time has come for the seal to be broken, the cork extracted, and the fragrant bouquet of deity to fill the earth so that, for a fleeting but festive moment, the world's parched lips might taste the kingdom of God.

That time coincides, appropriately, with a wedding.

For the overworked, the underpaid, and the punitively taxed, the wedding was a much-needed reprieve when they could relax with old friends and together share a little food, a little wine, a little laughter. But the laughter was beginning to wane. The poor family hosting the wedding had hoped the wine could be stretched by watering down what they had and by filling the goblets only half full. But now they were down to dregs at the bottom of the wine jars.

In an effort to spare the family any embarrassment or social disgrace, Jesus' mother comes to Him for help…

Jesus hesitates because He knows that if He meets this need by supernatural means, life will never be the same. Never again could He turn back the clock…

"Dear woman, why do you involve Me? My time has not yet come…

Jesus would hesitate again at a future request. "Father, if You are willing, take this cup from me." But with a trembling hand Jesus would take that cup. "Yet not my will, but Yours be done."

And so, just as He would submit to his father's request at Gethsemane, He would submit now to His mother's request at Cana…

So characteristic of the Savior that He would first reveal His glory here, in this way, and for this purpose…

The unveiled glory enlarged the disciples' faith. And it did one other thing. With that decision to reveal His glory, Jesus crossed the Rubicon – that river of no return.

The clock was wound. It would begin ticking down to the final hour of His destiny and set in motion the gears that would ultimately enmesh Him and cost Him His life. For the wine he provided at Cana would hasten the cup He would one day drink at the cross.[59]

AND WHEN THEY HAD CROSSED OVER, they came to the land of the Gennes'art And when the men of that place recognized Him, they sent round to all that region and brought to Him all that were sick, and

---

[59] Gire, Moments with the Savior, 71-74.

besought Him that they might only touch the fringe of His garment; and as many as touched it were made well. (Matthew 14:34-36 RSV)

GIVING THE BLESSING, A TRANSFORMING TOUCH, GARY SMALLEY AND JOHN TRENT, PHD

Some nursing homes can be dwellings of lonely despair. So can animal shelters. Residents of both can go for days or weeks without a meaningful touch. Thankfully, some nursing homes and animal shelters have made a dent in the loneliness by bringing seniors and pets together.

More often than not, these programs began as simple recreational activities. But it has quickly become apparent that nursing home residents who hold and touch pets live longer than those who don't. They also have a significantly more positive attitude about life. Those few hours a day when they have someone to touch, to talk to, to love, provide new life and energy for these aging folk.

We don't usually think of a mutt as being a source of blessing, but for some elderly people they are angels in disguise. Some nursing homes have even adopted their own "angels" to bring the blessings of touch to residents.

AFTER SIX DAYS JESUS TOOK WITH HIM PETER, JAMES, AND JOHN THE BROTHER OF JAMES, and led them up a high mountain by themselves. There He was transfigured before them. His face shone like the sun, and His clothes became as white as the light. Just then there appeared before them Moses and Elijah, talking with Jesus.

Peter said to Jesus, "Lord, it is good for us to be here. If You wish, I will put up three shelters—one for You, one for Moses and one for Elijah."

While He was still speaking, a bright cloud covered them, and a voice from the cloud said, "This is my Son, whom I love; with Him I am well pleased. Listen to Him!"

When the disciples heard this, they fell facedown to the ground, terrified. But Jesus came and touched them. "Get up," he said. "Don't be afraid." When they looked up, they saw no one except Jesus.

As they were coming down the mountain, Jesus instructed them, "Don't tell anyone what you have seen, until the Son of Man has been raised from the dead."

The disciples asked Him, "Why then do the teachers of the law say that Elijah must come first?"

Jesus replied, "To be sure, Elijah comes and will restore all things. But I tell you, Elijah has already come, and they did not recognize him, but have done to him everything they wished. In the same way the Son of Man is going to suffer at their hands." Then the disciples understood that He was talking to them about John the Baptist.

When they came to the crowd, a man approached Jesus and knelt before Him. "Lord, have mercy on my son," he said. "He has seizures and is suffering greatly. He often falls into the fire or into the water. I brought him to Your disciples, but they could not heal him."

"You unbelieving and perverse generation," Jesus replied, "how long shall I stay with you? How long shall I put up with you? Bring the boy here to me." Jesus rebuked the demon, and it came out of the boy, and he was healed at that moment.

Then the disciples came to Jesus in private and asked, "Why couldn't we drive it out?"

He replied, "Because you have so little faith. Truly I tell you, if you have faith as small as a mustard seed, you can say to this mountain, 'Move from here to there,' and it will move. Nothing will be impossible for you."

When they came together in Galilee, He said to them, "The Son of Man is going to be delivered into the hands of men. They will kill Him, and on the third day he will be raised to life." And the disciples were filled with grief.

After Jesus and his disciples arrived in Capernaum, the collectors of the two-drachma temple tax came to Peter and asked, "Doesn't your teacher pay the temple tax?"

"Yes, he does," he replied.

When Peter came into the house, Jesus was the first to speak. "What do you think, Simon?" he asked. "From whom do the kings of the earth collect duty and taxes—from their own children or from others?"

"From others," Peter answered.

"Then the children are exempt," Jesus said to him. "But so that we may not cause offense, go to the lake and throw out your line. Take the first fish you catch; open its mouth and you will find a four-drachma coin. Take it and give it to them for my tax and yours. (Matthew 17:1-27 NIV)

> ### *A PLACE OF HEALING: WRESTLING WITH THE MYSTERIES OF SUFFERING, PAIN, AND GOD'S SOVEREIGNTY, JONI EARECKSON TADA*
> He has chosen not to heal me, but to hold me.
> The more intense the pain, the closer His embrace.[60]

AS THEY WERE LEAVING JERICHO, A LARGE CROWD FOLLOWED HIM. And two people who were blind, sitting by the road, hearing that Jesus was passing by, cried out, "Lord, have mercy on us, Son of David!" But the crowd sternly warned them to be quiet; yet they cried out all the more, "Lord, Son of David, have mercy on us!" And Jesus stopped and called them, and said, "What do you want Me to do for you?" They said to Him, "Lord, we want our eyes to be opened." Moved with compassion, Jesus touched their eyes; and immediately they regained their sight and followed Him. (Matthew 20:29-34 NASB)

---

[60] Joni Eareckson Tada, A Place of Healing: Wrestling with the Mysteries of Suffering, Pain, and God's Sovereignty (Colorado Springs: Cook, 2010), 35.

A PLACE OF HEALING: WRESTLING WITH THE MYSTERIES OF SUFFERING, PAIN, AND GOD'S SOVEREIGNTY, JONI EARECKSON TADA

Here at our ministry, we refuse to present a picture of "gentle Jesus, meek and mild," a portrait that tugs at your sentiments or pulls at your heartstrings. That's because we deal with so many people who suffer, and when you're hurting hard, you're neither helped nor inspired by a syrupy picture of the Lord, like those sugary, sentimental images many of us grew up with. You know what I mean? Jesus with His hair parted down the middle, surrounded by cherubic children and bluebirds.

Come on. Admit it: when your heart is being wrung out like a sponge, when you feel like Morton's salt is being poured into your wounded soul, you don't want a thin, pale, emotional Jesus who relates only to lambs and birds and babies. You want a warrior Jesus. You want a battlefield Jesus. You want his rigorous and robust gospel to command your sensibilities to stand at attention.

To be honest, many of the sentimental hymns and gospel songs of our heritage don't do much to hone that image. One of the favorite words of hymn writers in days gone by was sweet. It's a term that doesn't have the edge on it that it once did.

When you're in a dark place, when lions surround you, when you need strong help to rescue you from impossibility, you don't want "sweet." You don't want faded pastels and honeyed softness. You want mighty. You want the strong arm and an unshakable grip of God, who will not let you go – no matter what.[61]

ON THAT DAY, WHEN EVENING CAME, HE SAID TO THEM, "LET'S GO OVER TO THE OTHER SIDE." After dismissing the crowd, they took Him along with them in the boat, just as He was; and other

---
[61] Ibid. 31.

boats were with Him. And a fierce gale of wind developed, and the waves were breaking over the boat so much that the boat was already filling with water. And yet Jesus Himself was in the stern, asleep on the cushion; and they woke Him and said to Him, "Teacher, do You not care that we are perishing?" And He got up and rebuked the wind and said to the sea, "Hush, be still." And the wind died down and it became perfectly calm. And He said to them, "Why are you afraid? Do you still have no faith?" They became very much afraid and said to one another, "Who, then, is this, that even the wind and the sea obey Him?" (Mark 5:35-41 NASB)

DR. JOSEPH HEATON, INTERNIST, SUMMIT COUNTY PARKINSON'S SUPPORT GROUP LEADER

I had been caring for an elderly patient who had an abrupt cardiac/respiratory collapse following hip surgery. A resuscitation ensued. I immediately spoke with the family and called the patient's daughter (as power of attorney) and informed her of the ominous outlook. She indicated that her mother would not have wanted heroic recovery efforts and to please stop the resuscitation. I went into the room and advised the team of the families' request. CPR was ended and all monitors were removed. About 15 minutes later I finished the paperwork, went into the room one last time, and, to my surprise, my patient sat up and asked me where she could get something to eat. Her following recovery was uneventful, and she went on to live a meaningful life.

Currently, I am dealing with the proverbial other side of the fence; I am the patient instead of the provider. I was diagnosed with Parkinson's eight years ago. The usual treatment with medication, trials, and escalations followed. I became unable to work due to the disease and its treatment. Eventually escalation of doses, side effects and concerns regarding quality of life ensued, prompting me to discuss Deep Brain Stimulation surgery, which I had last year. I was an unusual case, according to my Movement Disorders Specialist, and I have been able to eliminate all my medications. I still have Parkinson's, but the brain stimulator device is keeping my symptoms at bay. For nearly a year now, my wife, Sally, has participated in prayer groups on my behalf, and I know that there have been many others praying as well.

Healings in biblical times seemed miraculous and dramatic. Eyesight was restored, leprosy healed, and other miracles were dramatically recounted. Jesus healed nearly everyone who pleaded with Him for a miracle. What has happened in the last two centuries? We don't hear much about miracles anymore. Could it be that they still occur, but are not recognized and celebrated? Did the elderly lady who had the cardiac arrest experience divine intervention that brought her back to life? Was my recovery just performed by an exceptional surgeon or was it a miracle?

I suspect and would suggest to you that healings such as mine and the patient mentioned are as real and dramatic as the restoration of eyesight and the healing of leprosy. Let's open our eyes and recognize the miracles and healings that happen all around us.[62]

NOW JESUS WAS TEACHING IN ONE OF THE SYNAGOGUES ON THE SABBATH. And there was a woman who for eighteen years had had a sickness caused by a spirit; and she was bent over double, and could not straighten up at all. When Jesus saw her, He called her over and said to her, "Woman, you are freed from your sickness." And He laid His hands on her; and immediately she stood up straight again, and began glorifying God. But the synagogue leader, indignant because Jesus had healed on the Sabbath, began saying to the crowd in response, "There are six days during which work should be done; so come during them and get healed, and not on the Sabbath day." But the Lord answered him and said, "You hypocrites, does each of you on the Sabbath not untie his ox or donkey from the stall and lead it away to water it? And this woman, a daughter of Abraham as she is, whom Satan has bound for eighteen long years, should she not have

---

[62] Dr. Joseph Heaton, Denver internist, Summit County Parkinson's support group leader. personal friend of the author.

been released from this restraint on the Sabbath day?" And as He said this, all His opponents were being humiliated; and the entire crowd was rejoicing over all the glorious things being done by Him. (Luke 13:10-17 NASB)

> ### A PLACE OF HEALING: WRESTLING WITH THE MYSTERIES OF SUFFERING, PAIN, AND GOD'S SOVEREIGNTY, JONI EARECKSON TADA
> My wheelchair was the key to seeing all this happen—especially since God's power always shows up best in weakness. So here I sit … glad that I have not been healed on the outside, but glad that I have been healed on the inside. Healed from my own self-centered wants and wishes.[63]

ON THE THIRD DAY A WEDDING TOOK PLACE AT CANA IN GALILEE. Jesus' mother was there, and Jesus and His disciples had also been invited to the wedding. When the wine was gone, Jesus' mother said to Him, "They have no more wine."

"Woman, why do you involve me?" Jesus replied. "My hour has not yet come."

His mother said to the servants, "Do whatever He tells you."

Nearby stood six stone water jars, the kind used by the Jews for ceremonial washing, each holding from twenty to thirty gallons.

Jesus said to the servants, "Fill the jars with water"; so they filled them to the brim.

Then He told them, "Now draw some out and take it to the master of the banquet."

They did so, and the master of the banquet tasted the water that had been turned into wine. He did not realize where it had come from,

---

[63] Tada, A Place of Healing, 49.

though the servants who had drawn the water knew. Then he called the bridegroom aside and said, "Everyone brings out the choice wine first and then the cheaper wine after the guests have had too much to drink; but you have saved the best til now." What Jesus did here in Cana of Galilee was the first of the signs through which He revealed His glory; and His disciples believed in Him. After this he went down to Capernaum with His mother and brothers and His disciples. There they stayed for a few days. (John 2:1-12 NASB)

AFTER THIS, JESUS CROSSED OVER TO THE FAR SIDE OF THE SEA OF GALILEE, also known as the sea of Tiberias. A huge crowd kept following Him wherever He went, because they saw His miraculous signs as He healed the sick. Then Jesus climbed a hill and sat down with His disciples around Him. (It was nearly time for the Jewish Passover celebration.) Jesus soon saw a huge crowd of people coming to look for Him. Turning to Philip, he asked, "Where can we buy bread to feed all these people?" He was testing Philip, for He already knew what He was going to do.

Philip replied, "Even if we worked for months, we wouldn't have enough money to feed them!"

Then Andrew, Simon Peter's brother, spoke up. "There's a young boy here with five barley loaves and two fish. But what good is that with this huge crowd?"

"Tell everyone to sit down," Jesus said. So they all sat down on the grassy slopes. (The men alone numbered about 5,000.) Then Jesus took the loaves, gave thanks to God, and distributed them to the people. Afterward He did the same with the fish. And they all ate as much as they wanted. After everyone was full, Jesus told his disciples, "Now gather the leftovers, so that nothing is wasted." So they picked up the pieces and filled twelve baskets with scraps left by the people who had eaten from the five barley loaves.

When the people saw Him do this miraculous sign, they exclaimed, "Surely, He is the Prophet we have been expecting!" When Jesus saw that they were ready to force Him to be their king, He slipped away into the hills by Himself.

That evening Jesus' disciples went down to the shore to wait for Him. But as darkness fell and Jesus still hadn't come back, they got into the boat and headed across the lake toward Capernaum. Soon a gale swept down upon them, and the sea grew very rough. They had rowed three or four miles when suddenly they saw Jesus walking on the water toward the boat. They were terrified, but He called out to them, "Don't be afraid. I am here!" Then they were eager to let Him in the boat, and immediately they arrived at their destination!

The next day the crowd that had stayed on the far shore saw that the disciples had taken the only boat, and they realized Jesus had not gone with them. Several boats from Tiberias landed near the place where the Lord had blessed the bread and the people had eaten. So when the crowd saw that neither Jesus nor His disciples were there, they got into the boats and went across to Capernaum to look for Him. They found Him on the other side of the lake and asked, "Rabbi, when did you get here?" (John 6:1-25 NLT)

<u>I BELIEVE IN MIRACLES, JOHN PETERSON</u>

Creation shows the power of God
There's glory all around,
And those who see must stand in awe,
For miracles abound.
I believe in miracles
I've seen a soul set free,
Miraculous the change in one
Redeemed through Calvary;
I've seen the lily push its way
Up through the stubborn sod

> I believe in miracles
> For I believe in God![64]

THEN JOSHUA SPOKE TO THE LORD on the day when the Lord turned the Amorites over to the sons of Israel, and he said in the sight of Israel,

> "Sun, stand still at Gibeon,
> And moon, at the Valley of Aijalon!"
> So the sun stood still, and the moon stopped,
> Until the nation avenged themselves of their enemies.

Is it not written in the Book of Jashar? And the sun stopped in the middle of the sky and did not hurry to go down for about a whole day. There was no day like that before it or after it, when the Lord listened to the voice of a man; for the Lord fought for Israel.

Then Joshua and all Israel with him returned to the camp at Gilgal. (Joshua 10:12-15 NASB)

PATTI BURNETT

THESE ARE UNUSUAL DAYS; we are three years into the Coronavirus (COVID-19) pandemic. It's difficult to predict the outcome. Nearly six million people have died so far (1.1 million in the US alone); and there have been approximately 428 million reported cases worldwide. It is believed that this thing is far from finished with its deadly rampage. As I wrote this, we had just gotten back from dropping off lunch at one of our daughters' homes because she and her husband had symptoms.

During the early pandemic days, I spent a considerable amount of time in hospitals. I had every COVID symptom and tested negative

---

[64] John W. Peterson and Carlton C. Buck, arr. by Roger C. Wilson, I Believe in Miracles (Brentwood: New Spring Publishing Inc., 1948), from https://digitalsongsandhymns.com/songs/10385

every time; but my most deadly symptom was fear. As it turned out, I instead had pneumonia and a seriously infected kidney with two cysts the size of baseballs.

During my stints at various medical facilities, fighting for my life, I was completely alone. Because of the dark cloud of paranoia that paralyzed our world, there was scant to no support given to those who were hospitalized; and if a doctor or nurse actually entered a patient's room, they were clothed in a costume that rivaled that of a scientist working with radioactive elements. There were times when I truly felt radioactive.

Such is still the case in many facilities in the U.S. Probably one of the institutions most profoundly affected by these state and federal mandates are nursing homes and assisted living residences. It is believed that about one third of the US COVID-19 deaths can be linked to long-term care facilities; that amounts to about 200,000 of our dear parents and grandparents. It is estimated that approximately 1.4 million Americans live in nursing homes; and at one point approximately 450 residents of these facilities died every day from COVID-19.

These statistics are important to us. My Dad, during his vibrant years was a speed skater; hockey player, coach, and AHL official. He built and ran his own business; parented six children, had twenty grandchildren, thirty something great grandchildren; and was a competitive sailor. Until Dad's death this past fall, he remained in a nearly catatonic state while living in an adult community. He was not allowed to have social interaction with the other residents and the only touch he received was for the rudimentary practices of cleanliness and dressing. I am so grateful for my brother, Lanse, and his wife, Amy, who rescued Dad and relocated him to their home.

My mother-in-law, Lois, was in an entirely different situation. We were not allowed to enter her adult residence and our only means of communication was through a thick plexiglass wall. Mom B. begged us to allow her to hold her second great grandchild, but that was definitely against the rules and her wish was not granted before her time here on earth was tragically and needlessly ended.

Why the lengthy discourse on this particular subject? Because you who are reading are perhaps finally having an opportunity to care for the matriarchs and patriarchs of your families. Please tell them you love them and touch them in a meaningful way that conveys how much you appreciate them.

Jesus' touch changed lives. He touched the children who came to Him. He touched the leper and the woman with the issuance of blood, and they were healed. He touched the eyes of the blind man, and he could see. Jesus touched Peter's mother-in-law, a 12-year-old girl, a man who was deaf, the soldier whose ear Peter lopped off, the young son of a widow and another young boy. All of them left changed forever.

I love the stories of Mother Teresa as she cared for the lepers dying in the streets of Calcutta. Following are a few of her quotes:

- "Being unwanted, unloved, uncared for, forgotten by everybody, I think that is a much greater hunger, a much greater poverty than the person who has nothing to eat."
- "Let us touch the dying, the poor, the lonely and the unwanted according to the graces we have received and let us not be ashamed or slow to do the humble work."
- "Loneliness and the feeling of being unwanted is the most terrible poverty."
- "The biggest disease today is not leprosy or tuberculosis, but rather the feeling of being unwanted."
- "Our life of poverty is as necessary as the work itself. Only in heaven will we see how much we owe to the poor for helping us to love God better because of them."

Chapter 12

YA GOTTA HAVE FAITH

MY SOUL, WAIT IN SILENCE FOR GOD ALONE, for my hope is from Him. He alone is my rock and my salvation, My refuge; I will not be shaken. My salvation and my glory rest on God. The rock of my strength, my refuge is in God. (Psalm 62:5-7 NASB)

MY FAITH STORY, PATTI BURNETT

WHAT A LIFE! One of six children, our summers were filled with water-skiing, jumping on trampolines, fishing, and swimming. Winters included skiing, skating, more time with friends, and snow days which of course meant powder skiing. I had close friends, a great family, and not a care in the world. However, entering my teen years, current events took a turn for the worse.

1970, when I graduated from Brighton High, was a very disturbing time for our country. Protests occurred on every major university campus, opposing the United States' involvement in the Vietnam war and expansion into Cambodia. During a peace rally on May 4, 1970, four unarmed students were killed and nine injured by the Ohio National Guard. Crosby, Stills, Nash and Young sang about the Kent State massacre in "Four Dead in Ohio."

There was no question in any of my male classmates' minds that college was their only option; no one wanted to be assigned a field trip through Viet Nam. My boyfriend at the time got drafted onto a nuclear sub.

I majored in physical education and business at Ashland College, in Ohio. I enjoyed college life, with all the fraternity and sorority parties, cheerleading, and newfound freedom from my strict upbringing. It was also a distraction from the war.

After moving back home, my brothers and I started a Young Life club in Pittsford, NY. I had the privilege of discipling eight of the girls and I loved it when those young ladies, in turn, developed a burden for their classmates' spirituality. Recently I learned that many of them are leaving a legacy of faith, with their own children going into full time ministry opportunities, like Young Life.

Yet, despite all these Christian activities and fellowship, things were not right in my heart. I needed a change. I called Young Life headquarters, inquiring about jobs. They just happened to have an office manager and bookkeeper position at Trail West Ranch, so I moved to

Buena Vista, Colorado within a few weeks. I fell in love with the beautiful Colorado mountains and was either hiking or horseback riding every opportunity I got.

Shortly thereafter, I moved to Breckenridge to teach skiing. Drinking, drugs, and heavy partying was – and is – one of the occupational hazards of being a "ski bum." I shut God out of almost every aspect of my life, dating one guy seriously and becoming pregnant my first winter. I had never even thought through the consequences of an unplanned pregnancy; and abortion seemed my only option. My main concern was how it would devastate my parents if they found out. How deranged that I would not even consider how much more terrible it would be to rule a death sentence to my own flesh and blood.

That chapter of my life still replays as a nightmare. I blocked out the fact that I was killing the baby that I helped create! I do not remember being driven to the abortion clinic in Denver. To this day, it's almost as if it never happened – I had hardened my heart beyond belief. There was no counseling at the clinic, but I do remember the awful sound of the machine as it performed its deadly task. The next day I taught skiing as if it were just another day, hiding the spotting and terrible cramps I was experiencing. As I look back on that experience, I have a hard time understanding how I could have sunk so low. Since that time, I have had some opportunities to counsel post-abortive women. The emotional consequences are tragic, and healing can be a painful and extensive journey.

After the abortion, my life was pretty miserable. I knew that Jesus had taken the curse of my sin, even an abortion, when He died on the cross; but I needed to confess this to someone. I called a local church; and when I met with the pastor, I came clean – literally. It was freeing to have the burden of guilt removed from my heart. My behavior changed gradually as I surrounded myself with others who loved Christ. They helped me to walk in obedience to Him. And all along Jesus had been patiently waiting for me to turn to Him in my pain and sorrow.

I am so grateful that He never gave up on me and that His death and resurrection made it possible for me to repent of my sins and find forgiveness and release from the chains that were choking me from the inside out. God saves (redeems) those who turn to Him from sin, evil, trouble, bondage, and ultimately death. It is by His grace that we are rescued and restored.

The following year I started ski patrolling. Working in a male dominated field did not bother me because of my ski race history and having been raised with four brothers.

My life took a drastic change of direction when I blew out my knee. Suddenly, my old ski buddies weren't around. Not being able to ski while I rehabilitated meant I was less fun and that was when I learned who my real friends were. At the time it was hurtful; but now as I look back, I appreciate the fact that God replaced the old friends with a few Christians. I had much more time to think while I was off my feet and had many heart-to-heart conversations with the Lord. He gave me a hunger for His Word and for fellowship.

Another by-product of my immobilizing injury occurred when I got my obviously NOT four-wheel drive Toyota Celica, stuck in a snowbank in my driveway. Alicia, my best friend, had told me about a Christian guy who lived close by, so I hobbled up the street on my crutches to beg for help – something I have never been very good at. Dan, a real estate broker and search and rescue mission coordinator, was happy to help a "damsel in distress."

Our friendship developed gradually, neither of us interested in becoming seriously involved. We spent time going to Bible studies, sailing, skiing, volunteering with the search and rescue team, and just talking – but almost always in groups. I had never met a man so interested in deep conversations about spiritual matters. I had never met anyone who so freely expressed his emotions. Dan likes to say that, in our relationship, he's the girl, because he does most of the talking, which is uncharacteristic for a man. If you know Dan, you know that he loves to tell stories. It was a few years before we started dating, and even then, we were careful to take it slow.

Finally, in August 1984 Dan "popped the question." There was not a doubt in my mind or heart that he was the man God had provided for me. We were married four months later, a snowy December day when God created one new life out of two. Over the years we have grown to love each other more as we have each, individually and jointly, grown in our relationships with Jesus.

In 1986 we started trying to get pregnant. I knew that Dan would be a great dad, and at the age of 34, my biological clock ticked off the alarm that it was time. However, God was in a different time zone. So began the four-year-long infertility and adoption merry-go-round. We were both healthy, and the doctors could not pinpoint the reasons for our infertility. We tried medications, charting my temperature, scheduling intimacy, and receiving much unsolicited advice from our friends and family.

Guilt feelings about the abortion raised its ugly head again. Perhaps this was God's way of paying me back for killing my child. The God I had come to know forgave a truly repentant heart and yet, the Bible also says that a person reaps what he or she sows. I also wondered whether the abortion had produced scar tissue, making it more difficult to conceive.

We continually heard that the issues of adoption and infertility could be hard on marriages. The blessing through it all was that Dan's and my relationship grew stronger. It was fortunate that we had discussed the adoption option even before we realized we were infertile. We called Christian Family Services and started the endless stream of required paperwork. We participated in parenting classes and home studies and found that adoption is a veritable rollercoaster. Twice birth moms chose us and, subsequently, decided to keep their babies. With each disappointment, we renewed our fertility efforts, seeing yet another specialist. Whenever that route seemed hopeless, we renewed the adoption efforts once again.

Nothing changes a person's perspective on abortion as much as trying to adopt. Do you realize that since 1973, Roe v. Wade, there have been nearly 63,000,000 abortions? There are 125,000 abortions every day worldwide. So many babies being aborted – so many infertile parents desperate for a child.

Finally in 1990, we met with a 17-year-old young lady. Becky's parents completely supported her decision to place her baby for adoption. They demonstrated incredible love for their daughter; and during one of our counseling sessions, Becky's Dad told Mike, the birth father, how much he loved him. Mike broke down in tears and admitted that no one had ever shown him that kind of love. Becky's due date was about six weeks away; and so began another waiting game. Having met Becky face to face, I had peace that this situation would be different from the others.

During this time of anticipation, we were soon to get another surprise. I missed one of my monthly cycles and an early pregnancy test yielded positive results. Doubtful, I conducted two more tests, both positive. Still skeptical, a blood test and listening to my baby's heartbeat removed the last vestiges of doubts. We were ecstatic and hid our little secret from everyone except the adoption agency. We did not want to in any way take away from the joy of our first child's arrival.

And what a joyous occasion it was! We got the call around 11 PM that Becky had delivered a 7-lb 6oz baby girl. We named her Bethany and Becky gave her the middle name of Kayla. We arrived the next morning to take our little miracle home – finally. At the dedication in the hospital chapel, we all expressed our gratitude to God and asked Him to bless Bethany. As we walked out to the car together, and Becky placed her in my arms, Dan and I both received a fresh appreciation of unconditional love. It must be so hard to carry a baby to term and then release her to another family. I also received a new understanding of God's grace. He had done a new work in our family, despite my miserable past failures.

An added blessing arrived when we learned that we may have conceived the very day that we first met with Becky. There is no end to

God's sense of humor and timing. He wanted to make sure that people realized that He was the one who controlled this situation, not my stress and female hormones. Rachel Hope was born seven and a half months after Bethany.

The two were friends from the start and to this day they are having children at the same time, sharing baby clothes, parenting ideas, and child-care duties (me too, which is perfectly fine by me). I was able to express milk for Bethany so that she received the same antibodies Rachel got. At our ages, God was good in blessing us with babies so "parent friendly." Both slept through the night within a few months. Being doubly blessed, we asked our friends to stop praying that God would fill our quiver.

Throughout all this family expansion, I patrolled during the six winter months, and was quickly promoted to supervisor. I took a little flak from friends though, wondering why I was working with two children so young. This was a constant topic of discussion between me and Dan. We had sought God's guidance, and each time He confirmed that we were doing the right thing. Dan could spend more time with the girls during the winters when real estate business was slower. I think that there are few dads bonded with their daughters as well.

The winter of 1985, with the support of the Copper Mountain administration, I initiated the search and rescue dog program in our county. These programs have grown exponentially over the years, especially at the Colorado Ski Resorts. Because of their "scent-abilities," dogs are well suited for finding people lost in the wilderness, buried in avalanche deposition, or drowned in rivers. As my experience increased over the thirty years of handling dogs, I had the privilege of speaking and training hundreds of dog teams around the world. I also published "Avalanche! Hasty Search," a book that gives instructions on how to train an avalanche dog, along with many stories of missions in which the dogs participated.

Overall, I would have to say that I've had a pretty good run; but life has not necessarily been easy sailing since learning to walk faithfully with my God. Lately there have been many bumps and falls, trying to navigate Parkinson's; but I am learning that each time I stumble, God picks me up and draws me closer to Himself. Every scar more clearly illustrates the truth that God's power is made stronger in weakness, and I choose to be in the center of His plan for my life.

PAUL, A SERVANT OF CHRIST JESUS, called to be an apostle, set apart for the Gospel of God, which He promised beforehand through His prophets in the holy Scriptures, concerning His Son, who was descended from David according to the flesh and was declared to be the Son of God in power according to the Spirit of holiness by His resurrection from the dead, Jesus Christ our Lord, through Whom we have received grace and apostleship to bring about the obedience of faith for the sake of His name among all the nations, including you who are called to belong to Jesus Christ,

To all those in Rome who are loved by God and called to be saints:

Grace to you and peace from God our Father and the Lord Jesus Christ.

First, I thank my God through Jesus Christ for all of you, because your faith is proclaimed in all the world. For God is my witness, whom I serve with my spirit in the gospel of His Son, that without ceasing I mention you always in my prayers, asking that somehow by God's will I may now at last succeed in coming to you. For I long to see you, that I may impart to you some spiritual gift to strengthen you—that is, that we may be mutually encouraged by each other's faith, both yours and mine. I do not want you to be unaware, brothers, that I have often intended to come to you (but thus far have been prevented), in order that I may reap some harvest among you as well as among the rest of the Gentiles. I am under obligation both to Greeks and to barbarians, both to the wise and to the foolish. So I am eager to preach the gospel to you also who are in Rome.

For I am not ashamed of the gospel, for it is the power of God for salvation to everyone who believes, to the Jew first and also to the Greek. (Romans 1:1-16 ESV)

> ### *C.S. LEWIS*
> Faith is the art of holding on to things your reason has once accepted, in spite of your changing moods.[65]

WITH THE ARRIVAL OF JESUS, THE MESSIAH, that fateful dilemma is resolved. Those who enter into Christ's being-here-for-us no longer have to live under a continuous, low-lying black cloud. A new power is in operation. The Spirit of life in Christ, like a strong wind, has magnificently cleared the air, freeing you from a fated lifetime of brutal tyranny at the hands of sin and death.

God went for the jugular when He sent His own Son. He didn't deal with the problem as something remote and unimportant. In His Son, Jesus, he personally took on the human condition, entered the disordered mess of struggling humanity in order to set it right once and for all. The law code, weakened as it always was by fractured human nature, could never have done that.

The law always ended up being used as a Band-Aid on sin instead of a deep healing of it. And now what the law code asked for, but we couldn't deliver, is accomplished as we, instead of redoubling our own efforts, simply embrace what the Spirit is doing in us.

Those who think they can do it on their own, end up obsessed with measuring their own moral muscle but never get around to exercising it in real life. Those who trust God's action in them find that God's Spirit is in them—living and breathing God! Obsession with self in these

---

[65] C.S. Lewis, Mere Christianity (London: Geoffrey Bles, 1952), 106.

matters is a dead end; attention to God leads us out into the open, into a spacious, free life. Focusing on the self is the opposite of focusing on God. Anyone completely absorbed in self, ignores God, ends up thinking more about self than God. That person ignores who God is and what He is doing. And God isn't pleased at being ignored.

But if God Himself has taken up residence in your life, you can hardly be thinking more of yourself than of Him. Anyone, of course, who has not welcomed this invisible but clearly present God, the Spirit of Christ, won't know what we're talking about. But for you who welcome Him, in whom He dwells—even though you still experience all the limitations of sin—you yourself experience life on God's terms. It stands to reason, doesn't it, that if the alive-and-present God who raised Jesus from the dead moves into your life, He'll do the same thing in you that He did in Jesus, bringing you alive to Himself? When God lives and breathes in you (and He does, as surely as He did in Jesus), you are delivered from that dead life. With His Spirit living in you, your body will be as alive as Christ's!

So don't you see that we don't owe this old do-it-yourself life one red cent. There's nothing in it for us, nothing at all. The best thing to do is give it a decent burial and get on with your new life. God's Spirit beckons. There are things to do and places to go!

This resurrection life you received from God is not a timid, grave-tending life. It's adventurously expectant, greeting God with a childlike "What's next, Papa?" God's Spirit touches our spirits and confirms who we really are. We know who He is, and we know who we are: Father and children. And we know we are going to get what's coming to us—an unbelievable inheritance! We go through exactly what Christ goes through. If we go through the hard times with Him, then we're certainly going to go through the good times with Him!

That's why I don't think there's any comparison between the present hard times and the coming good times. The created world itself can hardly wait for what's coming next. Everything in creation is being more or less held back. God reins it in until both creation and all the creatures are ready and can be released at the same moment into the glorious times ahead. Meanwhile, the joyful anticipation deepens.

All around us we observe a pregnant creation. The difficult times of pain throughout the world are simply birth pangs. But it's not only around us; it's within us. The Spirit of God is arousing us within. We're also feeling the birth pangs. These sterile and barren bodies of ours are yearning for full deliverance. That is why waiting does not diminish us, any more than waiting diminishes a pregnant mother. We are enlarged in the waiting. We, of course, don't see what is enlarging us. But the longer we wait, the larger we become, and the more joyful our expectancy.

Meanwhile, the moment we get tired in the waiting, God's Spirit is right alongside helping us along. If we don't know how or what to pray, it doesn't matter. He does our praying in and for us, making prayer out of our wordless sighs, our aching groans. He knows us far better than we know ourselves, knows our pregnant condition, and keeps us present before God. That's why we can be so sure that every detail in our lives of love for God is worked into something good.

God knew what He was doing from the very beginning. He decided from the outset to shape the lives of those who love Him along the same lines as the life of His Son. The Son stands first in the line of humanity He restored. We see the original and intended shape of our lives there in Him. After God made that decision of what His children should be like, he followed it up by calling people by name. After He called them by name, He set them on a solid basis with Himself. And then, after getting them established, He stayed with them to the end, gloriously completing what He had begun.

So, what do you think? With God on our side like this, how can we lose? If God didn't hesitate to put everything on the line for us, embracing our condition and exposing Himself to the worst by sending His own Son, is there anything else He wouldn't gladly and freely do for us?

And who would dare tangle with God by messing with one of God's chosen? Who would dare even to point a finger? The one who died for us—who was raised to life for us!—is in the presence of God at this very moment sticking up for us. Do you think anyone is going to be able to drive a wedge between us and Christ's love for us? There is no way! Not trouble, not hard times, not hatred, not hunger, not homelessness, not bullying threats, not backstabbing, not even the worst sins listed in Scripture:

> They kill us in cold blood because they hate you.
> We're sitting ducks; they pick us off one by one.

None of this fazes us because Jesus loves us. I'm absolutely convinced that nothing—nothing living or dead, angelic or demonic, today or tomorrow, high or low, thinkable or unthinkable—absolutely nothing can get between us and God's love because of the way that Jesus our Master has embraced us. (Romans 8:1-39 Message)

J.R.R. TOLKIEN
Faithless is he that says farewell when the road darkens.[66]

AT THE SAME TIME, YOU NEED TO KNOW that I carry with me at all times a huge sorrow. It's an enormous pain deep within me, and I'm never free of it. I'm not exaggerating – Christ and the Holy Spirit are my witnesses. It's the Israelites … If there were any way I could be cursed by the Messiah so they could be blessed by Him, I'd do it in a minute. They're my family. I grew up with them. They had everything going for them—family, glory, covenants, revelation, worship, promises, to say nothing of being the race that produced the Messiah, the Christ, who is God over everything, always. Oh, yes!

---

[66] J.R.R. Tolkien, The Fellowship of the Ring (London: George Allen and Unwin, 1954), 111.

Don't suppose for a moment, though, that God's Word has malfunctioned in some way or other. The problem goes back a long way. From the outset, not all Israelites of the flesh were Israelites of the spirit. It wasn't Abraham's sperm that gave identity here, but God's promise. Remember how it was put: "Your family will be defined by Isaac?" That means that Israelite identity was never racially determined by sexual transmission, but it was God-determined by promise. Remember that promise, "When I come back next year at this time, Sarah will have a son?"

And that's not the only time. To Rebecca, also, a promise was made that took priority over genetics. When she became pregnant by our one-of-a-kind ancestor, Isaac, and her babies were still innocent in the womb—incapable of good or bad—she received a special assurance from God. What God did in this case made it perfectly plain that His purpose is not a hit-or-miss thing dependent on what we do or don't do, but a sure thing determined by His decision, flowing steadily from His initiative. God told Rebecca, "The firstborn of your twins will take second place." Later that was turned into a stark epigram: "I loved Jacob; I hated Esau."

Is that grounds for complaining that God is unfair? Not so fast, please. God told Moses, "I'm in charge of mercy. I'm in charge of compassion." Compassion doesn't originate in our bleeding hearts or moral sweat, but in God's mercy. The same point was made when God said to Pharaoh, "I picked you as a bit player in this drama of my salvation power." All we're saying is that God has the first word, initiating the action in which we play our part for good or ill.

Are you going to object, "So how can God blame us for anything since He's in charge of everything? If the big decisions are already made, what say do we have in it?"

Who in the world do you think you are to second-guess God? Do you for one moment suppose any of us knows enough to call God into question? Clay doesn't talk back to the fingers that mold it, saying, "Why did you shape me like this?" Isn't it obvious that a potter has a perfect right to shape one lump of clay into a vase for holding flowers and another into a pot for cooking beans? If God needs one style of pottery especially designed to show His angry displeasure and another style carefully crafted to show His glorious goodness, isn't that all right? Either or both happens to Jews, but it also happens to the other people. Hosea put it well:

> I'll call nobodies and make them somebodies;
> > I'll call the unloved and make them beloved.
> In the place where they yelled out, "You're nobody!"
> > they're calling you "God's living children."

Isaiah maintained this same emphasis:

> If each grain of sand on the seashore were numbered
> > and the sum labeled "chosen of God,"
> They'd be numbers still, not names;
> salvation comes by personal selection.
> God doesn't count us; He calls us by name.
> > Arithmetic is not His focus.

Isaiah had looked ahead and spoken the truth:

> If our powerful God
> > had not provided us a legacy of living children,
> We would have ended up like ghost towns,
> > like Sodom and Gomorrah.

How can we sum this up? All those people who didn't seem interested in what God was doing actually embraced what God was doing as He straightened out their lives. And Israel, who seemed so interested in reading and talking about what God was doing, missed it. How could they miss it? Because instead of trusting God, they took over. They were absorbed in what they themselves were doing. They were so absorbed in their "God projects" that they didn't notice God right in front of them, like a huge rock in the middle of the road. And so they stumbled into Him and went sprawling. Isaiah (again!) gives us the metaphor for pulling this together:

Careful! I've put a huge stone on the road to Mount Zion,
    a stone you can't get around.
But the stone is me! If you're looking for me,
    you'll find me on the way, not in the way. (Romans 9:1-33 Message)

> ### HELEN KELLER
> Faith is the strength by which a shattered world shall emerge into the light.[67]

"FOR THROUGH THE LAW I DIED TO THE LAW so that I might live for God. I have been crucified with Christ and I no longer live, but Christ lives in me. The life I now live in the body, I live by faith in the Son of God, who loved me and gave Himself for me. I do not set aside the grace of God, for if righteousness could be gained through the law, Christ died for nothing. (Galatians 2:19-21 NASB)

DRAW THE CIRCLE, MARK BATTERSON

Jesus and his disciples were leaving Jericho when two blind men begged Him for mercy. The disciples couldn't be bothered but Jesus stopped and asked them what they wanted from Him, even though it was pretty obvious that they wanted Him to heal them of their blindness.

---

[67] Anonymous quoting Helen Keller, God Grant Me: More Meditations from the Authors of Keep It Simple (Center City: Hazelden Publishing, 2009), 10.

Jesus wanted to make sure that they knew what they wanted. What if Jesus asked you the same question? What do you want Me to do for you? Would you be able to spell out the promises, miracles, and dreams God has put in your heart? ... The great irony, of course, is that if we can't answer the question, then we're as blind spiritually as these men were physically. Most of us don't get what we want simply because we don't know what we want.

If faith is being sure of what we hope for, then not being sure of what we hope for is the exact opposite of faith, isn't it?[68]

NOW FAITH IS CONFIDENCE IN WHAT WE HOPE FOR and assurance about what we do not see. This is what the ancients were commended for. By faith we understand that the universe was formed at God's command, so that what is seen was not made out of what was visible.

By faith Abel brought God a better offering than Cain did. By faith he was commended as righteous, when God spoke well of his offerings. And by faith Abel still speaks, even though he is dead.

By faith Enoch was taken from this life, so that he did not experience death: "He could not be found, because God had taken him away." For before he was taken, he was commended as one who pleased God. And without faith it is impossible to please God, because anyone who comes to Him must believe that He exists and that He rewards those who earnestly seek Him.

By faith Noah, when warned about things not yet seen, in holy fear built an ark to save his family. By his faith he condemned the world and became heir of the righteousness that is in keeping with faith.

By faith Abraham, when called to go to a place he would later receive as his inheritance, obeyed and went, even though he did not know where he was going. By faith he made his home in the promised land like a stranger in a foreign country; he lived in tents, as did

---

[68] Batterson, Draw the Circle, 171.

Isaac and Jacob, who were heirs with him of the same promise. For he was looking forward to the city with foundations, whose architect and builder is God. And by faith even Sarah, who was past childbearing age, was enabled to bear children because she considered Him faithful who had made the promise. And so from this one man, and he as good as dead, came descendants as numerous as the stars in the sky and as countless as the sand on the seashore.

All these people were still living by faith when they died. They did not receive the things promised; they only saw them and welcomed them from a distance, admitting that they were foreigners and strangers on earth. People who say such things show that they are looking for a country of their own. If they had been thinking of the country they had left, they would have had opportunity to return.

Instead, they were longing for a better country—a heavenly one. Therefore, God is not ashamed to be called their God, for He has prepared a city for them.

> By faith Abraham, when God tested him, offered Isaac as a sacrifice. He who had embraced the promises was about to sacrifice his one and only son, even though God had said to him, "It is through Isaac that your offspring will be reckoned." Abraham reasoned that God could even raise the dead, and so in a manner of speaking he did receive Isaac back from death.
>
> By faith Isaac blessed Jacob and Esau in regard to their future.
>
> By faith Jacob, when he was dying, blessed each of Joseph's sons, and worshiped as he leaned on the top of his staff.
>
> By faith Joseph, when his end was near, spoke about the exodus of the Israelites from Egypt and gave instructions concerning the burial of his bones.

By faith Moses' parents hid him for three months after he was born, because they saw he was no ordinary child, and they were not afraid of the king's edict.

By faith Moses, when he had grown up, refused to be known as the son of Pharaoh's daughter. He chose to be mistreated along with the people of God rather than to enjoy the fleeting pleasures of sin. He regarded disgrace for the sake of Christ as of greater value than the treasures of Egypt, because he was looking ahead to his reward. By faith he left Egypt, not fearing the king's anger; he persevered because he saw Him who is invisible. By faith he kept the Passover and the application of blood, so that the destroyer of the firstborn would not touch the firstborn of Israel.

By faith the people passed through the Red Sea as on dry land; but when the Egyptians tried to do so, they were drowned.

By faith the walls of Jericho fell, after the army had marched around them for seven days.

By faith the prostitute Rahab, because she welcomed the spies, was not killed with those who were disobedient.

And what more shall I say? I do not have time to tell about Gideon, Barak, Samson and Jephthah, about David and Samuel and the prophets, who through faith conquered kingdoms, administered justice, and gained what was promised; who shut the mouths of lions, quenched the fury of the flames, and escaped the edge of the sword; whose weakness was turned to strength; and who became powerful in battle and routed foreign armies. Women received back their dead, raised to life again. There were others who were tortured, refusing to be released so that they might gain an even better resurrection. Some faced jeers and flogging, and even chains and imprisonment. They were put to death by stoning; they were sawed in two; they were killed by the sword. They went about in sheepskins and goatskins, destitute, persecuted and mistreated—the world was not worthy of them. They wandered in deserts and mountains, living in caves and in holes in the ground.

These were all commended for their faith, yet none of them received what had been promised, since God had planned something better for us so that only together with us would they be made perfect. (Hebrews 11:1-40 NASB)

MARY MCLEOD BETHUNE
Faith is the first factor in a life devoted to service. Without faith, nothing is possible. With it, nothing is impossible.[69]

FOR THIS IS CONTAINED IN SCRIPTURE:
"Behold, I am laying in Zion a choice stone, a precious cornerstone,
And the one who believes in Him will not be put to shame."
This precious value, then, is for you who believe; but for unbelievers,
"A stone which the builders rejected,
This became the chief cornerstone,"
and, "A stone of stumbling and a rock of offense"; for they stumble because they are disobedient to the word, and to this they were also appointed.

But you are a chosen people, a royal priesthood, a holy nation, a people for God's own possession, so that you may proclaim the excellencies of Him who has called you out of darkness into His marvelous light; for you once were not a people, but now you are the people of God; you had not received mercy, but now you have received mercy.

---

[69] Mary McLeod Bethune, Building a Better World (Bloomington: Indiana University Press, 2001), 60.

Beloved, I urge you as foreigners and strangers to abstain from fleshly lusts, which wage war against the soul. Keep your behavior excellent among the Gentiles, so that in the thing in which they slander you as evildoers, they may because of your good deeds, as they observe them, glorify God on the day of visitation. (1 Peter 2:6-12 NASB)

> ### WALTER BRUEGGEMAN
> Faith does, on occasion arise – partly because of us and partly in spite of us.[70]

DRAW THE CIRCLE, MARK BATTERSON

Standing beneath a giant sequoia is like standing in the shadow of the Creator. It was absolutely awe-inspiring on my first visit to Yosemite National Park. These magnificent creations can measure more than twenty feet wide and three hundred feet tall. The root system goes down about twelve feet and stretches out into an area about eighty feet in diameter. Their resistance to disease, insect damage, and fire, make them almost indestructible. And their built-in ability to recycle and regenerate contributes to their two-thousand-year life span.

Now here is the amazing thing: the giant sequoia was once a seed. And that sequoia seed is no bigger than the seed that produces a tomato plant. That is the power of a single seed. And one sequoia, when it matures, will produce 400,000 seeds of its own every year. So, in every seed, there isn't just a tree; there is a forest of trees.

Then God said, "Let the land sprout with vegetation—every sort of seed-bearing plant, and trees that grow seed-bearing fruit. These seeds will then produce the kinds of plants and trees from which they came." And we just keep reading the Genesis account as if nothing happened.

---

[70] Walter Brueggeman, Biblical Perspectives on Evangelism (Nashville: Abingdon Press, 1993).

Granted, there are more spectacular creations than the simple seed—the sun, moon, and stars, for example. But the seed may be the most amazing example of God's prolific creativity. And we certainly owe God a thank-you for every kind of seed every time we bite into the fruit they produce—orange seeds, apple seeds, strawberry seeds, grapefruit seeds, pomegranate seeds, watermelon seeds. Can you imagine life without any of these seeds?

William Jennings Bryan, famous for his role in the Scopes Monkey Trial in 1925, once likened the mystery of God to a watermelon seed:

> I have observed the watermelon seed. It has the power of drawing from the ground and through itself 200,000 times its weight: and when you can tell me how it takes this material and out of it colors an outside surface beyond the imitation of art, and then forms in it a white rind and within that again a side of red heart, thickly inlaid with black seeds, each one of which in turn is capable of drawing through itself 200,000 times its weight—when you can explain to me the mystery of a watermelon, you can ask me to explain the mystery of God.

If we are going to understand the potential of faith, we have to understand the power of a seed. Jesus spoke of our faith in relation to a mustard seed, the smallest known garden seed in that culture. Like every seed, it needs to germinate, and this seed can take up to ten days to germinate.

Some plants, like some dreams, take a lot longer. My dream of writing had to germinate for thirteen years! And some of my goals will take decades to accomplish! Faith is what keeps those dreams alive, even when it seems as though they are dead and buried. But that is the very nature of seeds. They go underground. They disappear. And while it may seem like they are dead, they are not. They're just germinating beneath the surface!

If you saw a mustard seed but didn't know what it was, you would have a hard time imagining what it could become. The potential is disguised in an awfully small package. You would have no clue that the mustard you put on your hot dog is the by-product of a tiny seed that was planted in the ground. You would have no idea what the seed would grow to become or how big it could get. And that is true of every seed. Would you guess that an acorn would become an oak? You'd never guess that a black seed would become a green watermelon with a red interior that tastes amazing! In case you were wondering, the tiny mustard seed contains all the nutrients you need to survive. It's packed with vitamins B1, B6, C, E, and K. It's a source of calcium, iron, magnesium, phosphorus, potassium, selenium, and zinc.

Faith is a lot like that. It doesn't look like much, but we never know what it can become. A little faith goes a long way; in fact, a little faith will last an eternity. If we do the little things like they are big things, then God will do the big things like they are little things.[71]

---

[71] Batterson, Draw the Circle, 73-75

Chapter 13

TRUST AND OBEY

***TRUST IN THE LORD WITH ALL YOUR HEART** and lean not on your own understanding; in all your ways submit to Him, and He will make your paths straight. (Proverbs 3:5-6 NIV)*

PATTI BURNETT

"You're gonna have to trust somebody."

Our good friend, Maggie, was telling us that she felt as though a lot of the fear mongering that is occurring now during the COVID-19 pandemic is directly proportional to a lack of trust in God. As a retired army officer, she certainly views our present world situation from a different perspective.

People will often place their faith in something or someone else if they don't know God. In fact, the Washington Times ran a story in August of 2019, even before COVID, entitled "Democrats ready to replace worship of God with worship of the state." However, I am not sure that this supposition is more overwhelmingly true of one party than the other.

I do think that there are factions inside and outside our government, as well as the media, that love to take advantage of intimidating methods of persuasion. Even social media is not outside their window of influence. It must make our politicians feel powerful when they can give millions of dollars to Americans with no expectations. Additionally, those who hate our country and everything it stands for must enjoy destroying law and order as they attempt to remove any vestiges of peace and safety from the homes and hearts of Americans.

The question is "How do we establish a faith that overcomes the fear so prevalent today?" The Bible says that our faith is increased by hearing God's Word. We can also counteract worry and anxiety by worshiping God and praying. King David's life was plagued with trauma and drama. If it wasn't King Saul or the Philistines trying to take his life, it was his own sons. The theme throughout his Psalms was that when he was afraid, he would trust in God.

On the website "Got Questions – Your Questions. Biblical Answers," in "Faith vs. fear," it is made clear that hardship is a necessary component of our faith building. "God is kind and understanding toward our weaknesses, but He requires us to go forward in faith; and the Bible is clear that faith does not mature and strengthen without trials. Adversity is God's most effective tool to develop a strong faith. That pattern is evident in scripture. God takes each one of us through fearful situations; and, as we learn to obey His Word and allow it to saturate our thoughts, we find each trial becomes a steppingstone to a stronger and deeper faith. It gives us that ability to say, He sustained me in the past, He'll carry me through today and he'll uphold me in the future."

As Christians, we are called to be bold and courageous. Could we not gently make it clear to those we love that our God is in control and our future government is already established in heaven. In God we trust!

> **FOR TO US A CHILD IS BORN,**
> to us a Son is given,
> and the government will be on His shoulders.
> And He will be called
> Wonderful Counselor, Mighty God,
> Everlasting Father, Prince of Peace.
> Of the greatness of His government and peace
> there will be no end.
> He will reign on David's throne
> and over his kingdom,
> establishing and upholding it
> with justice and righteousness
> from that time on and forever.
> The zeal of the LORD Almighty
> will accomplish this. (Isaiah 9:6-7)

> **BOB DYLAN**
> You're gonna have to serve somebody.[72]

---

[72] Bob Dylan, Gotta Serve Somebody, Jerry Wexler (producer), distributed by Columbia, track 1 on Slow Train Coming album, 1979.

NOW AS THEY WERE TRAVELING ALONG, HE ENTERED A VILLAGE; and a woman named Martha welcomed Him into her home. She had a sister called Mary, who was seated at the Lord's feet, listening to His word. But Martha was distracted with all her preparations; and she came up to Him and said, "Lord, do You not care that my sister has left me to do all the serving alone? Then tell her to help me." But the Lord answered and said to her, "Martha, Martha, you are worried and bothered about so many things; but only one thing is necessary, for Mary has chosen the good part, which shall not be taken away from her." (Luke 10:38-42 NASB)

<u>TRUST AND OBEY, JOHN SAMMIS</u>
When we walk with the Lord
In the light of His Word,
What a glory He sheds on our way;
While we do His good will,
He abides with us still,
And with all who will trust and obey.

Trust and obey, for there's no other way
To be happy in Jesus, but to trust and obey.

Not a shadow can rise,
Not a cloud in the skies,
But His smile quickly drives it away;
Not a doubt or a fear, not a sigh or a tear,
Can abide while we trust and obey.

Not a burden we bear,
Not a sorrow we share,
But our toil He doth richly repay;
Not a grief or a loss,
Not a frown or a cross,
But is blest if we trust and obey.

> But we never can prove
> The delights of His love,
> Until all on the altar we lay;
> For the favor He shows,
> And the joy He bestows,
> Are for them who will trust and obey.
>
> Then in fellowship sweet
> We will sit at His feet,
> Or we'll walk by His side in the way;
> What He says we will do;
> Where He sends we will go,
> Never fear, only trust and obey.[73]

PHILIP SAID, "LORD, SHOW US THE FATHER and that will be enough for us." Jesus answered: "Don't you know Me, Philip, even after I have been among you such a long time? Anyone who has seen Me has seen the Father. How can you say, 'Show us the Father'? Don't you believe that I am in the Father, and that the Father is in Me? The words I say to you I do not speak on My own authority. Rather, it is the Father, living in Me, who is doing His work. Believe Me when I say that I am in the Father and the Father is in Me; or at least believe on the evidence of the works themselves. Very truly I tell you, whoever believes in Me will do the works I have been doing, and they will do even greater things than these, because I am going to the Father. And I will do whatever you ask in My name, so that the Father may be glorified in the Son. You may ask Me for anything in My name, and I will do it.

"If you love Me, keep my commands. And I will ask the Father, and He will give you another advocate to help you and be with you forever—the Spirit of truth. The world cannot accept Him, because it neither sees Him nor knows Him. But you know Him, for He lives with you and will

---

[73] John Sammis, Trust and Obey, Hymns Old and New, United Methodist Hymnal, 1887.

be in you. I will not leave you as orphans; I will come to you. Before long, the world will not see Me anymore, but you will see me. Because I live, you also will live. On that day you will realize that I am in my Father, and you are in Me, and I am in you. Whoever has My commands and keeps them is the one who loves Me. The one who loves Me will be loved by my Father, and I too will love them and show Myself to them."

Then Judas (not Judas Iscariot) said, "But, Lord, why do You intend to show Yourself to us and not to the world?"

Jesus replied, "Anyone who loves Me will obey my teaching. My Father will love them, and We will come to them and make our home with them. Anyone who does not love me will not obey My teaching. These words you hear are not My own; they belong to the Father who sent Me.

"All this I have spoken while still with you. But the Advocate, the Holy Spirit, whom the Father will send in My name, will teach you all things and will remind you of everything I have said to you. Peace I leave with you; My peace I give you. I do not give to you as the world gives. Do not let your hearts be troubled and do not be afraid.

"You heard me say, 'I am going away and I am coming back to you.' If you loved Me, you would be glad that I am going to the Father, for the Father is greater than I. I have told you now before it happens, so that when it does happen you will believe. I will not say much more to you, for the prince of this world is coming. He has no hold over me, but he comes so that the world may learn that I love the Father and do exactly what my Father has commanded me. "Come now; let us leave." (John 14:8-31 NIV)

NEW MORNING MERCIES, PAUL DAVID TRIPP
Your rest is not to be found in figuring your life out, but in trusting the One who has it all figured out for your good and His glory.[74]

---

[74] Tripp, New Morning Mercies, 2.

"I HAVE THE RIGHT TO DO ANYTHING," you say – but not everything is beneficial. "I have the right to do anything"—but I will not be mastered by anything. (I Corinthians 6:12 NIV)

JESUS CALLING, JANUARY 4th, SARAH YOUNG

I want you to learn a new habit. Try saying, "I trust You, Jesus" in response to whatever happens to you.

If there is time, think about who I am in all My Power and Glory; ponder also the depth and breadth of My Love for you.

This simple practice will help you see Me in every situation, acknowledging My sovereign control over the universe. When you view events from this perspective – through the Light of My universal Presence – fear loses its grip on you. Adverse circumstances become growth opportunities when you affirm your trust in Me no matter what. You receive blessings gratefully, realizing they flow directly from My hand of grace. Your continual assertion of trusting Me will strengthen our relationship and keep you close to Me.[75]

THEREFORE, I, THE PRISONER OF THE LORD, urge you to walk in a manner worthy of the calling with which you have been called, with all humility and gentleness, with patience, bearing with one another in love, being diligent to keep the unity of the Spirit in the bond of peace. There is one body and one Spirit, just as you also were called in one hope of your calling; one Lord, one faith, one baptism, one God and Father of all Who is over all and through all and in all. (Ephesians 4:1-6 NASB)

---

[75] Sarah Young, Jesus Calling (Nashville: Thomas Nelson, 2004), 5.

> ### _JESUS CALLING, JANUARY 10th, SARAH YOUNG_
> Every time you affirm your trust in Me, you put a coin into My treasury. Thus, you build up equity in preparation for days of trouble. I keep safely in My heart all trust invested in Me, with interest compounded continuously. The more you trust Me, the more I empower you to do so.
>
> Practice trusting Me during quiet days, when nothing much seems to be happening. Then when storms come, your trust balance will be sufficient to see you through. Store up for yourself treasure in heaven, through placing your trust in Me. This practice will keep you in My Peace.[76]

PAUL AND TIMOTHY, bond-servants of Christ Jesus, to all the saints in Christ Jesus who are in Philippi, including the overseers and deacons: Grace to you and peace from God our Father and the Lord Jesus Christ.

I thank my God in all my remembrance of you, always offering prayer with joy in my every prayer for you all, in view of your participation in the gospel from the first day until now. For I am confident of this very thing, that He who began a good work in you will perfect it until the day of Christ Jesus. For it is only right for me to feel this way about you all, because I have you in my heart, since both in my imprisonment and in the defense and confirmation of the gospel, you all are partakers of grace with me. For God is my witness, how I long for you all with the affection of Christ Jesus. And this I pray, that your love may abound still more and more in real knowledge and all discernment, so that you may approve the things that are excellent, in order to be sincere and blameless until the day of Christ; having been filled with the

---
[76] Ibid, 11.

fruit of righteousness which comes through Jesus Christ, to the glory and praise of God.

Now I want you to know, brethren, that my circumstances have turned out for the greater progress of the gospel, so that my imprisonment in the cause of Christ has become well known throughout the whole praetorian guard and to everyone else, and that most of the brethren, trusting in the Lord because of my imprisonment, have far more courage to speak the word of God without fear. Some, to be sure, are preaching Christ even from envy and strife, but some also from good will; the latter do it out of love, knowing that I am appointed for the defense of the gospel; the former proclaim Christ out of selfish ambition rather than from pure motives, thinking to cause me distress in my imprisonment. What then? Only that in every way, whether in pretense or in truth, Christ is proclaimed; and in this I rejoice.

Yes, and I will rejoice, for I know that this will turn out for my deliverance through your prayers and the provision of the Spirit of Jesus Christ, according to my earnest expectation and hope, that I will not be put to shame in anything, but that with all boldness, Christ will even now, as always, be exalted in my body, whether by life or by death. For to me, to live is Christ and to die is gain.

But if I am to live on in the flesh, this will mean fruitful labor for me; and I do not know which to choose. But I am hard-pressed from both directions, having the desire to depart and be with Christ, for that is very much better; yet to remain on in the flesh is more necessary for your sake. Convinced of this, I know that I will remain and continue with you all for your progress and joy in the faith, so that your proud confidence in me may abound in Christ Jesus through my coming to you again.

Only conduct yourselves in a manner worthy of the gospel of Christ, so that whether I come and see you or remain absent, I will hear of you that you are standing firm in one spirit, with one mind striving together for the faith of the gospel; in no way alarmed by your opponents—which is a sign of destruction for them, but of salvation for you, and that too, from God. For to you it has been granted for Christ's sake, not only to believe in Him, but also to suffer for His sake, experiencing the same conflict which you saw in me, and now hear to be in me. (Philippians 1:1-30 NASB)

> ### *JESUS CALLING, JANUARY 12th, SARAH YOUNG*
> Let Me prepare you for the day that stretches out before you. I know exactly what this day will contain, whereas you have only vague ideas about it. You would like to see a map, showing all the twists and turns of your journey. You'd feel more prepared if you could somehow visualize what is on the road ahead. However, there is a better way to be prepared for whatever you will encounter today: spend quality time with Me.
>
> I will not show you what is on the road ahead, but I will thoroughly equip you for the journey. My living Presence is your Companion each step of the way. Stay in continual communication with Me, whispering My Name whenever you need to redirect your thoughts. Thus, you can walk through this day with your focus on Me. My abiding Presence is the best road map[77]

AT THAT TIME THE LORD SAID TO ME, 'Cut out for yourself two tablets of stone like the first two, and come up to Me on the mountain, and make an ark of wood for yourself. Then I will write on the tablets the words that were on the first tablets which you smashed to pieces, and you shall put them in the ark.' So I made an ark of acacia wood and cut out two tablets of stone like the first two, and I went up on the mountain with the two tablets in my hand. Then He wrote on the tablets, like the first writing, the Ten Commandments which the Lord had

---
[77] Ibid, 13.

spoken to you on the mountain from the midst of the fire on the day of the assembly; and the Lord gave them to me. Then I turned and came down from the mountain, and I put the tablets in the ark which I had made; and they are there, just as the Lord commanded me."

(Now the sons of Israel set out from Beeroth Bene-jaakan to Moserah. There Aaron died and there he was buried, and his son Eleazar served as priest in his place. From there they set out to Gudgodah, and from Gudgodah to Jotbathah, a land of streams of water. At that time the Lord singled out the tribe of Levi to carry the ark of the covenant of the Lord, to stand before the Lord to serve Him and to bless in His name, until this day. Therefore, Levi does not have a portion or inheritance with his brothers; the Lord is his inheritance, just as the Lord your God spoke to him.)

"I, moreover, stayed on the mountain for forty days and forty nights like the first time, and the Lord listened to me that time also; the Lord was not willing to destroy you. Then the Lord said to me, 'Arise, proceed on your journey ahead of the people, so that they may go in and take possession of the land which I swore to their fathers to give them.'

"And now, Israel, what does the Lord your God require of you, but to fear the Lord your God, to walk in all His ways and love Him, and to serve the Lord your God with all your heart and with all your soul, and to keep the Lord's commandments and His statutes which I am commanding you today for your good. Behold, to the Lord your God belong heaven and the highest heavens, the earth and all that is in it. Yet the Lord set His affection on your fathers, to love them, and He chose their descendants after them, you over all the other peoples, as it is this day. So circumcise your heart, and do not stiffen your neck any longer. For the Lord your God is the God of gods and the Lord of lords, the great, the mighty, and the awesome God, who does not show partiality, nor take a bribe. He executes justice for the orphan and the widow, and shows His love for the stranger by giving him food and clothing. So show your love for the stranger, for you were strangers in the land of Egypt. You shall fear the Lord your God; you shall serve Him, and cling to Him, and you shall swear by His name. He is your glory and He is your God, who has done these great and awesome things for you which your eyes have seen. Your fathers went down to Egypt seventy persons in all, and now the Lord your God has made you as numerous as the stars of heaven. (Deuteronomy 10:1-22 NASB)

RUN YOUR RACE TO WIN!, PASTOR LEE ALLEN JENKINS, EAGLES NEST CHURCH, FCA MAGAZINE

One of the most embarrassing and proudest moments of my life happened in the early 1980s when I was running track for the University of Tennessee. I was elated to make it to the finals of the 200-meter dash where I raced against world-class sprinters, some of whom were already household names.

When the race started, I exploded out of the blocks, then moved swiftly around the curve. Then things suddenly changed. Those world-class sprinters evidently had a gear I did not. Coming out of the curve, they pulled away from me like I was standing still. A few seconds later, I ran through the finish line … in last place. I was devastated and mortified by my performance – that is, until I heard my time. You see, although I came in dead last, I ran the fastest 200 meters I'd ever run! When the announcer called my name as the last-place finisher, I jumped for joy! Most people thought I lost that day, but to me and to God, I was a winner! Consider this: winning is not what you have done compared to someone else. Winning is what you have done compared to what you were created to do.

Mark 12:30 sums up the formula for a winning Christian life this way: "Love the Lord your God with all your heart and with all your soul and with all your mind and with all your strength." Just after this verse, Jesus offers another important command. It's of such importance that He mentions it after the greatest command of all. "The second is this: 'Love your neighbor as yourself.' There is no commandment greater than these "(Mark 12:31, NIV).

For Christians, "winning" means giving ourselves totally to the Lord – 100% - and letting His love overflow through us onto others…

Hebrews 12:1 refers to a "huge crowd of witnesses" when talking about living a life of faith. This is a great place to start when reading about the lives of heroes of the faith and how to model their faithful steps in our own lives.

"Let us strip off every weight that slows us down, especially the sin that so easily trips us up. And let us run with endurance the race God has set before us" (Hebrews 12:1b). A life of discipleship can easily be paralleled with running. Just like today, Greek runners dressed as lightly as possible, so clothes didn't slow them down. As Christians, we should be eager to rid ourselves of all that hinders our Christian lives. This applies to anything preventing us from doing our best for Jesus Christ.

To become all we need to be, our ultimate example is the Lord Himself, Jesus Christ. Look at what Hebrews 12:2-3 says: "We do this by keeping our eyes on Jesus, the champion who initiates and perfects our faith. Because of the joy awaiting Him, He endured the cross, disregarding its shame. Now He is seated in the place of honor beside God's throne. Think of all the hostility He endured from sinful people; then you won't become weary and give up."

Jesus is the epitome of a winner! As you run your race and disciple others to step more fully into their God-given assignments, remember this: God will give you the grace to run your race. What is last place to man can be first place to God.[78]

NOW IT CAME ABOUT AFTER THE DEATH OF MOSES THE SERVANT OF THE LORD, that the Lord spoke to Joshua the son of Nun, Moses' servant, saying, "Moses My servant is dead; so now arise, cross this Jordan, you and all this people, to the land which I am giving to them, to the sons of Israel. Every place on which

---

[78] Lee Allen Jenkins, Run Your Race to Win, Fellowship of Christian Athletes, April 8, 2021, https://www.fca.org/fca-in-action/2021/04/08/run-your-race-to-win!.

the sole of your footsteps, I have given it to you, just as I spoke to Moses. From the wilderness and this Lebanon, even as far as the great river, the river Euphrates, all the land of the Hittites, and as far as the Great Sea toward the setting of the sun will be your territory. No one will be able to oppose you all the days of your life. Just as I have been with Moses, I will be with you; I will not desert you nor abandon you. Be strong and courageous, for you shall give this people possession of the land which I swore to their fathers to give them. Only be strong and very courageous; be careful to do according to all the Law which Moses My servant commanded you; do not turn from it to the right or to the left, so that you may achieve success wherever you go. This Book of the Law shall not depart from your mouth, but you shall meditate on it day and night, so that you may be careful to do according to all that is written in it; for then you will make your way prosperous, and then you will achieve success. Have I not commanded you? Be strong and courageous! Do not be terrified nor dismayed, for the Lord your God is with you wherever you go."

Then Joshua commanded the officers of the people, saying, "Pass through the midst of the camp and command the people, saying, 'Prepare provisions for yourselves, for within three days you are going to cross this Jordan, to go in to take possession of the land which the Lord your God is giving you, to possess it.'"

But to the Reubenites, to the Gadites, and to the half-tribe of Manasseh, Joshua said, "Remember the word which Moses the servant of the Lord commanded you, saying, 'The Lord your God is giving you rest, and will give you this land.' Your wives, your little ones, and your livestock shall remain in the land which Moses gave you beyond the Jordan, but you shall cross ahead of your brothers in battle formation, all your valiant warriors, and shall help them, until the Lord gives your brothers rest, as He is giving you, and they also possess the land which the Lord your God is giving them. Then you may return to your own land, and take possession of that which

Moses the servant of the Lord gave you beyond the Jordan toward the sunrise."

They answered Joshua, saying, "All that You have commanded us we will do, and wherever You send us we will go. Just as we obeyed Moses in all things, so we will obey You; only may the Lord your God be with you as He was with Moses. Anyone who rebels against your command and does not obey your words in all that you command him, shall be put to death; only be strong and courageous. (Joshua 1:1-18 NASB)

<u>MY UTMOST FOR HIS HIGHEST, OSWALD CHAMBERS</u>
Naturally, we are inclined to be so mathematical and calculating that we look upon uncertainty as a bad thing … Certainty is the mark of the common-sense life. To be certain of God means that we are uncertain in all our ways, we do not know what a day may bring forth. This is generally said with a sigh of sadness; it should rather be an expression of breathless expectation."[79]

AS DAVID'S TIME TO DIE DREW NEAR, he commanded his son Solomon, saying, "I am going the way of all the earth. So be strong and prove yourself a man. Do your duty to the Lord your God, to walk in His ways, to keep His statutes, His commandments, His ordinances, and His testimonies, according to what is written in the Law of Moses, so that you may succeed in all that you do and wherever you turn, so that the Lord may fulfill His promise which He spoke regarding me, saying, 'If your sons are careful about their way, to walk before Me in truth with all their heart and all their soul, you shall not be deprived of a man to occupy the throne of Israel.' (I Kings 2:1-4 NASB)

---

[79] Hannah West and Jennifer Wild quoting Oswald Chambers, The Westminster Collection of Christian Meditations (Westminster: John Knox Press, 2000), 216.

> **_DAILY WITH THE KING, W.G. EVANS_**
> I will seek holiness (which results in wholeness), without which no man can see the Lord, at all times. Wholeness is God centeredness, the "one thing needful," the one thing I desire and seek after, "the one thing I do." I will not pray for peace, power, success, or fruit, for they are by-products of a relationship, not its conditions. They are God's responsibility, not mine. [80]

NOW WHEN SOLOMON HAD FINISHED PRAYING, fire came down from heaven and consumed the burnt offering and the sacrifices and the glory of the Lord filled the house. The priests could not enter into the house of the Lord because the glory of the Lord filled the Lord's house. All the sons of Israel, seeing the fire come down and the glory of the Lord upon the house, bowed down on the pavement with their faces to the ground, and they worshiped and gave praise to the Lord, saying, "Truly He is good, truly His lovingkindness is everlasting."

Then the king and all the people offered sacrifice before the Lord. King Solomon offered a sacrifice of 22,000 oxen and 120,000 sheep. Thus the king and all the people dedicated the house of God. The priests stood at their posts, and the Levites also, with the instruments of music to the Lord, which King David had made for giving praise to the Lord—"for His lovingkindness is everlasting"—whenever he gave praise by their means, while the priests on the other side blew trumpets; and all Israel was standing.

Then Solomon consecrated the middle of the court that was before the house of the Lord, for there he offered the burnt offerings and the fat of the peace offerings because the bronze altar which Solomon had made was not able to contain the burnt offering, the grain offering and the fat.

---

[80] W.G. Evans, Daily with the King: 366 Daily Devotions (Chicago: Moody Publishers, 1979), 5.

So Solomon observed the feast at that time for seven days, and all Israel with him, a very great assembly who came from the entrance of Hamath to the brook of Egypt. On the eighth day they held a solemn assembly, for the dedication of the altar they observed seven days and the feast seven days. Then on the twenty-third day of the seventh month he sent the people to their tents, rejoicing and happy of heart because of the goodness that the Lord had shown to David and to Solomon and to His people Israel.

Thus Solomon finished the house of the Lord and the king's palace, and successfully completed all that he had planned on doing in the house of the Lord and in his palace.

Then the Lord appeared to Solomon at night and said to him, "I have heard your prayer and have chosen this place for Myself as a house of sacrifice. If I shut up the heavens so that there is no rain, or if I command the locust to devour the land, or if I send pestilence among My people, and My people who are called by My name humble themselves and pray and seek My face and turn from their wicked ways, then I will hear from heaven, will forgive their sin and will heal their land. Now My eyes will be open and My ears attentive to the prayer offered in this place. For now I have chosen and consecrated this house that My name may be there forever, and My eyes and My heart will be there perpetually. As for you, if you walk before Me as your father David walked, even to do according to all that I have commanded you, and will keep My statutes and My ordinances, then I will establish your royal throne as I covenanted with your father David, saying, 'You shall not lack a man to be ruler in Israel.'

"But if you turn away and forsake My statutes and My commandments which I have set before you, and go and serve other gods and worship them, then I will uproot you from My land which I have given you, and this house which I have consecrated for My name I will cast out of My sight and I will make it a proverb and a byword among all peoples. As for this house, which was exalted, everyone who passes by it will be astonished and say, 'Why has the Lord done thus to this land

and to this house?' And they will say, 'Because they forsook the Lord, the God of their fathers who brought them from the land of Egypt, and they adopted other gods and worshiped them and served them; therefore He has brought all this adversity on them.'" (2 Chronicles 7:1-22 NASB)

> ### *THE DIVINE EMBRACE, KEN GIRE*
> Jesus' feelings about Mary's devotion are captured in a scene from Goethe's novel The Sorrows of Young Werther, in which the main character is captivated by a woman he sees on the dance floor. "You should see her dance? She concentrates so completely – heart and soul – on the dance itself; her whole body is in harmony, as carefree and as ingenuous as if nothing else mattered, as if she had no other thoughts or feelings; and I am certain that at those moments everything else vanishes from her sight."
>
> That is how I want to dance with Jesus. That is the kind of focus I want. As if nothing else mattered. As if everything else vanished from sight. For I would rather see His face and have everything else blur in my peripheral vision than to have every peripheral thing in focus and miss seeing Him.[81]

---

[81] Gire, The Divine Embrace, 39.

Trust And Obey

BE GRACIOUS TO ME, O GOD, for man has trampled upon me.
Fighting all day long he oppresses me.
My foes have trampled upon me all day long,
For they are many who fight proudly against me.
When I am afraid,
I will put my trust in You.
In God, whose word I praise,
In God I have put my trust;
I shall not be afraid.
What can mere man do to me?
All day long they distort my words;
All their thoughts are against me for evil.
They attack, they lurk,
They watch my steps,
As they have waited to take my life.
Because of wickedness, cast them forth,
In anger put down the peoples, O God!
You have taken account of my wanderings;
Put my tears in Your bottle.
Are they not in Your book?
Then my enemies will turn back in the day when I call;
This I know, that God is for me.
In God, whose word I praise,
In the Lord, whose word I praise,
In God I have put my trust, I shall not be afraid.
What can man do to me?
Your vows are binding upon me, O God;
I will render thank offerings to You.
For You have delivered my soul from death,
Indeed, my feet from stumbling,
So that I may walk before God
In the light of the living. (Psalm 56:1-13 NASB)

> ## *MY UTMOST FOR HIS HIGHEST, JANUARY 14th, OSWALD CHAMBERS*
> God did not direct His call to Isaiah—Isaiah overheard God saying, "… who will go for Us?" The call of God is not just for a select few but for everyone. Whether I hear God's call or not depends on the condition of my ears, and exactly what I hear depends upon my spiritual attitude.[82]

MY SON, DO NOT FORGET MY TEACHING,
But have your heart comply with My commandments;
For length of days and years of life
And peace they will add to you.
Do not let kindness and truth leave you;
Bind them around your neck,
Write them on the tablet of your heart.
So you will find favor and a good reputation
In the sight of God and man.
Trust in the LORD with all your heart
And do not lean on your own understanding.
In all your ways acknowledge Him,
And He will make your paths straight.
Do not be wise in your own eyes;
Fear the LORD and turn away from evil.
It will be healing to your body
And refreshment to your bones.
Honor the LORD from your wealth,
And from the first of all your produce;
Then your barns will be filled with plenty,
And your vats will overflow with new wine.

---

[82] Chambers, My Utmost for His Highest, January 14th.

Trust And Obey

My son, do not reject the discipline of the LORD
Or loathe His rebuke,
For whom the LORD loves He disciplines,
Just as a father disciplines the son in whom he delights.

Blessed is a person who finds wisdom,
And one who obtains understanding.
For her profit is better than the profit of silver,
And her produce better than gold.
She is more precious than jewels,
And nothing you desire compares with her.
Long life is in her right hand;
In her left hand are riches and honor.
Her ways are pleasant ways,
And all her paths are peace.
She is a tree of life to those who take hold of her,
And happy are those who hold on to her.
The LORD founded the earth by wisdom,
He established the heavens by understanding.
By His knowledge the ocean depths were burst open,
And the clouds drip with dew.
My son, see that they do not escape from your sight;
Comply with sound wisdom and discretion,
And they will be life to your soul
And adornment to your neck.
Then you will walk in your way securely,
And your foot will not stumble.
When you lie down, you will not be afraid;
When you lie down, your sleep will be sweet.
Do not be afraid of sudden danger,
Nor of trouble from the wicked when it comes;
For the LORD will be your confidence,
And will keep your foot from being caught.

Do not withhold good from those to whom it is due,
When it is in your power to do it.
Do not say to your neighbor, "Go, and come back,
And tomorrow I will give it to you,"
When you have it with you.
Do not devise harm against your neighbor,
While he lives securely beside you.
Do not contend with a person for no reason,
If he has done you no harm.
Do not envy a violent person,
And do not choose any of his ways.
For the devious are an abomination to the Lord;
But He is intimate with the upright.
The curse of the Lord is on the house of the wicked,
But He blesses the home of the righteous.
Though He scoffs at the scoffers,
Yet He gives grace to the needy.
The wise will inherit honor,
But fools increase dishonor. (Proverbs 3:1-35 NASB)

> **_MY UTMOST FOR HIS HIGHEST, MARCH 19th,_**
> **_OSWALD CHAMBERS_**
> The life of faith is not a life of mounting up with wings,
> but a life of walking and not fainting.[83]

---

[83] Ibid. March 19.

Trust And Obey

> ### MARGERY HANFELT, US ARMY COLONEL (RETIRED)
> I was selected for command of a unit beyond my capability and experience. I prayed for guidance; and the Lord reminded me that for every situation in which He places us, our simple response should be to trust and obey. In my 22 years of military experience and in the world's eyes, there is still always someone more prepared, better trained, more educated, and better appreciated. Comparing myself to others does no good. The fact is, God chose me, and I need to act secure in the knowledge that He will always give me the confidence to fulfill my responsibilities in any particular mission; and He will receive the glory. The other truth, even now, is that I am never actually in command - God is. From my experience, I know that He will give me what I need when I need it to tackle the mission to His glory. My job is simply to pray, obey, and trust the outcome to God. He's never failed me yet.[84]

NEVER ENVY THE WICKED! Soon they fade away like grass and disappear. Trust in the Lord instead. Be kind and good to others; then you will live safely here in the land and prosper, feeding in safety.

Be delighted with the Lord. Then He will give you all your heart's desires. Commit everything you do to the Lord. Trust Him to help you do it, and He will. Your innocence will be clear to everyone. He will vindicate you with the blazing light of justice shining down as from the noonday sun.

Rest in the Lord; wait patiently for Him to act. Don't be envious of evil men who prosper.

Stop your anger! Turn off your wrath. Don't fret and worry—it only leads to harm. For the wicked shall be destroyed, but those who trust

---

[84] Margery Hanfelt, US Army Colonel and veterinarian (retired), good friend of author.

the Lord shall be given every blessing. Only a little while and the wicked shall disappear. You will look for them in vain. But all who humble themselves before the Lord shall be given every blessing and shall have wonderful peace.

The Lord is laughing at those who plot against the godly, for He knows their judgment day is coming. Evil men take aim to slay the poor; they are ready to butcher those who do right. But their swords will be plunged into their own hearts, and all their weapons will be broken.

It is better to have little and be godly than to own an evil man's wealth; for the strength of evil men shall be broken, but the Lord takes care of those He has forgiven.

Day by day the Lord observes the good deeds done by godly men, and gives them eternal rewards. He cares for them when times are hard; even in famine, they will have enough. But evil men shall perish. These enemies of God will wither like grass and disappear like smoke. Evil men borrow and "cannot pay it back"! But the good man returns what he owes with some extra besides. Those blessed by the Lord shall inherit the earth, but those cursed by Him shall die.

The steps of good men are directed by the Lord. He delights in each step they take. If they fall, it isn't fatal, for the Lord holds them with His hand.

I have been young and now I am old. And in all my years I have never seen the Lord forsake a man who loves Him; nor have I seen the children of the godly go hungry. Instead, the godly are able to be generous with their gifts and loans to others, and their children are a blessing.

So if you want an eternal home, leave your evil, low-down ways and live good lives. For the Lord loves justice and fairness; He will never abandon His people. They will be kept safe forever; but all who love wickedness shall perish.

The godly shall be firmly planted in the land and live there forever. The godly man is a good counselor because he is just and fair and knows right from wrong.

Evil men spy on the godly, waiting for an excuse to accuse them and then demanding their death. But the Lord will not let these evil men succeed, nor let the godly be condemned when they are brought before the judge.

Don't be impatient for the Lord to act! Keep traveling steadily along His pathway and in due season He will honor you with every blessing, and you will see the wicked destroyed. I myself have seen it happen: a proud and evil man, towering like a cedar of Lebanon, but when I looked again, he was gone! I searched but could not find him! But the good man—what a different story! For the good man—the blameless, the upright, the man of peace—he has a wonderful future ahead of him. For him there is a happy ending. But evil men shall be destroyed, and their posterity shall be cut off.

The Lord saves the godly! He is their salvation and their refuge when trouble comes. Because they trust in Him, He helps them and delivers them from the plots of evil men. (Psalm 37:1-40 TLB)

> ### MARTIN LUTHER KING, JR.
> Use me, God. Show me how to take who I am, who I want to be, and what I can do, and use it for a purpose greater than myself.[85]

MY UTMOST FOR HIS HIGHEST, JANUARY 1st, LET US KEEP TO THE POINT, OSWALD CHAMBERS

"My Utmost for His Highest... My earnest expectation and hope that in nothing I shall be ashamed..." We will all feel very much ashamed if we do not yield to Jesus the areas of our lives He has asked us to yield to Him. It's as if Paul were saying, "My determined purpose is to be my utmost for His highest – my best for His glory." To each that level of determination is a matter of the will, not of debate or of reasoning. It is

---

[85] Oprah Winfrey quoting Martin Luther King, Jr., The Wisdom of Sundays (New York: MacMillan Audio, 2017), 174.

absolutely an irrevocable surrender of the will at that point. An undue amount of thought and consideration for ourselves is what keeps us from making that decision, although we cover it up with the pretense that it is others we are considering. When we think seriously about what it will cost others if we obey the call of Jesus, we tell God He doesn't know what our obedience will mean. Keep to the point – He does know. Shut out every other thought and keep yourself before God in this one thing only – my utmost for His highest. I am determined to be absolutely and entirely for Him and Him alone.

My unstoppable Determination for His Holiness. "Whether it means life or death – it makes no difference!" Paul was determined that nothing would stop him from doing exactly what God wanted. But before we choose to follow God's will, a crisis must develop in our lives. This happens because we tend to be unresponsive to God's gentler nudges. He brings us to the place where He asks us to be our utmost for Him and we begin to debate. He then providentially produces a crisis where we have to decide – for or against. That moment becomes a great crossroads in our lives. If a crisis has come to you on any front, surrender your will to Jesus absolutely and irrevocably. [86]

---

[86] Chambers, My Utmost for His Highest, January 1.

Chapter 14

DON'T ALLOW YOUR PAIN TO ECLIPSE GOD'S BLESSINGS

***IF YOU LISTEN OBEDIENTLY TO THE VOICE OF GOD, YOUR GOD,** and heartily obey all His commandments that I command you today, God, your God, will place you on high, high above all the nations of the world. All these blessings will come down on you and spread out beyond you because you have responded to the Voice of God, your God: God's blessing inside the city, God's blessing in the country; God's blessing on your children, the crops of your land, the young of your livestock, the calves of your herds, the lambs of your flocks. God's blessing on your basket and bread bowl; God's blessing in your coming in, God's blessing in your going out. (Deuteronomy 28:1-6 Message)*

PATTI BURNETT

IT WOULD BE EASY to let pain negatively impact every aspect of our thoughts, actions, and motivations. Every day we can choose to either allow suffering to gnaw away at us and make us **bitter**, or we can welcome the opportunity to share in Christ's pain as He makes us **better**. 1st Peter 4 says that in direct proportion to the extent which we suffer for our Lord, we will someday share in His glory. That's good news to me.

My best friend and greatest blessing is Dan, my husband of 39 years. In our marriage, God has developed a higher level of trust, love, and vulnerability than I ever realized possible. Early in our friendship, the one characteristic that set our relationship apart was exceptionally profound self-disclosure – primarily from Dan's promptings and encouragement.

We became acquainted through our best friends, Bill and Alicia; and our relationship grew slowly, with no ulterior motives or expectations. Eventually, a fair amount of our time together was spent sailboat racing and volunteering for search and rescue. Few environments have the potential to create such extreme volatility and anxiety as sailing regattas and search and rescue missions. Even severe weather conditions and life-threatening circumstances rarely ruffled Dan's feathers. In fact, I would not be lying if I told you he thrived in those situations.

And yet, it took years before I felt comfortable totally baring my soul to him. I still suffered tremendous guilt and shame from some of my earlier lapses in judgment. I was especially hesitant to reveal one secret that was trapped in a dark dungeon in my heart. Yet I knew that if I was not transparent with him, even with this particularly traumatic event, marriage was out of the question. When I finally came clean, Dan's empathy, support, and love were overwhelming. In him, I found a man who would unconditionally accept me with all my imperfections – as I was and as I am. I guess you could say that God turned my deepest heart-breaking failure into a blessing.

The greatest test to our friendship came in our first six years of marriage. We wanted to have children and spent much time, energy, and finances trying to solve the infertility and adoption enigmas. Our relationship grew stronger as we depended on each other and the Lord more fully, while struggling to understand the whys and wherefores. Again, God turned our challenges into the sweet blessings named Bethany and Rachel. Patti Johnson, a psychologist, and creator of the anxiety relief app Emma recommends that the next time you feel overwhelmed with the trials of your life, make a list of specific things for which you are grateful —those blessings in disguise.

With all the worthwhile endeavors we can invest our time and effort in, we need to take care that we do not neglect those people God has placed in our lives for a significant purpose. A great marriage takes work, but the dividends return 100-fold. No effort is too great to ensure the continuing love and friendship that God has so generously bestowed on me and Dan; and no matter the situation, I know I speak for both of us that we will continually fight for our marriage.

PAUL, AN APOSTLE OF CHRIST JESUS BY THE WILL OF GOD, to the saints who are at Ephesus and are faithful in Christ Jesus: Grace to you and peace from God our Father and the Lord Jesus Christ.

Blessed be the God and Father of our Lord Jesus Christ who has blessed us with every spiritual blessing in the heavenly places in Christ, just as He chose us in Him before the foundation of the world, that we would be holy and blameless before Him. In love He predestined us to adoption as sons and daughters through Jesus Christ to Himself, according to the good pleasure of His will, to the praise of the glory of His grace, with which He favored us in the Beloved. In Him we have redemption through His blood, the forgiveness of our wrongdoings, according to the riches of His grace which He lavished on us. In all wisdom and insight He made known to us the mystery of His will, according to His good pleasure which He set forth in Him, regarding His plan of the fullness of the times, to bring all things together in Christ, things in the heavens and things on the earth. In Him we also have obtained an inheritance, having been predestined according to the purpose of Him who works all things in accordance with the plan of His will, to the end that we who were the first to hope in the Christ would be to the praise of His glory. In Him, you also, after listening to the message of truth, the gospel of your salvation—having also believed, you were sealed in Him with the Holy Spirit of the promise, who is a first installment of our inheritance, in regard to the redemption of God's own possession, to the praise of His glory.

For this reason I too, having heard of the faith in the Lord Jesus which exists among you and your love for all the saints, do not cease giving thanks for you, while making mention of you in my prayers; that the God of our Lord Jesus Christ, the Father of glory, may give you a spirit of wisdom and of revelation in the knowledge of Him. I pray that the eyes of your heart may be enlightened, so that you will know what is the hope of His calling, what are the riches of the glory of His inheritance in the saints, and what is the boundless greatness of His power toward us who believe. These are in accordance with the working of the strength of His might which He brought about in Christ, when He raised Him from the dead and seated Him at His right hand in the heavenly places, far above all rule and authority and power and dominion, and every name that is named, not only in this age but also in the one to come. And He put all things in subjection under His feet, and made Him head over all things to the church, which is His body, the fullness of Him who fills all in all. (Ephesians 1:1-23 NASB)

> **WILLIE NELSON**
> When I started counting my blessings, my whole life turned around.[87]

FOR THIS REASON I BEND MY KNEES BEFORE THE FATHER, from whom every family in heaven and on earth derives its name, that He

---

[87] Dominique M. Williams quoting Willie Nelson, Count Your Blessings (Morrisville: Lulu.com, 2019), 55.

would grant you, according to the riches of His glory, to be strengthened with power through His Spirit in the inner self, so that Christ may dwell in your hearts through faith; and that you, being rooted and grounded in love, may be able to comprehend with all the saints what is the width and length and height and depth, and to know the love of Christ which surpasses knowledge, that you may be filled to all the fullness of God.

Now to Him, who is able to do far more abundantly beyond all that we ask or think, according to the power that works within us, to Him be the glory in the church and in Christ Jesus to all generations forever and ever. Amen. (Ephesians 3:14-21 NASB)

> **OSCAR WILDE**
> What seems to us bitter trials are often blessings in disguise.[88]

PAUL AND SILVANUS AND TIMOTHY, to the Church of the Thessalonians in God the Father and the Lord Jesus Christ: Grace to you and peace.

We give thanks to God always for all of you, making mention of you in our prayers; constantly bearing in mind your work of faith and labor of love and steadfastness of hope in our Lord Jesus Christ in the presence of our God and Father, knowing, brethren beloved by God, His choice of you; for our gospel did not come to you in word only, but also in power and in the Holy Spirit and with full conviction; just as you know what kind of men we proved to be among you for your sake. You also became imitators of us and of the Lord, having received the word in much tribulation with the joy of the Holy Spirit, so that you became an example to all the believers in Macedonia and in Achaia. For the word of the Lord has sounded forth from you, not only in Macedonia and Achaia, but also in every place your faith toward God has gone forth, so

---

[88] Oscar Wilde, The Importance of Being Earnest (Woodstock: Dramatic Publishing Company 1984), 41.

that we have no need to say anything. For they themselves report about us what kind of a reception we had with you, and how you turned to God from idols to serve a living and true God, and to wait for His Son from heaven, whom He raised from the dead, that is Jesus, who rescues us from the wrath to come. (1 Thessalonians 1:1-10 NASB)

BLESSINGS, LAURA STORY
We pray for blessings, we pray for peace,
Comfort for family, protection while we sleep.
We pray for healing, for prosperity.
We pray for Your mighty hand to ease our suffering.

And all the while You hear each spoken need,
Yet love us way too much to give us lesser things.

When friends betray us, when darkness seems to win,
We know that pain reminds this heart,
That this is not, this is not our home.
It's not our home.

'Cause what if Your blessings come through raindrops?
What if Your healing comes through tears?
And what if a thousand sleepless nights are what it takes to know
You're near?

What if my greatest disappointments
Or the aching of this life,
Is the revealing of a greater thirst this world can't satisfy?

And what if trials of this life
The rain, the storms, the hardest nights
Are Your mercies in disguise?[89]

---

[89] Laura Story, Blessings," Nathan Nockels (producer), distributed by INO Records, track 5 on Blessings album, 2011.

THEN JACOB WAS LEFT ALONE; and a man wrestled with him until daybreak. When the man saw that he had not prevailed against him, he touched the socket of Jacob's hip; and the socket of Jacob's hip was dislocated while he wrestled with him. Then he said, "Let me go, for the dawn is breaking." But he said, "I will not let you go unless you bless me." So he said to him, "What is your name?" And he said, "Jacob." Then he said, "Your name shall no longer be Jacob, but Israel; for you have contended with God and with men, and have prevailed." And Jacob asked him and said, "Please tell me your name." But he said, "Why is it that you ask my name?" And he blessed him there. So Jacob named the place Peniel, for he said, "I have seen God face to face, yet my life has been spared." Now the sun rose upon him just as he crossed over Penuel, and he was limping on his hip. Therefore, to this day the sons of Israel do not eat the tendon of the hip which is on the socket of the hip, because he touched the socket of Jacob's hip in the tendon of the hip. (Genesis 32:24-32 NASB)

> ## JOHN CALVIN
> However many blessings we expect from God,
> His infinite liberality will always exceed all our wishes
> and our thoughts.[90]

THEN THE LORD SPOKE TO MOSES, SAYING,
"Speak to Aaron and to his sons, saying, 'Thus you shall bless the sons of Israel. You shall say to them:
The Lord bless you, and keep you;
The Lord make His face shine on you,
And be gracious to you;
The Lord lift up His countenance on you,

---

[90] Taiwo Adesina quoting John Calvin, *You Are Blessed* (Morrisville: Lulu.com, 2013), 11.

And give you peace.'
So they shall invoke My name on the sons of Israel, and I then will bless them." (Numbers 6:22-27 NASB)

LOUIE GIGLIO

I'm convinced that once we're in heaven we will never regret letting go of wrongs and forgiving others in the same way our Father has forgiven us. We will only regret the bitterness we harbored and the anger we held onto while on earth. When we see the risen Jesus, scars still marking His wrists and side, we will wish we'd trusted Him more to empower us to turn the tide of hate and loss and take our place as agents of a better kingdom. When we see the mighty throne of God, and understand fully that all justice rests in His hands, we'll wish we had extended more olive branches of peace to those around us.

For now, I simply encourage you to park under the waterfall of a better blessing. Remember from the outset it's a blessing you didn't earn or deserve. It's the blessing of a perfect Father with extravagant love, a Father who has never lost sight of you and will never let you go. He is a perfect Abba who will not leave you powerless, but who will make you powerful – powerful enough to extend to others the blessing He is extending to you.[91]

PETER MARSHALL
God will not permit any troubles to come upon us, unless He has a specific plan by which great blessing can come out of the difficulty.[92]

---

[91] Louie Giglio, visionary, architect, author, and director of the Passion Movement.

[92] Thomas Nelson quoting Peter Marshall, NKJV, Ancient-Modern Bible (Nashville: Thomas Nelson, 2019), 717.

Chapter 15

EMPTIED OF ALL BUT HIM

***AND HE SUMMONED THE CROWD** together with His disciples, and said to them, "If anyone wants to come after Me, he must deny himself, take up his cross, and follow Me. For whoever wants to save his life will lose it, but whoever loses his life for My sake and the gospel's will save it. For what does it benefit a person to gain the whole world, and forfeit his soul? For what could a person give in exchange for his soul? (Mark 8:34-37 NASB)*

PATTI BURNETT

AS WAS THE CASE FOR MOST OF MY HIGH SCHOOL COHORT, I could have worked 12 months of the year, 50 or 60 hours a week, wearing high heels and uncomfortable clothes, confined to a tiny cubicle, where I pounded on computer keys and talked incessantly about matters of little consequence.

But instead, I had possibly the best job ever – custom made just for me. As a ski patrol supervisor, get this, they actually paid me to ski powder, drive a snowmobile, help injured people, assist parents in reconnecting with lost children, transport avalanche dogs via chairlifts, toboggans, and snowmobiles, teach school children about avalanche safety, ride in helicopters to avalanche accidents, and enjoy views of possibly the most majestic mountain ranges in the world.

Our avalanche dog program was a pretty big deal - the first in Colorado. Consequently, other ski areas and search and rescue groups sought us out for our advice about how to train avalanche dogs in the lower 48 states as well as Europe and Alaska. My book, "Avalanche, Hasty Search!," provides detailed information for training an avalanche dog and starting a program.

BUT … out of the blue I was "let go;" it was more a case of forced to go; and don't let the door hit you on the way out.

I was crushed and confused. My entire identity was wrapped up in that job. I loved going to work every day. Every performance review reflected my history of innovation, supervising with fairness, excellent communication skills, and exceeding expectations.

Sorry to sound so braggadocio, but a person gets defensive when they feel they've been mistreated, even attacked.

After leaving my job, I checked the weather and new snow depths daily, just to commiserate over what I was missing. Ok, so maybe I didn't miss the minus 20-degree wind chill days. I listened to my radio and watched the Flight for Life helicopter fly over our home, wondering how the patient was doing. There was a huge hole in my heart.

At this time, Bethany and Rachel were entering middle school and my health was starting to take a downward spin – I'm not sure which event was more traumatic. Not so coincidentally, I was invited to join a small women's accountability group.

Spending time in God's word, I gradually came to the realization that my identity was far more than Patti Burnett, ski patrol supervisor. Being emptied of the one thing I valued most, caused me to reevaluate what God said about me. What I did was not as important as who I was. It was not about performance; it was all about the ultimate sacrifice God made. He loved me so much that He sent His only Son to come and die for me so that I could have a relationship with God, the Father.

I came face to face with how much my more than full time job affected our family. I was shocked to find that being a wife, mother, spiritual advisor, coach, chauffeur, counselor, shopper, teacher, cook, cleaning lady, cheerleader, and home organizer took at least two parents. To contemplate that fact, that Dan assumed all of those responsibilities during the six winter months, was mind boggling.

Of greater significance, now that He had my attention, God was showing me that He had plans for my life; and my new meaningful identity had more to do with being a new creation in Christ – Him directing each step of my life. I am still in the process, slowly grasping what it means to be a human being, not a human doing.

What I had viewed as the end of my life, was possibly the most transformative event in my life.

BEFORE THE PASSOVER CELEBRATION, Jesus knew that His hour had come to leave this world and return to His Father. He had loved His disciples during His ministry on earth, and now He loved them to the very end. It was time for supper, and the devil had already prompted Judas, son of Simon Iscariot, to betray Jesus.

Jesus knew that the Father had given Him authority over everything and that He had come from God and would return to God. So He got up from the table, took off His robe, wrapped a towel around His waist, and poured water into a basin. Then He began to wash the disciples' feet, drying them with the towel He had around Him.

When Jesus came to Simon Peter, Peter said to Him, "Lord, are you going to wash my feet?"

Jesus replied, "You don't understand now what I am doing, but someday you will."

"No," Peter protested, "you will never ever wash my feet!"

Jesus replied, "Unless I wash you, you won't belong to Me."

Simon Peter exclaimed, "Then wash my hands and head as well, Lord, not just my feet!"

Jesus replied, "A person who has bathed all over does not need to wash, except for the feet, to be entirely clean. And you disciples are clean, but not all of you." For Jesus knew who would betray Him. That is what He meant when He said, "Not all of you are clean."

After washing their feet, He put on His robe again and sat down and asked, "Do you understand what I was doing? You call me 'Teacher' and 'Lord,' and you are right, because that's what I am. And since I, your Lord and Teacher, have washed your feet, you ought to wash each other's feet. I have given you an example to follow. Do as I have done to you. I tell you the truth, slaves are not greater than their master. Nor is the messenger more important than the one who sends the message. Now that you know these things, God will bless you for doing them. (John 13:1-17 NLT)

> ### UPWARD FALL, BRIAN MYERS
> Your life is a moment, one that transforms you, making your soul longings come true. I am forever with you, in you in every ounce of labor, every drop of blood, every tear. In everything, I waste nothing. In everything. He's making room for one thing: the fullness of deity through a bride emptied of all but Him."[93]

EVEN THOUGH I AM FREE OF THE DEMANDS AND EXPECTATIONS OF EVERYONE, I have voluntarily become a servant to any and all in order to reach a wide range of people: religious, non-religious, meticulous moralists, loose-living immoralists, the defeated, the demoralized—whoever. I didn't take on their way of life. I kept my bearings in Christ—but I entered their world and tried to experience things from their point of view. I've become just about every sort of servant there is in my attempts to lead those I meet into a God-saved life. I did all this because of the Message. I didn't just want to talk about it; I wanted to be in on it!

You've all been to the stadium and seen the athletes' race. Everyone runs; one wins. Run to win. All good athletes train hard. They do it for a gold medal that tarnishes and fades. You're after one that's gold eternally.

I don't know about you, but I'm running hard for the finish line. I'm giving it everything I've got. No lazy living for me! I'm staying alert and in top condition. I'm not going to get caught napping, telling everyone else all about it and then missing out myself. (1 Corinthians 9:19-27 Message)

---

[93] Brian Myers, The Upward Fall: Our Pilgrim Journey through Groaning to Glory (Portland: Dawson Media, 2013), 7.

<u>NEW MORNING MERCIES, MAY 24th, P.D. TRIPP</u>

Whenever you name something in creation as the thing that will satisfy you, you are asking that thing to be your personal savior. This means that, in a very practical, street-level way, you are looking horizontally for what will only ever be yours vertically. In other words, you are asking something in creation to do for you what only God can do. Now, the physical, created world was designed to be glorious, and it is. It is a sight-sound-touch-taste-feel symphony of multifaceted physical glories, but these glories cannot satisfy your heart. If you ask them to, your heart will be empty, and you will be frustrated and discouraged. No, the earthly glories that God created are to be like signposts that point us to the one glory that will ever satisfy our hearts.

The reality is this – God is the peace that you're looking for. He is the satisfaction that your heart seeks. He is the rest that you crave, the joy you long for, and the comfort your heart desires. All those things that you and I say we need, we don't really need. All those things that we think will bring us contentment and joy will fail to deliver. What we need in life is Him, and by grace, He is with us, in us, and for us. Our hearts can rest because, by grace, we have been given everything we could ever need, in Him.[94]

FOR YOU KNOW THE GRACE OF OUR LORD JESUS CHRIST, that though He was rich, yet for your sake He became poor, so that you through His poverty might become rich. (2 Corinthians 8:9 NASB)

---

[94] Tripp, New Morning Mercies, May 24th.

A.W. TOZER

Father, I want to know Thee, but my cowardly heart fears to give up its toys. I cannot part with them without inward bleeding, and I do not try to hide from Thee the terror of the parting. I come trembling, but I do come. Please root from my heart all those things which I have cherished so long, and which have become a very part of my living self, so that Thou mayest enter and dwell there without a rival.[95]

FOR THE GRACE OF GOD HAS APPEARED BRINGING SALVATION TO ALL PEOPLE, instructing us to deny ungodliness and worldly desires and to live sensibly, righteously, and in a godly manner in the present age, looking for the blessed hope and the appearing of the glory of our great God and Savior, Christ Jesus, who gave Himself for us to redeem us from every lawless deed, and to purify for Himself a people for His own possession, eager for good deeds. (Titus 2:11-14 NASB)

THE LIFE YOU'VE ALWAYS WANTED, JOHN ORTBERG

Imagine a group of people coming to your home and interrupting your Twinkie-eating, TV-watching routine with an urgent message. 'Good news! We're from the United States Olympic Committee. We've been looking for someone to run the marathon in the next Olympics. We have statistics on every person in the entire nation on computer. We have checked everybody's records – their performance in the president's physical fitness test in grade school, body type, bone structure, right down to their current percentage of body fat. We have determined that out of 2 hundred million people, you are the one person in America with a chance to bring home the gold medal in the marathon. So, you are on the squad. You will run the race. This is the chance of a lifetime.

---

[95] A.W. Tozer, The Pursuit of God: The Human Thirst For The Divine (Camp Hill: Wing Spread, 2006), 30.

You are surprised by this because the farthest you have ever run is from the couch to the refrigerator. But after the first shock passes, you are gripped by the realization of what's happening in your life. You picture yourself mingling with the elite athletes of the world. You allow yourself to imagine that maybe you do have what it takes. At night you dream about standing on the podium after the race and hearing the national anthem, seeing the flag raised, and bending low to receive the gold medal.

You begin to feel a sense of urgency. It will be your body wearing the red, white and blue singlet, with a billion people watching on TV. But greater than any external pressure is the internal drive that says, "This is the race I was created to run. This is my destiny. This is why I was born. Here's my chance."

This race becomes the great passion of your life. It dominates your mind and every waking moment. To run the race – and perhaps even win it – becomes the central focus of your existence. It is what gets you out of bed in the morning. It's what you live for. It is the chance of a lifetime.

Then it dawns on you. Right now you cannot run a marathon even if you try really, really hard. If you are serious about seizing this chance of a lifetime, you will have to enter into a life of training. You must arrange your life around certain practices that will enable you to do what you cannot do now by willpower alone."[96]

THEREFORE IT WAS NECESSARY for the copies of the things in the heavens to be cleansed with these things, but the heavenly things themselves with better sacrifices than these. For Christ did not enter a holy place made by hands, a mere copy of the true one, but into heaven itself, now to appear in the presence of God for us; nor was it that He would offer Himself often, as the high priest enters the Holy Place year by year with blood that is not his own. Otherwise, He would have

---

[96] John Ortberg, The Life You've Always Wanted: Spiritual Disciplines for Ordinary People (Grand Rapids: Zondervan, 1997), 45

needed to suffer often since the foundation of the world; but now once at the consummation of the ages He has been revealed to put away sin by the sacrifice of Himself. And just as it is destined for people to die once, and after this comes judgment, so Christ also, having been offered once to bear the sins of many, will appear a second time for salvation without reference to sin, to those who eagerly await Him. (Hebrews 9:23-28 NASB)

> ## BROTHER LAWRENCE
> You need not cry very loud; He is nearer to us than we think.[97]

O LOVING AND KIND GOD, HAVE MERCY. Have pity upon me and take away the awful stain of my transgressions. Oh, wash me, cleanse me from this guilt. Let me be pure again. For I admit my shameful deed—it haunts me day and night. It is against You and You alone I sinned and did this terrible thing. You saw it all, and Your sentence against me is just. But I was born a sinner, yes, from the moment my mother conceived me. You deserve honesty from the heart; yes, utter sincerity and truthfulness. Oh, give me this wisdom.

Sprinkle me with the cleansing blood and I shall be clean again. Wash me and I shall be whiter than snow. And after You have punished me, give me back my joy again. Don't keep looking at my sins—erase them from Your sight. Create in me a new, clean heart, O God, filled with clean thoughts and right desires. Don't toss me aside, banished forever from Your presence. Don't take Your Holy Spirit from me. Restore to me again the joy of Your salvation, and make me willing to obey You. Then I will teach Your ways to other sinners, and they—guilty like me—will repent and return to You. Don't sentence me to death. O

---

[97] Alan Vermile quoting Brother Lawrence, The Practice of the Presence of God: A 40-Day Devotion Based on Brother Lawrence's The Practice of the Presence of God (Mount Juliet: Brown Chair Books, 2021), 20.

my God, You alone can rescue me. Then I will sing of Your forgiveness, for my lips will be unsealed—oh, how I will praise You.

You don't want penance; if You did, how gladly I would do it! You aren't interested in offerings burned before You on the altar. It is a broken spirit You want—remorse and penitence. A broken and a contrite heart, O God, You will not ignore. (Psalm 51:1-17 TLB)

> *LARA CASEY*
> She believed she couldn't, so God did.[98]

GIVE THANKS TO THE LORD, FOR HE IS GOOD!
    His faithful love endures forever.
Has the LORD redeemed you? Then speak out!
    Tell others He has redeemed you from your enemies.
For He has gathered the exiles from many lands,
    from east and west,
    from north and south.
Some wandered in the wilderness,
    lost and homeless.
Hungry and thirsty,
    they nearly died.
"LORD, help!" they cried in their trouble,
    and He rescued them from their distress.
He led them straight to safety,
    to a city where they could live.
Let them praise the LORD for His great love
    and for the wonderful things He has done for them.
For he satisfies the thirsty
    and fills the hungry with good things.

---

[98] Lara Casey, Cultivate: A Grace-Filled Guide to Growing an Intentional Life (Nashville: Thomas Nelson, Inc., 2017), 104.

Some sat in darkness and deepest gloom,
    imprisoned in iron chains of misery.
They rebelled against the words of God,
    scorning the counsel of the Most High.
That is why He broke them with hard labor;
    they fell, and no one was there to help them.
"Lord, help!" they cried in their trouble,
    and He saved them from their distress.
He led them from the darkness and deepest gloom;
    He snapped their chains.

Let them praise the Lord for His great love
    and for the wonderful things He has done for them.
For He broke down their prison gates of bronze;
    He cut apart their bars of iron.
Some were fools; they rebelled
    and suffered for their sins.
They couldn't stand the thought of food,
    and they were knocking on death's door.
"Lord, help!" they cried in their trouble,
    and He saved them from their distress.
He sent out His word and healed them,
    snatching them from the door of death.
Let them praise the Lord for His great love
    and for the wonderful things He has done for them.
Let them offer sacrifices of thanksgiving
    and sing joyfully about His glorious acts.

Some went off to sea in ships,
    plying the trade routes of the world.
They, too, observed the Lord's power in action,
    His impressive works on the deepest seas.
He spoke, and the winds rose,
    stirring up the waves.

Their ships were tossed to the heavens
    and plunged again to the depths;
    the sailors cringed in terror.
They reeled and staggered like drunkards
    and were at their wits' end.
"Lord, help!" they cried in their trouble,
    and He saved them from their distress.
He calmed the storm to a whisper
    and stilled the waves.
What a blessing was that stillness
    as he brought them safely into harbor!
Let them praise the Lord for his great love
    and for the wonderful things he has done for them.
Let them exalt Him publicly before the congregation
    and before the leaders of the nation.

He changes rivers into deserts,
    and springs of water into dry, thirsty land.
He turns the fruitful land into salty wastelands,
    because of the wickedness of those who live there.
But He also turns deserts into pools of water,
    the dry land into springs of water.
He brings the hungry to settle there
    and to build their cities.
They sow their fields, plant their vineyards,
    and harvest their bumper crops.
How He blesses them!
They raise large families there,
    and their herds of livestock increase.

When they decrease in number and
    become impoverished
        through oppression, trouble, and sorrow,

> the LORD pours contempt on their princes,
> > causing them to wander in trackless wastelands.
> But He rescues the poor from trouble
> > and increases their families like flocks of sheep.
>
> The godly will see these things and be glad,
> > while the wicked are struck silent.
> Those who are wise will take all this to heart;
> > they will see in our history the faithful love of the LORD.
>
> (Psalm 107:1-43 NLT)

<u>RETURNING TO YOUR FIRST LOVE: PUTTING GOD BACK IN FIRST PLACE, TONY EVANS</u>

I want to take you to Philippians 2:7. Christ did more than simply lay aside the glory of heaven: He "emptied Himself, taking the form of a bondservant, and being made in the likeness of men."

I love this verse because it means that what was thought out and decided in eternity, Christ acted on. So often, our thoughts, beliefs, and statements never get translated into actions.

But unless there is a corresponding action to my statement, then my statement is suspect. If I tell you I love you, but there follows nothing identifiable that makes my statement concrete, then it's just mumbo jumbo. Christ could have stayed in heaven and said, "I love you down there!" But Christ didn't stay in heaven.

What does the self-emptying of Christ mean? The theological doctrine is called the kenosis, from the Greek verb meaning "to empty." Did he empty Himself of His deity and become merely a man? No, the focus of His self-emptying is not heaven, but earth; that is, what Christ emptied Himself into.

He didn't empty out God and pour in man. Rather, He emptied all of God into man. In other words, He didn't stop being God. He didn't say, "Deity, I'm going to leave You in heaven and go down to become humanity."

What Jesus did was take all of His deity and pour it into humanity so that He became much more than mere man. He became the God-man-God poured into man. Let me tell you something important. When Jesus Christ did something about your sin and mine, He didn't give us the leftovers. He poured all that made Him God into man so that man would have all of God. There is nothing that belonged to God that man didn't have when Jesus emptied Himself into man.

So, when we look at the grace and blessings of God in our lives, we need to remember, and I do mean remember, who made it all possible.[99]

THEREFORE, IF THERE IS ANY ENCOURAGEMENT IN CHRIST, if any consolation of love, if any fellowship of the Spirit, if any affection and compassion, make my joy complete by being of the same mind, maintaining the same love, united in spirit, intent on one purpose. Do nothing from selfishness or empty conceit, but with humility consider one another as more important than yourselves; do not merely look out for your own personal interests, but also for the interests of others.

Have this attitude in yourselves which was also in Christ Jesus, who, as He already existed in the form of God, did not consider equality with God something to be grasped, but emptied Himself by taking the form of a bondservant and being born in the likeness of men. And being found in appearance as a man, He humbled Himself by becoming obedient to the point of death: death on a cross. For this reason also God highly exalted Him, and bestowed on Him the name which is above every name, so that at the name of Jesus every knee will bow, of those who are in heaven and on earth and under the earth, and that every tongue will confess that Jesus Christ is Lord, to the glory of God the Father. (Philippians 2:1-11 NASB)

---

[99] Tony Evans, Returning To Your First Love: Putting God Back in First Place (Vendor: Moody Publishers, 2008), 181.

Chapter 16

THE EXACT REPRESENTATION

THE SON IS THE IMAGE OF THE INVISIBLE GOD, the firstborn over all creation. For in Him all things were created: things in heaven and on earth, visible and invisible, whether thrones or powers or rulers or authorities; all things have been created through Him and for Him. He is before all things, and in Him all things hold together. And He is the head of the body, the church; He is the beginning and the firstborn from among the dead, so that in everything He might have the supremacy. For God was pleased to have all His fullness dwell in Him, and through Him to reconcile to Himself all things, whether things on earth or things in heaven, by making peace through His blood, shed on the cross. (Colossians 1:15-20 NIV)

PATTI BURNETT

IN EXODUS 3 WE READ THAT MOSES WAS PASTURING HIS FATHER-IN-LAW, JETHRO'S FLOCK, when he came upon a burning bush, from which God spoke to him "Moses, Moses." Moses said, "Here *I AM*." God introduced Himself by telling Moses "*I AM* the God of your father – the God of Abraham, the God of Isaac, and the God of Jacob." God told Moses, "*I AM* aware of My peoples' sufferings."

God told Moses that He was going to send him to Pharaoh to have him release the Children of Israel and bring them out of Egypt. But Moses said, "Who *AM I*, that I should go to Pharaoh, and that I should bring the sons of Israel out of Egypt?" When God assured Moses that He would be with him, Moses asked God who he should say sent him to Pharoah. God responded, "*I AM WHO I AM… I AM* has sent me to you."

It is easy for us to get depressed and down on ourselves, especially during this time in history following the Covid Pandemic. It might help if we could concentrate on our identity in Christ rather than our identity in 2023 USA.

The Bible is replete with descriptions of who Jesus is. Here you go:

BECAUSE CHRIST IS	**THEREFORE**,
The perfect Lamb of God who died for me	My sins are forever forgiven and forgotten.
My Good Shepherd	I am led, cared for, and protected.
The Great I Am	I am courageous, bold, and fearless.
The Christ	I am an overcomer.
The Door	I can enter in and dine and have fellowship with God.
The Resurrection and the Life	I have eternal life.

Heir of All Things	I am a joint heir with Christ and blessed with every spiritual blessing in the heavenlies.
The Great Physician	I am healed.
The Way	I am rescued and led.
The Truth	I am free from lies.
Son of God	I am God's daughter or son.
The Image of the Invisible God	I am an image bearer.
Firstborn of All Creation	I am born again.
Bread of Life	I have abundant life.
The Spirit of the Living God	I am His temple and filled with the Holy Spirit.
The True Vine	I am His branch to bear much fruit.
Head of the Body	I am a gifted member of the Body of Christ.
The Radiance of God's Glory	I am God's workmanship.
The Exact Representation of God's Nature	I am equipped to walk in His divine nature.
The Beginning and the End	I will live forever with Him in heaven.
The Alpha and the Omega	I am an overcomer.
Great High Priest	I am a member of the royal priesthood.
The Light of the World	I am light and salt, Christ's ambassador.
The Head Over All Rule and Authority	I am complete.

VERY TRULY I TELL YOU PHARISEES, anyone who does not enter the sheep pen by the gate, but climbs in by some other way, is a thief and a robber. The one who enters by the gate is the shepherd of the sheep. The gatekeeper opens the gate for Him, and the sheep listen to His voice. He calls His own sheep by name and leads them out. When

He has brought out all His own, He goes on ahead of them, and His sheep follow Him because they know His voice. But they will never follow a stranger; in fact, they will run away from Him because they do not recognize a stranger's voice." Jesus used this figure of speech, but the Pharisees did not understand what He was telling them.

Therefore Jesus said again, "Very truly I tell you, I am the gate for the sheep. All who have come before me are thieves and robbers, but the sheep have not listened to them. I am the gate; whoever enters through Me will be saved. They will come in and go out, and find pasture. The thief comes only to steal and kill and destroy; I have come that they may have life, and have it to the full.

"I am the good shepherd. The good shepherd lays down his life for the sheep. The hired hand is not the shepherd and does not own the sheep. So when he sees the wolf coming, he abandons the sheep and runs away. Then the wolf attacks the flock and scatters it. The man runs away because he is a hired hand and cares nothing for the sheep.

"I am the good shepherd; I know my sheep and my sheep know Me—just as the Father knows Me and I know the Father—and I lay down My life for the sheep. I have other sheep that are not of this sheep pen. I must bring them also. They too will listen to My voice, and there shall be one flock and one shepherd. The reason My Father loves Me is that I lay down My life—only to take it up again. No one takes it from Me, but I lay it down of My own accord. I have authority to lay it down and authority to take it up again. This command I received from My Father."

The Jews who heard these words were again divided. Many of them said, "He is demon-possessed and raving mad. Why listen to Him?"

But others said, "These are not the sayings of a man possessed by a demon. Can a demon open the eyes of the blind?"

Then came the Festival of Dedication at Jerusalem. It was winter, and Jesus was in the temple courts walking in Solomon's Colonnade. The Jews who were there gathered around Him, saying, "How long will you keep us in suspense? If You are the Messiah, tell us plainly."

Jesus answered, "I did tell you, but you do not believe. The works I do in My Father's name testify about Me, but you do not believe because you are not My sheep. My sheep listen to My voice; I know them, and they follow Me. I give them eternal life, and they shall never perish; no one will snatch them out of My hand. My Father, who has given them to Me, is greater than all; no one can snatch them out of My Father's hand. I and the Father are one."

Again his Jewish opponents picked up stones to stone Him, but Jesus said to them, "I have shown you many good works from the Father. For which of these do you stone Me?"

"We are not stoning You for any good work," they replied, "but for blasphemy, because You, a mere man, claim to be God."

Jesus answered them, "Is it not written in your Law, 'I have said you are "gods"'? If he called them 'gods,' to whom the word of God came—and Scripture cannot be set aside—what about the One whom the Father set apart as His very own and sent into the world? Why then do you accuse Me of blasphemy because I said, 'I am God's Son'? Do not believe Me unless I do the works of My Father. But if I do them, even though you do not believe Me, believe the works, that you may know and understand that the Father is in Me, and I in the Father." Again they tried to seize Him, but He escaped their grasp.

Then Jesus went back across the Jordan to the place where John had been baptizing in the early days. There He stayed, and many people came to Him. They said, "Though John never performed a sign, all that John said about this man was true." And in that place many believed in Jesus. (John 10:1-42 NIV)

> **MATT CHANDLER**
> The context of the gospel message is not our benefit or our salvation; the context of the gospel is the supremacy of Christ and the glory of God. This story of the good news is personal, but it is also cosmic.[100]

ALL IN ALL, NICHOLE NORDEMAN[101]

You are my strength when I am weak
You are the treasure that I seek
You are my all in all
Seeking You as a precious jewel
Lord, to give up I'd be a fool
You are my all in all

Jesus, Lamb of God
Worthy is Your name
Jesus, Lamb of God
Worthy is Your name

GOD, AFTER HE SPOKE LONG AGO TO THE FATHERS in the prophets in many portions and in many ways, in these last days has spoken to us in His Son, whom He appointed heir of all things, through whom He also made the world. And He is the radiance of His glory and the exact representation of His nature, and upholds all things by the word of His power. When He had made purification of sins, He sat down at the right hand of the Majesty on high, having become so much better than the angels, to the extent that He has inherited a more excellent name than they.

---

[100] Matt Chandler, The Explicit Gospel (Wheaton: Crossway, 2014), 4.

[101] Nichole Nordeman (Album Side Eyed, Star Song Records and Sparrow Records, 1998).

For to which of the angels did He ever say,
"You are My Son,
Today I have fathered You?"
And again,
"I will be a Father to Him
And He will be a Son to Me?"
And when He again brings the firstborn into the world, He says,
"And let all the angels of God worship Him."
And regarding the angels He says,
"He makes His angels winds,
And His ministers a flame of fire."
But regarding the Son He says,
"Your throne, God, is forever and ever,
And the scepter of righteousness is the scepter of His kingdom.
You have loved righteousness and hated lawlessness;
Therefore God, Your God, has anointed You
With the oil of joy above Your companions."
And,
"You, Lord, in the beginning laid the foundation of the earth,
And the heavens are the works of Your hands;
They will perish, but You remain;
And they all will wear out like a garment,
And like a robe You will roll them up;
Like a garment they will also be changed.
But You are the same,
And Your years will not come to an end."
But to which of the angels has He ever said,
"Sit at My right hand,
Until I make Your enemies
A footstool for Your feet?"
Are they not all ministering spirits, sent out to provide service for the sake of those who will inherit salvation? (Hebrews 1:1-14 NASB)

> ## QUEEN VICTORIA
> That Book, the Bible, accounts for the supremacy of England. England has become great and happy by the knowledge of the true God through Jesus Christ.[102]

---

[102] William J. Federer quoting Queen Victoria, America's God and Country: Encyclopedia of Quotations (Fort Myers: Amerisearch, 2000), 624.

Chapter 17

PAIN COMPOUNDS FEAR EXPONENTIALLY

BUT JOSEPH SAID TO THEM, "DO NOT BE AFRAID, for am I in God's place? As for you, you meant evil against me, but God meant it for good in order to bring about this present result, to keep many people alive. So therefore, do not be afraid; I will provide for you and your little ones." So he comforted them and spoke kindly to them. (Genesis 50:19-21 NASB)

PATTI BURNETT

IT WAS MY FIFTIETH BIRTHDAY, May 24, 2002, and I was scheduled to give lectures to dog handlers attending the National Search Dog Conference in Colorado Springs.

The two-hour drive from our home that morning was especially stressful. Road rage was rampant; so, I was relieved when we finally exited I-25. As I waited in the left turning lane to enter the hotel parking lot, the traffic coming from the other direction was rush hour, standstill and backed up; and those drivers waved us into the hotel's entry road.

Just as I started to turn in, a small car whipped around one of the waiting cars and hit my front right bumper, totaling my car. I should mention that this was a brand-new car to us; in fact, the insurance company didn't even know about it. At the time, it appeared that there were no injuries. Even Sandy, my young search dog, seemed no worse for the wear despite being flung into the front seat as our car came to an abrupt stop against a yield sign. Even with my seatbelt in place, my head must have hit the windshield, causing a spider web pattern.

God gave me a supernatural calm in the middle of this crisis. Once my husband, Dan, had secured Sandy, I responded to the driver of the other car, aware that her airbag had inflated, potentially causing injury. After a thorough medical appraisal, she appeared to be fine.

It must have seemed strange to conference participants as they watched us unload luggage and dog from a totally crumpled car being pulled by a tow truck.

I was so grateful that God gave me the grace and strength to follow through with my weekend commitments. I could have been easily gripped by fear and anxiety, especially the next day, when whiplash set in. I'm not sure whether that was the result of contacting the windshield or Sandy hitting the back of my head when he flew into the front seats. Whatever the mechanism, it resulted in herniated and bulging discs and eventually a C5-7 neck fusion.

Let there be no doubt that our Heavenly Father has our backs, and our necks.

Pain Compounds Fear Exponentially

Since we are talking about fear and speaking, it is a well-known fact that glossophobia, fear of public speaking, is the greatest social angst, even more than darkness, spiders, and dying. It affects 75% of the population. In fact, surveys place death as fourth down the list. Public speakers fear being judged negatively, having their material questioned and their delivery scrutinized.

To make a long story hopefully shorter, the impetus for my public speaking began in 1983 when one of our much loved and respected senior ski patrollers died in an out of bounds avalanche. Micky's body was located rapidly with an avalanche beacon, but we realized that if a member of the public were to be buried, they might not be wearing a beacon. Thus began our quest for the perfect search and rescue dog. Once we had located Hasty, a male golden retriever, Avalanche Puppy Training 101 commenced in earnest. Was he the perfect dog? Definitely not. Highly motivated and focused? He was all we could ever have hoped for.

As our program grew and became recognized for its effectiveness and innovation, we were invited to visit other search and rescue and ski patrol organizations to help them develop similar programs. Many of the television networks and print media picked up on the novelty of this beautiful, majestic golden retriever, who could find people buried under meters of snow. Some of the media outlets that featured stories about Hasty were Good Morning America, Dateline, PBS' Extraordinary Dogs, Unsolved Mysteries, Mountain Zone, The Summit Daily, The Spirit of Colorado, and the Denver Post front page.

In the 80's, other than a few books concerning general search and rescue, there was not much information available to a person intent on training an avalanche dog. Friends and associates encouraged me to write a book, but with two young children and a full-time winter job, a book was out of the question. However, my veterinarian and I produced a video about avalanche dog training, geared especially toward SAR dog handlers. It was also a useful tool for presentations. With all this information, experience and ideas swirling around in my head, I did eventually write "Avalanche! Hasty Search" in 1999.

As I reflected on this dynamic season in my life, I repeatedly asked myself - "Was my passion for loving my family and sharing my faith as great as it was for SAR dogs?" Maybe that is one of the reasons for this book. The root word for enthusiasm is THEOS, which means GOD IN. I share the Apostle Paul's conviction that the most important message we will ever communicate to others is the Gospel. Speaking publicly has provided opportunities that I would not have had otherwise, to share my faith with people who need the Lord. I try to be prepared whenever I communicate God's Word. Paul urges us to "Preach the Word; be prepared in season and out of season; correct, rebuke and encourage – with great patience and careful instruction" (II Timothy 4:2 NIV).

Even if public speaking is your number one phobia, do not fear! You have been given the same courage and strength that motivated Rahab to heroically hide the Israeli spies, that led Moses and the Children of Israel valiantly through the Red Sea, that brought Stephen to the point where he could share the gospel with an angry mob as they stoned him, that inspired Jesus to bravely overthrow the tables of the money changers, and then, hanging from a cross, declare "Father, forgive them. They know not what they do" (Luke 23:34 KJV).

Step up and speak out, ye of little faith. Be brave and courageous. The battle is the Lord's.

ELEANOR ROOSEVELT

You gain strength, courage, and confidence by every experience in which you really stop to look fear in the face. You are able to say to yourself, 'I lived through this horror. I can take the next thing that comes along.' You must do the thing you think you cannot do.[103]

---

[103] Joe Batten and Leonard Hudson quoting Eleanor Roosevelt, Dare to Live Passionately (Eugene: Resource Publications, 2003), 62.

BUT MOSES SAID TO THE PEOPLE, "DO NOT FEAR! Stand by and see the salvation of the Lord which He will accomplish for you today; for the Egyptians whom you have seen today, you will never see them again forever. The Lord will fight for you while you keep silent."

Then the Lord said to Moses, "Why are you crying out to Me? Tell the sons of Israel to go forward. As for you, lift up your staff and stretch out your hand over the sea and divide it, and the sons of Israel shall go through the midst of the sea on dry land. As for Me, behold, I will harden the hearts of the Egyptians so that they will go in after them; and I will be honored through Pharaoh and all his army, through his chariots and his horsemen. Then the Egyptians will know that I am the Lord, when I am honored through Pharaoh, through his chariots and his horsemen."

The angel of God, who had been going before the camp of Israel, moved and went behind them; and the pillar of cloud moved from before them and stood behind them. So it came between the camp of Egypt and the camp of Israel; and there was the cloud along with the darkness, yet it gave light at night. Thus the one did not come near the other all night.

Then Moses stretched out his hand over the sea; and the Lord swept the sea back by a strong east wind all night and turned the sea into dry land, so the waters were divided. The sons of Israel went through the midst of the sea on the dry land, and the waters were like a wall to them on their right hand and on their left. Then the Egyptians took up the pursuit, and all Pharaoh's horses, his chariots and his horsemen went in after them into the midst of the sea. At the morning watch, the Lord looked down on the army of the Egyptians through the pillar of fire and cloud and brought the army of the Egyptians into confusion. He caused their chariot wheels to swerve, and He made them drive with difficulty; so the Egyptians said, "Let us flee from Israel, for the Lord is fighting for them against the Egyptians."

Then the Lord said to Moses, "Stretch out your hand over the sea so that the waters may come back over the Egyptians, over their chariots and their horsemen." So Moses stretched out his hand over the sea, and the sea returned to its normal state at daybreak, while the Egyptians were fleeing right into it; then the Lord overthrew the Egyptians in the midst of the sea. The waters returned and covered the chariots and the horsemen, even Pharaoh's entire army that had gone into the sea after them; not even one of them remained. But the sons of Israel walked on dry land through the midst of the sea, and the waters were like a wall to them on their right hand and on their left.

Thus the Lord saved Israel that day from the hand of the Egyptians, and Israel saw the Egyptians dead on the seashore. When Israel saw the great power which the Lord had used against the Egyptians, the people feared the Lord, and they believed in the Lord and in His servant Moses. (Exodus 14:13-31 NASB)

MY UTMOST FOR HIS HIGHEST, THE DELIGHT OF DESPAIR, MAY 24th, OSWALD CHAMBERS

It may be that, like the apostle John, you know Jesus Christ intimately, when suddenly He appears with no familiar characteristic at all, and the only thing you can do is to fall at His feet as dead. There are times when God cannot reveal Himself in any other way than in His majesty, and it is the awfulness of the vision which brings you to the delight of despair; if you are ever to be raised up, it must be the hand of God.

"He laid his right hand upon me." In the midst of the awfulness, a touch comes, and you know it is the right hand of Jesus Christ. The right hand not of restraint nor of correction nor of chastisement, but the right hand of the Everlasting Father. Whenever His is laid upon you, it is ineffable peace and comfort, the sense that "underneath are the everlasting arms," full of sustaining and comfort and strength. When once His touch comes, nothing at all can cast you into fear again. In the midst of all His ascended glory the Lord Jesus comes to speak to an insignificant disciple, and to say – "Fear not." His tenderness is ineffably sweet. Do I know Him like that?

Watch some of the things that strike despair. There is despair in which there is no delight, no horizon, no hope of anything, but the delight of despair comes when I know that "in me (that is, in my flesh) dwelleth no good thing." I delight to know that there is that in me which must fall prostrate before God when He manifests Himself, and if I am ever to be raised up, it must be by the hand of God. God can do nothing for me until I get to the limit of the possible.[104]

FRANKLIN D. ROOSEVELT
The only thing we have to fear is fear itself.[105]

THE PHILISTINES DREW UP THEIR TROOPS FOR BATTLE. They deployed them at Socoh in Judah, and set up camp between Socoh and Azekah at Ephes Dammim. Saul and the Israelites came together, camped at Oak Valley, and spread out their troops in battle readiness for the Philistines. The Philistines were on one hill, the Israelites on the opposing hill, with the valley between them.

A giant nearly ten feet tall stepped out from the Philistine line into the open, Goliath from Gath. He had a bronze helmet on his head and was dressed in armor—126 pounds of it! He wore bronze shin guards and carried a bronze sword. His spear was like a fence rail—the spear tip alone weighed over fifteen pounds. His shield bearer walked ahead of him.

Goliath stood there and called out to the Israelite troops, "Why bother using your whole army? Am I not Philistine enough for you? And you're all committed to Saul, aren't you? So, pick your best fighter and pit him against me. If he gets the upper hand and kills me, the Philistines will all become your slaves. But if I get the upper hand and

---

[104] Oswald Chambers, My Utmost for His Highest, May 24th.

[105] Jonathan Alter quoting Franklin D. Roosevelt, The Defining Moment; FDR's Hundred Days and the Triumph of Hope (Manhattan: Simon & Schuster, 2007).

kill him, you'll all become our slaves and serve us. I challenge the troops of Israel this day. Give me a man. Let us fight it out together!"

When Saul and his troops heard the Philistine's challenge, they were terrified and lost all hope.

Enter David. He was the son of Jesse the Ephrathite from Bethlehem in Judah. Jesse, the father of eight sons, was himself too old to join Saul's army. Jesse's three oldest sons had followed Saul to war. The names of the three sons who had joined up with Saul were Eliab, the firstborn; next, Abinadab; and third, Shammah. David was the youngest son. While his three oldest brothers went to war with Saul, David went back and forth from attending to Saul to tending his father's sheep in Bethlehem.

Each morning and evening for forty days, Goliath took his stand and made his speech.

One day, Jesse told David his son, "Take this sack of cracked wheat and these ten loaves of bread and run them down to your brothers in the camp. And take these ten wedges of cheese to the captain of their division. Check in on your brothers to see whether they are getting along all right; and let me know how they're doing—Saul and your brothers, and all the Israelites in their war with the Philistines in the Oak Valley."

David was up at the crack of dawn and, having arranged for someone to tend his flock, took the food and was on his way just as Jesse had directed him. He arrived at the camp just as the army was moving into battle formation, shouting the war cry. Israel and the Philistines moved into position, facing each other, battle-ready. David left his bundles of food in the care of a sentry, ran to the troops who were deployed, and greeted his brothers. While they were talking together, the Philistine champion, Goliath of Gath, stepped out from the front lines of the Philistines, and gave his usual challenge. David heard him.

The Israelites, to a man, fell back the moment they saw the giant—totally frightened. The talk among the troops was, "Have you ever seen anything like this, this man openly and defiantly challenging Israel?

Pain Compounds Fear Exponentially

The man who kills the giant will have it made. The king will give him a huge reward, offer his daughter as a bride, and give his entire family a free ride."

David, who was talking to the men standing around him, asked, "What's in it for the man who kills that Philistine and gets rid of this ugly blot on Israel's honor? Who does he think he is, anyway, this uncircumcised Philistine, taunting the armies of God-Alive?"

They told him what everyone was saying about what the king would do for the man who killed the Philistine.

Eliab, his older brother, heard David fraternizing with the men and lost his temper: "What are you doing here! Why aren't you minding your own business, tending that scrawny flock of sheep? I know what you're up to. You've come down here to see the sights, hoping for a ringside seat at a bloody battle!"

"What is it with you?" replied David. "All I did was ask a question." Ignoring his brother, he turned to someone else, asked the same question, and got the same answer as before.

The things David was saying were picked up and reported to Saul. Saul sent for him.

"Master," said David, "don't give up hope. I'm ready to go and fight this Philistine."

Saul answered David, "You can't go and fight this Philistine. You're too young and inexperienced—and he's been at this fighting business since before you were born."

David said, "I've been a shepherd, tending sheep for my father. Whenever a lion or bear came and took a lamb from the flock, I'd go after it, knock it down, and rescue the lamb. If it turned on me, I'd grab it by the throat, wring its neck, and kill it. Lion or bear, it made no difference—I killed it. And I'll do the same to this Philistine pig who is taunting the troops of God-alive. God, who delivered me from the teeth of the lion and the claws of the bear, will deliver me from this Philistine."

Saul said, "Go. And God help you!"

Then Saul outfitted David as a soldier in armor. He put his bronze helmet on his head and belted his sword on him over the armor. David tried to walk but he could hardly budge.

David told Saul, "I can't even move with all this stuff on me. I'm not used to this." And he took it all off.

Then David took his shepherd's staff, selected five smooth stones from the brook, and put them in the pocket of his shepherd's pack, and with his sling in his hand approached Goliath.

As the Philistine paced back and forth, his shield bearer in front of him, he noticed David. He took one look down on him and sneered—a mere youngster, apple-cheeked and peach-fuzzed.

The Philistine ridiculed David. "Am I a dog that you come after me with a stick?" And he cursed him by his gods.

"Come on," said the Philistine. "I'll make roadkill of you for the buzzards. I'll turn you into a tasty morsel for the field mice."

David answered, "You come at me with sword and spear and battle-ax. I come at you in the name of God-of-the-Angel-Armies, the God of Israel's troops, whom you curse and mock. This very day God is handing you over to me. I'm about to kill you, cut off your head, and serve up your body and the bodies of your Philistine buddies to the crows and coyotes. The whole earth will know that there's an extraordinary God in Israel. And everyone gathered here will learn that God doesn't save by means of sword or spear. The battle belongs to God—He's handing you to us on a platter!"

That roused the Philistine, and he started toward David. David took off from the front line, running toward the Philistine. David reached into his pocket for a stone, slung it, and hit the Philistine hard in the forehead, embedding the stone deeply. The Philistine crashed, face down in the dirt.

That's how David beat the Philistine—with a sling and a stone. He hit him and killed him. No sword for David!

Then David ran up to the Philistine and stood over him, pulled the giant's sword from its sheath, and finished the job by cutting off his head. When the Philistines saw that their great champion was dead, they scattered, running for their lives.

The men of Israel and Judah were up on their feet, shouting! They chased the Philistines all the way to the outskirts of Gath and the gates of Ekron. Wounded Philistines were strewn along the Shaaraim road all the way to Gath and Ekron. After chasing the Philistines, the Israelites came back and looted their camp. David took the Philistine's head and brought it to Jerusalem. But the giant's weapons he placed in his own tent.

When Saul saw David go out to meet the Philistine, he said to Abner, commander of the army, "Tell me about this young man's family."

Abner said, "For the life of me, O King, I don't know."

The king said, "Well, find out the lineage of this raw youth."

As soon as David came back from killing the Philistine, Abner brought him, the Philistine's head still in his hand, straight to Saul.

Saul asked him, "Young man, whose son are you?"

"I'm the son of your servant Jesse," said David, "the one who lives in Bethlehem." (1 Samuel 17:1-58 MESSAGE)

NEW MORNING MERCIES, JANUARY 31st, _PAUL DAVID TRIPP_

If you're God's child, it's no more you against the world than it was David, by himself, against the great warrior Goliath.

Remember, these Israelite soldiers were the army of the Most High God, the Lord Almighty, who had promised that He would deliver these enemies into their hands…

Why didn't these soldiers stand up to Goliath's challenge? Why didn't they fight in the name of the Lord? The answer is clear and unavoidable – they were an army of identity amnesiacs. Because they had forgotten who they were, they were filled with fear and drew a fallacious spiritual conclusion. They compared their puny selves to this massive warrior and concluded there was no path to victory…

What identity will you assign to yourself today? Will you deal with life based on what you assess you bring to the table or based on who you now are as a child of the King of kings and Lord of lords – the Savior who is always with you in power and grace? Will you live in timidity and fear or the courage of hope? Will you avoid challenges of faith in fear or move toward them, resting not in your own ability but in the presence, power and grace of the One who rules all and has become your Father? May God, give you grace to remember your identity as His child in those moments when remembering is essential.[106]

FEAR: FALSE EVIDENCE APPEARING REAL

GIVE THANKS TO THE LORD, FOR HE IS GOOD;
    His love endures forever.
Let Israel say:
    "His love endures forever."
Let the house of Aaron say:
    "His love endures forever."
Let those who fear the Lord say:
    "His love endures forever."
When hard pressed, I cried to the Lord;
    He brought me into a spacious place.
The Lord is with me; I will not be afraid.
    What can mere mortals do to me?
The Lord is with me; He is my helper.
    I look in triumph on my enemies.
It is better to take refuge in the Lord
    than to trust in humans.
It is better to take refuge in the Lord
    than to trust in princes.

---

[106] Paul Davis Tripp, New Morning Mercies, January 31st.

Pain Compounds Fear Exponentially

All the nations surrounded me,
    but in the name of the Lord I cut them down.
They surrounded me on every side,
    but in the name of the Lord I cut them down.
They swarmed around me like bees,
    but they were consumed as quickly as burning thorns;
    in the name of the Lord I cut them down.
I was pushed back and about to fall,
    but the Lord helped me.

The Lord is my strength and my defense;
    He has become my salvation.
Shouts of joy and victory
    resound in the tents of the righteous:

"The Lord's right hand has done mighty things!
The Lord's right hand is lifted high;
    the Lord's right hand has done mighty things!"
I will not die but live,
    and will proclaim what the Lord has done.
The Lord has chastened me severely,
    but He has not given me over to death.
Open for me the gates of the righteous;
    I will enter and give thanks to the Lord.
This is the gate of the Lord
    through which the righteous may enter.
I will give You thanks, for You answered me;
    You have become my salvation.
The stone the builders rejected
    has become the cornerstone;
the Lord has done this,
    and it is marvelous in our eyes.
The Lord has done it this very day;

    let us rejoice today and be glad.
Lord, save us!
    Lord, grant us success!
Blessed is he who comes in the name of the Lord.
    From the house of the Lord we bless you.
The Lord is God,
    and He has made His light shine on us.
With boughs in hand, join in the festal procession
    up to the horns of the altar.
You are my God, and I will praise You;
    You are my God, and I will exalt You.

Give thanks to the Lord, for He is good;
    His love endures forever. (Psalm 118:1-29 NIV)

NEW MORNING MERCIES, FEBRUARY 4th,
PAUL DAVID TRIPP

Every day you preach to yourself some kind of gospel – a false "I can't do this" gospel or the true "I have all I need in Christ" gospel.

You are preaching to yourself a gospel that produces fear and timidity or one that propels you with courage and hope. You are preaching to yourself of a God who is distant, passive, and uncaring or of a God who is near, caring, and active. You are always preaching to yourself a gospel that causes you to rest in His wisdom or a gospel that produces a bit of panic because it seems as if there are no answers to be found…

When you are tempted to give way to despondency or fear, what will you say to you? When life seems hard and unfair, what gospel will you preach to you? When parenting or your marriage seems difficult and overwhelming, what will you share with you? When your dreams elude your grasp, what will you say to you? When you face a disease that you thought you'd never face, what gospel will you preach to you?

It really is true – no one talks to you more than you do. So, God in His grace has given you His word so that you may preach to yourself what is true in those moments when the only one talking to you is you.[107]

JESUS CALLING, JANUARY 21<u>st</u>, SARAH YOUNG

I want you to be all Mine. I am weaning you from other dependencies. Your security rests in Me alone – not in other people, not in circumstances. Depending only on Me may feel like walking on a tightrope, but there is a safety net underneath: the everlasting arms. So don't be afraid of falling. Instead, look ahead to Me. I am always before you, beckoning you on – one step at a time. Neither height nor depth, nor anything else in all creation, can separate you from My loving Presence.[108]

---

[107] Ibid., February 4th.

[108] Sarah Young, Jesus Calling, 22.

Chapter 18

RESCUE ME

THIS IS HOW WE KNOW THAT WE LIVE IN HIM AND HE IN US: He has given us of His Spirit. And we have seen and testify that the Father has sent His Son to be the Savior of the world. If anyone acknowledges that Jesus is the Son of God, God lives in them and they in God. And so we know and rely on the love God has for us. God is love. Whoever lives in love lives in God, and God in them. (1 John 4:13-16 NIV)

PATTI BURNETT

FOR A LARGE PORTION OF MY LIFE, I was a part of the emergency services world. I supervised Copper Mountain Ski Patrol and handled search dogs with the Summit County Rescue Group, Search and Rescue Dogs of Colorado, Copper, and the FEMA Task Force.

I saw stuff, lots of stuff and even today, years later, I have lingering emotions and thoughts I cannot erase.

I've done CPR on multiple people, but the first one was perhaps the most poignant. An exceptionally proficient backcountry skier had ventured onto Grizzly Peak in October with a friend – they were members of the infamous Ski to Die club. They triggered a slide that buried one of them, and the victim's buddy called 911 for help. We arrived and were fortunate to be able to locate him with a probe line. This was before we had search dogs. As we exposed his head, the Flight for Life nurse asked us to initiate CPR, even though he had been buried for at least three or four hours.

At the nurse's request, everyone in our group stepped back except me; and I realized that, by omission, I had just volunteered to do respirations. In those days we did not have pocket masks to protect us; and as I blew oxygen into his lungs, I heard a gurgling noise. I wondered whether this meant my rescue breathing was helping. Unfortunately, such was not the case; and it was with deep sadness that I experienced my first encounter with the angel of death. I am sure that I had post-traumatic stress. I could not erase from my memory the expression of terror etched on Turbo's face.

Another tragic memory was when I had just started handling search and rescue (SAR) dogs. Hasty was very young, but we were the only search dog team in our county at the time. To set the stage for you, we were called to Berthoud Pass; and I think it may have been New Year's Day. The previous day a cross country group had been touring the Second Creek area and came upon old avalanche debris that had been partially covered with new blowing snow. They noticed a ski protruding from the deposition; and when they dug it out, they found that it was still attached to a young man's frozen body. Sheriff's officers learned that this man and his girlfriend had been winter camping. They must have triggered the slide and buried themselves. They probably didn't have a chance – dry slab avalanches can reach speeds of 80 mph within about five seconds.

We were asked to meet a news helicopter at the top of Berthoud Pass early the next morning to hitch a ride to the avalanche site. As we waited for our ship, temperatures hovered around zero degrees with beautifully clear skies and not much wind – typical early morning Colorado weather. Suddenly two Labrador Retrievers, a large chocolate male and a small yellow female, ran up to Hasty. The male proceeded to chomp onto my dog's face and out of nowhere I watched this burley body with his puffy 40 below zero jacket pounce on the big lab and pin him to the ground.

About that time a petite woman, who happened to be the owner of Timberline Ski Area (at the top of Berthoud Pass), ran up to us and pleaded with my husband to release her dog. Dan said that he'd be glad to comply as soon as she placed her dog on a leash.

Shortly thereafter, the helicopter arrived. A ski patrol team was flown over the area surrounding the slide path to drop explosives and reduce any hang fire (remaining avalanche risk.) They produced a small slide which unknowingly further buried the young woman.

When the site commander determined that it was safe, Chester, Judy's Chesapeake Bay Retriever from Vail, and my dog, Hasty, began their search. "Are you ready to go to work? Go search."

I don't think I've ever seen dogs work so effectively and efficiently. After his mean dog encounter, adrenaline was racing through Hasty's veins. Within seconds of scanning the debris, Hasty pointed that amazing nose into the wind and acquired an air scent. He immediately worked a beautiful cone shaped grid as the light, steady winds helped him to methodically arrive at the point where the scent from the buried victim was strongest. We used ten-foot-long skinny metal poles to probe the area where Hasty was digging Someone yelled "strike." Someone had struck her body.

Since this verbiage may be foreign to you, I will help you to audit a quick avalanche dog class. When a person is buried in an avalanche, their scent rises to the surface of the snow. The colder the air temperature the faster the scent rises because there is a larger temperature gradient – the difference between air and ground temperature. The gradient causes heat, vapor, and scent to flow toward the lower temperature. The denser the avalanche debris, the slower the rise. Obviously, the scent will rise faster in powder slide deposition than in slab avalanches.

My state of Colorado is overwhelmingly responsible for the most avalanche deaths in the United States – 21% and approximately 6 per year. 90% of avalanche victims are men and the mean age is 33, while the mean age of women victims is about 38. Make sense? To learn more, read "Avalanche! Hasty Search."

Back to Second Creek. Chester came over to confirm our efforts and the little growl from my alpha male, Hasty, was proof enough that our suspicions were correct. The lost woman was under about seven feet of snow. Looking into the face of the first woman whose body we had recovered, I realized that years earlier, when I was ignorant of avalanche dangers, I could have been in her place. Because of missions such as this, I would have to say that Dan and I tend to be much more conservative than the rest of our friends when making decisions about the safety and viability of backcountry terrain.

These are just a few of the hundreds of traumatic scenarios to which we have responded. However, the most difficult combination of tragedies happened in 1994. Dan and I and some friends were attending the Mountain Community Fair and were approached by one of the Sheriff's officers working the event. He told us that he had just received word that a hiker with a leg injury was being evacuated from Mount Huron, a 14,000' peak outside our county's jurisdiction. The mission was located in such high terrain that, without helicopter assistance, it would have taken hours to get her down; and there would be increased potential for injuries to the Chaffee County responders.

The way I understand it, the site was located above timberline on some large scree (loose rocks also known as talus.) As Gary, the pilot, approached the scene, he carefully placed his skids on the surface of the rocks. The rocks must have shifted slightly causing a main rotor strike. In just seconds, Gary moved the inevitable helicopter crash away from the rescuers and patient, sacrificing his and Sandy's lives. I'm sure they died immediately.

I would be remiss if I failed to mention the beautiful, incredibly skilled, and compassionate Flight for Life nurse, Sandy. She was a Medical Volunteer Patroller with the Copper Ski Patrol and my good friend. I am reminded of the time I responded to an accident down one of Copper's expert trails. A young woman had skied into a tree and was unconscious. We attempted to place an oral airway in her throat to assist in performing CPR. The tubes we had were too large and we were unsuccessful.

Within seconds, Sandy was on scene and proceeded to work her magic. Despite the woman's state of unconsciousness, Sandy got right down next to her face and told her what she was going to do. We then apprised Sandy of the situation and how our airway tubes were too large and impossible to insert. The next words out of her mouth have been forever etched in my heart. She said, "Never say never," and with that Sandy expertly got that airway in just before the helicopter arrived to fly Michelle to a Denver hospital.

Around the time of the Mount Huron helicopter accident, there was a major forest fire in the South Canyon on Storm King Mountain, near Glenwood Springs. In a tragic turn of events, the winds picked up and changed directions; and the wildland firefighters, each carrying 30 to 60 pounds of gear, could not outrun the fire as it up sloped. Fourteen "hotshot" firefighters lost their lives on July 6, 1994.

If you are ever in Colorado, I encourage you to visit the Storm King Firefighters Memorial trail, constructed as a tribute to these men and women.

Vail search and rescue group members were dispatched to evacuate the bodies of these brave firefighters. It must have been a horrendous scene. I was asked to conduct a critical incident stress debrief for the rescuers who carried the firefighters' bodies out of the field.

But – the timing was bad. That same day, the day after the helicopter accident on Huron, Dan and I hiked up the mountain to recover some of Sandy and Gary's gear. We saw awful things and realized that we had made a mistake in going there so soon after their accident. I found Sandy's hiking boot wedged between some rocks. I found her trauma shears and other medical equipment scattered over the area. I located many memories of my friends – tears run freely as I write this.

Talk about emotional overload – I was not the person to be doing a CISD that night.

Now, 29 years later, I still carry around in my mind and heart a picture of the mountain that stole our friends' lives. My counselor, Julie, has tried to help me work through the scars that remain. I am sure that in our medical responses, since that day in July of 1994, my compassion has increased 100-fold, knowing that there is often a very thin thread that separates life and death.

I try to imagine what it must have been like for my Savior, Jesus Christ, to take on Himself all the pain and hurt that we try to carry on our own. This world is filled with suffering. Only the perfect One, God who became Man, can bear this tremendous burden. We all need a Savior – the ultimate Rescuer.

JESUS ENTERED JERICHO AND WAS PASSING THROUGH. And there was a man called by the name of Zacchaeus; he was a chief tax collector and he was rich. Zaccheus was trying to see who Jesus was, and he was unable due to the crowd, because he was short in stature. So he ran on ahead and climbed up a sycamore tree in order to see Him, because He was about to pass through that way. And when Jesus came to the place, He looked up and said to him, "ZACCHEUS, hurry and come down, for today I must stay at your house." And he hurried and came down and received Him joyfully. When the people saw this, they all began to complain, saying, "He has gone in to be the guest of a man who is a sinner!" But Zacchaeus stopped and said to the Lord, "Behold, Lord, half of my possessions I am giving to the poor, and if I have extorted anything from anyone, I am giving back four times as much." And Jesus said to him, "Today salvation has come to this house, because he, too, is a son of Abraham. For the Son of Man has come to seek and to save that which was lost." (Luke 19:1-10 NASB)

THERE IS A REDEEMER, KEITH GREEN

There is a Redeemer,
Jesus, God's own Son,
Precious Lamb of God, Messiah,
Holy One.

Jesus my Redeemer,
Name above all names,
Precious Lamb of God, Messiah,
Hope for sinners slain.

Thank You oh my Father,
For giving us Your Son,
And leaving Your Spirit,
'Til the work on earth is done.

When I stand in glory,
I will see His face,
And there I'll serve my King forever,
In that holy place.

Thank You oh my Father,
For giving us Your Son,

And leaving Your Spirit,
'Til the work on earth is done.[109]

WE MUST PAY THE MOST CAREFUL ATTENTION, therefore, to what we have heard, so that we do not drift away. For since the message spoken through angels was binding, and every violation and disobedience received its just punishment, how shall we escape if we ignore so great a salvation? This salvation, which was first announced by the Lord, was confirmed to us by those who heard Him. God also testified to it by signs, wonders and various miracles, and by gifts of the Holy Spirit distributed according to His will.

It is not to angels that he has subjected the world to come, about which we are speaking. But there is a place where someone has testified:

"What is mankind that you are mindful of them,
A son of man that you care for him?
You made them a little lower than the angels;
You crowned them with glory and honor
And put everything under their feet."

In putting everything under them, God left nothing that is not subject to them. Yet at present we do not see everything subject to them. But we do see Jesus, who was made lower than the angels for a little while, now crowned with glory and honor because He suffered death, so that by the grace of God He might taste death for everyone.

In bringing many sons and daughters to glory, it was fitting that God, for whom and through whom everything exists, should make the pioneer of their salvation perfect through what He suffered. Both the one who makes people holy and those who are made holy are of the same family. So Jesus is not ashamed to call them brothers and sisters. He says,

---

[109] Keith Green, There is a Redeemer, Melody Green (writer), distributed by Birdwing Music, track 6 on Songs for the Shepherd, 1977, cassette.

"I will declare Your name to my brothers and sisters;
in the assembly I will sing Your praises."
And again,
"I will put My trust in Him."
And again He says,
"Here am I, and the children God has given Me."
Since the children have flesh and blood, He too shared in their humanity so that by His death He might break the power of him who holds the power of death—that is, the devil—and free those who all their lives were held in slavery by their fear of death. For surely it is not angels He helps, but Abraham's descendants. For this reason He had to be made like them, fully human in every way, in order that he might become a merciful and faithful high priest in service to God, and that he might make atonement for the sins of the people. Because He Himself suffered when He was tempted, He is able to help those who are being tempted. (Hebrews 2:1-18 NIV)

I WILL PRAISE THE LORD AT ALL TIMES.
    I will constantly speak His praises.
I will boast only in the Lord;
    let all who are helpless take heart.
Come, let us tell of the Lord's greatness;
    let us exalt His name together.
I prayed to the Lord, and He answered me.
    He freed me from all my fears.
Those who look to Him for help will be
    Radiant with joy;
    No shadow of shame will darken their faces.
In my desperation I prayed, and the Lord listened;
    He saved me from all my troubles.
For the angel of the Lord is a guard;
    He surrounds and defends all who fear Him .
Taste and see that the Lord is good.

Oh, the joys of those who take refuge in Him!
Fear the Lord, you His godly people,
>   for those who fear Him will have all they need.
Even strong young lions sometimes go hungry,
>   but those who trust in the Lord
>   will lack no good thing.
Come, my children, and listen to me,
>   and I will teach you to fear the Lord.
Does anyone want to live a life
>   that is long and prosperous?
Then keep your tongue from speaking evil
>   and your lips from telling lies!
Turn away from evil and do good.
Search for peace, and work to maintain it.
The eyes of the Lord watch over those who do right;
>   His ears are open to their cries for help.
But the Lord turns his face against those who do evil;
He will erase their memory from the earth.
The Lord hears His people when they call to Him for help.
He rescues them from all their troubles.
The Lord is close to the brokenhearted;
He rescues those whose spirits are crushed.
The righteous person faces many troubles,
>   but the Lord comes to the rescue each time.
For the Lord protects the bones of the righteous;
>   not one of them is broken!
Calamity will surely destroy the wicked,
>   and those who hate the righteous will be punished.
But the Lord will redeem those who serve Him.
No one who takes refuge in Him will be condemned. (Psalm 34:1-22 NLT)

Rescue Me

> **BILLY GRAHAM**
> Jesus Christ is the Savior of the world because He is the only one who can bridge the gap between heaven and earth.[110]

I LOVE THE LORD BECAUSE HE HEARS MY VOICE
    and my prayer for mercy.
Because He bends down to listen,
    I will pray as long as I have breath!
Death wrapped its ropes around me;
    the terrors of the grave overtook me.
I saw only trouble and sorrow.
Then I called on the name of the Lord:
"Please, Lord, save me!"
How kind the Lord is! How good He is!
So merciful, this God of ours!
The Lord protects those of childlike faith;
I was facing death, and He saved me.
Let my soul be at rest again,
    for the Lord has been good to me.
He has saved me from death,
    my eyes from tears,
    my feet from stumbling.
And so I walk in the Lord's presence
    as I live here on earth!
I believed in You, so I said,
"I am deeply troubled, Lord."
In my anxiety I cried out to You,
"These people are all liars!"
What can I offer the Lord
    for all He has done for me?

---

[110] Billy Graham, The Heaven Answer Book (Nashville: Thomas Nelson, 2012), 30.

I will lift up the cup of salvation
    and praise the Lord's name for saving me.
I will keep my promises to the Lord
    in the presence of all His people.
The Lord cares deeply
    when his loved ones die.
O Lord, I am your servant;
    yes, I am your servant, born into your household;
    you have freed me from my chains.
I will offer you a sacrifice of thanksgiving
    and call on the name of the Lord.
I will fulfill my vows to the Lord
    in the presence of all His people—
    in the house of the Lord
    in the heart of Jerusalem.
Praise the Lord! (Psalm 116:1-19 NLT)

MOMENTS WITH THE SAVIOR, KEN GIRE

As a front piece to his gospel, Matthew places a family tree. The tree is rooted in Israel's greatest patriarch, Abraham, and in its greatest king, David.

The fruit of the tree is Jesus.

Throughout Matthew's gospel is this pattern of root and fruit. The root of Old Testament prophecies. The fruit of New Testament fulfillment. Rachel weeping for her children becomes the collective tears of Bethlehem's mothers for the infants slaughtered by Herod. The voice crying in the wilderness, of which Isaiah speaks, becomes the preaching of John the Baptist. The striking down of the shepherd and the scattering of the sheep, recorded in Zechariah, are fulfilled the night of Jesus' betrayal.

Writing to the Jews, Matthew quotes the Old Testament more than any other gospel writer. He sees, within the richly furrowed lines of the Psalms, rows of truth rooting below the surface. And within the seemingly fallow words of the prophets, fields of seeds lying dormant in the soil.

Dormant but expectant.

For ever since the ruin of Eden, all creation has awaited its Savior, the promised seed that would one day restore paradise. Season after season it has waited. Century after century. Millennium after millennium…

The Savior would come from a royal line. That much everyone knew. The line would originate with Abraham and branch through David. Yet despite how sturdy its trunk and how spreading its limbs the Savior's family tree had its share of blight and barrenness, of bent twigs and broken branches.

- Abraham, for example. A man of faith. But a man who also lied, sending his wife into the arms of Pharaoh and putting the promised seed in jeopardy…
- And there was David. He was, the Scriptures tell us, a man after God's own heart. But he was also a man after other things. Bathsheba, for one…
- Rahab was a harlot…
- Ruth was a foreigner, an unexpected graft…
- Uriah's wife goes unnamed in Matthew's list, but she is Bathsheba…
- Then there's the forked branch of Judah. And the twisted branch of Manasseh. And when we've gone through the entire line, we're left scratching our heads, wondering, what are we to make of this tree through whose branches came the Savior of the world? What are we to make of all the sin, all the imperfection, all the failure?

Simply this. That God's purposes are not thwarted by our humanity, however weak and wayward it may be. That He works in us and through us and, more often than not, in spite of us. That He works with us, as a gardener works with his garden. Lifting. Pruning. Watering. Weeding. Whatever it takes to bring it to fruition. Or however long it takes.

This is our hope. That season after season he walks the uncultivated fields of each generation. His providential hands at work in the dark, cloddy soil. His careful eyes watch over the growth. Watching over the budding faith of the young and over the branching influence of the old. So that something beautiful may blossom from our frail and nubby reach for the sky.[111]

"COME NOW, AND LET US REASON TOGETHER,"
  Says the Lord,
"Though your sins are as scarlet,
  They will be as white as snow;
  Though they are red like crimson,
  They will be like wool.
"If you consent and obey,
  You will eat the best of the land;
"But if you refuse and rebel,
  You will be devoured by the sword."
  Truly, the mouth of the Lord has spoken. (Isaiah 1:18-20 NASB)

<u>PATTI BURNETT</u>

AT THIS TIME THERE ARE ONLY A FEW SERVICE DOGS specifically trained to aid people living with Parkinson's. There is a young gal who lives in the Netherlands who is working to remedy this situation. Her doctoral thesis is dedicated to the goal of bringing these wonderful creatures alongside my fellow Parkinsonians.

This is an excellent idea for a number of reasons. For one, people who are lonely tend to go downhill more rapidly in both cognitive and movement symptoms. Various surveys have confirmed this theory. In ways that we don't understand, dogs are able to reduce our stress and

---

[111] Gire, *Moments with the Savior*, 15-17.

anxiety levels and provide a boost in self-esteem and social connection. Dogs somehow bring total strangers together, in a magical, magnetic way. Our ski patrollers especially enjoyed walking the avalanche dogs around the tops of chairlifts where the dogs were transformed into "chick magnets."

A second advantage of having a service dog is that if a person with Parkinson's has balance or freezing problems, the dogs, if large enough, can provide a stable back to lean upon, as well as a driving force of momentum when a body thinks it does not want to move on. People who have freezing as a PD symptom, at times feel as though their feet are frozen to the floor.

Service dogs are also able to help pull a wheelchair, open doors, turn lights on and off, and pick up objects. If someone falls, the dog can act as a brace for the person to lean on and get off the floor. The dog may even be able to prevent an impending fall.

I have a six-year-old Golden Retriever named Cadence who I am hoping will someday provide this type of assistance to me should the need arise. He is already a certified therapy dog and the bond between us is awesome. We have visited libraries, elderly day care facilities, hospitals, and schools. We are also in the process of becoming Hope Dog certified so that we can respond to EMS scenarios where victims, friends, and family members need a soft Golden Retriever's head to love on.

THE LORD GAVE ANOTHER MESSAGE TO JEREMIAH. He said, this is what the Lord, the God of Israel, says: Write down for the record everything I have said to you, Jeremiah. For the time is coming when I will restore the fortunes of my people of Israel and Judah. I will bring them home to this land that I gave to their ancestors, and they will possess it again. I, the LORD, have spoken!"

This is the message the LORD gave concerning Israel and Judah. This is what the LORD says:

"I hear cries of fear;
    there is terror and no peace.
Now let me ask you a question:
    Do men give birth to babies?
Then why do they stand there, ashen-faced,
    hands pressed against their sides
    like a woman in labor?
In all history there has never been such a time of terror.
It will be a time of trouble for My people Israel.
Yet in the end they will be saved!
For in that day,"
    says the LORD of Heaven's Armies,
  "I will break the yoke from their necks
    and snap their chains.
Foreigners will no longer be their masters.
For My people will serve the LORD their God
    and their king descended from David—
    the king I will raise up for them.

"So do not be afraid, Jacob, my servant;
    do not be dismayed, Israel,"
    says the LORD.
"For I will bring you home again from distant lands,
    and your children will return from their exile.
Israel will return to a life of peace and quiet,
    and no one will terrorize them.
For I am with you and will save you,"
    says the LORD.
"I will completely destroy the nations where
    I have scattered you,
    but I will not completely destroy you.
I will discipline you, but with justice;
    I cannot let you go unpunished." ...

I will give you back your health
    and heal your wounds," says the LORD.
"For you are called an outcast—
    'Jerusalem for whom no one cares.'"

This is what the LORD says:
"When I bring Israel home again from captivity
    and restore their fortunes,
    Jerusalem will be rebuilt on its ruins,
    and the palace reconstructed as before.
There will be joy and songs of thanksgiving,
    and I will multiply My people, not diminish them;
I will honor them, not despise them.
Their children will prosper as they did long ago.
I will establish them as a nation before me,
    and I will punish anyone who hurts them.
They will have their own ruler again,
    and he will come from their own people.
I will invite him to approach me," says the LORD,
    "for who would dare to come unless invited?
You will be My people,
    and I will be your God."
Look! The LORD's anger bursts out like a storm,
    a driving wind that swirls down on the heads of the wicked.
The fierce anger of the LORD will not diminish
    until it has finished all He has planned.
In the days to come
    you will understand all this. (Jeremiah 30:1-11, 17-24 NLT)

Chapter 19

HE IS MY REFUGE AND FORTRESS IN THE STORM

WHOEVER DWELLS IN THE SHELTER OF THE MOST HIGH will rest in the shelter of the almighty. I will say of the Lord, "He is my refuge and my fortress, my God, in whom I trust." Surely He will save you from the fowler's snare and from the deadly pestilence. (Psalm 9:1-3 NIV)

PATTI BURNETT

WHEN WE ARE WALKING IN OBEDIENCE TO GOD and trials come our way, it's not unusual to assume that one of three things is going on. Either God is not in control; or He doesn't care that this is happening to me; or He's got a greater good in mind. This was definitely the case when I was first diagnosed with Parkinson's.

Rather than doubting our Lord's goodness and asking "WHY?" Maybe the question we should ask is "WHAT?" God, what do You want to do through this situation? Do I have some rough edges that You want to chisel away so that You can use me more effectively in my family and community? Are there people who can be reached with the gospel when they see that I continue to glorify and walk with You despite major roadblocks and detours?

Do I like God's ways and means? Not necessarily. But I do like the fact that He is the only God; and He has His reasons – reasons I will probably not understand until I stand before His throne. I know that nothing touches me that has not first been filtered through the loving hands of the Great I Am. I know that He will give me the strength needed to handle even this.

THEN DAVID SPOKE TO THE LORD THE WORDS OF THIS SONG, on the day when the LORD had delivered him from the hand of all his enemies, and from the hand of Saul. And he said:

> "The LORD is my rock and my fortress and my deliverer;
> The God of my strength, in whom I will trust;
> My shield and the horn of my salvation,
> My stronghold and my refuge;
> My Savior, You save me from violence.
> I will call upon the LORD, who is worthy to be praised;
> So shall I be saved from my enemies.
> "When the waves of death surrounded me,

He Is My Refuge And Fortress In The Storm

The floods of ungodliness made me afraid.
The sorrows of Sheol surrounded me;
The snares of death confronted me.
In my distress I called upon the LORD,
And cried out to my God;
He heard my voice from His temple,
And my cry entered His ears.
"Then the earth shook and trembled;
The foundations of heaven quaked and were shaken,
Because He was angry.
Smoke went up from His nostrils,
And devouring fire from His mouth;
Coals were kindled by it.
He bowed the heavens also, and came down
With darkness under His feet.
He rode upon a cherub, and flew;
And He was seen upon the wings of the wind.
He made darkness canopies around Him,
Dark waters and thick clouds of the skies.
From the brightness before Him
Coals of fire were kindled.
"The LORD thundered from heaven,
And the Most High uttered His voice.
He sent out arrows and scattered them;
Lightning bolts, and He vanquished them.
Then the channels of the sea were seen,
The foundations of the world were uncovered,
At the rebuke of the LORD,
At the blast of the breath of His nostrils.
"He sent from above, He took me,
He drew me out of many waters.
He delivered me from my strong enemy,
From those who hated me;

For they were too strong for me.
They confronted me in the day of my calamity,
But the Lord was my support.
He also brought me out into a broad place;
He delivered me because He delighted in me.
"The Lord rewarded me according to my righteousness;
According to the cleanness of my hands
He has recompensed me.
For I have kept the ways of the Lord,
And have not wickedly departed from my God.
For all His judgments were before me;
And as for His statutes, I did not depart from them.
I was also blameless before Him,
And I kept myself from my iniquity.
Therefore the Lord has recompensed me according to my righteousness,
According to my cleanness in His eyes.
"With the merciful You will show Yourself merciful;
With a blameless man You will show Yourself blameless;
With the pure You will show Yourself pure;
And with the devious You will show Yourself shrewd.
You will save the humble people;
But Your eyes are on the haughty, that You may bring them down.
"For You are my lamp, O Lord
The Lord shall enlighten my darkness.
For by You I can run against a troop;
By my God I can leap over a wall.
As for God, His way is perfect;
The word of the Lord is proven;
He is a shield to all who trust in Him.
"for who is God, except the Lord?
And who is a rock, except our God?
God is my strength and power,

And He makes my way perfect.
He makes my feet like the feet of deer,
And sets me on my high places.
He teaches my hands to make war,
So that my arms can bend a bow of bronze.
"You have also given me the shield of Your salvation;
Your gentleness has made me great.
You enlarged my path under me;
So my feet did not slip.
"The Lord lives!
Blessed be my Rock!
Let God be exalted,
The Rock of my salvation!
It is God who avenges me,
And subdues the peoples under me;
He delivers me from my enemies.
You also lift me up above those who rise against me;
You have delivered me from the violent man.
Therefore I will give thanks to You, O Lord, among the Gentiles,
And sing praises to Your name.
"He is the tower of salvation to His king,
And shows mercy to His anointed,
To David and his descendants forevermore."
(2 Samuel 22:1-37, 47-51 NKJV)

SADHU SUNDER SINGH

One day after a long journey I rested in front of a house. Suddenly a sparrow came towards me blown helplessly by a strong wind. From another direction, an eagle dived to catch the panicky sparrow. Threatened from different directions, the sparrow flew into my lap. By choice, it would not ordinarily do that. However, the little bird was seeking refuge from a great danger.

KEEP ME SAFE, MY GOD,
for in You I take refuge.
I say to the Lord, "You are my Lord;
    apart from You I have no good thing."
I say of the holy people who are in the land,
"They are the noble ones in whom is all my delight."
Those who run after other gods will suffer more and more.
I will not pour out libations of blood to such gods
    or take up their names on my lips.
Lord, You alone are my portion and my cup;
    you make my lot secure.
The boundary lines have fallen for me in
Pleasant places;
Surely I have a delightful inheritance.
I will praise the Lord, who counsels me;
    even at night my heart instructs me.
I keep my eyes always on the Lord.
With Him at my right hand, I will not be shaken.
Therefore my heart is glad and my tongue rejoices;
    my body also will rest secure,
        because you will not abandon me to the realm of the dead,
        nor will you let your faithful one see decay.
You make known to me the path of life;
    you will fill me with joy in Your presence,
    with eternal pleasures at Your right hand. (Psalm 16:1-11 NIV)

A.C. DIXON

In Jesus Christ on the Cross there is refuge; there is safety; there is shelter; and all the power of sin upon our track cannot reach us when we have taken shelter under the Cross that atones for our sins.[112]

---

[112] Stephen Arterburn and Nick Harrison quoting A.C. Dixon, The One Year Life Recovery Prayer Devotional (Carol Stream: Tyndale Momentum, 2021) 2.

THE LORD IS MY LIGHT AND MY SALVATION -
Whom shall I fear?
The LORD is the refuge and fortress of my life—
Whom shall I dread?
When the wicked came against me to eat up my flesh,
My adversaries and my enemies, they stumbled and fell.
Though an army encamp against me,
My heart will not fear;
Though war arise against me,
Even in this I am confident.
One thing I have asked of the Lord, and that I will seek:
That I may dwell in the house of the Lord [in His presence] all the days of my life,
To gaze upon the beauty [the delightful loveliness and majestic grandeur] of the Lord
And to meditate in His temple.
For in the day of trouble He will hide me in His shelter;
In the secret place of His tent He will hide me;
He will lift me up on a rock.
And now my head will be lifted up above my enemies around me,
In His tent I will offer sacrifices with shouts of joy;
I will sing, yes, I will sing praises to the LORD.
Hear, O LORD, when I cry aloud;
Be gracious and compassionate to me and answer me.
When You said, "Seek My face [in prayer, require My presence as your greatest need]," my heart said to You,
"Your face, O LORD, I will seek [on the authority of Your word]."
Do not hide Your face from me,
Do not turn Your servant away in anger;
You have been my help;
Do not abandon me nor leave me,
O God of my salvation!
Although my father and my mother have abandoned me,
Yet the LORD will take me up [adopt me as His child].
Teach me Your way, O LORD,
And lead me on a level path

Because of my enemies [who lie in wait].
Do not give me up to the will of my adversaries,
For false witnesses have come against me;
They breathe out violence.
I would have despaired had I not believed that I would see the goodness of the Lord
In the land of the living.
Wait for and confidently expect the Lord;
Be strong and let your heart take courage;
Yes, wait for and confidently expect the LORD. (Psalm 27:1-14 AMP)

GOD WITH SKIN ON, GIVING THE BLESSING, GARY SMALLEY AND JOHN TRENT, PH.D.

A little girl became frightened one night during a thunderstorm. After one particularly loud clap of thunder, she burst into her parents' room. Jumping into the middle of the bed, she sought her parents' arms for comfort and assurance.

"Don't worry, honey," her father said, trying to calm her fears. "The Lord will protect you." The little girl snuggled closer. "I know that, Daddy, but right now I need someone with skin on!"

This little one did not doubt her heavenly Father's ability to protect her, but she also knew He had given her an earthly father. She knew she could run to this one God had made and entrusted with a special gift to bring her comfort, security, and personal acceptance – the blessing of meaningful touch.[113]

BUT THOSE WHO WANT THE BEST FOR ME,
Let them have the last word—a glad shout!
    and say, over and over and over,
"God is great—everything works
    together for good for His servant.

---

[113] Smalley and Trent, Giving the Blessing, 59.

I'll tell the world how great and good you are,
   I'll shout Hallelujah all day, every day.
(Psalm 35:27-28 Message)

> ## JOHN NEWTON
> If the Lord be with us, we have no cause of fear. His eye is upon us, His arm over us, His ear open to our prayer - His grace sufficient, His promise unchangeable.[114]

GOD IS OUR REFUGE AND STRENGTH [MIGHTY AND IMPENETRABLE],
A very present and well-proved help in trouble.

Therefore we will not fear, though the earth should change
And though the mountains be shaken and slip into the heart of the seas,

Though its waters roar and foam,
Though the mountains tremble at its roaring. Selah.

There is a river whose streams make glad the city of God,
The holy dwelling places of the Most High.

God is in the midst of her [His city], she will not be moved;
God will help her when the morning dawns.

The nations made an uproar, the kingdoms tottered and were moved;
He raised His voice, the earth melted.

---

[114] John Newton, The Works of the Rev. John Newton (London: Hamilton, Adams & Co., 1820), 272.

The Lord of hosts is with us;
The God of Jacob is our stronghold [our refuge, our high tower]. Selah.

Come, behold the works of the Lord,
Who has brought desolations and wonders on the earth.

He makes wars to cease to the end of the earth;
He breaks the bow into pieces and snaps the spear in two;
He burns the chariots with fire.

"Be still and know (recognize, understand) that I am God.
I will be exalted among the nations! I will be exalted in the earth.
The Lord of hosts is with us;
The God of Jacob is our stronghold [our refuge, our high tower].
Selah. (Psalm 46:1-11 AMP)

FRANCIS FRANGIPANE

Beloved, I say, let your fears go, lest they make you fainthearted. Stop inspiring fear in those around you and now take your stand in faith. God has been good and He will continue to manifest His goodness. Let us approach these days expecting to see the goodness of the Lord manifest. Let us be strong and of good courage, for the Lord will fight for us if we stand in faith[115]

HE WHO DWELLS IN THE SHELTER OF THE MOST HIGH,
Will remain secure and rest in the shadow of the Almighty
[whose power no enemy can withstand].
I will say of the Lord, "He is my refuge and my fortress,

---

[115] Marcia Ford quoting Francis Frangipane, Essentials for Life: Your Back to Basics Guide to What Matters Most (New York: Harper Collins Publishers, 2010), 114.

He Is My Refuge And Fortress In The Storm

My God, in whom I trust [with great confidence, and on whom I rely]!"
For He will save you from the trap of the fowler,
And from the deadly pestilence.
He will cover you and completely protect you with His pinions,
and under His wings you will find refuge;
His faithfulness is a shield and a wall.
You will not be afraid of the terror of night,
Nor of the arrow that flies by day,
Nor of the pestilence that stalks in darkness,
Nor of the destruction (sudden death) that lays waste at noon.
A thousand may fall at your side
And ten thousand at your right hand,
But danger will not come near you
You will only [be a spectator as you] look on with your eyes
And witness the [divine] repayment of the wicked [as you watch safely from the shelter of the Most High].
Because you have made the LORD, [who is] my refuge,
Even the Most High, your dwelling place,
No evil will befall you,
Nor will any plague come near your tent
For He will command His angels in regard to you,
To protect and defend and guard you in all your ways [of obedience and service].
They will lift you up in their hands,
So that you do not [even] strike your foot against a stone.
You will tread upon the lion and cobra;
The young lion and the serpent you will trample underfoot.
"Because he set his love on Me, therefore I will save him;
I will set him [securely] on high,
because he knows My name [he confidently trusts and relies on Me,
knowing I will never abandon him, no, never].

"He will call upon Me, and I will answer him;
I will be with him in trouble;
I will rescue him and honor him.
"With a long life I will satisfy him
And I will let him see My salvation." (Psalm 91:1-16 AMP)

> ### ON EAGLE'S WINGS, MICHAEL JONCAS
> You who dwell in the shelter of the Lord, who abide in His shadow for life, say to the Lord: "My refuge, my rock in whom I trust!" And he will raise you up on eagles' wings, bear you on the breath of dawn, make you to shine like the sun, and hold you in the palm of His hand.[116]

I WILL LIFT UP MY EYES TO THE HILLS –
From whence comes my help?
My help comes from the LORD,
Who made heaven and earth.
He will not allow your foot to be moved;
He who keeps you will not slumber.
Behold, He who keeps Israel
Shall neither slumber nor sleep.
The LORD is your keeper;
The LORD is your shade at your right hand.
The sun shall not strike you by day,
Nor the moon by night.
The LORD shall preserve you from all evil;
He shall preserve your soul.
The LORD shall preserve your going out and your coming in
From this time forth, and even forevermore. (Psalm 121:1-8 NKJV)

---

[116] Michael Joncas (composer) (1976 or 1979), Eagle's Wings, Michael Crawford (performer), distributed by OCP Publications, track 4 on On Eagle's Wings, 1998, cassette.

<u>YOU RAISE ME UP, GRAHAM BRENDAN JOSEPH, LOVLAND ROLF</u>

When I am down and, oh my soul, so weary
When troubles come and my heart burdened be
Then, I am still and wait here in the silence
Until You come and sit awhile with me.

You raise me up, so I can stand on mountains
You raise me up, to walk on stormy seas
I am strong, when I am on your shoulders
You raise me up to more than I can be.[117]

THE NAME OF THE LORD IS A STRONG TOWER. The righteous runs into it and is safe. (Proverbs 18:10 NASB)

> ### <u>SOMETIMES REJECTION IS GOD'S PROTECTION</u>

---

[117] Secret Garden, You Raise Me Up, Steven Mercurio (conductor), Brendan Graham (lyricist), Rolf Lovland (orchestrated by), Brian Kennedy and Tracey Campbell-Nation (vocals), distributed by Universal Music AS, Norway, track 2 on Once in a Red Moon, 2002, album.

Chapter 20

PTL

"BELIEVE ME, WOMAN, the time is coming when you Samaritans will worship the Father neither here at this mountain nor there in Jerusalem. You worship guessing in the dark; we Jews worship in the clear light of day. God's way of salvation is made available through the Jews. But the time is coming—it has, in fact, come—when what you're called will not matter and where you go to worship will not matter. "It's who you are and the way you live that count before God ...

Your worship must engage your spirit in the pursuit of truth. That's the kind of people the Father is out looking for: those who are simply and honestly themselves before Him in their worship. God is sheer being itself—Spirit. Those who worship Him must do it out of their very being, their spirits, their true selves, in adoration." John 4:21-24 (Message)

PATTI BURNETT

WHEN GOD TOLD THE ISRAELITES that they should have no other gods before Him, He was serious. In fact, "You shall have no other gods before me" is the first commandment and in probability, the one we break most often. It made sense that the Egyptians would worship other gods; their entire culture and history revolved around the worship of many other gods. But the Israelites? God's chosen people? We are talking about the same people God carried safely through the wilderness and protected from the advancing army of Pharoah. God repeatedly made a way of escape when it appeared that the odds were highly stacked against them.

Much like the Israelites, we place other people, possessions, money, sports figures, jobs, reputations, sex, and great leaders on our podiums of praise. We imitate them, dress like them, and even adopt their hair styles and manners of speech. We name our kids after them.

If all that's not bad enough, we are even more likely to idolize ourselves. Much like our grandchildren, we think the universe revolves around us. And no, you cannot get a pass for idolizing your grandkids. They may be grand, but they're not God.

I wonder if the reason we have all these idols is because we have not positioned our Lord God in His proper place in our lives. The Four Spiritual Laws have been used by Campus Crusade for decades as an evangelical tool for presenting the Gospel to people. The fourth law explains how to receive Christ and place Him on the throne of our lives. Our God is so big that there's no room for other things in that position. He will not share Lordship with any other god.

I remember a professor in Bible college teaching us that our checkbooks told the story of who our gods were. Food? Travel? Fancy Cars? Beautiful Houses? Alimony? Coffee? "No one can serve two masters; for either he will hate the one and love the other, or he will be devoted to one and despise the other. You cannot serve God and wealth" (Matthew 6:24 NASB). We often comment about the things we love; i.e., our dog, that new dress, a song, another person.

And it's okay to be grateful to God for the gifts He bestows on us. But – if those gifts replace the Giver, push Him off the throne of our lives, we can easily become guilty of idolatry.

NOW WHEN THEY DREW NEAR TO JERUSALEM, AND CAME TO BETHPHAGE, at the Mount of Olives, then Jesus sent two disciples, saying to them, "Go into the village opposite you, and immediately you will find a donkey tied, and a colt with her. Loose them and bring them to Me. And if anyone says anything to you, you shall say, 'The Lord has need of them,' and immediately he will send them."

All this was done that it might be fulfilled which was spoken by the prophet, saying:

"Tell the daughter of Zion,
'Behold, your King is coming to you,
Lowly, and sitting on a donkey,
A colt, the foal of a donkey.'"

So the disciples went and did as Jesus commanded them. They brought the donkey and the colt, laid their clothes on them, and set Him on them. And a very great multitude spread their clothes on the road; others cut down branches from the trees and spread them on the road. Then the multitudes who went before and those who followed cried out, saying:

"Hosanna to the Son of David!
'Blessed is He who comes in the name of the LORD!'
Hosanna in the highest!"

And when He had come into Jerusalem, all the city was moved, saying, "Who is this?"
So the multitudes said, "This is Jesus, the prophet from Nazareth of Galilee." (Matthew 21:1-11 NKJV)

> ### THE GLORY OF CHRIST – BEHELD!
> ### CHARLES SPURGEON
> Do I perceive His glory? Have I seen something of the splendor of God in the humble man of Nazareth? Have I learned to magnify Him in my soul, and have I desired to glorify Him in my life, as my God, my life, my love, my all in all, though once despised and rejected of men? … Oh! Let us be astonished at the sovereignty of God, let us be filled with gratitude at His compassion; let us pray that if ever we know something of the glory, we may know more of it day by day, and may set it forth among the sons of men, that they too may by-and-by perceive His glory.[118]

"NOW, THEREFORE, FEAR THE LORD and serve Him in sincerity and truth; and do away with the gods which your fathers served beyond the Euphrates River and in Egypt, and serve the Lord. But if it is disagreeable in your sight to serve the Lord, choose for yourselves today whom you will serve: whether the gods which your fathers served, which were beyond the Euphrates River, or the gods of the Amorites in whose land you are living; but as for me and my house, we will serve the Lord."

The people answered and said, "Far be it from us that we would abandon the Lord to serve other gods; for the Lord our God is He who brought us and our fathers up out of the land of Egypt, from the house of slaves, and did these great signs in our sight and watched over us through all the way in which we went and among all the peoples through whose midst we passed. The Lord drove out from before us all the peoples, even the Amorites who lived in the land. We also will serve the Lord, for He is our God."

Then Joshua said to the people, "You will not be able to serve the Lord, for He is a holy God. He is a jealous God; He will not forgive your

---

[118] Charles Spurgeon, *Sermons on the Gospel of John* (Grand Rapids: Zondervan, 1966), 11.

wrongdoing or your sins. If you abandon the Lord and serve foreign gods, then He will turn and do you harm and destroy you after He has done good to you." And the people said to Joshua, "No, but we will serve the Lord." So Joshua said to the people, "You are witnesses against yourselves that you have chosen for yourselves the Lord, to serve Him." And they said, "We are witnesses." "Now then, do away with the foreign gods which are in your midst, and incline your hearts to the Lord, the God of Israel." And the people said to Joshua, "We will serve the Lord our God and obey His voice." So Joshua made a covenant with the people that day, and made for them a statute and an ordinance in Shechem. And Joshua wrote these words in the Book of the Law of God; and he took a large stone and set it up there under the oak that was by the sanctuary of the Lord. Then Joshua said to all the people, "Behold, this stone shall be a witness against us, because it has heard all the words of the Lord which He spoke to us; so it shall be a witness against you, so that you do not deny your God." Then Joshua dismissed the people, each to his inheritance.

Now it came about after these things that Joshua the son of Nun, the servant of the Lord, died, being 110 years old. And they buried him in the territory of his inheritance, in Timnath-serah, which is in the hill country of Ephraim, on the north of Mount Gaash.

Israel served the Lord all the days of Joshua and all the days of the elders who survived Joshua, and had known every deed of the Lord which He had done for Israel. (Joshua 24:14-31 NASB)

<u>JONI EARECKSON TADA</u>

Whatever troubles are weighing you down, they are featherweight when compared to the glory yet to come.
With a sweep of a prayer and the praise of a child's heart,
God can strip away any cobweb.[119]

---

[119] Gary Schutz, quoting Joni Eareckson Tada, From Victim to Victory (Bloomington: Author Solutions, LLC, 2012) 75.

I WILL EXTOL YOU, O LORD, FOR YOU HAVE LIFTED ME UP,
And have not let my foes rejoice over me.
O Lord my God, I cried out to You,
And You healed me.
O Lord, You brought my soul up from the grave;
You have kept me alive, that I should not go down to the pit.
Sing praise to the Lord, you saints of His,
And give thanks at the remembrance of His holy name.
For His anger is but for a moment,
His favor is for life;
Weeping may endure for a night,
But joy comes in the morning.
Now in my prosperity I said,
"I shall never be moved."
Lord, by Your favor You have made my mountain stand strong;
You hid Your face, and I was troubled.
I cried out to You, O Lord;
And to the Lord I made supplication:
"What profit is there in my blood,
When I go down to the pit?
Will the dust praise You?
Will it declare Your truth?
Hear, O Lord, and have mercy on me;
Lord, be my helper!"
You have turned for me my mourning into dancing;
You have put off my sackcloth and clothed me with gladness,
To the end that my glory may sing praise to You and not be silent.
O Lord my God, I will give thanks to You forever. (Psalm 30:1-12 NKJV)

> ### RICK WARREN
> The deepest level of worship is praising God in spite of pain, trusting Him during a trial, surrendering while suffering, and loving Him when he seems distant.[120]

HAVE MERCY ON ME, O GOD, HAVE MERCY!
I look to You for protection.
I will hide beneath the shadow of Your wings
until the danger passes by.
I cry out to God Most High,
to God who will fulfill His purpose for me.
He will send help from heaven to rescue me,
disgracing those who hound me. Interlude
My God will send forth His unfailing love
and faithfulness.
I am surrounded by fierce lions
who greedily devour human prey—
whose teeth pierce like spears and arrows,
and whose tongues cut like swords.
Be exalted, O God, above the highest heavens!
May Your glory shine over all the earth.
My enemies have set a trap for me.
I am weary from distress.
They have dug a deep pit in my path,
but they themselves have fallen into it.
My heart is confident in You, O God;
my heart is confident.
No wonder I can sing Your praises!
Wake up, my heart!
Wake up, O lyre and harp!

---
[120] Rick Warren, The Purpose Driven Life: What on Earth Am I Here For? (Grand Rapids: Zondervan, 2002), 22.

I will wake the dawn with my song.
I will thank You, Lord, among all the people.
I will sing Your praises among the nations.
For Your unfailing love is as high as the heavens.
Your faithfulness reaches to the clouds.
Be exalted, O God, above the highest heavens.
May Your glory shine over all the earth. (Psalm 57:1-11 NLT)

> ## MATT REDMAN
> We can always find a reason to praise.
> Situations change for better and for worse,
> but God's worth never changes.[121]

BUT AS FOR ME, I WILL SING OF YOUR STRENGTH
For You have been my refuge
And a place of refuge on the day of my distress.
My strength, I will sing praises to You;
For God is my refuge, the God who shows me favor.
(Psalm 59:16-17 NASB)

JAMES MONTGOMERY
Songs of praise the angels sang, Heav'n with alleluias rang, when creation was begun, when God spoke and it was done.[122]

YOU, GOD, ARE MY GOD,
earnestly I seek You;
I thirst for You,
my whole being longs for You,

---

[121] Heather Holleman quoting Matt Redman, Chosen for Christ: Stepping into the Life You've Been Missing (Chicago: Moody Publishers, 2018).

[122] Catholic Church quoting James Montgomery, The Liturgy of the Hours: Advent Season. Christmas Season (Totowa: Catholic Book Publishing, 1975), 389.

in a dry and parched land
 where there is no water.
I have seen You in the sanctuary
 and beheld Your power and Your glory.
Because Your love is better than life,
 my lips will glorify You.
I will praise You as long as I live,
 and in Your name I will lift up my hands.
I will be fully satisfied as with the richest of foods;
 with singing lips my mouth will praise You.
On my bed I remember You;
 I think of You through the watches of the night.
Because You are my help,
 I sing in the shadow of Your wings.
I cling to You;
 Your right hand upholds me.
Those who want to kill me will be destroyed;
 they will go down to the depths of the earth.
They will be given over to the sword
 and become food for jackals.
But the king will rejoice in God;
 all who swear by God will glory in Him,
  while the mouths of liars will be silenced. (Psalm 63:1-11 NIV)

DAVID JEREMIAH

In a sense, we are better prepared to praise God than the angels are, for angels have never known the joy of redemption.[123]

I WILL SING OF THE LORD'S UNFAILING LOVE FOREVER!
Young and old will hear of Your faithfulness.

---

[123] David Jeremiah, from https://quotefancy.com/quote/791947/David-Jeremiah-In-a-sense-we-are-better-prepared-to-praise-God-than-the-angels-are-for.

Your unfailing love will last forever.
Your faithfulness is as enduring as the heavens.
The LORD said, "I have made a covenant with David,
    my chosen servant.
I have sworn this oath to him:
'I will establish your descendants as kings forever;
    they will sit on your throne from now until eternity.'"
All heaven will praise Your great wonders, LORD;
    myriads of angels will praise You for
    Your faithfulness.
For who in all of heaven can compare with the LORD?
What mightiest angel is anything like the LORD?
The highest angelic powers stand in awe of God.
He is far more awesome than all who
    surround His throne.
O LORD God of Heaven's Armies!
Where is there anyone as mighty as You, O LORD?
You are entirely faithful.
You rule the oceans.
You subdue their storm-tossed waves.
You crushed the great sea monster.
You scattered Your enemies with Your mighty arm.
The heavens are Yours, and the earth is Yours;
    everything in the world is Yours—You created it all.
You created north and south.
Mount Tabor and Mount Hermon praise Your name.
Powerful is Your arm!
Strong is Your hand!
Your right hand is lifted high in glorious strength.
Righteousness and justice are the foundation
    of Your throne.
Unfailing love and truth walk before You
    as attendants.
Happy are those who hear the joyful call to worship,

for they will walk in the light of Your presence, LORD.
They rejoice all day long in Your wonderful reputation.
They exult in Your righteousness.
You are their glorious strength.
It pleases You to make us strong.
Yes, our protection comes from the Lord,
    And He, the Holy One of Israel, has given us our king.
Long ago You spoke in a vision to Your faithful people.
You said, "I have raised up a warrior.
I have selected him from the common people
    to be king.
I have found my servant David.
I have anointed him with My holy oil.
I will steady him with My hand;
    with My powerful arm I will make him strong.
His enemies will not defeat him,
    nor will the wicked overpower him.
I will beat down his adversaries before him
    and destroy those who hate him.
My faithfulness and unfailing love will be with him,
    and by My authority he will grow in power.
I will extend his rule over the sea,
    his dominion over the rivers.
And he will call out to Me, 'You are my Father,
    my God, and the Rock of my salvation.'
I will make him My firstborn son,
    the mightiest king on earth.
I will love him and be kind to him forever;
My covenant with him will never end.
I will preserve an heir for him;
    his throne will be as endless as the days of heaven.
But if his descendants forsake My instructions
    and fail to obey My regulations,
    if they do not obey My decrees
    and fail to keep My commands,

> then I will punish their sin with the rod,
>> and their disobedience with beating.
> But I will never stop loving him
>> nor fail to keep My promise to him.
> No, I will not break My covenant;
> I will not take back a single word I said.
> I have sworn an oath to David,
>> and in My holiness I cannot lie:
> His dynasty will go on forever;
>> his kingdom will endure as the sun.
> It will be as eternal as the moon,
>> My faithful witness in the sky!"

(Psalm 89:1-37 NLT)

STORMIE OMARTIAN

In the darkest times of your life, your praise to God should be the loudest. It will not only turn on the floodlights, but it will strengthen your faith and let the enemy know you're not afraid of the dark.[124]

LET ALL THAT I AM PRAISE THE LORD;
> with my whole heart, I will praise His holy name.
> Let all that I am praise the LORD;
>> may I never forget the good things He does for me.
> He forgives all my sins
>> and heals all my diseases.
> He redeems me from death
>> and crowns me with love and tender mercies.
> He fills my life with good things.

---

[124] Stormie Omartian, The Prayer That Changes Everything (Eugene: Harvest House Publishers, 2012), 152.

My youth is renewed like the eagle's!
The LORD gives righteousness
   and justice to all who are treated unfairly.
He revealed his character to Moses
   and His deeds to the people of Israel.
The LORD is compassionate and merciful,
   slow to get angry and filled with unfailing love.
He will not constantly accuse us,
   nor remain angry forever.
He does not punish us for all our sins;
He does not deal harshly with us, as we deserve.
For His unfailing love toward those who fear Him
Is as great as the height of the heavens
Above the earth.
He has removed our sins as far from us
As the east is from the west.
The LORD is like a father to His children,
   tender and compassionate to those who fear Him.
For He knows how weak we are;
He remembers we are only dust.
Our days on earth are like grass;
   like wildflowers, we bloom and die.
The wind blows, and we are gone—
   as though we had never been here.
But the love of the LORD remains forever
   with those who fear Him.
His salvation extends to the children's children
   of those who are faithful to His covenant,
   of those who obey His commandments!
The LORD has made the heavens His throne;
   from there He rules over everything.
Praise the LORD, you angels,
   you mighty ones who carry out His plans,

listening for each of His commands.
Yes, praise the LORD, you armies of angels
    who serve Him and do His will!
Praise the LORD, everything He has created,
    everything in all His kingdom.
Let all that I am praise the LORD.
(Psalm 103:1-22 NLT)

MARTIN LUTHER KING, JR.

I may not be the man I want to be; I may not be the man I ought to be; I may not be the man I could be; I may not be the man I truly can be; but praise God, I'm not the man I once was.[125]

PRAISE THE LORD.
Praise the LORD, you His servants;
    praise the name of the LORD.
Let the name of the LORD be praised,
    both now and forevermore.
From the rising of the sun to the place where it sets,
    the name of the LORD is to be praised.
The LORD is exalted over all the nations,
    His glory above the heavens.
Who is like the LORD our God,
    the One who sits enthroned on high,
who stoops down to look
    on the heavens and the earth?
He raises the poor from the dust
    and lifts the needy from the ash heap;
He seats them with princes,

---

[125] Tim Hansel quoting Martin Luther King, Jr., Holy Sweat (Nashville: W Pub Group, 1989), 55.

with the princes of His people.
He settles the childless woman in her home
    as a happy mother of children.
Praise the Lord. (Psalm 113:1-9 NIV)

AMAZING LOVE/YOU ARE MY KING, NEWSBOYS

    I'm forgiven because You were forsaken
    I'm accepted, You were condemned
    I'm alive and well, Your Spirit is within me
    Because You died and rose again

    Amazing love, how can it be
    That You, my King, should die for me?
    Amazing love, I know it's true
    It's my joy to honor You
    In all I do, to honor You[126]

O ISRAEL, TRUST IN THE LORD;

He is their help and their shield.
O house of Aaron, trust in the Lord;
He is their help and their shield.
You who fear the Lord, trust in the Lord;
He is their help and their shield.

The Lord has been mindful of us;
He will bless us;
He will bless the house of Israel;
He will bless the house of Aaron.
He will bless those who fear the Lord,
Both small and great.

---

[126] Billy James Foote (writer), You are My King (Amazing Love), originally released by Phillips, Craig & Dean on Let My Words be Few (2001), then released by Newsboys on Adoration: The Worship Album (2003).

May the Lord give you increase more and more,
You and your children.
May you be blessed by the Lord,
Who made heaven and earth.
The heaven, even the heavens, are the Lord's;
But the earth He has given to the children of men.

The dead do not praise the Lord,
Nor any who go down into silence.
But we will bless the Lord
From this time forth and forevermore.
Praise the Lord! (Psalm 115:9-18 NKJV)

HOLY IS THE LORD, CHRIS TOMLIN

We stand and lift up our hands
For the joy of the Lord is our strength
We bow down and worship Him now
How great, how awesome is He
And together we sing
Holy is the Lord God Almighty
The earth is filled with His glory
Holy is the Lord God Almighty
The earth is filled with His glory[127]

THANK YOU! EVERYTHING IN ME SAYS "THANK YOU!"

    Angels listen as I sing my thanks.
I kneel in worship facing Your holy temple
    and say it again: "Thank You!"
Thank You for your love,
    thank You for Your faithfulness;

---

[127] Chris Tomlin, Holy is the Lord, distributed by Sixsteps/Sparrow, Arriving, 2004, album.

Most holy is Your name,
> most holy is Your Word.

The moment I called out, You stepped in;
> You made my life large with strength.

When they hear what You have to say, God,
> all earth's kings will say "Thank You."

They'll sing of what You've done
> "How great the glory of God!"

And here's why: God, high above, sees far below;
> no matter the distance, He knows everything about us.

When I walk into the thick of trouble,
> keep me alive in the angry turmoil.

With one hand
> strike my foes,

With Your other hand
> save me.

Finish what you started in me, God. Your love is eternal—
> don't quit on me now.

(Psalm 138:1-8 Message)

A.W. TOZER
Go to church once a week and nobody pays attention. Worship God seven days a week and you become strange.[128]

I WILL EXTOL YOU, MY GOD, O KING;
And I will bless Your name forever and ever.
Every day I will bless you,
And I will praise your name forever and ever.

---

[128] Lauren Barlow quoting Aiden Wilson Tozer, *Inspired by Tozer: 59 Artists, Writers and Leaders Share the Insight and Passion They've Gained from A.W. Tozer* (Raleigh, Regal, 2011), 142.

CHRONIC HOPE

Great is the Lord, and greatly to be praised;
And His greatness is unsearchable.

One generation shall praise Your works to another,
And shall declare Your mighty acts.
I will meditate on the glorious splendor of Your majesty,
And on Your wondrous works.
Men shall speak of the might of Your awesome acts,
And I will declare Your greatness.
They shall utter the memory of Your great goodness,
And shall sing of Your righteousness.

The Lord is gracious and full of compassion,
Slow to anger and great in mercy.
The Lord is good to all,
And His tender mercies are over all His works.

All Your works shall praise You, O Lord,
And Your saints shall bless You.
They shall speak of the glory of Your kingdom,
And talk of Your power,
To make known to the sons of men His mighty acts,
And the glorious majesty of His kingdom.
Your kingdom is an everlasting kingdom,
And Your dominion endures throughout all generations.
The Lord upholds all who fall,
And raises up all who are bowed down.
The eyes of all look expectantly to You,
And You give them their food in due season.
You open Your hand
And satisfy the desire of every living thing.

The LORD is righteous in all His ways,
Gracious in all His works.
The LORD is near to all who call upon Him,
To all who call upon Him in truth.
He will fulfill the desire of those who fear Him;
He also will hear their cry and save them.
The LORD preserves all who love Him,
But all the wicked He will destroy.
My mouth shall speak the praise of the LORD,
And all flesh shall bless His holy name
Forever and ever. (Psalm 145:1-21 NKJV)

> ### *FRANCIS CHAN*
> Isn't it a comfort to worship a God we cannot exaggerate?[129]

THEN THE MYSTERY WAS REVEALED TO DANIEL in a night vision. Then Daniel blessed the God of heaven; Daniel said,
"Let the name of God be blessed forever and ever,
For wisdom and power belong to Him.
"It is He who changes the times and the epochs;
He removes kings and establishes kings;
He gives wisdom to wise men
And knowledge to men of understanding.
"It is He who reveals the profound and hidden things;
He knows what is in the darkness,
And the light dwells with Him.
"To You, O God of my fathers, I give thanks and praise,
For You have given me wisdom and power;
Even now You have made known to me what we requested of You,

---

[129] Francis Chan, Forgotten God: Reversing Our Tragic Neglect of the Holy Spirit (Colorado Springs: David C. Cook, 2014), 179.

For You have made known to us the king's matter." (Daniel 2:19-23 NASB)

RICK WARREN

Happy moments, PRAISE GOD. Difficult moments, SEEK GOD. Quiet moments, WORSHIP GOD. Painful moments, TRUST GOD. Every moment, THANK GOD.[130]

---

[130] Mike Beck quoting Rick Warren, Living in a Body. Mike Beck quoting Rick Warren, Living in a Body with a Mind of Its Own (Bloomington: AuthorHouse, 2013), 87.

Chapter 21

IT TAKES THE BODY OF CHRSIT

IN THIS WAY we are like the various parts of a human. Each part gets its meaning from the body as a whole, not the other way around. The body we're talking about is Christ's body of chosen people. Each of us finds our meaning and function as a part of His body. But as a chopped-off finger or cut-off toe, we wouldn't amount to much, would we? So, since we find ourselves fashioned into all these excellently formed and marvelously functioning parts in Christ's body, let's just go ahead and be what we were made to be, without enviously or pridefully comparing ourselves with each other, or trying to be something we aren't. (Romans12:4-7 Message)

PATTI BURNETT

WE WERE NEVER MEANT to walk this path of life alone. As believers, we are each given spiritual gifts to exercise within the framework of the Body of Christ. Each member is necessary for the Body to function effectively; and if a gift is missing, the whole Body suffers. I find it interesting and comforting that 1 Corinthians 12 says that the weaker parts of the Body are just as necessary as the other parts and that we should honor those parts that are less presentable. We are warned to diligently maintain unity and faithfully care for each other.

"And if one part of the body suffers, all the parts suffer with it; if a part is honored, all the parts rejoice with it" (1 Corinthians 12:26 NASB). I have noticed that at times when my knee hurts, it can cause problems in my hip, foot, or even neck. Recently I broke both baby toes, with no mechanism of injury, at least none that I could recall. In other words, I have no idea how it happened. After a few months of hobbling around with crutches, my lower back started acting up too, which of course sent shooting nerve pain all the way down my leg. I hate it when the toe bone is connected to the … clap … back bone.

For a reason unknown to me, Parkinson's tends to exacerbate pain intensity and duration. The National Institute of Health researchers reported that "Compared to the general population of similar age, PD patients suffer from a significantly higher level and prevalence of pain… The types of chronic pain are musculoskeletal, cystonic (dystonic), nerve, primary, akathitic (restlessness needing movement), and gastrointestinal pain."

There are times when it feels as though every part of my body has issues. It can be difficult to assess which of the following culprits is to blame.

- Parkinson's
- Side effect of medications
- Injury

- Inactivity
- Non-motor co-morbidities
- Poor decision making
- Just growing older

However, if I can pay special attention to a painful part, perhaps doing yoga to decrease rigidity, it will often positively affect other body systems and functions.

Back to the toe bone connected to the backbone. I had an MRI a few years ago and … the envelope please. I had badly degenerated disk disease and stenosis (narrowing or constriction) in my lumbar region (my lower back.) The other concern was the 8x10mm cyst at L4-L5.

I made the unfortunate decision to open this information from my patient portal just prior to bedtime. This was not wise bedtime reading. I journaled for a while, hoping that by giving it to the Lord I would be able to sleep. Such was not the case. My mind raced with the fear of yet again imposing upon the Body of Christ. How would at least one and possibly two surgeries impact those who often helped with meals and transportation? Who would pick up one month old baby girl Emerson when her nap was over? Who would make sure that Maverick had enough snacks? Who would play trash trucks and fire trucks with Noah, and who would tell Jax stories as he fell asleep? It is humbling to ask family, friends, and prayer chains to help us out even one more time.

We should share in each other's successes and celebrations just as much as we should commiserate with each other's failures and tragedies. The phrase "I feel your pain" is often used flippantly; and yet, within the Body of Christ, this is in fact a mandate. If we truly function as a Body, we will feel each other's pain and we will help to carry each other's burdens.

Patti, I am allowing these maladies for a reason unknown to you. It's My desire to continue molding and shaping you into something unrecognizably beautiful and resembling My Son. I want others to see how the Body of Christ springs into action when there is an intense need. Sincerely, God

Father, it's me again. It's my prayer that you will cause all things to work in harmony for the furtherance of Your Kingdom. Replace my pain with joy. Where I once complained and whined give me the supernatural ability to find contentment and overwhelming comfort in the fact that nothing touches me without Your knowledge. I worship You, Lord. Sincerely, Patti

THEY WERE CONTINUALLY DEVOTING THEMSELVES to the Apostles' teaching and to fellowship, to the breaking of bread and to prayer.

Everyone kept feeling a sense of awe; and many wonders and signs were taking place through the apostles. And all the believers were together and had all things in common; and they would sell their property and possessions and share them with all, to the extent that anyone had need. Day by day continuing with one mind in the temple, and breaking bread from house to house, they were taking their meals together with gladness and sincerity of heart, praising God and having favor with all the people. And the Lord was adding to their number day by day those who were being saved. (Acts 2:42-47 NASB)

> ### THE COST OF DISCIPLESHIP, DIETRICH BONHOEFFER
> The temple of God is the holy people in Jesus Christ. The Body of Christ is the living temple of God and of the new humanity.[131]

---

[131] Dietrich Bonhoeffer, The Cost of Discipleship - For the 21st Century (Morrisville: Lulu Press, 2020). 276.

THEREFORE I URGE YOU, BROTHERS AND SISTERS, by the mercies of God, to present your bodies as a living and holy sacrifice, acceptable to God, which is your spiritual service of worship. And do not be conformed to this world, but be transformed by the renewing of your mind, so that you may prove what the will of God is, that which is good and acceptable and perfect.

For through the grace given to me I say to everyone among you not to think more highly of himself than he ought to think; but to think so as to have sound judgment, as God has allotted to each a measure of faith. For just as we have many parts in one body and all the body's parts do not have the same function, so we, who are many, are one body in Christ, and individually parts of one another. However, since we have gifts that differ according to the grace given to us, each of us is to use them properly: if prophecy, in proportion to one's faith; if service, in the act of serving; or the one who teaches, in the act of teaching; or the one who exhorts, in the work of exhortation; the one who gives, with generosity; the one who is in leadership, with diligence; the one who shows mercy, with cheerfulness.

Love must be free of hypocrisy. Detest what is evil; cling to what is good. Be devoted to one another in brotherly love; give preference to one another in honor, not lagging behind in diligence, fervent in spirit, serving the Lord; rejoicing in hope, persevering in tribulation, devoted to prayer, contributing to the needs of the saints, practicing hospitality.

Bless those who persecute you; bless and do not curse. Rejoice with those who rejoice, and weep with those who weep. Be of the same mind toward one another; do not be haughty in mind, but associate with the lowly. Do not be wise in your own estimation. Never repay evil for evil to anyone. Respect what is right in the sight of all people. If possible, so far as it depends on you, be at peace with all people. Never take your own revenge, beloved, but leave room for the wrath of God, for it is written: "Vengeance is Mine, I will repay," says the Lord. "But if your enemy is hungry, feed him; if he is thirsty, give him a drink; for in so doing you will heap burning coals on his head." Do not be overcome by evil, but overcome evil with good. (Romans 12:1-21 NASB)

> ### *MOTHER TERESA*
> I know I am touching the living body of Christ
> in the broken bodies of the hungry and the suffering.[132]

THOSE OF US WHO ARE STRONG and able in the faith need to step in and lend a hand to those who falter, and not just do what is most convenient for us. Strength is for service, not status. Each one of us needs to look after the good of the people around us, asking ourselves, "How can I help?"

That's exactly what Jesus did. He didn't make it easy for Himself by avoiding people's troubles, but waded right in and helped out. "I took on the troubles of the troubled," is the way Scripture puts it. Even if it was written in Scripture long ago, you can be sure it's written for us. God wants the combination of His steady, constant calling and warm, personal counsel in Scripture to come to characterize us, keeping us alert for whatever He will do next. May our dependably steady and warmly personal God develop maturity in you so that you get along with each other as well as Jesus gets along with us all. Then we'll be a choir—not our voices only, but our very lives singing in harmony in a stunning anthem to the God and Father of our Master Jesus!

So reach out and welcome one another to God's glory. Jesus did it; now you do it! Jesus, staying true to God's purposes, reached out in a special way to the Jewish insiders so that the old ancestral promises would come true for them. As a result, the non-Jewish outsiders have been able to experience mercy and to show appreciation to God.

---

[132]Mother Teresa, The Pope Speaks 2004 - Volume 49 (Huntington: Our Sunday Visitor, Inc., 2004), 108.

Just think of all the Scriptures that will come true in what we do! For instance:

> Then I'll join outsiders in a hymn-sing;
> I'll sing to Your name!
> And this one:
> Outsiders and insiders, rejoice together!
> And again:
> People of all nations, celebrate God!
> All colors and races, give hearty praise!
> And Isaiah's word:
> There's the root of our ancestor Jesse,
> breaking through the earth and growing tree tall,
> Tall enough for everyone everywhere to see and take hope!

Oh! May the God of green hope fill you up with joy, fill you up with peace, so that your believing lives, filled with the life-giving energy of the Holy Spirit, will brim over with hope!

Personally, I've been completely satisfied with who you are and what you are doing. You seem to me to be well-motivated and well-instructed, quite capable of guiding and advising one another. So, my dear friends, don't take my rather bold and blunt language as criticism. It's not criticism. I'm simply underlining how very much I need your help in carrying out this highly focused assignment God gave me, this priestly and gospel work of serving the spiritual needs of the non-Jewish outsiders so they can be presented as an acceptable offering to God, made whole and holy by God's Holy Spirit.

Looking back over what has been accomplished and what I have observed, I must say I am most pleased—in the context of Jesus, I'd even say proud, but only in that context. I have no interest in giving you a chatty account of my adventures, only the wondrously powerful and transformingly present words and deeds of Christ in me that triggered a believing response among the outsiders. In such ways I have trailblazed a preaching of the Message of Jesus all the way from Jerusalem far into northwestern Greece. This has all been pioneer work, bringing the Message only into those places where Jesus was not yet known and worshiped. My text has been,

> Those who were never told of Him—
>   They'll see Him!
> Those who've never heard of Him—
>   They'll get the message!

And that's why it has taken me so long to finally get around to coming to you. But now that there is no more pioneering work to be done in these parts, and since I have looked forward to seeing you for many years, I'm planning my visit. I'm headed for Spain, and expect to stop off on the way to enjoy a good visit with you, and eventually have you send me off with God's blessing.

First, though, I'm going to Jerusalem to deliver a relief offering to the followers of Jesus there. The Greeks—all the way from the Macedonians in the north to the Achaians in the south—decided they wanted to take up a collection for the poor among the believers in Jerusalem. They were happy to do this, but it was also their duty. Seeing that they got in on all the spiritual gifts that flowed out of the Jerusalem community so generously, it is only right that they do what they can to relieve their poverty. As soon as I have done this—personally handed over this "fruit basket"—I'm off to Spain, with a stopover with you in Rome. My hope is that my visit with you is going to be one of Christ's more extravagant blessings.

I have one request, dear friends: Pray for me. Pray strenuously with and for me—to God the Father, through the power of our Master Jesus, through the love of the Spirit—that I will be delivered from the lions' den of unbelievers in Judea. Pray also that my relief offering to the Jerusalem believers will be accepted in the spirit in which it is given. Then, God willing, I'll be on my way to you with a light and eager heart, looking forward to being refreshed by your company. God's peace be with all of you. Oh, yes! (Romans 15:1-33 Message)

> ### COFFEE SHOP DEVOS: DAILY DEVOTIONAL PICK-ME-UP FOR TEEN GIRLS, TESSA EMILY HALL
> "He's not going to applaud us for becoming famous during our lifetimes; He's going to ask us how we used our spotlight to bring Him glory. He's not going to ask us how many trophies and awards we received; He's going to ask us how we used our gifts to build the body of Christ."[133]

NOW CONCERNING SPIRITUAL GIFTS. BRETHREN, I DO NOT WANT YOU TO BE UNAWARE. You know that when you were pagans, you were led astray to the mute idols, however you were led. Therefore I make known to you that no one speaking by the Spirit of God says, "Jesus is accursed"; and no one can say, "Jesus is Lord," except by the Holy Spirit.

Now there are varieties of gifts, but the same Spirit. And there are varieties of ministries, and the same Lord. There are varieties of effects, but the same God who works all things in all persons. But to each one is given the manifestation of the Spirit for the common good. For to one is given the word of wisdom through the Spirit, and to another the word of knowledge according to the same Spirit; to another faith by the same Spirit, and to another gifts of healing by the one Spirit, and to another the effecting of miracles, and to another prophecy, and to another the distinguishing of spirits, to another various kinds of tongues, and to another the interpretation of tongues. But one and the

---

[133] Tessa Emily Hall, Coffee Shop Devos: Daily Devotional Pick-Me-Ups for Teen Girls (Bloomington: Bethany House Publishers, 2018).

same Spirit works all these things, distributing to each one individually just as He wills.

For even as the body is one and yet has many members, and all the members of the body, though they are many, are one body, so also is Christ. For by one Spirit we were all baptized into one body, whether Jews or Greeks, whether slaves or free, and we were all made to drink of one Spirit.

For the body is not one member, but many. If the foot says, "Because I am not a hand, I am not a part of the body," it is not for this reason any the less a part of the body. And if the ear says, "Because I am not an eye, I am not a part of the body," it is not for this reason any the less a part of the body. If the whole body were an eye, where would the hearing be? If the whole were hearing, where would the sense of smell be? But now God has placed the members, each one of them, in the body, just as He desired. If they were all one member, where would the body be? But now there are many members, but one body. And the eye cannot say to the hand, "I have no need of you"; or again the head to the feet, "I have no need of you." On the contrary, it is much truer that the members of the body which seem to be weaker are necessary; and those members of the body which we deem less honorable, on these we bestow more abundant honor, and our less presentable members become much more presentable, whereas our more presentable members have no need of it. But God has so composed the body, giving more abundant honor to that member which lacked, so that there may be no division in the body, but that the members may have the same care for one another. And if one member suffers, all the members suffer with it; if one member is honored, all the members rejoice with it.

Now you are Christ's body, and individually members of it. And God has appointed in the church, first apostles, second prophets, third teachers, then miracles, then gifts of healings, helps, administrations, various kinds of tongues. All are not apostles, are they? All are not prophets, are they? All are not teachers, are they? All are not workers of miracles, are they? All do not have gifts of healings, do they? All do not speak with tongues, do they? All do not interpret, do they? But earnestly desire the greater gifts. And I show you a still more excellent way. (1 Corinthians 12:1-31 NASB)

> **UNDERSTANDING YOUR BLESSINGS IN CHRIST: EPHESIANS, ELIZABETH GEORGE**
> Our conduct is an advertisement for or against Jesus Christ. That's why unity in the body of Christ is so important."[134]

BUT TO EACH ONE OF US GRACE WAS GIVEN according to the measure of Christ's gift. Therefore it says,

"When He ascended on high,
He led captive the captives,
and He gave gifts to people."

(Now this expression, "He ascended," what does it mean except that He also had descended into the lower parts of the earth? He who descended is Himself also He who ascended far above all the heavens, so that He might fill all things.) And He gave some as apostles, some as prophets, some as evangelists, some as pastors and teachers, for the equipping of the saints for the work of ministry, for the building up of the body of Christ; until we all attain to the unity of the faith, and of the knowledge of the Son of God, to a mature man, to the measure of the stature which belongs to the fullness of Christ. As a result, we are no longer to be children, tossed here and there by waves and carried about by every wind of doctrine, by the trickery of people, by craftiness in deceitful scheming; but speaking the truth in love, we are to grow up in all aspects into Him who is the head, that is, Christ, from whom the whole body, being fitted and held together by what every joint supplies,

---
[134]Elizabeth George, Understanding your Blessings in Christ: Ephesians, (Eugene: Harvest House Publishers, 2008), 71.

according to the proper working of each individual part, causes the growth of the body for the building up of itself in love.

So I say this, and affirm in the Lord, that you are to no longer walk just as the Gentiles also walk, in the futility of their minds, being darkened in their understanding, excluded from the life of God because of the ignorance that is in them, because of the hardness of their heart; and they, having become callous, have given themselves up to indecent behavior for the practice of every kind of impurity with greediness. But you did not learn Christ in this way, if indeed you have heard Him and have been taught in Him, just as truth is in Jesus, that, in reference to your former way of life, you are to rid yourselves of the old self, which is being corrupted in accordance with the lusts of deceit, and that you are to be renewed in the spirit of your minds, and to put on the new self, which in the likeness of God has been created in righteousness and holiness of the truth.

Therefore, ridding yourselves of falsehood, speak truth each one of you with his neighbor, because we are parts of one another. Be angry, and yet do not sin; do not let the sun go down on your anger, and do not give the devil an opportunity. The one who steals must no longer steal; but rather he must labor, producing with his own hands what is good, so that he will have something to share with the one who has need. Let no unwholesome word come out of your mouth, but if there is any good word for edification according to the need of the moment, say that, so that it will give grace to those who hear. Do not grieve the Holy Spirit of God, by whom you were sealed for the day of redemption. All bitterness, wrath, anger, clamor, and slander must be removed from you, along with all malice. Be kind to one another, compassionate, forgiving each other, just as God in Christ also has forgiven you. (Ephesians 4:7-32 NASB)

> ### **GREG GORDON**
> The hordes of demonic activity at times can take advantage of those who are wounded by others in the body of Christ. When we allow any hurt, we can be used of the enemy to sow discord into God's work and His body.[135]

SO THEN, MY BELOVED, JUST AS YOU HAVE ALWAYS OBEYED, not in my presence only, but now much more in my absence, work out your own salvation with fear and trembling; for it is God who is at work in you, both to desire and to work for His good pleasure.

Do all things without complaining or arguments; so that you will prove yourselves to be blameless and innocent, children of God above reproach in the midst of a crooked and perverse generation, among whom you appear as lights in the world, holding firmly the word of life, so that on the day of Christ I can take pride because I did not run in vain nor labor in vain. But even if I am being poured out as a drink offering upon the sacrifice and service of your faith, I rejoice and share my joy with you all. You too, I urge you, rejoice in the same way and share your joy with me.

But I hope, in the Lord Jesus, to send Timothy to you shortly, so that I also may be encouraged when I learn of your condition. For I have no one else of kindred spirit who will genuinely be concerned for your welfare. For they all seek after their own interests, not those of Christ Jesus. But you know of his proven character, that he served with me in the furtherance of the gospel like a child serving his father. Therefore I hope to send him immediately, as soon as I see how things go with me; and I trust in the Lord that I myself will also be coming shortly. But I thought it necessary to send to you Epaphroditus, my brother and

---

[135] Greg Gordon , Founder of SermonIndex.net, Author of The Following of Christ (Rome, Aeterna Press, 2015), from https://www.goodreads.com/quotes/7046033-the-hordes-of-demonic-activity-at-times-can-take-advantage

fellow worker and fellow soldier, who is also your messenger and minister to my need, because he was longing for you all and was distressed because you had heard that he was sick. For indeed he was sick to the point of death, but God had mercy on him, and not only on him but also on me, so that I would not have sorrow upon sorrow. Therefore I have sent him all the more eagerly, so that when you see him again you may rejoice and I may be less concerned about you. Receive him then in the Lord with all joy, and hold people like him in high regard, because he came close to death for the work of Christ, risking his life to compensate for your absence in your service to me. (Philippians 2:12-30 NASB)

> ### *WILL DAVIS JR.*
> Give other Christians permission to be different from you. You're not the only Christ-follower in the world, and neither are you the most committed. Your way of loving Jesus is neither the only way or the best. If you don't know that, your Christian world is way too small.[136]

THE SAME GOES FOR YOU WIVES: be good wives to your husbands, responsive to their needs. There are husbands who, indifferent as they are to any words about God, will be captivated by your life of holy beauty. What matters is not your outer appearance—the styling of your hair, the jewelry you wear, the cut of your clothes—but your inner disposition.

Cultivate inner beauty, the gentle, gracious kind that God delights in. The holy women of old were beautiful before God that way, and were good, loyal wives to their husbands. Sarah, for instance, taking care of Abraham, would address him as "my dear husband." You'll be true daughters of Sarah if you do the same, unanxious and unintimidated.

---

[136] Will Davis Jr., 10 Things Jesus Never Said and Why You Should Stop Believing Them (Ada: Revell, 2011), 101.

The same goes for you husbands: Be good husbands to your wives. Honor them, delight in them. As women they lack some of your advantages. But in the new life of God's grace, you're equals. Treat your wives, then, as equals so your prayers don't run aground.

Summing up: be agreeable, be sympathetic, be loving, be compassionate, be humble. That goes for all of you, no exceptions. No retaliation. No sharp-tongued sarcasm. Instead, bless—that's your job, to bless. You'll be a blessing and also get a blessing.

> Whoever wants to embrace life,
>> and see the day fill up with good,
> Here's what you do:
>> Say nothing evil or hurtful;
> Snub evil and cultivate good;
>> run after peace for all you're worth.
> God looks on all this with approval,
>> listening and responding well to what He's asked;
> But he turns his back
>> on those who do evil things.

If with heart and soul you're doing good, do you think you can be stopped? Even if you suffer for it, you're still better off. Don't give the opposition a second thought. Through thick and thin, keep your hearts at attention, in adoration before Christ, your Master. Be ready to speak up and tell anyone who asks why you're living the way you are, and always with the utmost courtesy. Keep a clear conscience before God so that when people throw mud at you, none of it will stick. They'll end up realizing that they're the ones who need a bath. It's better to suffer for doing good, if that's what God wants, then to be punished for doing bad. That's what Christ did definitively: suffered because of others' sins, the Righteous One for the unrighteous ones. He went through it all—was put to death and then made alive—to bring us to God.

He went and proclaimed God's salvation to earlier generations who ended up in the prison of judgment because they wouldn't listen. You know, even though God waited patiently all the days that Noah built his ship, only a few were saved then, eight to be exact—saved from the water by the water. The waters of baptism do that for you, not by washing away dirt from your skin but by presenting you through Jesus' resurrection before God with a clear conscience. Jesus has the last wise word on everything and everyone, from angels to armies. He's standing right alongside God, and what he says goes. (I Peter 3:1-22 Message)

> ### C.S. LEWIS
> For the church is not a human society of people united by their natural affinities but the Body of Christ, in which all members, however different, (and He rejoices in their differences and by no means wishes to iron them out) must share the common life, complementing and helping one another precisely by their differences[137]

STAY ON GOOD TERMS WITH EACH OTHER, held together by love. Be ready with a meal or a bed when it's needed. Why, some have extended hospitality to angels without ever knowing it! Regard prisoners as if you were in prison with them. Look on victims of abuse as if what happened to them had happened to you. Honor marriage, and guard the sacredness of sexual intimacy between wife and husband. God draws a firm line against casual and illicit sex.

Don't be obsessed with getting more material things. Be relaxed with what you have. Since God assured us, "I'll never let you down, never walk off and leave you," we can boldly quote,

---

[137] C.S. Lewis, Yours, Jack: Spiritual Direction from C.S. Lewis (San Francisco: HarperOne, 2008), 151.

God is there, ready to help;
I'm fearless no matter what.
Who or what can get to me?

Appreciate your pastoral leaders who gave you the Word of God. Take a good look at the way they live, and let their faithfulness instruct you, as well as their truthfulness. There should be a consistency that runs through us all. For Jesus doesn't change—yesterday, today, tomorrow, he's always totally Himself.

Don't be lured away from Him by the latest speculations about Him. The grace of Christ is the only good ground for life. Products named after Christ don't seem to do much for those who buy them.

The altar from which God gives us the gift of Himself is not for exploitation by insiders who grab and loot. In the old system, the animals are killed and the bodies disposed of outside the camp. The blood is then brought inside to the altar as a sacrifice for sin. It's the same with Jesus. He was crucified outside the city gates—that is where He poured out the sacrificial blood that was brought to God's altar to cleanse His people.

So let's go outside, where Jesus is, where the action is—not trying to be privileged insiders, but taking our share in the abuse of Jesus. This "insider world" is not our home. We have our eyes peeled for the City about to come. Let's take our place outside with Jesus, no longer pouring out the sacrificial blood of animals but pouring out sacrificial praises from our lips to God in Jesus' name.

Make sure you don't take things for granted and go slack in working for the common good; share what you have with others. God takes particular pleasure in acts of worship—a different kind of "sacrifice"—that take place in kitchen and workplace and on the streets.

Be responsive to your pastoral leaders. Listen to their counsel. They are alert to the condition of your lives and work under the strict supervision of God. Contribute to the joy of their leadership, not its drudgery. Why would you want to make things harder for them?

Pray for us. We have no doubts about what we're doing or why, but it's hard going and we need your prayers. All we care about is living well before God. Pray that we may be together soon.

> May God, who puts all things together,
>   makes all things whole,
> Who made a lasting mark through the sacrifice of Jesus,
>   the sacrifice of blood that sealed the eternal covenant,
> Who led Jesus, our Great Shepherd,
>   up and alive from the dead,
> Now put you together, provide you
>   with everything you need to please Him,
> Make us into what gives Him most pleasure,
>   by means of the sacrifice of Jesus, the Messiah.
> All glory to Jesus forever and always!
>   Oh, yes, yes, yes.

Friends, please take what I've written most seriously. I've kept this as brief as possible; I haven't piled on a lot of extras. You'll be glad to know that Timothy has been let out of prison. If he leaves soon, I'll come with him and get to see you myself.

Say hello to your pastoral leaders and all the congregations. Everyone here in Italy wants to be remembered to you.

Grace be with you, everyone. (Hebrews 13:1-25 Message)

Chapter 22

THE GREATEST OF THESE IS LOVE

THEREFORE, ENCOURAGE ONE ANOTHER and build one another up, just as you also are doing. But we ask you, brothers and sisters, to recognize those who diligently labor among you and are in leadership over you in the Lord, and give you instruction, and that you regard them very highly in love because of their work. Live in peace with one another. We urge you, brothers and sisters, admonish the unruly, encourage the fainthearted, help the weak, be patient with everyone. See that no one repays another with evil for evil, but always seek what is good for one another and for all people. (1 Thessalonians 5:11-15 NASB)

PATTI BURNETT

I HAD THE PRIVILEGE of hearing Joni Erickson Tada speak at a Young Life Convention years ago. I will forever marvel at her beautiful smile and the power of the Resurrected Christ, who reveals Himself so beautifully through her twisted body. I remember her saying that she would never trade in her wheelchair and quadriplegic frame for an uninjured version if it meant one less person knowing Jesus. What wondrous love! Can you imagine the difficulty and frustration of living in a body that does not move?

While not nearly as crippling as paralysis, Parkinson's (PD) is a progressive neurologic disease. My dream of growing old gracefully dissolved into the atmosphere of the neurologist's office when I received that diagnosis.

People with Parkinson's tend to have a body riddled with rigidity and slow movement initially. However, after a number of years on Levodopa medication, a person can develop dyskinesias, which are involuntary, erratic, writhing movements of the face, arms, legs, or trunk. They can be smooth and almost dance-like or they may involve rapid jerking or extended muscle spasms.

As is true for most people with Parkinson's, my body doesn't work well, but I'm grateful for not having some of the less tolerable PD symptoms. When I first wrote this, I was nursing an extremely painful SI nerve that radiated down to my ankle; and I had a series of pain mitigating injections. It appears now that the pain is gone, and I may not need surgery. The best news of all is that it's probably not dystonia, a Parkinson's symptom that cannot be fixed with surgery or an injection.

My most recent symptom has been Burning Mouth Syndrome (BMS.) Almost 24-7 my tongue, teeth, lips, and gums are tingly, swollen, and painful. I get a metallic or rubbery taste and I can't stop licking my lips because my gums stick to my teeth. My teeth feel like they're going to fall out and I am worried about ruining tooth enamel. It's a nearly intolerable condition.

Visits with my Dentist, ENT, Gastroenterologist, Thoracic Surgeon, Pulmonologist, Nephrologist, Movement Disorder Specialist, Chiropractor, Physical Therapist and GP have not proved beneficial. Even appointments with a Mayo Clinic oral dermatologist brought no answers.

My most recent appointment was with the Thoracic surgeon. He confirmed that I have a hiatal hernia – basically a portion of my stomach has worked its way up through my diaphragm and it is causing many symptoms; but the most disturbing is the presence of acid in my mouth.

The concerning part of this story is that I had numerous tests performed by a Gastro Enterologist two and a half years ago. One of those tests was wireless reflux monitoring. It indicated that I had a total distal esophageal acid exposure of 13.1%. Normal individuals maintain an esophageal pH a little above 4%. My Thoracic surgeon was the one who brought these test results to our attention. We should have been notified two and a half years ago. Not only would I possibly not have had BMS for 1 ½ years, but that much acid could cause esophageal cancer. It can also lead to inflammation, bleeding and ulcers.

They ran a few more tests and then I had surgery two weeks ago. Wish I could tell you that the hiatal surgery made all the difference but I'd be lying. It could be that the jury's still out since I still have quite a bit of healing to do. I pray that the issue would be resolved and that I could live a little more normal life. I'm sure this is a common mantra for PPD (People with Parkinson's.)

I wrote in my journal last night that I want my life to be characterized by gratitude, contentment – and NO WHINING!

As I was biking around Lake Dillon last summer, God brought to my mind the Bible passage where the Apostle Paul mentions that our bodies are the temple of the Holy Spirit. How bazaar that His plan would include a member of the Triune Deity living inside of me. I felt ashamed and humbled that I would criticize God's house. I have friends who have ministries to very poor people and have chosen to live in their neighborhoods, to better identify with them. Isn't that part of the reason that God chose to live in our bodies? So that we could more effectively share the gospel with others who have similar challenges in their lives.

I spoke with a woman recently diagnosed with PD who is seriously depressed. In a moment of weakness and vulnerability she stated that she would take her own life rather than live as an invalid, shaking, hunched over, slurring her speech, and humiliated by cognitive decline. Lord, speak words of life and hope to this dearly beloved of Yours.

In many passages, the Bible states that we should anticipate suffering in our lives as Christians. Jesus sweated agonizing drops of blood when He pleaded with God to take this cup of torture from Him. He was whipped and beaten beyond recognition. Our Lord stumbled up Calvary's hill and was humbled to the point of death – death on a cross. The word excruciating is derived from the word crucifixion, and it was one of the slowest, most painful methods of killing.

That's the path Jesus chose so that we could be redeemed or freed from our bondage to sin. He made the ultimate sacrifice – all because He loved you and me. In my painstaking edit of this manuscript, I worked on this particular chapter two years in a row over Easter. What the Father God did by sending His Son to die, so that I could have eternal life, is incomprehensible.

Jesus' entire purpose in coming to earth as a man was to take upon Himself human disease, human sin, and human pain and suffering. He never looked down His nose at a person, no matter their level of sin or disease. He loved every single one He met. I want that to be said of me. That I had empathy. That I always took the time to help a person in need, especially if they were living with a progressive disease like Parkinson's.

I am not expecting to grow old gracefully; but I do want to grow old gratefully. It's my prayer that God would make me a vessel who conveys **Chronic Hope** to people. Father, help me to communicate to others about your redeeming presence in the midst of pain.

"I AM THE TRUE VINE, AND MY FATHER IS THE GARDENER. He cuts off every branch in me that bears no fruit, while every branch that does bear fruit He prunes so that it will be even more fruitful. You are already clean because of the word I have spoken to you. Remain in me, as I also remain in you. No branch can bear fruit by itself; it must remain in the vine. Neither can you bear fruit unless you remain in Me.

"I am the vine; you are the branches. If you remain in Me and I in you, you will bear much fruit; apart from Me you can do nothing. If you do not remain in Me, you are like a branch that is thrown away and withers; such branches are picked up, thrown into the fire and burned. If you remain in Me and my words remain in you, ask whatever you wish, and it will be done for you. This is to my Father's glory, that you bear much fruit, showing yourselves to be My disciples.

"As the Father has loved me, so have I loved you. Now remain in my love. If you keep My commands, you will remain in My love, just as I have kept My Father's commands and remain in His love. I have told you this so that My joy may be in you and that your joy may be complete. My command is this: Love each other as I have loved you. Greater love has no one than this: to lay down one's life for one's friends. You are my friends if you do what I command. I no longer call you servants, because a servant does not know his master's business. Instead, I have called you friends, for everything that I learned from my Father I have made known to you. You did not choose me, but I chose you and appointed you so that you might go and bear fruit—fruit that will last—and so that whatever you ask in My name the Father will give you. This is My command: Love each other.

"If the world hates you, keep in mind that it hated Me first. If you belonged to the world, it would love you as its own. As it is, you do not belong to the world, but I have chosen you out of the world. That is why the world hates you. Remember what I told you: 'A servant is not greater than his master.' If they persecuted Me, they will persecute you also. If they obeyed My teaching, they will obey yours also. They will treat you this way because of My name, for they do not know the one who sent Me. If I had not come and spoken to them, they would not be guilty of sin; but now they have no excuse for their sin. Whoever hates me hates my Father as well. If I had not done among them the works no one else did, they would not be guilty of sin. As it is, they have seen, and yet they have hated both Me and My Father. But this is to fulfill what is written in their Law: 'They hated Me without reason.'

"When the Advocate comes, whom I will send to you from the Father—the Spirit of truth who goes out from the Father—he will testify about Me. And you also must testify, for you have been with Me from the beginning. (John 15:1-27 NIV)

LATER ON, JESUS SHOWED HIMSELF again to his disciples on the shore of lake Tiberias, and he did it in this way. Simon Peter, Thomas (called the Twin), Nathanael from Cana in Galilee, the sons of Zebedee and two other disciples were together, when Simon Peter said, "I'm going fishing." "All right," they replied, "we'll go with you." So they went out and got into the boat and during the night caught nothing at all. But just as dawn began to break, Jesus stood there on the beach, although the disciples had no idea that it was Jesus.

"Have you caught anything, lads?" Jesus called out to them. "No," they replied.

"Throw the net on the right side of the boat," said Jesus, "and you'll have a catch." So they threw out the net and found that they were now not strong enough to pull it in because it was so full of fish! At this, the disciple that Jesus loved said to Peter, "It is the Lord!"

Hearing this, Peter slipped on his clothes, for he had been naked, and plunged into the sea. The other disciples followed in the boat, for they were only about a hundred yards from the shore, dragging in the net full of fish. When they had landed, they saw that a charcoal fire was burning, with a fish placed on it, and some bread. Jesus said to them, "Bring me some of the fish you've just caught." So Simon Peter got into the boat and hauled the net ashore full of large fish, one hundred and fifty-three altogether. But in spite of the large number the net was not torn.

Then Jesus said to them, "Come and have your breakfast." None of the disciples dared to ask Him who he was; they knew it was the Lord.

Jesus went and took the bread and gave it to them and gave them all fish as well. This is already the third time that Jesus showed Himself to his disciples after his resurrection from the dead.

When they had finished breakfast Jesus said to Simon Peter, "Simon, son of John, do you love me more than these others?" "Yes, Lord," he replied, "you know that I am your friend."

"Then feed my lambs," returned Jesus. Then he said for the second time, "Simon, son of John, do you love me?" "Yes, Lord," returned Peter. "You know that I am your friend."

"Then care for my sheep," replied Jesus. Then for the third time, Jesus spoke to him and said, "Simon, son of John, are you my friend?" Peter was deeply hurt because Jesus' third question to him was "Are you my friend?", and he said, "Lord, you know everything. You know that I am your friend!"

"Then feed my sheep," Jesus said to him. "I tell you truly, Peter, that when you were younger, you used to dress yourself and go where you liked, but when you are an old man, you are going to stretch out your hands and someone else will dress you and take you where you do not want to go."

(He said this to show the kind of death—by crucifixion—by which Peter was going to honor God.) Then Jesus said to him, "You must follow me."

Then Peter turned round and noticed the disciple whom Jesus loved following behind them. (He was the one who had his head on Jesus' shoulder at supper and had asked, "Lord, who is the one who is going to betray you?") So he said, "Yes, Lord, but what about him?"

"If it is my wish," returned Jesus, "for him to stay until I come, is that your business, Peter? You must follow me."

This gave rise to the saying among the brothers that this disciple would not die. Yet, of course, Jesus did not say, "He will not die," but simply, "If it is my wish for him to stay until I come, is that your business?"

Now it is this same disciple who is hereby giving his testimony to these things and has written them down. We know that his witness is reliable. Of course, there are many other things which Jesus did, and I suppose that if each one were written down in detail, there would not be room in the whole world for all the books that would have to be written. (John 21:1-25 PHILLIPS)

> ### STUART BRISCOE
> Try concentrating on the other person's good points and on your bad points (if you have any). This is contrary to nature but in accord with bible teaching. Look at it this way: if your bad points are better than his or her good points, you must be almost ready for heaven, and your opponent is in much need of help. So, you, being so close to perfect, are the obvious person to give her the help she needs. On the other hand, if her good points are better than your bad points, she could conceivably have something to teach you.[138]

IF I COULD SPEAK ALL THE LANGUAGES OF EARTH AND OF ANGELS, but didn't love others, I would only be a noisy gong or a clanging cymbal. If I had the gift of prophecy, and if I understood all of God's secret plans and possessed all knowledge, and if I had such faith that I could move mountains, but didn't love others, I would be nothing. If I gave everything I have to the poor and even sacrificed my body, I could boast about it; but if I didn't love others, I would have gained nothing.

---

[138] Stuart Briscoe, Bound for Joy, Philippians: Paul's Letter from Prison (Grand Rapids: G/L Publications, 1975), 54.

Love is patient and kind. Love is not jealous or boastful or proud or rude. It does not demand its own way. It is not irritable, and it keeps no record of being wronged. It does not rejoice about injustice but rejoices whenever the truth wins out. Love never gives up, never loses faith, is always hopeful, and endures through every circumstance.

Prophecy and speaking in unknown languages and special knowledge will become useless. But love will last forever! Now our knowledge is partial and incomplete, and even the gift of prophecy reveals only part of the whole picture! But when the time of perfection comes, these partial things will become useless.

When I was a child, I spoke and thought and reasoned as a child. But when I grew up, I put away childish things. Now we see things imperfectly, like puzzling reflections in a mirror, but then we will see everything with perfect clarity. All that I know now is partial and incomplete, but then I will know everything completely, just as God now knows me completely.

Three things will last forever—faith, hope, and love—and the greatest of these is love. (1 Corinthians 13:1-13 NLT)

WILLIAM PURKEY

"You've gotta dance like there's nobody watching.
Love like you'll never be hurt.
Sing like there's nobody listening.
And live like it's heaven on earth."[139]

SO I DECIDED that I would not bring you grief with another painful visit. For if I cause you grief, who will make me glad? Certainly not someone I have grieved. That is why I wrote to you as I did, so that when I do come, I won't be grieved by the very ones who ought to give

---

[139] Holly Shantara quoting William Purkey, Live Like A Life Star, (Morrisville, Lulu.com, 2013), 1.

me the greatest joy. Surely you all know that my joy comes from your being joyful. I wrote that letter in great anguish, with a troubled heart and many tears. I didn't want to grieve you, but I wanted to let you know how much love I have for you.

I am not overstating it when I say that the man who caused all the trouble hurt all of you more than he hurt me. Most of you opposed him, and that was punishment enough. Now, however, it is time to forgive and comfort him. Otherwise he may be overcome by discouragement. So I urge you now to reaffirm your love for him.

I wrote to you as I did to test you and see if you would fully comply with my instructions. When you forgive this man, I forgive him, too. And when I forgive whatever needs to be forgiven, I do so with Christ's authority for your benefit, so that Satan will not outsmart us. For we are familiar with his evil schemes.

When I came to the city of Troas to preach the Good News of Christ, the Lord opened a door of opportunity for me. But I had no peace of mind because my dear brother Titus hadn't yet arrived with a report from you. So I said good-bye and went on to Macedonia to find him.

But thank God! He has made us his captives and continues to lead us along in Christ's triumphal procession. Now He uses us to spread the knowledge of Christ everywhere, like a sweet perfume. Our lives are a Christ-like fragrance rising up to God. But this fragrance is perceived differently by those who are being saved and by those who are perishing. To those who are perishing, we are a dreadful smell of death and doom. But to those who are being saved, we are a life-giving perfume. And who is adequate for such a task as this?

You see, we are not like the many hucksters who preach for personal profit. We preach the word of God with sincerity and with Christ's authority, knowing that God is watching us. (2 Corinthians 2:1-17 NLT)

A TESTAMENT OF HOPE: THE ESSENTIAL WRITINGS AND SPEECHES, MARTIN LUTHER KING JR.
Darkness cannot drive out darkness: only light can do that. Hate cannot drive out hate: only love can do that.[140]

BEAR ONE ANOTHER'S BURDENS, and thereby fulfill the law of Christ. (Galatians 6:2 NASB)

> ## MARTIN LUTHER KING JR.
> Love is the only force capable of transforming an enemy into a friend.[141]

THEREFORE, my fellow believers, whom I love and long for, my delight and crown [my wreath of victory], in this way stand firm in the Lord, my beloved.

I urge Euodia and I urge Syntyche to agree and to work in harmony in the Lord. Indeed, I ask you too, my true companion, to help these women [to keep on cooperating], for they have shared my struggle in the [cause of the] gospel, together with Clement and the rest of my fellow workers, whose names are in the Book of Life.

Rejoice in the Lord always [delight, take pleasure in Him]; again I will say, rejoice! Let your gentle spirit [your graciousness, unselfishness, mercy, tolerance, and patience] be known to all people. The Lord is near. Do not be anxious or worried about anything, but in everything [every circumstance and situation] by prayer and petition with thanksgiving, continue to make your [specific] requests known to God. And the peace

---

[140] Martin Luther King Jr., The Martin Luther King, Jr. Companion (New York: St. Martin's Press, 1993),56.

[141] Marcia Ford quoting Martin Luther King, Jr., The Sacred Art of Forgiveness Forgiving Ourselves and Others Through God's Grace (Woodstock: Skylight Paths, 2006), 8.

of God [that peace which reassures the heart, that peace] which transcends all understanding, [that peace which] stands guard over your hearts and your minds in Christ Jesus [is yours].

Finally, believers, whatever is true, whatever is honorable and worthy of respect, whatever is right and confirmed by God's word, whatever is pure and wholesome, whatever is lovely and brings peace, whatever is admirable and of good repute; if there is any excellence, if there is anything worthy of praise, think continually on these things [center your mind on them, and implant them in your heart]. The things which you have learned and received and heard and seen in me, practice these things [in daily life], and the God [who is the source] of peace and well-being will be with you.

I rejoiced greatly in the Lord, that now at last you have renewed your concern for me; indeed, you were concerned about me before, but you had no opportunity to show it. Not that I speak from [any personal] need, for I have learned to be content [and self-sufficient through Christ, satisfied to the point where I am not disturbed or uneasy] regardless of my circumstances. I know how to get along and live humbly [in difficult times], and I also know how to enjoy abundance and live in prosperity. In any and every circumstance I have learned the secret [of facing life], whether well-fed or going hungry, whether having an abundance or being in need. I can do all things [which He has called me to do] through Him who strengthens and empowers me [to fulfill His purpose—I am self-sufficient in Christ's sufficiency; I am ready for anything and equal to anything through Him who infuses me with inner strength and confident peace.] Nevertheless, it was right of you to share [with me] in my difficulties.

And you Philippians know that in the early days of preaching the gospel, after I left Macedonia, no church shared with me in the matter of giving and receiving except you alone; for even in Thessalonica you sent a gift more than once for my needs. Not that I seek the gift itself, but I do seek the profit which increases to your [heavenly] account [the blessing which is accumulating for you]. But I have received everything in full and more; I am amply supplied, having received from Epaphroditus the gifts you sent me. They are the fragrant aroma of an offering, an acceptable sacrifice which God welcomes and in which He delights. And my God will liberally supply (fill until full) your every need according to His riches in glory in Christ Jesus. To our God and Father be the glory forever and ever. Amen.

Remember me to every saint in Christ Jesus. The brothers who are with me greet you. All God's people wish to be remembered to you, especially those of Caesar's household.

The grace of the Lord Jesus Christ be with your spirit. (Philippians 4:1-23 AMP)

> ### THE KINDLY ONES, NEIL GAIMAN
> Have you ever been in love? Horrible isn't it? It makes you so vulnerable. It opens your chest and it opens up your heart and it means that someone can get inside you and mess you up.[142]

DO NOT LIE TO ONE ANOTHER, since you stripped off the old self with its evil practices, and have put on the new self, which is being renewed to a true knowledge according to the image of the One who created it—a renewal in which there is no distinction between Greek and Jew, circumcised and uncircumcised, barbarian, Scythian, slave, and free, but Christ is all, and in all.

So, as those who have been chosen of God, holy and beloved, put on a heart of compassion, kindness, humility, gentleness, and patience; bearing with one another, and forgiving each other, whoever has a complaint against anyone; just as the Lord forgave you, so must you do also. In addition to all these things put on love, which is the perfect bond of unity. Let the peace of Christ, to which you were indeed called in

---

[142] Steve Stewart-Williams quoting Neil Gaiman, The Ape That Understood the Universe (Cambridge: Cambridge University Press, 2018) 138.

one body, rule in your hearts, and be thankful. Let the word of Christ richly dwell within you, with all wisdom teaching and admonishing one another with psalms, hymns, and spiritual songs, singing with thankfulness in your hearts to God. Whatever you do in word or deed, do everything in the name of the Lord Jesus, giving thanks through Him to God the Father. (Colossians 3:9-17 NASB)

<u>MOTHER TERESA</u>
Our life of poverty is as necessary as the work itself. Only in heaven will we see how much we owe to the poor for helping us to love God better because of them.[143]

BUT WE PROVED TO BE GENTLE AMONG YOU. AS A NURSING MOTHER TENDERLY CARES FOR HER CHILDREN, in the same way we had a fond affection for you and were delighted to share with you not only the gospel of God, but also our own lives, because you had become very dear to us.

For you recall, brothers and sisters, our labor and hardship: it was by working night and day so as not to be a burden to any of you, that we proclaimed to you the gospel of God. You are witnesses, and so is God, of how devoutly and rightly and blamelessly we behaved toward you believers; just as you know how we were exhorting and encouraging and imploring each one of you as a father would his own children, so that you would walk in a manner worthy of the God who calls you into His own kingdom and glory. (I Thessalonians 2:7-12 NASB)

<u>DAVID WILKERSON</u>
Love is not something you feel. It's something you do.[144]

---

[143] Mother Teresa, Dorothy S. Hunt, Love, a Fruit Always in Season (San Francisco: Ignatius Press, 1987), 159.

[144] Candy Chand quoting David Wilkerson, Love is Patient, Love is Kind (Beverly: Fair Winds Press, 2004), 44.

CONSIDER THE INCREDIBLE LOVE THAT THE FATHER HAS SHOWN US in allowing us to be called "children of God"—and that is not just what we are called, but what we are. Our heredity on the Godward side is no mere figure of speech—which explains why the world will no more recognize us than it recognized Christ.

Oh, dear children of mine (forgive the affection of an old man!), have you realized it? Here and now we are God's children. We don't know what we shall become in the future. We only know that, if reality were to break through, we should reflect His likeness, for we should see Him as He really is!

Everyone who has at heart a hope like that keeps himself pure, for he knows how pure Christ is.

Everyone who commits sin breaks God's law, for that is what sin is, by definition—a breaking of God's law. You know, moreover, that Christ became man for the purpose of removing sin, and He Himself was quite free from sin. The man who lives "in Christ" does not habitually sin. The regular sinner has never seen or known Him.

You, my children, are younger than I am, and I don't want you to be taken in by any clever talk just here. The man who lives a consistently good life is a good man, as surely as God is good. But the man whose life is habitually sinful is spiritually a son of the devil, for the devil is behind all sin, as he always has been. Now the Son of God came to earth with the express purpose of liquidating the devil's activities. The man who is really God's son does not practice sin, for God's nature is in him, for good, and such a heredity is incapable of sin.

Here we have a clear indication as to who are the children of God and who are the children of the devil. The man who does not lead a good life is no son of God, nor is the man who fails to love his brother.

For the original command, as you know, is that we should love one another. We are none of us to have the spirit of Cain, who was a son of the devil and murdered his brother. Have you realized his motive? It was just because he realized the goodness of his brother's life and the rottenness of his own. Don't be surprised, therefore, if the world hates you.

We know that we have crossed the frontier from death to life because we do love our brothers. The man without love for his brothers is living in death already. The man who actively hates his brother is a potential murderer, and you will readily see that the eternal life of God cannot live in the heart of a murderer.

We know and, to some extent realize, the love of God for us because Christ expressed it in laying down His life for us. We must in turn express our love by laying down our lives for those who are our brothers. But as for the well-to-do man who sees his brothers in want but shuts his eyes—and his heart—how could anyone believe that the love of God lives in him? My children, let us not love merely in theory or in words—let us love in sincerity and in practice!

If we live like this, we shall know that we are children of the truth and can reassure ourselves in the sight of God, even if our own hearts make us feel guilty. For God is infinitely greater than our hearts, and He knows everything.

And if, dear friends of mine, when we realize this our hearts no longer accuse us, we may have the utmost confidence in God's presence. We receive whatever we ask for, because we are obeying His orders and following His plans. His orders are that we should put our trust in the name of His Son, Jesus Christ, and love one another—as we used to hear Him say in person.

The man who does obey God's commands lives in God and God lives in him, and the guarantee of His presence within us is the Spirit He has given us. (I John 3:1-24 PHILLIPS)

> ### *LEO BUSCAGLIA*
> Love is always bestowed as a gift—freely, willingly, and without expectation...
> We don't love to be loved; we love to love.[145]

---

[145] Leo Buscaglia, Born for Love (New York City, Ballantine Books, 1994), 245.

The Greatest Of These Is Love

BELOVED, DO NOT BELIEVE EVERY SPIRIT [speaking through a self-proclaimed prophet]; instead test the spirits to see whether they are from God, because many false prophets and teachers have gone out into the world. By this you know and recognize the Spirit of God: every spirit that acknowledges and confesses [the fact] that Jesus Christ has [actually] come in the flesh [as a man] is from God [God is its source]; and every spirit that does not confess Jesus [acknowledging that He has come in the flesh, but would deny any of the Son's true nature] is not of God; this is the spirit of the antichrist, which you have heard is coming, and is now already in the world. Little children (believers, dear ones), you are of God and you belong to Him and have [already] overcome them [the agents of the antichrist]; because He who is in you is greater than he (Satan) who is in the world [of sinful mankind]. They [who teach twisted doctrine] are of the world and belong to it; therefore they speak from the [viewpoint of the] world [with its immoral freedom and baseless theories—demanding compliance with their opinions and ridiculing the values of the upright], and the [gullible one of the] world listens closely and pays attention to them. We [who teach God's word] are from God [energized by the Holy Spirit], and whoever knows God [through personal experience] listens to us [and has a deeper understanding of Him]. Whoever is not of God does not listen to us. By this we know [without any doubt] the spirit of truth [motivated by God] and the spirit of error [motivated by Satan].

Beloved, let us [unselfishly] love and seek the best for one another, for love is from God; and everyone who loves [others] is born of God and knows God [through personal experience]. The one who does not love has not become acquainted with God [does not and never did know Him], for God is love. [He is the originator of love, and it is an enduring attribute of His nature.] By this the love of God was displayed in us, in that God has sent His [One and] only begotten Son [the One who is truly unique, the only One of His kind] into the world so that we might live through Him. In this is love, not that we loved God, but that He loved us and sent His Son to be the propitiation [that is, the atoning sacrifice, and the satisfying offering] for our sins [fulfilling God's requirement for justice against sin and placating His wrath. Beloved, if God so loved us [in this incredible way], we also ought to love one another. No one has seen God at any time. But if we love one another [with unselfish concern], God abides in us, and His love [the love that is His essence abides in us and] is completed and perfected in us. By this we know [with confident assurance] that we abide in Him and He in us, because He has given to us His [Holy] Spirit. We [who were with Him in person] have seen and testify [as eyewitnesses] that the Father has sent the Son to be the Savior of the world.

Whoever confesses and acknowledges that Jesus is the Son of God, God abides in him, and he in God. We have come to know [by personal observation and experience], and have believed [with deep, consistent faith] the love which God has for us. God is love, and the one who abides in love abides in God, and God abides continually in him. In this [union and fellowship with Him], love is completed and perfected with us, so that we may have confidence in the day of judgment [with assurance and boldness to face Him]; because as He is, so are we in this world. There is no fear in love [dread does not exist]. But perfect (complete, full-grown) love drives out fear, because fear involves [the expectation of divine] punishment, so the one who is afraid [of God's judgment] is not perfected in love [has not grown into a sufficient understanding of God's love]. We love, because He first loved us. If anyone says, "I love God," and hates (works against) his [Christian] brother he is a liar; for the one who does not love his brother whom he has seen, cannot love God whom he has not seen. And this commandment we have from Him, that the one who loves God should also [unselfishly] love his brother and seek the best for him. (1 John 4:1-21 AMP)

FREDERICK BUECHNER

Of all the powers, love is the most powerful and the most powerless. It is the most powerful because it alone can conquer that final and most impregnable stronghold which is the human heart. It is the most powerless because it can do nothing except by consent. To say that love is God is romantic idealism; to say that God is love is either the last straw or the ultimate truth.

In the Christian sense, love is not primarily an emotion, but an act of the will. When Jesus tells us to love our neighbors, He is not telling us to love them in the sense of responding to them with a cozy emotional feeling. You can as well produce a cozy emotional feeling as you can a yawn or a sneeze.

On the contrary, He is telling us to love our neighbors in the sense of being willing to work for their well-being to that end, even if it means just leaving them alone.

Thus in Jesus' terms we can love our neighbors without necessarily liking them. In fact, liking them may stand in the way of loving them by making us overprotective sentimentalists instead of reasonably honest friends.

When Jesus talked to the Pharisees, He didn't say, "There, there. Everything's going to be alright." He said, "You brood of vipers! How can you speak good when you are evil!" And He said that to them because He loved them.

This does not mean that liking may not be a part of loving, only that it doesn't have to be. Sometimes liking follows on the heels of loving. It is hard to work for somebody's well-being very long without coming in the end to rather like him too."[146]

---

[146] Frederick Buechner, Faith That Matters: 365 Devotions from Classic Christian Leaders (San Francisco: HarperOne, 2018), 135.

BEHOLD, HOW GOOD AND HOW PLEASANT IT IS
For brothers to live together in unity!
It is like the precious oil on the head,
Running down upon the beard,
As on Aaron's beard,
The oil which ran down upon the edge of his robes. It is like the dew of Hermon.
Coming down upon the mountains of Zion;
For the Lord commanded the blessing there—life forever.
(Psalm 133:1-3 NASB)

ELISABETH ELLIOT

We want to avoid suffering, death, sin, ashes. But we live in a world crushed and broken and torn, a world God Himself visited to redeem. We receive His poured-out life, and being allowed the high privilege of suffering with Him, may then pour ourselves out for others.[147]

---

[147] Elisabeth Elliot, A Lamp Unto My Feet: The Bible's Light For Your Daily Walk (Ada: Baker Publishing Group, 2021), 19.

Chapter 23

MY GRACE IS SUFFICIENT FOR YOU

IN ORDER THAT IN THE COMING ages He might show the incomparable riches of His grace, expressed in His kindness to us in Christ Jesus. For it is by grace you have been saved, through faith—and this is not from yourselves, it is the gift of God—not by works, so that no one can boast. For we are God's handiwork, created in Christ Jesus to do good works, which God prepared in advance for us to do. (Ephesians 2:7-10 NIV)

PATTI BURNETT

MY MOM GREW UP IN A CHURCH THAT SELDOM MENTIONED THE GOSPEL, God's unconditional love, or the work of the Holy Spirit. So, when Mom met Dad and started hearing words like grace and born again, she had some questions and needed to play catchup. But you can be sure of this – once she understood that Christ loved her while she was still His enemy, she became His most outspoken advocate for grace.

Mom would say "I used to think that grace was just a nice name for a girl, but once I received the free gift of God's grace, I found it was far more than that; grace has made all the difference in my life and in the world."

CONSEQUENTLY, JUST AS CONDEMNATION FOR ALL people came through one transgression, so too through the one righteous act came righteousness leading to life for all people. For just as through the disobedience of the one man many were constituted sinners, so also through the obedience of one man many will be constituted righteous. Now the law came in so that the transgression may increase, but where sin increased, grace multiplied all the more, so that just as sin reigned in death, so also grace will reign through righteousness to eternal life through Jesus Christ our Lord. (Romans 5:18-21 NET)

NEW MORNING MERCIES, FEBRUARY 1st, PAUL DAVID TRIPP

Sure, you'll face difficulty. God is prying open your fingers, so you'll let go of your dreams, rest in His comforts, and take up His call.

Think about the words penned by Peter near the beginning of his New Testament letter: "Now for a little while, if necessary, you have been grieved by various trials, so that the tested genuineness of your faith – more precious than gold that perishes though it is tested by fire – may be found to result in praise and glory and honor at the revelation of Jesus Christ." (I Peter 1:6-7 ESV) …

Of all the words that he could use to describe what God is doing now, he selects these three: grieved, trials, and tested. These are three words that most of us hope would never describe our lives. None of us gets up in the morning and prays, "Lord, if you love me, you will send more suffering my way today." Rather, when we are living in the middle of difficulty, we are tempted to view it as a sign of God's unfaithfulness or inattention.

Peter, however, doesn't see moments of difficulty as objects in the way of God's plan or indications of the failure of God's plan… rather than being signs of his inattention, they are sure signs of the zeal of His redemptive love. In grace, He leads you where you didn't plan to go in order to produce in you what you couldn't achieve on your own…

God is working right now, but not so much to give us predictable, comfortable, and pleasurable lives. He isn't so much working to transform our circumstances as He is working through hard circumstances to transform you and me. Perhaps in hard moments, when we are tempted to wonder where God's grace is, it is grace that we are getting, but not grace in the form of a soft pillow or a cool drink. Rather, in those moments, we are being blessed with the heart-transforming grace of difficulty because the God who loves us knows that this is exactly the grace we need.[148]

FOR I DELIVERED TO YOU AS OF FIRST IMPORTANCE what I also received: that Christ died for our sins in accordance with the Scriptures, that he was buried, that he was raised on the third day in accordance with the Scriptures, and that he appeared to Cephas, then to the twelve. Then he appeared to more than five hundred brothers at one time, most of whom are still alive, though some have fallen asleep. Then he appeared to James, then to all the apostles. Last of all, as to one untimely born, he appeared also to me. For I am the least of the apostles, unworthy to be called an apostle, because I persecuted the church

---

[148] Paul David Tripp, New Morning Mercies, 1.

of God. But by the grace of God I am what I am, and His grace toward me was not in vain. On the contrary, I worked harder than any of them, though it was not I, but the grace of God that is with me. Whether then it was I or they, so we preach and so you believed. (1 Corinthians 15:1-11 ESV)

> ### *FCA MAGAZINE – TALENTS, TIME AND OPPORTUNITY, STEVE SPAGNUOLO, DEFENSIVE COORDINATOR, KANSAS CITY CHIEFS*
> Our talents are God's gift to us ;
> what we do with them is our gift back to God![149]

I THANK HIM WHO HAS GIVEN ME STRENGTH, Christ Jesus our Lord, because He judged me faithful, appointing me to His service, though formerly I was a blasphemer, persecutor, and insolent opponent. But I received mercy because I had acted ignorantly in unbelief, and the grace of our Lord overflowed for me with the faith and love that are in Christ Jesus. The saying is trustworthy and deserving of full acceptance, that Christ Jesus came into the world to save sinners, of whom I am the foremost. But I received mercy for this reason, that in me, as the foremost, Jesus Christ might display His perfect patience as an example to those who were to believe in Him for eternal life. To the King of the ages, immortal, invisible, the only God, be honor and glory forever and ever. Amen. (1 Timothy 1:12-17 ESV)

---

[149] Steve Spagnuolo, Talents, Time and Opportunities, The Fellowship of Christian Athletes, December 30, 2020, https://www.fca.org/fca-in-action/2020/12/30/talents-time-and-opportunity.

AMAZING GRACE, JOHN NEWTON

Amazing grace! How sweet the sound
That saved a wretch like me!
I once was lost, but now am found;
Was blind, but now I see.

'Twas grace that taught my heart to fear,
And grace my fears relieved;
How precious did that grace appear
The hour I first believed!

Through many dangers, toils and snares,
I have already come;
'Tis grace hath brought me safe thus far,
And grace will lead me home.

The Lord has promised good to me,
His Word my hope secures;
He will my Shield and Portion be,
As long as life endures.

Yea, when this flesh and heart shall fail,
And mortal life shall cease,
I shall possess, within the veil,
A life of joy and peace.

The earth shall soon dissolve like snow,
The sun forbear to shine;
But God, Who called me here below,
Will be forever mine.

When we've been there ten thousand years,
Bright shining as the sun,
We've no less days to sing God's praise
Then when we'd first begun.[150]

---

[150] John Newton, Amazing Grace (published in 1371 hymnals, 1779).

THEREFORE, SINCE WE HAVE A GREAT HIGH PRIEST who has passed through the heavens, Jesus the Son of God, let's hold firmly to our confession. For we do not have a high priest who cannot sympathize with our weaknesses, but One who has been tempted in all things just as we are, yet without sin. Therefore let's approach the throne of grace with confidence, so that we may receive mercy and find grace for help at the time of our need. (Hebrews 4:14-16 NASB)

JOHN CALVIN
Joy is a quiet gladness of heart as one contemplates the goodness of God's saving grace in Christ Jesus.[151]

~

CHARLES SPURGEON
I sometimes wonder that you do not get tired of my preaching, because I do nothing but hammer away on this one nail. With me it is, year after year, "None but Jesus!" Oh, you great saints, if you have outgrown the need of a sinner's trust in the Lord Jesus, you have outgrown your sins, but you have also outgrown your grace, and your saintship has ruined you![152]

---

[151] John Calvin, from https://www.azquotes.com/quote/1288659, French theologian, pastor, and reformer in Geneva during Protestant Reformation.
[152] Charles Spurgeon, Spurgeon at His Best (Grand Rapids Baker Book House, 2013), 110.

Chapter 24

POST TRAUMATIC GROWTH

WE NOW HAVE THIS LIGHT shining in our hearts, but we ourselves are like fragile clay jars containing this great treasure. This makes it clear that our great power is from God, not from ourselves.

We are pressed on every side by troubles, but we are not crushed. We are perplexed, but not driven to despair. We are hunted down, but never abandoned by God. We get knocked down, but we are not destroyed. Through suffering, our bodies continue to share in the death of Jesus so that the life of Jesus may also be seen in our bodies.

Yes, we live under constant danger of death because we serve Jesus, so that the life of Jesus will be evident in our dying bodies. So we live in the face of death, but this has resulted in eternal life for you. (2 Corinthians 4:7-12 NLT)

PATTI BURNETT

FOLLOWING THE VIETNAM WAR, psychiatric professionals discovered that many veterans suffered from a crippling disturbance labeled "Post Traumatic Stress Disorder." Soon thereafter, it was learned that a similar form of stress was debilitating emergency medical service (EMS) providers. A critical incident is any situation that causes first responders to experience unusually strong emotions that can potentially interfere with their ability to function, either at the scene or later. According to research, it was crucial for an individual to have the opportunity to air his or her feelings and reactions in a healthy, safe environment with caring peers and counselors. A Critical Incident Stress Debrief (CISD) team consists of at least one mental health professional and two or three peer counselors. A peer is an emergency responder, i.e., fire fighter, ambulance attendant, search and rescue member, ski patroller, sheriff, dispatcher, etc.

I was a member of the High Country CISD. We held debriefs for the deaths of children, multiple car and victim accidents, burns or excessive loss of bodily fluids, paralysis patients, etc. I participated as a ski patroller and search and rescue dog handler peer. This was in no way a technical debriefing. It was my job to help EMS responders talk about what happened, their feelings, their disappointments, and self-doubts. If unable to normalize these emotions, they were often destined to a shortened EMS career, quitting because of burnout.

My interest in CISD was triggered nearly 40 years ago. As newlyweds, Dan and I were asleep and awakened to the cries of sirens and emergency lights flashing on our bedroom walls. As a newly certified emergency EMT, I felt obligated to discover the nature of the situation and assist, if necessary. Several firefighters were attending to a mother and her three children in the lobby. Three men were performing CPR on a three-year-old, and two others were attending to a one-year-old and a five-year-old. They had me assume care of the youngest child. The family had sustained carbon monoxide poisoning while driving a car with a faulty exhaust system. The three-year-old died, and an ambulance transported the rest of the family to Denver for further medical treatment and observation.

A few days later, I attended a CISD. At this, my first debriefing, I was impressed with the professionalism of the team as they explained normal responses to this type of stress. This knowledge helped me to understand the importance of dealing with each potentially stressful response so that it did not become cumulatively detrimental to my job performance.

Most people have heard of post traumatic stress, but post traumatic growth might be a new concept. Do we buy in to the idea that, "Whatever doesn't kill you, makes you stronger?" I think it's fair to say that we'd rather not. But I also do not want to, like Job's wife, recommend that we "curse God and die."

Wikipedia

> "Post-traumatic growth (PTG) or "benefit finding" is positive psychological change experienced as a result of adversity and other challenges, in order to rise to a higher level of functioning. These circumstances represent significant challenges to the adaptive resources of the individual and pose significant challenges to their way of understanding the world and their place in it."

Christianity and many other teachings agree that suffering is a necessary detour to our eternal destination. Many who have traveled this lonesome road will acknowledge that life changing challenges caused them to be more optimistic; to gain a greater appreciation for life; to develop a resilience that they had never experienced before; and to love and empathize with those who were less fortunate.

I, PAUL, AN APOSTLE (SPECIAL MESSENGER, PERSONALLY CHOSEN REPRESENTATIVE) of Christ Jesus (the Messiah) by the will of God, and Timothy our brother, To the church of God which is at Corinth, and to all the saints (God's people) throughout Achaia (southern Greece):

Grace to you and peace [inner calm and spiritual well-being] from God our Father and the Lord Jesus Christ.

Blessed [gratefully praised and adored] be the God and Father of our Lord Jesus Christ, the Father of mercies and the God of all comfort, who comforts and encourages us in every trouble so that we will be able to comfort and encourage those who are in any kind of trouble, with the comfort with which we ourselves are comforted by God.

For just as Christ's sufferings are ours in abundance [as they overflow to His followers], so also our comfort [our reassurance, our encouragement, our consolation] is abundant through Christ [it is truly more than enough to endure what we must]. But if we are troubled and distressed, it is for your comfort and salvation; or if we are comforted and encouraged, it is for your comfort, which works [in you] when you patiently endure the same sufferings which we experience. And our hope for you [our confident expectation of good for you] is firmly grounded [assured and unshaken], since we know that just as you share as partners in our sufferings, so also you share as partners in our comfort.

For we do not want you to be uninformed, brothers and sisters, about our trouble in [the west coast province of] Asia [Minor], how we were utterly weighed down, beyond our strength, so that we despaired even of life [itself]. Indeed, we felt within ourselves that we had received the sentence of death [and were convinced that we would die, but this happened] so that we would not trust in ourselves, but in God who raises the dead. He rescued us from so great a threat of death, and will continue to rescue us. On Him we have set our hope. And He will again rescue us [from danger and draw us near], while you join in helping us by your prayers. Then thanks will be given by many persons on our behalf for the gracious gift [of deliverance] granted to us through the prayers of many [believers].

This is our [reason for] proud confidence: our conscience testifies that we have conducted ourselves in the world [in general], and especially toward you, with pure motives and godly sincerity, not in human wisdom, but in the grace of God [that is, His gracious lovingkindness that leads people to Christ and spiritual maturity]. For we write you nothing other than what you read and understand [there is no double meaning in what we say]. And I hope you will [accurately] understand [divine things] until the end; just as you have [already] partially understood us, [and one day will recognize] that you can be proud of us just as we are of you, in the day of our Lord Jesus.

It was with this confidence that I planned at first to visit you, so that you might receive twice a token of grace; that is, [I wanted] to visit you on my way to Macedonia, and [then] to come back to you [on my return] from Macedonia, and have you send me on my way to Judea. So then, was I indecisive or capricious when I was [originally] planning this? Or the things I plan, do I plan [in a self-serving way like a worldly man, ready to say, "Yes, yes" and "No, no" [at the same time]? But [as surely as] God is faithful and means what He says, our message to you is not "Yes" and "No" [at the same time]. For the Son of God, Jesus Christ, who was preached among you by us, by me, Silvanus, and Timothy, was not "Yes" and "No," but has proved to be "Yes" in Him [true and faithful, the divine "Yes" affirming God's promises]. For as many as are the promises of God, in Christ they are [all answered] "Yes." So through Him we say our "Amen" to the glory of God. Now it is God who establishes and confirms us [in joint fellowship] with you in Christ, and who has anointed us [empowering us with the gifts of the Spirit]; it is He who has also put His seal on us [that is, He has appropriated us and certified us as His] and has given us the [Holy] Spirit in our hearts as a pledge [like a security deposit to guarantee the fulfillment of His promise of eternal life].

But I call on God as my soul's witness, that it was to spare you [pain and discouragement] that I did not come again to Corinth—not that we rule [like dictators] over your faith, but rather we work with you for [the increase of] your joy; for in your faith you stand firm [in your strong conviction that Jesus of Nazareth—the Messiah—is the Son of God, through whom we obtain eternal salvation]. (2 Corinthians 1:1-24 AMP)

> ### *SCREWTAPE LETTERS, C.S. LEWIS*
> Screwtape, the Senior Demon, warns Wormwood, his disciple in the devilish business, that he worry most when a follower of the enemy (God) endures a season when all trace of God's presence and goodness disappears. It is then, he laments, that the most transforming victories for the other side are won.[153]

BUT HAVING THE SAME SPIRIT OF FAITH, according to what is written, "I believed, therefore I spoke," we also believe, therefore we also speak, knowing that He who raised the Lord Jesus will raise us also with Jesus and will present us with you. For all things are for your sakes, so that the grace which is spreading to more and more people may cause the giving of thanks to abound to the glory of God.

Therefore, we do not lose heart, but though our outer man is decaying, yet our inner man is being renewed day by day. For momentary, light affliction is producing for us an eternal weight of glory far beyond all comparison, while we look not at the things which are seen, but at the things which are not seen; for the things which are seen are temporal, but the things which are not seen are eternal. (2 Corinthians 4:13-18 NASB)

---

[153] C.S. Lewis, Screwtape Letters (Kings Place: The Guardian, 1941).

UPWARD FALL, BRIAN MYERS

Truth be told, for young and old, the upward call of God in Christ Jesus can have the look and feel of an upward fall.[154]

BECAUSE OF THE SURPASSING greatness and extraordinary nature of the revelations [which I received from God], for this reason, to keep me from thinking of myself as important, a thorn in the flesh was given to me, a messenger of Satan, to torment and harass me—to keep me from exalting myself!

So I am well pleased with weaknesses, with insults, with distresses, with persecutions, and with difficulties, for the sake of Christ; for when I am weak [in human strength], then I am strong [truly able, truly powerful, truly drawing from God's strength]. (2 Corinthians 12:7, 10 AMP)

STREAMS IN THE DESERT, APRIL 8th, L.B. COWMAN

The literal translation of this verse (II Corinthians 12:10) adds a startling emphasis to it, allowing it to speak for itself with power we have probably never realized. It is as follows: "Therefore I take pleasure in being without strength, being insulted, experiencing emergencies, and being chased and forced into a corner for Christ's sake; for when I am without strength, I am dynamite."

The secret of knowing God's complete sufficiency is in coming to the end of everything in ourselves and our circumstances…

"Teach me, O Lord, to glory in my cross. Teach me the value of my thorns. Show me how I have climbed to You through the path of pain. Show me it is through my tears I have seen my rainbows."[155]

---

[154] Brian Myers, The Upward Fall: Our Pilgrim Journey through Groaning to Glory (Portland: Dawson Media, 2013), 1.

[155] L.B. Cowman, Streams in the Dessert (Grand Rapids: Zondervan, 1997), 455.

REMEMBER JESUS CHRIST, RISEN FROM THE DEAD, DESCENDANT OF DAVID, ACCORDING TO MY GOSPEL, for which I suffer hardship even to imprisonment as a criminal; but the word of God is not imprisoned. For this reason I endure all things for the sake of those who are chosen, so that they also may obtain the salvation which is in Christ Jesus and with it eternal glory. The statement is trustworthy:

> For if we died with Him, we will also live with Him;
> If we endure, we will also reign with Him;
> If we deny Him, He will also deny us;
> If we are faithless, He remains faithful, for He cannot deny Himself.
> (2 Timothy 2:8-13 NASB)

HEAL THE WOUND BUT LEAVE THE SCAR, POINT OF GRACE
>   I used to pray that You would take this shame away
>   Hide all the evidence of who I've been
>   But it's the memory of the place You brought me from
>   That keeps me on my knees and even though I'm free
>   Heal the wound but leave the scar
>   A reminder of how merciful you are
>   I am broken, torn apart, take the pieces of this heart
>   And heal the wound but leave the scar[156]

JAMES, SERVANT OF GOD AND OF THE LORD JESUS CHRIST, sends greetings to the twelve dispersed tribes. When all kinds of trials and temptations crowd into your lives my brothers, don't resent them as intruders, but welcome them as friends! Realize that they come to test your faith and to produce in you the quality of endurance. But let the process go on until that endurance is fully developed, and you will

---

[156] Point of Grace (performers), Heal the Wound, Clint Lagerberg and Nichole Nordeman (lyricists), distributed by Nashville, Word Records, track 8 on How You Live, 2007, album.

find you have become men of mature character with the right sort of independence. And if, in the process, any of you does not know how to meet any particular problem he has only to ask God—who gives generously to all men without making them feel foolish or guilty—and he may be quite sure that the necessary wisdom will be given him. But he must ask in sincere faith without secret doubts as to whether he really wants God's help or not. The man who trusts God, but with inward reservations, is like a wave of the sea, carried forward by the wind one moment and driven back the next. That sort of man cannot hope to receive anything from God, and the life of a man of divided loyalty will reveal instability at every turn.

The brother who is poor may be glad because God has called him to the true riches.

The rich may be glad that God has shown him his spiritual poverty. For the rich man, as such, will wither away as surely as summer flowers. One day the sunrise brings a scorching wind; the grass withers at once and so do all the flowers—all that lovely sight is destroyed. Just as surely will the rich man and all his extravagant ways fall into the blight of decay.

The man who patiently endures the temptations and trials that come to him is the truly happy man. For once his testing is complete, he will receive the crown of life which the Lord has promised to all who love Him.

A man must not say when he is tempted, "God is tempting me." For God has no dealings with evil, and does not Himself tempt anyone. No, a man's temptation is due to the pull of his own inward desires, which can be enormously attractive. His own desire takes hold of him, and that produces sin. And sin in the long run means death—make no mistake about that, brothers of mine!

But every good endowment that we possess and every complete gift that we have received must come from above, from the Father of all lights, with whom there is never the slightest variation or shadow of inconsistency. By His own wish He made us His own sons through the Word of truth that we might be, so to speak, the first specimens of His new creation.

In view of what He has made us then, dear brothers, let every man be quick to listen but slow to use his tongue, and slow to lose his temper. For man's temper is never the means of achieving God's true goodness.

Have done, then, with impurity and every other evil which touches the lives of others, and humbly accept the message that God has sown in your hearts, and which can save your souls. Don't, I beg you, only hear the message, but put it into practice; otherwise, you are merely deluding yourselves. The man who simply hears and does nothing about it is like a man catching the reflection of his own face in a mirror. He sees himself, it is true, but he goes on with whatever he was doing without the slightest recollection of what sort of person he saw in the mirror. But the man who looks into the perfect mirror of God's law, the law of liberty (or freedom), and makes a habit of so doing, is not the man who sees and forgets. He puts that law into practice, and he wins true happiness.

If anyone appears to be "religious" but cannot control his tongue, he deceives himself and we may be sure that his religion is useless.

Religion that is pure and genuine in the sight of God the Father will show itself by such things as visiting orphans and widows in their distress and keeping oneself uncontaminated by the world. (James 1:1-27 PHILLIPS)

> ### C.S. LEWIS
> When a man turns to Christ and seems to be getting on pretty well (in the sense that some of his bad habits are now corrected) he often feels that it would now be natural if things went fairly smoothly. When troubles come along—illnesses, money troubles, new kinds of temptation—he is disappointed. These things, he feels, might have been necessary to rouse him and make him repent in his bad old days; but why now? Because God is forcing him on, or up, to a higher level: putting him into situations where he will have to be very much braver, or more patient, or more loving, than he ever dreamed of being before. It seems to us all unnecessary: but that is because we haven't the slightest notion of the tremendous thing He means to make of us.[157]

FOR YOU HAVE BEEN CALLED FOR THIS PURPOSE, because Christ also suffered for you, leaving you an example, so that you would follow in His steps, He who committed no sin, nor was any deceit found in His mouth; and while being abusively insulted, He did not insult in return; while suffering, He did not threaten, but kept entrusting Himself to Him who judges righteously; and He himself brought our sins in His body up on the cross, so that we might die to sin and live for righteousness; by His wounds you were healed. For you were continually straying like sheep, but now you have returned to the shepherd and guardian of your souls. (I Peter 2:21-25 NASB)

---

[157] C.S. Lewis, The Complete C.S. Lewis Signature Classics (New York: HarperCollins Publications, 2007), 162.

C.S. LEWIS

God wants us to love and be loved – to grow up. Something must drive us out of the nursery into the world of others. That something is suffering."[158]

BELOVED, DO NOT BE SURPRISED AT THE FIERY ORDEAL AMONG YOU, which comes upon you for your testing, as though something strange were happening to you; but to the degree that you share the sufferings of Christ, keep on rejoicing, so that at the revelation of His glory you may also rejoice and be overjoyed. If you are insulted for the name of Christ, you are blessed, because the Spirit of glory, and of God, rests upon you. Make sure that none of you suffers as a murderer, or thief, or evildoer, or a troublesome meddler; but if anyone suffers as a Christian, he is not to be ashamed, but is to glorify God in this name. For it is time for judgment to begin with the household of God; and if it begins with us first, what will be the outcome for those who do not obey the gospel of God? And if it is with difficulty that the righteous is saved, what will become of the godless man and the sinner? Therefore, those also who suffer according to the will of God are to entrust their souls to a faithful Creator in doing what is right. (1 Peter 4:12-19 NASB)

PATTI BURNETT

FRONT RIGHT SIDE OF NECK, left front ribs, front torso, left lateral torso, lower abdomen twice, left wrist, nose, right cheek, back, left knee, both baby toes – these are the railroad tracks of scars I have acquired "all over my body." Each has a story to tell. These are not the scars of a couch potato; they result from:

---

[158] Christopher Wright quoting C.S. Lewis, God and Morality: Book 1 (New York: Oxford University Press, 2003), 56.

1. A car accident while driving to a search and rescue dog convention. The car was totaled, and I received cervical fractures and herniated disks and a fusion
2. A hiking accident that broke three ribs, punctured my lung, resulting in plates and screws
3. Kidney disease that caused near fatal infected cysts and destroyed 30% of one kidney
4. Bilateral inguinal hernia with entangling mesh
5. Emergency Cesarean section
6. Fractured wrist with plates and screws from a fall while standing on a wheeled swivel chair. I know – that's why they put warning signs on those things. Doctors and nurses must go to school for many years to learn how not to stand on their stools.
7. Broken nose from trail running
8. Frost bitten skin from 70 years of ski racing, ski instructing, water skiing, ski patrolling, and search and rescue dog handling
9. Multiple knee surgeries resulting in a total knee replacement
10. Laminectomy to remove a cyst on my lower back
11. Broken toes with an implanted screw in one
12. Deep Brain Stimulation Surgery resulting in the placement of a device that sends signals to implanted electrodes in the areas of the brain affected by Parkinson's

I was certainly the recipient of Post Traumatic Growth, and yet my most life altering scars are not visible to the naked eye. We all have emotional wounds that are the hardest to heal and extricate from our memory bank. The time I lost a job unfairly. The time I made particularly poor decisions. The time I put my own well-being ahead of others who needed the care and protection only I could provide.

Sure, we experience growth from even those situations; but I wonder whether it would benefit not just me, but others as well, if I were more transparent about my failures and heartaches. Being a Christian does not make us any less human; and being vulnerable will certainly help to make us each more approachable.

NOW MAY I WHO AM MYSELF AN ELDER say a word to you my fellow-elders? I speak as one who actually saw Christ suffer, and as one who will share with you the glories that are to be unfolded to us. I urge you then to see that your "flock of God" is properly fed and cared for. Accept the responsibility of looking after them willingly and not because you feel you can't get out of it, doing your work not for what you can make, but because you are really concerned for their well-being. You should aim not at being "little tin gods" but as examples of Christian living in the eyes of the flock committed to your charge. And then, when the chief shepherd reveals Himself, you will receive that crown of glory which cannot fade.

You younger members must also submit to the elders. Indeed all of you should defer to one another and wear the "overall" of humility in serving each other. 'God resists the proud, but gives grace to the humble'.

So, humble yourselves under God's strong hand, and in His own good time He will lift you up. You can throw the whole weight of your anxieties upon Him, for you are His personal concern.

Be self-controlled and vigilant always, for your enemy the devil is always about, prowling like a lion roaring for its prey. Resist him, standing firm in your faith and remember that the strain is the same for all your fellow-Christians in other parts of the world. And after you have borne these sufferings a very little while, God Himself (from whom we receive all grace and who has called you to share His eternal splendor through Christ) will make you whole and secure and strong. All power is His for ever and ever, amen!

I am sending this short letter by Silvanus, whom I know to be a faithful brother, to stimulate your faith and assure you that the above words represent the true grace of God. See that you stand fast in that grace!

Your sister-church here in "Babylon" sends you greetings, and so does my son Mark. Give each other a handshake all round as a sign of love. Peace be to all true Christians. (I Peter 5:1-14 PHILLIPS)

I AM THANKFUL FOR THE SCARS, I AM THEY

Waking up to a new sunrise
Looking back from the other side
I can see now with open eyes
Darkest water and deepest pain
I wouldn't trade it for anything
'Cause my brokenness brought me to You
And these wounds are a story You'll use
I'm thankful for the scars
'Cause without them I wouldn't know Your heart
And I know they'll always tell of who You are
So forever I am thankful for the scars[159]

NOW YOU FOLLOWED MY TEACHING, conduct, purpose, faith, patience and sufferings, such as happened to me at Antioch, at Iconium, and at Lystra; what persecutions I endured, and out of them all the Lord rescued me! Indeed, all who want to live in a godly way in Christ Jesus will be persecuted. (2 Timothy 3:10-12 NASB)

THE DIVINE EMBRACE, KEN GIRE

Not only are the days of our lives in God's hands, but also the shaping of our lives. All these incremental surrenderings of self are part of the process God uses in shaping us into the image of His Son. Jesus was a man of sorrows, we are told. That was part of His beauty. Our sorrows acquaint us with His sorrows. Apart from suffering, there is a part of Jesus we cannot know. If there is a part of Him we cannot

---

[159] I AM THEY (performers), Scars, distributed by Provident Music Group, track 4 on Trial & Triumph, 201, album.

know, there is a part of Him we cannot love. And if there is a part of Him we cannot love, there is a part of us that can never be beautiful. At least here on earth.[160]

> ### *HUDSON TAYLOR*
> At the timberline where the storms strike with the most fury, the sturdiest trees are found.[161]

BUT [IN FACT] HE HAS BORNE OUR GRIEFS,
And He has carried our sorrows and pains;
Yet we [ignorantly] assumed that He was stricken,
Struck down by God and degraded and humiliated [by Him].
But He was wounded for our transgressions,
He was crushed for our wickedness [our sin, our injustice, our wrongdoing];
The punishment [required] for our well-being fell on Him,
And by His stripes (wounds) we are healed.
All of us like sheep have gone astray,
We have turned, each one, to his own way;
But the Lord has caused the wickedness of us all [our sin, our injustice, our wrongdoing]
To fall on Him [instead of us].

He was oppressed and He was afflicted,
Yet He did not open His mouth [to complain or defend Himself];
Like a lamb that is led to the slaughter,
And like a sheep that is silent before her shearers,
So He did not open His mouth.

---
[160] Gire, The Divine Embrace, 208.

[161] David Scott quoting Hudson Taylor, The Pebble and the Tower (Maitland: Xulon Press, 2007), 179.

After oppression and judgment He was taken away;
And as for His generation [His contemporaries], who [among them] concerned himself with the fact
That He was cut off from the land of the living [by His death]
For the transgression of my people, to whom the stroke [of death] was due?

His grave was assigned with the wicked,
But He was with a rich man in His death,
Because He had done no violence,
Nor was there any deceit in His mouth.

Yet the LORD was willing
To crush Him, causing Him to suffer;
If He would give Himself as a guilt offering [an atonement for sin],
He shall see His [spiritual] offspring,
He shall prolong His days,
And the will (good pleasure) of the LORD shall succeed and prosper in His hand.

As a result of the anguish of His soul,
He shall see it and be satisfied;
By His knowledge [of what He has accomplished] the Righteous One,
My Servant, shall justify the many [making them righteous—upright before God, in right standing with Him],
For He shall bear [the responsibility for] their sins.

Therefore, I will divide and give Him a portion with the great [kings and rulers],
And He shall divide the spoils with the mighty,
Because He [willingly] poured out His life to death,
And was counted among the transgressors;

Yet He Himself bore and took away the sin of many,
And interceded [with the Father] for the transgressors. (Isaiah 53: 4-12 AMP)

VICTOR FRANKL, NAZI CONCENTRATION CAMP SURVIVOR
He who has a WHY to live can bear almost any HOW.[162]

JESUS CALLING, JANUARY 23rd, SARAH YOUNG

It's alright to be human. When your mind wanders while you are praying, don't be surprised or upset. Simply return your attention to Me. Share a secret smile with Me, knowing that I understand. Rejoice in My love for you, which has no limits or conditions. Whisper My name in loving contentment, assured that I will never leave you or forsake you. Intersperse these peaceful interludes abundantly throughout your day. This practice will enable you to attain a quiet and gentle spirit, which is pleasing to Me.

As you live in close contact with Me, the light of My presence filters through you to bless others. Your weakness and woundedness are the openings through which the light of the knowledge of My glory shines forth. My strength and power show themselves most effective in your weakness.[163]

---

[162] Victor Frankl, Man's Search for Meaning (Boston: Beacon Press, 2006), 9.
[163] Young, Jesus Calling, 24.

Chapter 25

PAIN – A CONDUIT FOR MOVING HEAD KNOWLEDGE TO HEART KNOWLEDGE

NOW THIS IS ETERNAL LIFE: that they know you, the only true God, and Jesus Christ, whom You have sent. (John 17:3 NIV)

A HEART LIKE HIS, PATTI BURNETT

IN THE LAST FEW DECADES medical science has become remarkably proficient in the field of cardiac transplant surgery. If man, in his finite abilities, can reach such heights, how much more is God able to implant us with a spiritual heart like His! That person would be characterized as having integrity, humility, obedience, forgiveness, accountability, trust, passion for the things God loves, and disdain for the things God abhors. Our standard must be the attributes of God alone.

God testified concerning King David, "I have found David the son of Jesse, a man after My own heart, who will do all My will" (Acts 13:22b NKJV). Not only is it feasible for us to have hearts like David's, but it is also God's promise and intention for His children. Jeremiah prophesied a new relationship – a new covenant between God and His people. "I will give them a heart to know Me, that I am the Lord. They will be My people, and I will be their God, for they will return to Me with all their hearts" (Jeremiah 24:7 NLT).

To qualify for a heart transplant, a patient must have some type of coronary disease or irregularity. God placed David in the crucible and crushed his heart frequently. David personally knew the value of a broken and contrite spirit and entreated God for an organ that was pure (Psalm 51:10, 17).

Mental anguish brought David's heart and mind into alignment with the desires of His Lord. He viewed himself as a tool to be utilized by God in whatever way He deemed best. David's prayer life included crying out to God in his deep despondency and praising God during times of hope and triumph. "Trust in Him at all times, you people; pour out your hearts to Him, for God is our refuge" (Psalm 62:8 NIV). David was a man who passionately sat at God's feet and worshiped Him amid his successes and failures.

David acquired sensitivity to the prompting of the Holy Spirit, and when his life got out of synchronization with God's, he was conscience-stricken and immediately took measures to clear the slate. One time his pride motivated him to take a census of the people of Israel, which incurred God's wrath and resulted in the deaths of 70,000 of his men. Remorseful and repentant, David heeded the prophet, Gad, and obediently built an altar to the Lord to conclude the plague on Israel.

The real estate and oxen at the location God indicated for the altar were the property of Araunah, and he offered them as a gift to David. "But the king replied to Araunah, 'No, I insist on paying you for it. I will not sacrifice to the Lord my God burnt offerings that cost me nothing'" (II Samuel 24:24 NIV). David would not be guilty again of stealing the "ewe lamb that belonged to the poor man" (II Samuel 12:4c NIV). An individual after God's heart is less than perfect, but he is teachable. David also recognized that his sin cost the lives of many innocent people he was obligated to protect. God accepted David's sacrifice and eventually chose the threshing floor of Araunah, also known as Mount Moriah, as the site for the temple, the house of the Lord God (I Chronicles 21:27-22:1). It is no coincidence that years earlier, this was also the site where Abraham was asked to sacrifice his son, Isaac. God always provides a propitiation (atonement) for an obedient heart.

In the case of spiritual heart transplants, there is no limit to their availability, but it is not unusual for recipients to reject the donor heart. God has had to repeatedly break my heart in the 50 years I have known Him. Often, I have challenged God as to whether I was willing and competent to undergo the surgical procedure and rehabilitation. My experience has been that God is a gentle Physician; and, though the pain is excruciating, His persevering bedside grace and love are more than sufficient for the task. I have been forgiven much!

Since Christ's death and resurrection and Pentecost, whenever a person asks Christ into his life, he is indwelt by God's Holy Spirit. "I pray that out of His glorious riches He may strengthen you with power through His Spirit in your inner being, so that Christ may dwell in your hearts through faith" (Ephesians 3:16-17a NIV). As He takes up residence in our hearts, He teaches us God's ways and conforms our desires to those of God. However, there must also be an effort on our part. A pure heart like God's results from:

1. Honesty and repentance to a holy God (Psalm 51:10)
2. Seeking and pursuing God's face (Psalm 24:3-6)
3. Living according to God's Word (Psalm 119:9)
4. Devotion to God (II Timothy 2:22)
5. Hoping in God's appearance (I John 3:3)

I am grateful that the Bible includes numerous chronicles of King David's life, even those times when he failed or disobeyed His Heavenly Father. God's message is crystal-clear; even I can be a woman after God's heart. David's name means "Beloved of God." It is my privilege to be counted amongst those also labeled "Beloved of God." As I grow in grace, those things that break God's heart, must break my heart. Like David, my aspiration is to know God, to regard Him as my everything, and to pursue Him with all my heart. "The Lord is my rock, my fortress and my deliverer; my God is my rock, in whom I take refuge, my shield and the horn of my salvation, my stronghold" (Psalm 18:2 NLT).

WHEN JESUS HAD SAID THESE WORDS, He raised His eyes to heaven and said, "Father, the hour has come. Glorify Your Son now so that He may bring glory to You, for You have given Him authority over all men to give eternal life for all that You have given to Him. And this is eternal life, to know You, the only true God, and Him whom You have sent—Jesus Christ.

"I have brought You honour upon earth, I have completed the task which You gave Me to do. Now, Father, honour Me in Your own presence with the glory that I knew with You before the world was made. I have shown Yourself to the men whom You gave me from the world. They were Your men and You gave them to Me, and they have accepted Your word. Now they realize that all that You have given me comes from You—and that every message that You gave me I have given them. They have accepted it all and have come to know in their hearts that I did come from You—they are convinced that You sent me.

"I am praying to You for them: I am not praying for the world but for the men whom You gave me, for they are Yours—everything that is Mine is Yours and Yours Mine—and they have done Me honor. Now I am no longer in the world, but they are in the world and I am returning to You. Holy Father, keep the men You gave Me by Your power that they may be one, as We are one. As long as I was with them I kept them by the power that You gave me; I guarded them, and not one of them was destroyed, except the son of destruction—that the scripture might come true.

"And now I come to You and I say these things in the world that these men may find My joy completed in themselves. I have given them Your word, and the world has hated them, for they are no more sons of the world than I am. I am not praying that You will take them out of the world but that You will keep them from the evil one. They are no more the sons of the world than I am—make them holy by the truth; for Your word is the truth. I have sent them to the world just as You sent me to the world and I consecrate Myself for their sakes that they may be made holy by the truth.

"I am not praying only for these men but for all those who will believe in Me through their message, that they may all be one. Just as You, Father, live in Me and I live in You, I am asking that they may live in Us, that the world may believe that You did send Me. I have given them the honour that You gave me, that they may be one, as We are one—I in them and You in Me, that they may grow complete into one, so that the world may realize that You sent me and have loved them as You loved Me. Father, I want those whom You have given Me to be with Me where I am; I want them to see that glory which You have made mine—for You loved me before the world began. Father of goodness and truth, the world has not known You, but I have known You and these men now know that You have sent Me. I have made Yourself known to them and

I will continue to do so that the love which You have had for Me may be in their hearts—and that I may be there also. (John 17:1-26 Phillips)

> ## BOUND FOR JOY, STUART BRISCOE
> When the little boy fell out of bed and his mother asked how it happened, he replied, I stayed too near where I got in. That's exactly how it is with many people in their spiritual experience. Satisfied that their sins are forgiven and that their reservations for heaven have been confirmed, they stay 'where they got in.' That's a sure way to spiritual boredom and ineffectiveness.[164]

FINALLY, MY BROTHERS AND SISTERS, REJOICE IN THE LORD. To write the same things again is no trouble for me, and it is a safeguard for you.

Beware of the dogs, beware of the evil workers, beware of the circumcision; for we are the true circumcision, who worship in the Spirit of God and take pride in Christ Jesus, and put no confidence in the flesh, although I myself could boast as having confidence even in the flesh. If anyone else thinks he is confident in the flesh, I have more reason: circumcised the eighth day, of the nation of Israel, of the tribe of Benjamin, a Hebrew of Hebrews; as to the Law, a Pharisee; as to zeal, a persecutor of the church; as to the righteousness which is in the Law, found blameless.

But whatever things were gain to me, these things I have counted as loss because of Christ. More than that, I count all things to be loss in view of the surpassing value of knowing Christ Jesus my Lord, for whom I have suffered the loss of all things, and count them mere rubbish, so that I may gain Christ, and may be found in Him, not having

---

[164]Stuart Briscoe, Bound for Joy (Memphis: G/L Publications, 1977).

a righteousness of my own derived from the law, but that which is through faith in Christ, the righteousness which comes from God on the basis of faith, that I may know Him and the power of His resurrection and the fellowship of His sufferings, being conformed to His death; if somehow I may attain to the resurrection from the dead.

Not that I have already grasped it all or have already become perfect, but I press on if I may also take hold of that for which I was even taken hold of by Christ Jesus. Brothers and sisters, I do not regard myself as having taken hold of it yet; but one thing I do: forgetting what lies behind and reaching forward to what lies ahead, I press on toward the goal for the prize of the upward call of God in Christ Jesus. Therefore, all who are mature, let's have this attitude; and if in anything you have a different attitude, God will reveal that to you as well; however, let's keep living by that same standard to which we have attained.

Brothers and sisters, join in following my example, and observe those who walk according to the pattern you have in us. For many walk, of whom I often told you, and now tell you even as I weep, that they are the enemies of the cross of Christ, whose end is destruction, whose god is their appetite, and whose glory is in their shame, who have their minds on earthly things. For our citizenship is in heaven, from which we also eagerly wait for a Savior, the Lord Jesus Christ; who will transform the body of our lowly condition into conformity with His glorious body, by the exertion of the power that He has even to subject all things to Himself. (Philippians 3:1-21 NASB)

KNOWING GOD, A.W. TOZER
The way to deeper knowledge of God is through the lonely valleys of soul poverty and abnegation of all things.[165]

---

[165] Tozer, The Pursuit of God, 72.

SIMON PETER, A BOND-SERVANT AND APOSTLE OF JESUS CHRIST, To those who have received a faith of the same kind as ours, by the righteousness of our God and Savior, Jesus Christ: Grace and peace be multiplied to you in the knowledge of God and of Jesus our Lord, for His divine power has granted to us everything pertaining to life and godliness, through the true knowledge of Him who called us by His own glory and excellence. Through these He has granted to us His precious and magnificent promises, so that by them you may become partakers of the divine nature, having escaped the corruption that is in the world on account of lust. Now for this very reason also, applying all diligence, in your faith supply moral excellence, and in your moral excellence, knowledge, and in your knowledge, self-control, and in your self-control, perseverance, and in your perseverance, godliness, and in your godliness, brotherly kindness, and in your brotherly kindness, love. For if these qualities are yours and are increasing, they do not make you useless nor unproductive in the true knowledge of our Lord Jesus Christ. For the one who lacks these qualities is blind or short-sighted, having forgotten his purification from his former sins. Therefore, brothers and sisters, be all the more diligent to make certain about His calling and choice of you; for as long as you practice these things, you will never stumble; for in this way the entrance into the eternal kingdom of our Lord and Savior Jesus Christ will be abundantly supplied to you.

Therefore, I will always be ready to remind you of these things, even though you already know them and have been established in the truth which is present with you. I consider it right, as long as I am in this earthly dwelling, to stir you up by way of reminder, knowing that the laying aside of my earthly dwelling is imminent, as also our Lord Jesus Christ has made clear to me. And I will also be diligent that at any time after my departure you will be able to call these things to mind.

For we did not follow cleverly devised tales when we made known to you the power and coming of our Lord Jesus Christ, but we were eyewitnesses of His majesty. For when He received honor and glory from God the Father, such a declaration as this was made to Him by the Majestic Glory: "This is My beloved Son with whom I am well pleased"—and we ourselves heard this declaration made from heaven when we were with Him on the holy mountain.

And so we have the prophetic word made more sure, to which you do well to pay attention as to a lamp shining in a dark place, until the day dawns and the morning star arises in your hearts. But know this first of all, that no prophecy of Scripture becomes a matter of someone's own interpretation, for no prophecy was ever made by an act of human will, but men moved by the Holy Spirit spoke from God. (2 Peter 1:1-21 NASB)

KNOWING YOU JESUS, GRAHAM KENDRICK
Oh, to know the power of Your risen life
And to know You in your sufferings
To become like You in your death, my Lord
So with You to live and never die
Knowing You, Jesus
Knowing You
There is no greater thing
You're my all, You're the best
You're my joy, my righteousness
And I love You, Lord[166]

THEREFORE, BELOVED, SINCE YOU LOOK FOR THESE THINGS, be diligent to be found spotless and blameless by Him, at peace, and regard the patience of our Lord as salvation; just as also our beloved brother Paul, according to the wisdom given him, wrote to you, as also in all his letters, speaking in them of these things, in which there are some things that are hard to understand, which the untaught and unstable distort, as they do also the rest of the Scriptures, to their own

---
[166] Graham Kendrick, "Knowing You (All I Once Held Dear)," distributed by Make Way Music, 1993, cassette.

destruction. You therefore, beloved, knowing this beforehand, be on your guard so that you are not carried away by the error of unscrupulous people and lose your own firm commitment, but grow in the grace and knowledge of our Lord and Savior Jesus Christ. To Him be the glory, both now and to the day of eternity. Amen. (2 Peter 3:14-18 NASB)

> ### *TURNING POINT, DR. DAVID JEREMIAH*
> Let's start with a riddle: What two partners live less than two feet apart but never meet? They're both CEOs of vast organizations with overlapping jurisdictions; they communicate instantly, and work in perfect coordination. One would perish without the other. One specializes in intellectual pursuits all day while the other pumps iron. These two allies work tirelessly for a lifetime without ever taking a vacation or a day off. Even the slightest interruption of their labors would be catastrophic, so they never sleep. They're both exactly the same age, inhabit the same territory, and never rest. Their combined efforts keep us alive and well.
>
> I'm talking, of course, about your brain and your heart. They both oversee complex systems that are necessary for life—the nervous system and the circulatory system. From before our birth until the moment we go to be with the Lord, they're on the job.[167]

MY LITTLE CHILDREN, I am writing these things to you so that you may not sin. And if anyone sins, we have an Advocate with the Father, Jesus Christ the righteous; and He Himself is the propitiation for our sins; and not for ours only, but also for the sins of the whole world.

---

[167] David Jeremiah, author, Bible teacher, founder of Turning Point for God, from https://www.oneplace.com/ministries/ turning-point/read/articles/from-head-to-heart-15538.html.

By this we know that we have come to know Him, if we keep His commandments. The one who says, "I have come to know Him," and does not keep His commandments, is a liar, and the truth is not in him; but whoever follows His word, in him the love of God has truly been perfected. By this we know that we are in Him: the one who says that he remains in Him ought, himself also, walk just as He walked. (1 John 2:1-6 NASB)

I KNOW, BIG DADDY WEAVE

I don't understand the sorrow
But You're calm within the storm
Sometimes this weight is overwhelming
But I don't carry it alone
You're still close when I can't feel You
I don't have to be afraid
And though my eyes have never seen You
I've seen enough to say

I know that You are good
I know that You are good
I know that You are kind
I know that You are so much more
Than what I leave behind

I know that I am loved
I know that I am safe
'Cause even in the fire, to live is Christ, to die is gain
I know that You are good[168]

---

[168] Big Daddy Weave, "I Know," distributed by Fervent Records, track 4 on When The Light Comes, album.

PATTI BURNETT

I OFTEN WONDER WHY IT TAKES PAIN to move certain truths from my head to my heart. I know that the Bible tells me I will experience suffering as a Christ follower and yet until I actually go through the pain, it is just a concept that's out there – applicable for other believers but not necessarily, or even necessary, for me.

A.W. Tozer writes that to know God deeply requires soul poverty and self-abnegation. I am sitting here in a hotel room in the middle of the night; it's 4 am. My mouth almost constantly hurts now, especially through my sleepless nights; and though I've never been addicted to any substance, I find myself begging for a quick fix. I say quick; I've had this Burning Mouth Syndrome now for a year and a half. I googled abnegation and it has to do with self-denial; this is a concept foreign to me.

In less than three hours from now I will have my "On/Off" test. It requires 18 hours with no Parkinson's medications on board at which time the doctors test the patient to evaluate their symptoms. Then they have the patient take their drugs and test them to compare symptoms. If the test results demonstrate a marked distinction between the two tests, meaning the patient is helped by the medications, they are considered a good candidate for Deep Brain Stimulation (DBS) surgery.

This is my last DBS test and it feels a lot like abnegation.

It would not especially surprise me if the Lord were working on my self-centeredness. My Friday morning friends' small group and I love to tag on to the end of our deeply spiritual discussions the phrase "After all, it is all about me." We'll even sing it to the tune of "It's all about You, Jesus." We laugh as though we're just joking, but perhaps there is more than just a sliver of truth to it.

Josh Squires writes that "belief in God's promises doesn't shield us from pain but rather redeems it." And isn't that the whole purpose for our existence here on earth? That God could work out His redemption plan through the Church, His Body, desiring that none should perish, and all would know Him personally and spend eternity with Him.

I wonder if many of our "dark nights of the soul" or "soul poverty" occur at 4 am.

Father, To the limited degree that I understand abnegation, take this flimsy, tear-stained, sleep deprived offering of abnegation and have Your way in me. It hurts like crazy, but I surrender to Your plan of redemption for my life.

Chapter 26
BE A WISE GUY

AT THAT TIME JESUS SAID, "I praise you, Father, Lord of heaven and earth, that You have hidden these things from the wise and intelligent and have revealed them to infants. Yes, Father, for this way was well-pleasing in Your sight. All things have been handed over to Me by My Father; and no one knows the Son except the Father; nor does anyone know the Father except the Son, and anyone to whom the Son wills to reveal Him.

"Come to Me, all who are weary and heavy-laden, and I will give you rest. Take My yoke upon you and learn from Me, for I am gentle and humble in heart, and you will find rest for your souls. For My yoke is easy and My burden is light." (Matthew 11:25-30 NASB)

ALL I REALLY NEED TO KNOW I LEARNED IN KINDERGARTEN, ROBERT FULGHUM

Most of what I really need to know about how to live, and what to do, and how to be, I learned in kindergarten. Wisdom was not at the top of the graduate school mountain,
but there in the sandbox at nursery school.
These are the things I learned …
Share everything.
Play fair.
Don't hit people.
Put things back where you found them.
Clean up your own mess.
Don't take things that aren't yours.
Say you're sorry when you hurt somebody.
Wash your hands before you eat.
Flush.
Warm cookies and cold milk are good for you.
Live a balanced life- learn some and think some
and draw and paint and sing and dance and work every day some.
Take a nap every afternoon. (As a college student I stress this one.)
When you go out into the world watch out for traffic, hold hands, and stick together.
Be aware of wonder.
Remember the little seed in the styrofoam cup.
The roots go down and the plant goes up and nobody really knows
how or why but we are all like that.
Goldfish and hamsters and white mice and even the little seed in the styrofoam cup - they all die.
So do we.
Remember to look around you.
Everything you need to know is in there somewhere.
The Golden Rule and love and basic sanitation.
Ecology and politics and equality and sane living.

Think of what a better world it would be if we all –
the whole world had cookies and milk about 3 o'clock
every afternoon
and then lay down with our blankets for a nap.
Or if we had a basic policy in our nation and other nations to always
put things back where we found them and cleaned up our
own messes.
And it is still true, no matter how old you are,
when you go out into the world, it is best to hold hands and stick
together.[169]

PATTI BURNETT

THE MAN WHO WROTE "All I Really Need to Know I learned in Kindergarten" was a pastor, philosopher, public speaker, cowboy, folksinger, IBM salesman, professional artist, bartender, teacher, and father.

I thought it would be fun to go through Pastor Fulghum's list of the virtues he learned when he was five years old and apply them to some of my 70 years of life lessons.

- Share everything – especially your heart. Be willing to be vulnerable if you expect your friendships to be deep and honest (II Corinthians 12:9-10).
- Play fair – Don't manipulate people for your own purposes. Instead help them to see themselves as God sees them (Matthew 7:15).
- Don't hit people – Will your mouth be an instrument of encouragement and love, or a cesspool of ugly lies and hatred (Ephesians 4:29)?

---

[169] Robert Fulghum, All I Really Need to Know I Learned in Kindergarten (Baltimore: Ivy Books, 1989), from https://www.google.com/books/edition/All_I_Really_Need_to_Know_I_Learned_in_K/tQZnwgEACAAJ?hl=en.

- Put things back where you found them and clean up your own mess – Ask forgiveness and be willing to forgive even before it is asked of you (Mark 11:25).
- Don't take things that are not yours – It is more blessed to give than to receive; in fact, give a blessing to your family and friends. Let them know how special they are to you every time you meet (Acts 20:35).
- Say you're sorry when you hurt somebody – Humble yourself in the sight of your Lord and your friends. Find ways to lift them up when they are feeling down and depressed (James 4:10).
- Wash your hands before you eat – Come clean. The more time you spend washed in the water of God's Word the more able you will be to offer the gospel to your friends and family who need Jesus (Ephesians 5:26).
- Flush – There is a lot of ugliness and division in this world today. Let there be none of that in you. Let there be a distinct difference between the One that you represent and all that we see going on in social media, the internet, and the news. In fact, it wouldn't hurt to take a fast from social media, the internet, and the news (II Corinthians 2:15).
- Warm cookies and cold milk are good for you. Feast on the Word of God so it penetrates your heart and bones, all the way to the marrow (Hebrews 5:12).
- Live a balanced life – God has beautifully gifted you. Make your life a testimony to His creativity and excellent workmanship (Ephesians 2:10).
- Nap everyday – Sleep well by immersing yourself in meditation and prayer before laying your head on your pillow (Proverbs 3:24).
- When you go out into the world watch out for traffic, hold hands, and stick together—Work as a team. We are the Body of Christ. Use your spiritual gifts to build something of beauty so that the world will see who Jesus is (Ephesians 4:1-32)

- Be aware of wonder – You are the Temple of the Holy Spirit – He wants to use you as an instrument of His grace and mercy (I Corinthians 3:16).
- Remember the little seed in the styrofoam cup – Die to yourself daily. Take up your cross and follow Jesus. When people see that you are still in love with Jesus even during the difficult times, they are seeing Him, not you (Galatians 2:20).
- Goldfish and hamsters and white mice and even the little seed in the styrofoam cup—they all die. So do we – Fear not. We have a mansion in heaven that God has prepared for us (John 14:2-3).
- Remember to look around you – Notice the miracles (Mark 10:27).
- Read the Bible - Everything you need to know is in there somewhere. The Golden Rule and love and basic sanitation. Ecology and politics and equality and sane living. Do unto others as you would have them do unto you and return a blessing for a curse (Matthew 7:12).

FOR THE WORD OF THE CROSS is foolishness to those who are perishing, but to us who are being saved it is the power of God. For it is written:

"I will destroy the wisdom of the wise, and the understanding of those who have understanding, I will confound."

Where is the wise person? Where is the scribe? Where is the debater of this age? Has God not made foolish the wisdom of the world? For since in the wisdom of God the world through its wisdom did not come to know God, God was pleased through the foolishness of the message preached to save those who believe. For indeed Jews ask for signs and Greeks search for wisdom; but we preach Christ crucified, to Jews a stumbling block, and to Gentiles foolishness, but to those who are the called, both Jews and Greeks, Christ the power of God and the wisdom of God. For the foolishness of God is wiser than mankind, and the weakness of God is stronger than mankind.

For consider your calling, brothers and sisters, that there were not many wise according to the flesh, not many mighty, not many noble; but God has chosen the foolish things of the world to shame the wise, and God has chosen the weak things of the world to shame the things which are strong, and the insignificant things of the world and the despised God has chosen, the things that are not, so that He may nullify the things that are, so that no human may boast before God. But it is due to Him that you are in Christ Jesus, who became to us wisdom from God, and righteousness and sanctification, and redemption, so that, just as it is written: "Let the one who boasts, boast in the Lord. (1 Corinthians 1:18-31 NASB)

AS YOU LIKE IT, WILLIAM SHAKESPEARE
The fool doth think he is wise, but the wise man knows himself to be a fool.[170]

THE HEAVENS ARE TELLING THE GLORY OF GOD; they are a marvelous display of His craftsmanship. Day and night they keep on telling about God. Without a sound or word, silent in the skies, their message reaches out to all the world. The sun lives in the heavens where God placed it and moves out across the skies as radiant as a bridegroom going to his wedding, or as joyous as an athlete looking forward to a race! The sun crosses the heavens from end to end, and nothing can hide from its heat.

God's laws are perfect. They protect us, make us wise, and give us joy and light. God's laws are pure, eternal, just. They are more desirable than gold. They are sweeter than honey dripping from a honeycomb. For they warn us away from harm and give success to those who obey them.

But how can I ever know what sins are lurking in my heart? Cleanse me from these hidden faults. And keep me from deliberate wrongs; help

---
[170] Stephen Lynch quoting William Shakespeare, As You Like It: A Guide To The Play (Santa Barbara: ABC-CLIO Publishing, 2003), 101.

me to stop doing them. Only then can I be free of guilt and innocent of some great crime.

May my spoken words and unspoken thoughts be pleasing even to You, O Lord my Rock and my Redeemer. (Psalm 19:1-14 TLB)

> ### MICHELANGELO
> The greater danger for most of us lies not in setting our aim too high and falling short; but in setting our aim too low, and achieving our mark.[171]

EVERY YOUNG MAN WHO LISTENS TO ME AND OBEYS MY INSTRUCTIONS will be given wisdom and good sense. Yes, if you want better insight and discernment, and are searching for them as you would for lost money or hidden treasure, then wisdom will be given you and knowledge of God Himself; you will soon learn the importance of reverence for the Lord and of trusting Him.

For the Lord grants wisdom! His every word is a treasure of knowledge and understanding. He grants good sense to the godly—His saints. He is their shield, protecting them and guarding their pathway. He shows how to distinguish right from wrong, how to find the right decision every time. For wisdom and truth will enter the very center of your being, filling your life with joy. You will be given the sense to stay away from evil men who want you to be their partners in crime—men who turn from God's ways to walk down dark and evil paths. (Proverbs 2:1-13 (TLB)

---

[171] Michelangelo, from https://www.brainyquote.com/quotes/michelangelo_108779

> **MRS. GOOSE, HER BOOK, MAURICE SWITZER**
> It is better to remain silent at the risk of being thought a fool, than to talk and remove all doubt of it.[172]

TO LEARN, YOU MUST WANT TO BE TAUGHT. TO REFUSE REPROOF IS STUPID.
The Lord blesses good men and condemns the wicked.

Wickedness never brings real success; only the godly have that.

A worthy wife is her husband's joy and crown; the other kind corrodes his strength and tears down everything he does.

A good man's mind is filled with honest thoughts; an evil man's mind is crammed with lies.

The wicked accuse; the godly defend.

The wicked shall perish; the godly shall stand.

Everyone admires a man with good sense, but a man with a warped mind is despised.

It is better to get your hands dirty—and eat, than to be too proud to work—and starve.

A good man is concerned for the welfare of his animals, but even the kindness of godless men is cruel.

---

[172] Maurice Switzer, Mrs. Goose, Her Book (London: Forgotten Books, 2018), 1.

Be A Wise Guy

Hard work means prosperity; only a fool idles away his time.

Crooks are jealous of each other's loot, while good men long to help each other.

Lies will get any man into trouble, but honesty is its own defense.

Telling the truth gives a man great satisfaction, and hard work returns many blessings to him.

A fool thinks he needs no advice, but a wise man listens to others.

A fool is quick-tempered; a wise man stays cool when insulted.

A good man is known by his truthfulness; a false man by deceit and lies.

Some people like to make cutting remarks, but the words of the wise soothe and heal.

Truth stands the test of time; lies are soon exposed.

Deceit fills hearts that are plotting for evil; joy fills hearts that are planning for good!

No real harm befalls the good, but there is constant trouble for the wicked.

God delights in those who keep their promises and abhors those who don't.

A wise man doesn't display his knowledge, but a fool displays his foolishness.

Work hard and become a leader; be lazy and never succeed.

Anxious hearts are very heavy, but a word of encouragement does wonders!

The good man asks advice from friends; the wicked plunge ahead—and fall.

A lazy man won't even dress the game he gets while hunting, but the diligent man makes good use of everything he finds.

The path of the godly leads to life. So why fear death? (Proverbs 12:1-28 TLB)

DANIEL, LIVES OF INTEGRITY, BETH MOORE

The lifeblood of integrity is becoming the same person no matter where we are – no matter who's around. When we become people of integrity, everything we are on the inside is obvious from the outside. The Latin word for "integrity" literally means "entire." The essence of the term is wholeness and completeness. Integrity is "the quality or state of being complete or undivided." You can see, therefore, how much integrity depends on consistency. Integrity not only calls us to live inside-out, it keeps the outside from coming in. Consistency in our walk and in our talk becomes a transportable cloak of protection around us, going anywhere we go. Life becomes so much simpler when there aren't so many costume changes.[173]

---

[173] Beth Moore, Daniel: Lives of Integrity, Words of Prophecy (Nashville: Lifeway Christian Resources, 2006), 25.

WE CAN MAKE OUR PLANS, BUT THE FINAL OUTCOME IS IN GOD'S HANDS.

We can always "prove" that we are right, but is the Lord convinced?
Commit your work to the Lord, then it will succeed.
The Lord has made everything for His own purposes—even the wicked for punishment.
Pride disgusts the Lord. Take my word for it—proud men shall be punished.
Iniquity is atoned for by mercy and truth; evil is avoided by reverence for God.
When a man is trying to please God, God makes even his worst enemies to be at peace with him.
A little gained honestly is better than great wealth gotten by dishonest means.
We should make plans—counting on God to direct us.
God will help the king to judge the people fairly; there need be no mistakes.
The Lord demands fairness in every business deal. He established this principle.
It is a horrible thing for a king to do evil. His right to rule depends upon his fairness.
The king rejoices when his people are truthful and fair.
The anger of the king is a messenger of death, and a wise man will appease it.
Many favors are showered on those who please the king.
How much better is wisdom than gold, and understanding than silver!
The path of the godly leads away from evil; he who follows that path is safe.
Pride goes before destruction and haughtiness before a fall.
Better poor and humble than proud and rich.
God blesses those who obey Him; happy the man who puts his trust in the Lord.

The wise man is known by his common sense, and a pleasant teacher is the best.
Wisdom is a fountain of life to those possessing it, but a fool's burden is his folly.
From a wise mind comes careful and persuasive speech.
Kind words are like honey—enjoyable and healthful.
Before every man there lies a wide and pleasant road he thinks is right, but it ends in death.
Hunger is good—if it makes you work to satisfy it!
Idle hands are the devil's workshop; idle lips are his mouthpiece.
An evil man sows strife; gossip separates the best of friends.
Wickedness loves company—and leads others into sin.
The wicked man stares into space with pursed lips, deep in thought, planning his evil deeds.
White hair is a crown of glory and is seen most among the godly.
It is better to be slow-tempered than famous; it is better to have self-control than to control an army.
We toss the coin, but it is the Lord who controls its decision. (Proverbs 16:1-33 TLB)

ARISTOTLE
Knowing yourself is the beginning of all wisdom.[174]

REFINING POT IS FOR SILVER AND THE FURNACE FOR GOLD,
But the Lord tests hearts.
Grandchildren are the crown of the old,
And the glory of sons is their fathers.
A friend loves at all times,
And a brother is born for adversity.
A joyful heart is good medicine,
But a broken spirit dries up the bones.

---
[174] Steven Slavropoulos quoting Aristotle, The Beginning of All Wisdom (New York City: Hachette Books, 2003), 47.

One who withholds his words has knowledge,
And one who has a cool spirit is a person of understanding.
Even a fool, when he keeps silent, is considered wise;
When he closes his lips, he is considered prudent. (Proverbs 17:3, 6, 17, 22, 27-28 NASB)

DAWN PSAROMATIC

There are three definitions of wisdom (noun): 1. The ability to discern or judge what is true, right, or lasting; insight. 2. Common sense; good judgement. 3. The sum of learning through the ages; knowledge.

While the definition of wisdom hasn't changed over time, it does take on different meanings at different stages of our lives. When we were young, we didn't really think about what it meant to be wise. It was a word we might have heard from our parents or elders, "a word to the wise" or "there's wisdom in that," but it was not a word commonly used or pondered in our lighthearted adolescence. However, as we aged, we began to truly grasp the value of wisdom – especially godly wisdom.

The word wisdom is mentioned 222 times in the Hebrew Bible. The Bible emphasizes that wisdom is one of the greatest qualities we can possess. It's an important and vital spiritual gift that provides us with common sense and good judgment to help us determine right from wrong according to God's standards; and it provides us with happiness and a long life (Proverbs 3:13-16).

Wisdom, the sum of learning through the ages, is reflected in Proverbs 16:31. Gray hair is a crown of glory; it is attained in the way of righteousness. Gray hair is representative of our garland of wisdom, the knowledge we've obtained through the years of joy and heartache, through the years of splendor and suffering, and through the years that God has given and taken away.

In 1 Kings 3:1-15, Solomon asks God to give him a discerning heart to govern God's people and to distinguish between right and wrong. Because Solomon didn't ask God for a long life or wealth, nor did he ask for the death of his enemies, God gave him more than he could have ever wished—a wise and discerning heart.

God wants us to be wise.

Seek God's Word and pray for wisdom. Only then can we discern what is true and what is right in the eyes of our Heavenly Father.[175]

> **PHILIP YANCEY**
> A God wise enough to create me and the world I live in is wise enough to watch out for me.[176]

---

[175] Dawn Psaromatis, wise personal friend of author.

[176] Philip Yancey, Where is God When It Hurts? (Grand Rapids: Zondervan, 1997), 115.

Chapter 27

THE MASTER TEACHER

NOW WHEN JESUS SAW THE CROWDS, He went up on a mountainside and sat down. His disciples came to Him, and He began to teach them.

He said:

"Blessed are the poor in spirit, for theirs is the kingdom of heaven. (Matthew 5:1-3 NIV)

PATTI BURNETT

DAN AND I had the privilege of touring the Holy Land in 2014 with my brother, Dave, and his wife, Cindy. It was amazing, humbling, and awe-inspiring to walk where Jesus had walked and to sing and take communion close to where He'd celebrated His last supper.

Probably the point of interest that struck me most intensely was the Wailing Wall.

For the last year, I had been pleading with God to explain how He planned to use Parkinson's in my life.

The morning we went to the wall, my devotional reading was from Matthew 6, about God's loving care for the flowers of the field and the birds of the air—they don't store up food and yet our heavenly Father feeds and cares for their every need.

As Cindy and I waited to take our prayer requests up to the wall, I watched as a mother sparrow brought food to a nest near the top. It was as though the Father was telling me personally that He had this thing. My PD did not surprise Him; but in fact, he had a strategy that would far and away exceed my plans to work with Him to grow the kingdom. The message from the mother sparrow was an unmistakable answer to the question I had scribbled on my tiny piece of paper and squished into a crack on the wall.

If God loves the birds of the air so fervently, won't He take even greater care of His human children? Our Father God made the ultimate sacrifice by sending His Son to die so we could be adopted into His family. He is so well acquainted with us that He knows how many hairs we have on our heads. He knows our thoughts, plans, weaknesses, strengths, and dreams. He is familiar with all our ways (Psalm 139:1-4). He molded me in Christ's image. I am His child. Surely, He cares even more for me than He cares for the birds, the lilies, and the grass.

Why should I worry?

"BLESSED ARE THOSE WHO MOURN, FOR THEY SHALL BE COMFORTED.

"Blessed are the gentle, for they shall inherit the earth.

"Blessed are those who hunger and thirst for righteousness, for they shall be satisfied.

"Blessed are the merciful, for they shall receive mercy.

"Blessed are the pure in heart, for they shall see God.

"Blessed are the peacemakers, for they shall be called sons of God.

"Blessed are those who have been persecuted for the sake of righteousness, for theirs is the kingdom of heaven.

"Blessed are you when people insult you and persecute you, and falsely say all kinds of evil against you because of Me. Rejoice and be glad, for your reward in heaven is great; for in the same way, they persecuted the prophets who were before you.

"You are the salt of the earth; but if the salt has become tasteless, how can it be made salty again? It is no longer good for anything, except to be thrown out and trampled underfoot by men.

"You are the light of the world. A city set on a hill cannot be hidden; nor does anyone light a lamp and put it under a basket, but on the lampstand, and it gives light to all who are in the house. Let your light shine before men in such a way that they may see your good works and glorify your Father who is in heaven.

"Do not think that I came to abolish the Law or the Prophets; I did not come to abolish but to fulfill. For truly I say to you, until heaven and earth pass-away, not the smallest letter or stroke shall pass from the Law until all is accomplished. Whoever then annuls one of the least of these commandments, and teaches others to do the same, shall be called least in the kingdom of heaven; but whoever keeps and teaches them, he shall be called great in the kingdom of heaven.

"You have heard that it was said, 'An eye for an eye, and a tooth for a tooth.' But I say to you, do not resist an evil person; but whoever slaps you on your right cheek, turn the other to him also. If anyone wants to sue you and take your shirt, let him have your coat also. Whoever forces you to go one mile, go with him two. Give to him who asks of you, and do not turn away from him who wants to borrow from you.

"You have heard that it was said, 'You shall love your neighbor and hate your enemy.' But I say to you, love your enemies and pray for those who persecute you, so that you may be sons of your Father who is in heaven; for He causes His sun to rise on the evil and the good, and sends rain on the righteous and the unrighteous. For if you love those who love you, what reward do you have? Do not even the tax collectors do the same? If you greet only your brothers, what more are you doing than others? Do not even the Gentiles do the same? Therefore, you are to be perfect, as your heavenly Father is perfect. (Matthew 5:4-19, 38-42 NASB)

> ### *JAN HUS*
> I hope, by God's grace, that I am truly a Christian, not deviating from the faith, and that I would rather suffer the penalty of a terrible death than wish to affirm anything outside of the faith or transgress the commandments of our Lord Jesus Christ.[177]

---

[177] Jan Hus, De Ecclesia: The Church (New York: New York Public Library, 1915) V.

The Master Teacher

"**BE CAREFUL** not to practice your righteousness in front of others to be seen by them. If you do, you will have no reward from your Father in heaven.

"So when you give to the needy, do not announce it with trumpets, as the hypocrites do in the synagogues and on the streets, to be honored by others. Truly I tell you, they have received their reward in full. But when you give to the needy, do not let your left hand know what your right hand is doing, so that your giving may be in secret. Then your Father, who sees what is done in secret, will reward you.

"And when you pray, do not be like the hypocrites, for they love to pray standing in the synagogues and on the street corners to be seen by others. Truly I tell you, they have received their reward in full. But when you pray, go into your room, close the door and pray to your Father, who is unseen. Then your Father, who sees what is done in secret, will reward you. And when you pray, do not keep on babbling like pagans, for they think they will be heard because of their many words. Do not be like them, for your Father knows what you need before you ask Him.

"This, then, is how you should pray:

> "'Our Father in heaven,
> hallowed be Your name,
> Your kingdom come,
> Your will be done,
> on earth as it is in heaven.
> Give us today our daily bread.
> And forgive us our debts,
> as we also have forgiven our debtors.
> And lead us not into temptation,
> but deliver us from the evil one.'

For if you forgive other people when they sin against you, your heavenly Father will also forgive you. But if you do not forgive others their sins, your Father will not forgive your sins.

"When you fast, do not look somber as the hypocrites do, for they disfigure their faces to show others they are fasting. Truly I tell you, they have received their reward in full. But when you fast, put oil on your head and wash your face, so that it will not be obvious to others that you are fasting, but only to your Father, who is unseen; and your Father, who sees what is done in secret, will reward you.

"Do not store up for yourselves treasures on earth, where moths and vermin destroy, and where thieves break in and steal. But store up for yourselves treasures in heaven, where moths and vermin do not destroy, and where thieves do not break in and steal. For where your treasure is, there your heart will be also.

"The eye is the lamp of the body. If your eyes are healthy, your whole body will be full of light. But if your eyes are unhealthy, your whole body will be full of darkness. If then the light within you is darkness, how great is that darkness!

"No one can serve two masters. Either you will hate the one and love the other, or you will be devoted to the one and despise the other. You cannot serve both God and money.

"Therefore I tell you, do not worry about your life, what you will eat or drink; or about your body, what you will wear. Is not life more than food, and the body more than clothes? Look at the birds of the air; they do not sow or reap or store away in barns, and yet your heavenly Father feeds them. Are you not much more valuable than they? Can any one of you by worrying add a single hour to your life?

"And why do you worry about clothes? See how the flowers of the field grow. They do not labor or spin. Yet I tell you that not even Solomon in all his splendor was dressed like one of these. If that is how God clothes the grass of the field, which is here today and tomorrow is thrown into the fire, will He not much more clothe you—you of little faith? So do not worry, saying, 'What shall we eat?' or 'What shall we drink?' or 'What shall we wear?' For the pagans run after all these things, and your heavenly Father knows that you need them. But seek first His kingdom and His righteousness, and all these things will be given to you as well. Therefore do not worry about tomorrow, for tomorrow will worry about itself. Each day has enough trouble of its own. (Matthew 6:1-34 NIV)

DALLAS WILLARD
The basic question 'will I obey Christ's teaching?'
is rarely taken as a serious issue.
For example, to take one of Jesus' commands,
that is relevant to contemporary life,
I don't know of any church that actually teaches a church
how to bless people who curse them,
yet this is a clear command.[178]

"*ASK, AND IT WILL BE GIVEN TO YOU; SEEK, AND YOU WILL FIND;* knock, and it will be opened to you. For everyone who asks receives, and he who seeks finds, and to him who knocks it will be opened. Or what man is there among you who, when his son asks for a loaf, will give him a stone? Or if he asks for a fish, he will not give him a snake, will he? If you then, being evil, know how to give good gifts to your children, how much more will your Father who is in heaven give what is good to those who ask Him!

"In everything, therefore, treat people the same way you want them to treat you, for this is the Law and the Prophets.

"Enter through the narrow gate; for the gate is wide and the way is broad that leads to destruction, and there are many who enter through it. For the gate is small and the way is narrow that leads to life, and there are few who find it.

"Therefore, everyone who hears these words of Mine and acts on them, may be compared to a wise man who built his house on the rock. And the rain fell, and the floods came, and the winds blew and slammed against that house; and yet it did not fall, for it had been founded on

---

[178] Dallas Willard, Following Jesus and Living in the Kingdom (Colorado Springs: NavPress, 2022).

the rock. Everyone who hears these words of Mine and does not act on them, will be like a foolish man who built his house on the sand. The rain fell, and the floods came, and the winds blew and slammed against that house; and it fell—and great was its fall."

When Jesus had finished these words, the crowds were amazed at His teaching; for He was teaching them as one having authority, and not as their scribes. (Matthew 7:7-29 NASB)

> ### GROUCHO MARX
> Blessed are the cracked, for they shall let in the light.[179]

HEARING THAT JESUS HAD SILENCED THE SADDUCEES, the Pharisees got together. One of them, an expert in the law, tested Him with this question: "Teacher, which is the greatest commandment in the Law?"

Jesus replied: "'Love the Lord your God with all your heart and with all your soul and with all your mind.' This is the first and greatest commandment. And the second is like it: 'Love your neighbor as yourself.' All the Law and the Prophets hang on these two commandments." (Matthew 22:34-40 NIV)

> ### TIMOTHY KELLER
> Jesus' teaching consistently attracted the irreligious while offending the Bible-believing, religious people of His day.[180]

---

[179] Jason Pegler quoting Groucho Marx, Mental Health Publishing and Empowerment (United Kingdom: Chipamunka Publishing Ltd, 2009), 63.

[180] Timothy Keller, The Prodigal God: Recovering the Heart of the Christian Faith (Westminster, London: Penguin, 2008), 18.

ONE SABBATH JESUS WAS GOING THROUGH THE GRAINFIELDS, and His disciples began to pick some heads of grain, rub them in their hands and eat the kernels. Some of the Pharisees asked, "Why are you doing what is unlawful on the Sabbath?"

Jesus answered them, "Have you never read what David did when he and his companions were hungry? He entered the house of God, and taking the consecrated bread, he ate what is lawful only for priests to eat. And he also gave some to his companions." Then Jesus said to them, "The Son of Man is Lord of the Sabbath."

On another Sabbath He went into the synagogue and was teaching, and a man was there whose right hand was shriveled. The Pharisees and the teachers of the law were looking for a reason to accuse Jesus, so they watched Him closely to see if He would heal on the Sabbath. But Jesus knew what they were thinking and said to the man with the shriveled hand, "Get up and stand in front of everyone." So he got up and stood there.

Then Jesus said to them, "I ask you, which is lawful on the Sabbath: to do good or to do evil, to save life or to destroy it?"

He looked around at them all, and then said to the man, "Stretch out your hand." He did so, and his hand was completely restored. But the Pharisees and the teachers of the law were furious and began to discuss with one another what they might do to Jesus.

One of those days Jesus went out to a mountainside to pray and spent the night praying to God. When morning came, He called his disciples to Him and chose twelve of them, whom He also designated apostles: Simon (whom he named Peter), his brother Andrew, James, John, Philip, Bartholomew, Matthew, Thomas, James son of Alphaeus, Simon who was called the Zealot, Judas son of James, and Judas Iscariot, who became a traitor.

He went down with them and stood on a level place. A large crowd of His disciples was there and a great number of people from all over Judea, from Jerusalem, and from the coastal region around Tyre and Sidon, who had come to hear Him and to be healed of their diseases.

Those troubled by impure spirits were cured, and the people all tried to touch Him, because power was coming from Him and healing them all.

Looking at his disciples, he said:

"Blessed are you who are poor,
for yours is the kingdom of God.
Blessed are you who hunger now,
for you will be satisfied.
Blessed are you who weep now,
for you will laugh.
Blessed are you when people hate you,
when they exclude you and insult you
and reject your name as evil,
because of the Son of Man.
"Rejoice in that day and leap for joy, because great is
your reward in heaven. For that is how
their ancestors treated the prophets.
"But woe to you who are rich,
for you have already received your comfort.
Woe to you who are well fed now,
for you will go hungry.
Woe to you who laugh now,
for you will mourn and weep.
Woe to you when everyone speaks well of you,
for that is how their ancestors treated
the false prophets.

"But to you who are listening I say: love your enemies, do good to those who hate you, bless those who curse you, pray for those who mistreat you. If someone slaps you on one cheek, turn to them the other also. If someone takes your coat, do not withhold your shirt from them. Give to everyone who asks you, and if anyone takes what belongs to you, do not demand it back. Do to others as you would have them do to you.

"If you love those who love you, what credit is that to you? Even sinners love those who love them. And if you do good to those who are good to you, what credit is that to you? Even sinners do that. And if you lend to those from whom you expect repayment, what credit is that to you? Even sinners lend to sinners, expecting to be repaid in full. But love your enemies, do good to them, and lend to them without expecting to get anything back. Then your reward will be great, and you will be children of the Most High, because He is kind to the ungrateful and wicked. Be merciful, just as your Father is merciful.

"Do not judge, and you will not be judged. Do not condemn, and you will not be condemned. Forgive, and you will be forgiven. (Luke 6:1-37 NIV)

> ### MARK DRISCOLL
> Don't believe false teaching that says you won't suffer if you really love Jesus. Jesus will end all suffering eventually, but on earth He suffered more than anyone.[181]

THEN HE SAID TO HIS DISCIPLES, "Therefore I say to you, do not worry about your life, what you will eat; nor about the body, what you will put on. Life is more than food, and the body is more than clothing. Consider the ravens, for they neither sow nor reap, which have neither storehouse nor barn; and God feeds them. Of how much more value are you than the birds? And which of you by worrying can add one cubit to his stature? If you then are not able to do the least, why are you anxious for the rest? Consider the lilies, how they grow: they neither toil nor spin; and yet I say to you, even Solomon in all his glory was not

---

[181] Mark Driscoll, Mars Hill Elder, American Evangelical pastor and author, from https://www.azquotes.com/quote/856846.

arrayed like one of these. If then God so clothes the grass, which today is in the field and tomorrow is thrown into the oven, how much more will He clothe you, O you of little faith?

"And do not seek what you should eat or what you should drink, nor have an anxious mind. For all these things the nations of the world seek after, and your Father knows that you need these things. But seek the kingdom of God, and all these things shall be added to you.

"Do not fear, little flock, for it is your Father's good pleasure to give you the kingdom. Sell what you have and give alms; provide yourselves money bags which do not grow old, a treasure in the heavens that does not fail, where no thief approaches nor moth destroys. For where your treasure is, there your heart will be also. (Luke 12:22-34 NKJV)

> **OSWALD CHAMBERS**
> The dearest friend on earth is a mere shadow compared to Jesus Christ.[182]

DEAR FRIENDS, I AM NOT WRITING YOU A NEW COMMAND but an old one, which you have had since the beginning. This old command is the message you have heard. Yet I am writing you a new command; its truth is seen in Him and in you, because the darkness is passing and the true light is already shining.

Anyone who claims to be in the light but hates a brother or sister is still in the darkness. Anyone who loves their brother and sister lives in the light, and there is nothing in them to make them stumble. But anyone who hates a brother or sister is in the darkness and walks around in the darkness. They do not know where they are going, because the darkness has blinded them.

---

[182] Randy Acorn quoting Oswald Chambers, It's All About Jesus (Bloomington: Westbow Press, 2022), 199.

I am writing to you, dear children,
because your sins have been forgiven on account of His name.
I am writing to you, fathers,
because you know Him who is from the beginning.
I am writing to you, young men,
because you have overcome the evil one.
I write to you, dear children,
because you know the Father.
I write to you, fathers,
because you know Him who is from the beginning.
I write to you, young men,
because you are strong,
and the word of God lives in you,
and you have overcome the evil one.

Do not love the world or anything in the world. If anyone loves the world, love for the Father is not in them. For everything in the world—the lust of the flesh, the lust of the eyes, and the pride of life—comes not from the Father but from the world. The world and its desires pass away, but whoever does the will of God lives forever.

Dear children, this is the last hour; and as you have heard that the antichrist is coming, even now many antichrists have come. This is how we know it is the last hour. They went out from us, but they did not really belong to us. For if they had belonged to us, they would have remained with us; but their going showed that none of them belonged to us.

But you have an anointing from the Holy One, and all of you know the truth. I do not write to you because you do not know the truth, but because you do know it and because no lie comes from the truth. Who is the liar? It is whoever denies that Jesus is the Christ. Such a person is the antichrist—denying the Father and the Son. No one who denies the Son has the Father; whoever acknowledges the Son has the Father also.

As for you, see that what you have heard from the beginning remains in you. If it does, you also will remain in the Son and in the Father. And this is what He promised us—eternal life.

I am writing these things to you about those who are trying to lead you astray. As for you, the anointing you received from Him remains in you, and you do not need anyone to teach you. But as His anointing teaches you about all things and as that anointing is real, not counterfeit—just as it has taught you, remain in Him.

And now, dear children, continue in Him, so that when He appears we may be confident and unashamed before Him at His coming.

If you know that He is righteous, you know that everyone who does what is right has been born of Him. (I John 2:7-29 NIV)

Chapter 28

TEACH YOUR CHILDREN (AND PARENTS) WELL

ONE DAY CHILDREN WERE BROUGHT TO JESUS in the hope that He would lay hands on them. The disciples shooed them off. But Jesus intervened: "Let the children alone, don't prevent them from coming to me. God's kingdom is made up of people like these." After laying hands on them, He left. (Matthew 19:13-15 Message)

PATTI BURNETT

THE SANDWICH GENERATION is comprised of adults at least 65 years old who have a living parent and are either raising a child under 18 or supporting a grown child. Now that Dan's and my parents are gone, Bethany and Rachel may at some point assume their sandwich generation positions.

At this time, we love helping to care for our grandkids: Noah, Jaxson, Maverick, and Emerson – hopefully easing the financial and schedule burdens for our daughters' families. It is our privilege to spend time with the most precious children in all of creation. I love that I can at times take care of baby Emerson so that Rachel can get some much needed rest. My generation has recently been described as the club sandwich generation, wedged between our 90 something year old parents and our grandchildren.

Not knowing what my future holds with Parkinson's, I pray that Bethany and Rachel do not have a difficult road ahead, partnering with Dan for my care. On a continual basis, I remind myself that this too is in God's hands. We must trust Him, while at the same time making responsible choices—planning long term care options, exercising, eating well, growing more and more in love with Jesus, and maintaining a strong network of friends and medical support.

Just three days ago I had my first of three Deep Brain Stimulation surgeries in the hopes that this will extend the number of years that God will grant me as I continue walking with Him. There are, of course, no guarantees. I look pretty scary right now – eyes swollen nearly shut, bloody incision on my head that makes it look as though I was just the victim of an axe murderer. The things we do for love.

Our children need to be aware of stressors that can plague their generation such as: care partner burnout; neglect for spouse and children; failure to schedule time for hobbies, fun, and work; as well as psychological issues.

Teach Your Children (and Parents) Well

Lastly, here are some tips that can make for a more positive care partnering experience:

1. Consider moving aging parents into your home to curb expenses and contribute to their continuing happiness, especially in their 12th hour.
2. Establish a medical alert system.
3. Hire outside assistance so that the care partner has time for rejuvenation and relaxation.
4. Have other family members contribute to financial and care responsibilities.
5. Ensure that aging parents have excellent hearing aid devices - it's amazing how much this small accessory contributes to cognition.

Not to be self-serving, but it wouldn't hurt for a care partner to get a copy of **CHRONIC HOPE: God's Redeeming Presence in the Midst of Pain.** This book may be an excellent help as both you and your loved one relax at the end of the day and prepare for sleep!

And I, of course, would not fail to mention our love for our three canine friends – Cadence, Yampa, and Teagan. Does that make this the hotdog generation? At this time, I guess between the grandkids and the grand dogs, it is our privilege to play the roles of care partners rather than care receivers.

AT THAT TIME THE DISCIPLES CAME TO JESUS AND SAID, "Who then is greatest in the kingdom of heaven?" And He called a child to Himself and set him among them, and said, "Truly I say to you, unless you change and become like children, you will not enter the kingdom of heaven. So whoever will humble himself like this child, he is the greatest in the kingdom of heaven. And whoever receives one such child in My name, receives Me; but whoever causes one of these little ones who believe in Me to sin, it is better for him that a heavy millstone be hung around his neck, and that he be drowned in the depths of the sea. (Matthew 18:1-6 NASB)

PATTI BURNETT

THERE IS NOTHING LIKE BEING A GRANDMA, at least that's the opinion of this "MiMi." I love my four grandchildren. They are the apple of my eye, and they almost always make me smile.

Many of my friends have said that the person who had the greatest spiritual influence on their lives was a grandparent. Why is that?

I think that the discipline of prayer has a lot to do with it. Shortly after the death of my dad, my sister-in-law, Jenn, paused to consider how blessed we were to have had parents who constantly covered our children and grandchildren with prayer. To this day, I have cherished in my heart the memory of my dad kneeling by his bed. Now it's our turn to receive the baton and run the race so that "those who come behind us find us faithful." I love praying for my future granddaughters and grandson-in-laws even though they are just babies or toddlers. We already love them.

Our grandsons are four and a half, three, two, and two months old. Dan and I had been praying for them long before the days their moms surprised us with ultrasound pictures. We also make a concerted effort to ensure that prayer is a part of our time together – before meals, at bedtime, surrounding special needs and travel mercies.

When our two daughters were young, Dan and I would sit on the floor in their bedroom doorway and read the Bible to them until they fell asleep. This is a practice I am trying to continue with our grandchildren whenever I can.

And perhaps my favorite and most effective "fair trick" is singing Christian songs to the children. I think we can all agree that Bible verse songs are a wonderful way to teach our children the significance of hiding God's Word in their little hearts. Almost always, when one of the boys is crying, singing stops the crying. And I love it when they try to repeat the words back to me. From the mouths of babes!

A few months ago there was a bomb threat at the high school where Bethany worked. I will forever remember Jaxson finding a place behind the couch where he prayed for her and her students. It must bring joy to the Father's heart when He hears these little ones' requests.

It fills me with an inexpressible joy to share another Jaxson story. I had put the boys down for an afternoon nap. Jaxson always asks me to lie down on the trundle bed next to his so that we can tell stories. I know it's just his ploy to not take a nap but I'm such a sucker for that kind of thing.

He asked me to tell him a scary story. So I told him that the Easter story started out as a pretty scary story. God sent His Son, Jesus, to earth so that we could become friends with God. The religious people were jealous of Jesus because He said He was God and because He gave us such a beautiful picture of who God is and how much He loves us.

The mean people who hated Jesus beat Him up and put Him on a cross and killed Him. Remember in the Easter story how Jesus' friends gently placed Him in a cave and then the soldiers put a stone over the cave's entrance so that no one would steal Jesus' body?

Well, now we get to the happy, unscary part of the Easter story. God brought Jesus back to life and Jesus walked right out of that cave. All along it had been God's plan that Jesus, His only Son, would be put to death - that's the very sad part. But the reason is the very happy part. In order for us, as children of God, to live forever, God needed to show that He had power over death.

But that's not the end of the story. We have a part to play. When we ask Jesus into our hearts, He comes and lives inside us. Jaxson told me that he had done that many times, but it didn't work. How do you explain the Holy Spirit to a four-year-old? I told Him that someday He would understand what it means to be a Christian more fully. But for now, as a child, all he really needed to know was that Jesus loved him.

Jaxson asked me to pray that Jesus would come into his heart, which I joyfully did. I then explained that God loves him so much that he would never break his promises to Jaxson. I also told him that because God conquered death and because Jax asked Jesus into his heart, death would have no power over him. Even now, Jesus is preparing a place in heaven for him to live forever and ever. End of the story.

AND THOSE WHO WERE BLIND AND THOSE WHO LIMPED came to Him in the temple area, He healed them. But when the chief priests and the scribes saw the wonderful things that He had done, and the children who were shouting in the temple area, "Hosanna to the Son of David," they became indignant, and they said to Him, "Do You hear what these children are saying?" And Jesus said to them, "Yes. Have you never read, 'From the mouths of infants and nursing babies You have prepared praise for Yourself'?" And He left them and went out of the city to Bethany, and spent the night there. (Matthew 21:14-17 NASB)

> ### HERBERT HOOVER
> Children are our most valuable resource.[183]

AND THEY WERE BRINGING CHILDREN TO HIM so that he might touch them; but the disciples rebuked them. But when Jesus saw this, He was indignant and said to them, "Permit the children to come to Me; do not hinder them; for the kingdom of God belongs to such as these. Truly I say to you, whoever does not receive the kingdom of God like a child will not enter it at all." And He took them in His arms and began blessing them, laying His hands on them. (Mark 10:13-16 NASB)

---

[183] Peggy Caruso quoting Herbert Hoover, Revolutionize Your Child's Life (New York City: Morgan James Publishing, 2014), 88.

IT'S TIME FOR SLEEPY TIME, PSALTY

It's time for sleepy time.
It's time to rest your head,
To snuggle up and get
Cozy in your bed.
To dream of happy things,
And how much God loves you,
'Cause you're His special child.
It's sleepy time.[184]

YOU, HOWEVER, continue in the things you have learned and been convinced of, knowing from whom you have learned them, and that from childhood you have known the sacred writings which are able to give you the wisdom that leads to salvation through faith which is in Christ Jesus. All Scripture is inspired by God and beneficial for teaching, for rebuke, for correction, for training in righteousness; so that the man or woman of God may be fully capable, equipped for every good work. (II Timothy 3:14-17 NASB)

BILLY GRAHAM
The greatest legacy one can pass on to one's children and grandchildren is not money or other material things accumulated in one's life, but rather a legacy of character and faith.[185]

---

[184] Debby Kerner Rettino and Ernie Rettino (performers), "It's Time for Sleepytime," Psalty.com, Rettino/Kerner Publishing, 1990, https://www.psalty.com/track/694951/8-sleepytime-theme-extro.

[185] Robin Bertram quoting Billy Graham, No Regrets: How Loving Deeply and Living Passionately Can Impact Your Legacy Forever (New York City: Morgan James Publishing, 2017), 148.

"NOW THIS IS THE COMMANDMENT, THE STATUTES, and the judgments which the Lord your God has commanded me to teach you, so that you may do them in the land where you are going over to take possession of it, so that you, your son, and your grandson will fear the Lord your God, to keep all His statutes and His commandments which I command you, all the days of your life, and that your days may be prolonged. Now Israel, you shall listen and be careful to do them, so that it may go well for you and that you may increase greatly, just as the Lord, the God of your fathers, has promised you, in a land flowing with milk and honey.

"Hear, Israel! The Lord is our God, the Lord is one! And you shall love the Lord your God with all your heart and with all your soul and with all your strength. These words, which I am commanding you today, shall be on your heart. And you shall repeat them diligently to your sons and speak of them when you sit in your house, when you walk on the road, when you lie down, and when you get up. You shall also tie them as a sign to your hand, and they shall be as frontlets on your forehead. You shall also write them on the doorposts of your house and on your gates.

"Then it shall come about when the Lord your God brings you into the land that He swore to your fathers, to Abraham, Isaac, and Jacob, to give you, great and splendid cities which you did not build, and houses full of all good things which you did not fill, and carved cisterns which you did not carve out, vineyards and olive trees which you did not plant, and you eat and are satisfied, be careful that you do not forget the Lord who brought you out of the land of Egypt, out of the house of slavery. You shall fear only the Lord your God; and you shall worship Him and swear by His name. You shall not follow other gods, any of the gods of the peoples who surround you, for the Lord your God who is in the midst of you is a jealous God; so follow Him, or else the anger of the Lord your God will be kindled against you, and He will wipe you off the face of the earth.

"You shall not put the Lord your God to the test, as you tested Him at Massah. You shall diligently keep the commandments of the Lord your God, and His provisions and His statutes which He has commanded you. You shall do what is right and good in the sight of the Lord, so that it may go well for you and that you may go in and take possession of the good land which the Lord swore to give your fathers, by driving out all your enemies from you, as the Lord has spoken.

"When your son asks you in time to come, saying, 'What do the provisions and the statutes and the judgments mean which the Lord our God commanded you?' then you shall say to your son, 'We were slaves to Pharaoh in Egypt, and the Lord brought us out of Egypt with a mighty hand. Moreover, the Lord provided great and terrible signs and wonders before our eyes against Egypt, Pharaoh, and all his household; He brought us out of there in order to bring us in, to give us the land which He had sworn to our fathers.' So the Lord commanded us to follow all these statutes, to fear the Lord our God for our own good always and for our survival, as it is today. And it will be righteousness for us if we are careful to follow all this commandment before the Lord our God, just as He commanded us. (Deuteronomy 6:1-25 NASB)

POSITIVE IMPACT: WHY GRANDPARENTS ARE KEY TO CHILDRENS' DEVELOPMENT, ALTURA LEARNING

Grandparents fill an irreplaceable role in a child's development. Pillars of wisdom and sources of support, they possess a unique understanding of a family's history and traditions. They love their grandchildren with unconditional affection that matches that of a child's own parents, and though some families are separated by distance or circumstance, being able to connect with a grandchild frequently fosters a relationship that can influence a child to define values, flourish in self-confidence and strengthen the bonds of family. Here is why Grandparents are key to children's development.

Grandparents Are Wise. A lifetime of experiences has shaped a grandparent into who he or she is. A grandparent can quell the urgency of a seemingly disastrous event with the quiet reassurance of perspective, providing a stability that allows a grandchild to navigate hardships with renewed confidence…

Grandparents Are Essential. As a member of the family, the love that grandparents feel for their grandchildren is especially strong, amplified by the love they bear for their own children. The relationship is one of blood and history, and grandparents are part of the formation and maintenance of the traditions that define a family…

Grandparents Are Fun. While it is easy for new parents to feel pressured by the burdens of their responsibility, grandparents can offer a relaxed perspective and remind a family to remain light-hearted. Family game night can be a fun and unifying experience, introducing grandchildren to card or board games that they might not otherwise have learned…

Grandparents Are Connected. Though distance may separate some families from frequent in-person interaction, technology allows grandparents to remain a highly connected part of grandchildren's lives. Social media platforms like Facebook or Twitter allow for the sharing of images, messages, or life events, and programs like Skype or Zoom let families interact face-to-face…

The positive influence that grandparents can have on their grandchildren's development is profound. By offering love and guidance, imparting wisdom, passing on traditions, and making memories, grandparents can leave behind a legacy that their grandchildren will value for the rest of their lives…[186]

---

[186] Altura Blog, "Positive Impact: Why Grandparents are Key to Children's Development" Altura Learning, March 14, 2017, https://www.alturalearning.com/positive-impact-why-grandparents-are-key-to-childrens-development/.

UNLESS THE LORD BUILDS A HOUSE,
They who build it labor in vain;
Unless the Lord guards a city,
The watchman stays awake in vain.
It is futile for you to rise up early,
To stay up late,
To eat the bread of painful labor;
This is how He gives to His beloved sleep.
Behold, children are a gift of the Lord,
The fruit of the womb is a reward.
Like arrows in the hand of a warrior,
So are the children of one's youth.
Blessed is the man whose quiver is full of them;
They will not be ashamed
When they speak with their enemies in the gate.
(Psalm 127:1-5 NASB)

GIVING THE BLESSING, I GOT TO HEAR IT, GARY SMALLEY AND JOHN TRENT, PH.D.

I (John) grew up without a father at home. For a time, my grandfather was a father figure for me and my brothers. Grandfather was stern with white hair and a big beard (he looked a little like Robert E. Lee), and he was a firm disciplinarian. I was always a little afraid of him.

One day I had broken a rule and received the standard punishment – two swats with Grandfather's belt. I was still nursing my pride when I was sent to call Grandfather to dinner. I started to knock on his door, then saw it was open a crack. I pushed the door open. Grandfather was sitting on the edge of the bed, crying. I just knew I was in more trouble for catching him crying. But he beckoned me to him and took me in his arms. "John," he said, "I just want you to know, it hurts me so much to have to discipline you boys. But I love you so much, and I want you to grow up to be good young men."

Grandfather died eight months later. But before he left us, I got to hear the love and commitment in my grandfather's heart. That day is still a red-letter day in my memory.[187]

A GENTLE RESPONSE DEFIES ANGER,
    but a sharp tongue kindles a temper-fire.
Knowledge flows like spring water from the wise;
    fools are leaky faucets, dripping nonsense.
God doesn't miss a thing—
    he's alert to good and evil alike.
Kind words heal and help;
    cutting words wound and maim.
Moral dropouts won't listen to their elders;
    welcoming correction is a mark of good sense.
The lives of God-loyal people flourish;
    a misspent life is soon bankrupt.
Perceptive words spread knowledge;
    fools are hollow—there's nothing to them.
God can't stand pious poses,
    but he delights in genuine prayers.
A life frittered away disgusts God;
He loves those who run straight for the finish line.
A cheerful heart brings a smile to your face;
A sad heart makes it hard to get through the day.
An intelligent person is always eager to take in more truth;
Fools feed on fast-food fads and fancies.
A miserable heart means a miserable life;
A cheerful heart fills the day with song.
A simple life in the Fear-of-God
Is better than a rich life with a ton of headaches.

---

[187] Smalley and Trent, Giving the Blessing, from https://www.sweetstudy.com/files/the-blessing-giving-the-gift-of-unconditional-love-and-acceptance-by-john-trent-gary-smalley-z-lib-org-mobi-pdf-6783023

Teach Your Children (and Parents) Well

Better a bread crust shared in love
    than a slab of prime rib served in hate.
Hot tempers start fights;
    a calm, cool spirit keeps the peace.
The path of lazy people is overgrown with briers;
    the diligent walk down a smooth road.
Intelligent children make their parents proud;
    lazy students embarrass their parents.
The empty-headed treat life as a plaything;
    the perceptive grasp its meaning and make a go of it.
Refuse good advice and watch your plans fail;
    take good counsel and watch them succeed.
Congenial conversation—what a pleasure!
The right word at the right time—beautiful!
Life ascends to the heights for the thoughtful—
    it's a clean about-face from descent into hell.
God smashes the pretensions of the arrogant;
He stands with those who have no standing.
God can't stand evil scheming,
    but He puts words of grace and beauty on display.
A greedy and grasping person destroys community;
    those who refuse to exploit live and let live.
Prayerful answers come from God-loyal people;
    the wicked are sewers of abuse.
God keeps His distance from the wicked;
He closely attends to the prayers of God-loyal people.
A twinkle in the eye means joy in the heart,
And good news makes you feel fit as a fiddle.
Listen to good advice if you want to live well,
    an honored guest among wise men and women.
An undisciplined, self-willed life is puny;
    an obedient, God-willed life is spacious.
Fear-of-God is a school in skilled living—
    first you learn humility, then you experience glory. (Proverbs 15:1-9, 13-33 Message)

PARENTING THROUGH ADOPTION, PATTI BURNETT

Very few experiences equip a couple for parenting as well as adoption. The unconditional love and grace of birth parents beautifully exemplifies the sacrificial provision that God demonstrated when He gave His only Son. Through our infertility and adoption struggles, we learned that God's design is the ultimate "Family Plan."

Dan and I were married at the ages of 28 and 32 respectively; and after a few years realized that if we were to have children, we needed to get started. However, we discovered that getting pregnant was not as easy as we had hoped. Once our doctors diagnosed "infertility," we began the laborious task of trying to discover why. Charting my temperature, altering my diet, and numerous procedures and tests were unable to answer our myriad of questions.

Infertility is a time of deep introspection for couples. The emotional roller coaster speeds up exponentially with fertility drugs. This was all foreign to me; I considered myself a relatively stable person. I was always the stoic one when everyone else was crying at sad movies and funerals. Suddenly, I did not recognize the stranger I had become.

I questioned why God was asking us to bear this cross. I could relate to the Apostle Paul and his thorn in the flesh. Was my active lifestyle not allowing my body the rest and replenishment it needed to conceive? Was this the Lord's way of punishing me for wrong decisions earlier in life. Newspaper articles jumped out at me with stories of child abuse and abandonment. God, don't You care about these suffering babies? Don't you see how much love and security we could provide to just one of these unwanted infants?

When relatives and friends shared that they were expecting, I was overwhelmed with jealousy. I am from a family of eight; and naturally, all of my siblings were as "fertile as rabbits." I did not experience the joy I should have when I visited nieces and nephews.

I could not sit through a Mother's Day sermon without it tearing at my heart. It hurt that my mother-in-law was grieving her loss of a grandchild. I was too self-absorbed to empathize with her feelings. What was God doing?

Even before we knew we were infertile, we had discussed the adoption option. We joined a parenting class at Christian Family Services and began filling our file with testimonies, autobiographies, photos, letters to the baby, and letters to the birth mother. Equipped with this information, a birthmother would choose a couple to parent her baby. Thus, began the seemingly endless waiting game. We had two "situations" in which the birthmothers chose us and then decided to keep their babies. With the second one, as we hastily drove down to Denver, we informed co-workers, family, and friends that our baby had been born. We made it all the way to the hospital lobby, fully armed with our shiny new baby car seat and diaper bag. As we waited expectantly, our adoption counselor, Pam, informed us tearfully that Diane had changed her mind. We were overwhelmed with shock and disappointment. I tried to place myself in the shoes of this young woman, who, after carrying her baby for nine months, found that when she looked into his face, there'd be no way she could say goodbye.

The following day we received cards and gifts from friends; and in response, we had to inform them that the adoption had fallen through.

They say that "three's a charm." Such was the case for us. Vacationing in Florida and trying to get our minds off babies, we received a call from the adoption agency; they had yet another "situation." Becky, a 17-year-old Christian teen, had chosen us to parent her baby. We met with her in early May, and it was immediately apparent why the other two "situations" had failed – God had a better plan. Sitting between her parents, Becky, much 'with child,' explained why she had chosen adoption for her baby.

During one of the meetings the birth father joined us. Mike was from a broken family; and I will always remember the love that Becky's father expressed to him. In his troubled youth, he had never experienced such grace and forgiveness.

As if things were not exciting enough, just before Becky's due date I missed a cycle. Early pregnancy and blood tests confirmed that I also was "with child." Not wanting to steal from the joy of Becky's delivery, we only shared this news with the adoption agency.

On June 26, we received a call in the middle of the night that a healthy baby girl had just entered the world. Becky let us hold her beautiful child and our hearts welled with admiration and respect for this brave young woman, who chose the more difficult, less popular path; Becky chose life for her child. She arranged a dedication service at the hospital chapel so that we could all commit ourselves to raising Bethany Kayla Burnett in the love of the Lord.

From the time we first contacted the agency to the time that Bethany was born, the adoption process took nine months – just like any other pregnancy. I love God's timing—it is so much better than ours. Bethany's final adoption hearing was December 20, 1990, at 1:45 PM in the Arapahoe County District Court. Rachel was born on February 6, 1991.

"As the heavens are higher than the earth, so are My ways higher than your ways and My thoughts than your thoughts" (Isaiah 55:9 NASB). Dan and I learned that God wanted to bring us to the place where we recognized that He was the Provider. Remember Paul's thorn in the flesh? "Three times I pleaded with the Lord to take it away from me. But He said to me, 'My grace is sufficient for you, for My power is made perfect in weakness'" (II Corinthians 12:8-9a NIV).

When all our strength was exhausted, we finally turned to Him; He proved to be more than adequate for the task at hand. I can just imagine Him saying, "Well, if you are done now, do you want to step aside to see what I have planned? I have a blueprint so much better than anything your minds could manufacture."

We were stunned when we realized that we conceived Rachel within days of our first appointment with Becky. God wanted us to know that the reason we were infertile was so that Bethany would be part of the

Burnett household, in God's timing—not ours. This was just one of many times He had to school us.

We received new insight into parenting preparation and training through the adoption process. It is odd that, in many cases, people must invest more time and energy into getting a driver's license than having a baby. A person cannot accidentally get a driver's license, and yet some babies are considered accidents or mistakes!

Another parenting lesson I will never forget was the way Becky's parents walked alongside her through the thick and thin of pregnancy and delivery. Even Becky's grandmother, an orphan herself, joined the celebration by making a beautiful quilt for Bethany.

There are parents who inform their unwed teens that unless they have an abortion, they will be out on the street. Even Christian parents are guilty of this attitude. Apparently, many of them care more about their own reputations than the irreparable damage they are inflicting upon their precious little girls. I think that more unwed moms would choose adoption over abortion if they knew that their friends and families would not abandon them.

There must have been times when Bethany questioned why Becky chose adoption. Children often think that they must have done something wrong and that it is their fault they could not stay with their birth parents. Bethany must understand without question that it was love that motivated Becky's decision not to raise her baby herself.

A generation ago many families kept adoption a secret. If a child learned about their adoption from someone other than the parents, they felt deceived and hurt. Dan and I have always tried to communicate with Bethany at her comfort level. We have always tried to answer any of her questions directly, honestly, and at the appropriate age. Children fear the unknown, as do adults. We have always tried to keep the unknown factor to a minimum.

When I tell our family story and get to the part about becoming pregnant after the adoption, people love interjecting that they know of similar situations. Everyone has a rationalization for why this happens.

They explain that I was able to conceive because I no longer had the stress of trying so hard to get pregnant. I would rather accept that it was a result of God's perfect timing.

As I was proofreading this chapter of the book, we were vacationing at Moab with our two adult daughters, their husbands, and our grandchildren. Bethany was mid-way through her pregnancy with our third grandson. Special? Yes. A Miracle? Yes. God's ultimate gift of love and mercy. I love the Father's sense of humor.

> **TRAIN UP A CHILD IN THE WAY HE SHOULD GO,**
> even when he grows older he will not abandon it.
> (Proverbs 22:6 NASB)

~

> **MARIANNE WILLIAMSON**
> Children are happy because they don't have a file in their minds called "All the things that could go wrong."[188]

LISTEN TO ME, YOU ISLANDS;
    hear this, you distant nations:
Before I was born the LORD called me;
    from my mother's womb He has spoken my name.
He made my mouth like a sharpened sword,
    in the shadow of His hand He hid me;
He made me into a polished arrow
    and concealed me in His quiver.

---

[188] Marianne Williamson, Illuminata: Thoughts, Prayers, Rites of Passage (New York: Random House Inc., 1994), 88.

He said to me, "You are my servant,
    Israel, in whom I will display my splendor."
But I said, "I have labored in vain;
I have spent my strength for nothing at all.
Yet what is due me is in the Lord's hand,
    And my reward is with my God."
And now the LORD says—
He who formed me in the womb to be His servant
    to bring Jacob back to Him
    and gather Israel to Himself,
    for I am honored in the eyes of the LORD
    and my God has been my strength—
He says:
"It is too small a thing for you to be my servant
    to restore the tribes of Jacob
    and bring back those of Israel I have kept.
I will also make you a light for the Gentiles,
    that My salvation may reach to the ends of the earth."
This is what the LORD says—
    the Redeemer and Holy One of Israel—
    to Him who was despised and abhorred by the nation,
    to the servant of rulers:
"Kings will see You and stand up,
    princes will see and bow down,
    because of the LORD, who is faithful,
    the Holy One of Israel, who has chosen you."
This is what the LORD says:
"In the time of My favor I will answer you,
    and in the day of salvation I will help you;
I will keep you and will make you
    to be a covenant for the people,
    to restore the land
    and to reassign its desolate inheritances,

    to say to the captives, 'Come out,'
       and to those in darkness, 'Be free!'
"They will feed beside the roads
       and find pasture on every barren hill.
They will neither hunger nor thirst,
       nor will the desert heat or the sun beat down on them.
He who has compassion on them will guide them
       and lead them beside springs of water.
I will turn all my mountains into roads,
       and my highways will be raised up.
See, they will come from afar—
       some from the north, some from the west,
       some from the region of Aswan."
Shout for joy, you heavens;
       rejoice, you earth;
       burst into song, you mountains!
For the LORD comforts His people
       and will have compassion on His afflicted ones.
But Zion said, "The LORD has forsaken me,
       the Lord has forgotten me."
"Can a mother forget the baby at her breast
       and have no compassion on the child she has borne?
Though she may forget,
       I will not forget you!
See, I have engraved you on the palms of My hands;
Your walls are ever before Me.
Your children hasten back,
       and those who laid you waste depart from you.
Lift up your eyes and look around;
All your children gather and come to you.
As surely as I live," declares the Lord,
    "You will wear them all as ornaments;
       You will put them on, like a bride.

"Though you were ruined and made desolate
    and your land laid waste,
    now you will be too small for your people,
    and those who devoured you will be far away.
The children born during your bereavement
    will yet say in your hearing,
'This place is too small for us;
    give us more space to live in.'
Then you will say in your heart,
    'Who bore me these?
I was bereaved and barren;
    I was exiled and rejected.
Who brought these up?
I was left all alone,
    but these—where have they come from?'"
This is what the Sovereign LORD says:
"See, I will beckon to the nations,
    I will lift up my banner to the peoples;
    they will bring your sons in their arms
    and carry your daughters on their hips.
Kings will be your foster fathers,
    and their queens, your nursing mothers.
They will bow down before you with their faces to the ground;
    they will lick the dust at your feet.
Then you will know that I am the LORD;
    those who hope in Me will not be disappointed."
Can plunder be taken from warriors,
    or captives be rescued from the fierce?
But this is what the LORD says:
"Yes, captives will be taken from warriors,
    and plunder retrieved from the fierce;
I will contend with those who contend with you,
    and your children I will save. (Isaiah 49:1-25 NIV)

CHRONIC HOPE

> ### *MARTIN LUTHER KING, JR.*
> I have a dream that my four little children will one day live in a nation where they will not be judged by the color of their skin, but by the content of their character.[189]

CHILDREN LEARN WHAT THEY LIVE, DOROTHY LAW NOLTE AND RACHEL HARRIS

If children live with criticism, they learn to condemn.
If children live with hostility, they learn to fight.
If children live with ridicule, they learn to be shy.
If children live with shame, they learn to feel guilty.
If children live with encouragement, they learn confidence.
If children live with tolerance, they learn to be patient.
If children live with praise, they learn to appreciate.
If children live with acceptance, they learn to love.
If children live with approval, they learn to like themselves.
If children live with honesty, they learn truthfulness.
If children live with security,
they learn to have faith in themselves and others.
If children live with friendliness,
they learn the world is a nice place in which to live.[190]

---

[189] Elizabeth Sirimarco quoting Martin Luther King, Jr., The Civil Rights Movement (Singapore: Marshall Cavendish, 2005), 122.

[190] Linda LaTourelle quoting Dorothy Law Nolte and Rachel Harris, The Ultimate Guide to Celebrating Kids: Birth Through Preschool (Georgetown: Gold House Publishing, 2004), 14.

Chapter 29

HER WORTH IS FAR ABOVE JEWELS

AN EXCELLENT WIFE, WHO CAN FIND HER?
For her worth is far above jewels.
The heart of her husband trusts in her,
And he will have no lack of gain.
She does him good and not evil
All the days of her life.
She looks for wool and linen,
And works with her hand in delight.
She is like merchant ships;
She brings her food from afar.
And she rises while it is still night
And gives food to her household,
And portions to her attendants.
She considers a field and buys it;
From her earnings she plants a vineyard.
She surrounds her waist with strength
And makes her arms strong.
She senses that her profit is good;
Her lamp does not go out at night.
She stretches out her hands to the distaff,

And her hands grasp the spindle.
She extends her hand to the poor,
And she stretches out her hands to the needy.
She is not afraid of the snow for her household,
For all her household are clothed with scarlet.
She makes coverings for herself;
Her clothing is fine linen and purple.
Her husband is known in the gates,
When he sits among the elders of the land.
She makes linen garments and sells them,
And supplies belts to the tradesmen.
Strength and dignity are her clothing,
And she smiles at the future.
She opens her mouth in wisdom,
And the teaching of kindness is on her tongue.
She watches over the activities of her household,
And does not eat the bread of idleness.
Her children rise up and bless her;
Her husband also, and he praises her, saying:
"Many daughters have done nobly,
But you excel them all."
Charm is deceitful and beauty is vain,
But a woman who fears the Lord, she shall be praised.
Give her the product of her hands,
And let her works praise her in the gates. (Proverbs 31:10-31 NASB)

THOU SHALT NOT YANK OUT THINE GRAY HAIRS, PATTI BURNETT

WHEN QUESTIONED BY THE PHARISEES as to the greatest commandment, Jesus replied, "'Love the Lord your God with all your heart and with all your soul and with all your mind.' This is the first and greatest commandment. And the second is like it: 'Love your neighbor as yourself'" (Matthew 22:37-39 [J.B. Phillips]).

In contrast, the Pharisees had 613 mitzvot (commandments) compiled in the Torah. One of the laws pertaining to grooming was that a woman could not look in a mirror on the Sabbath. Notice that this ordinance applied exclusively to the female gender. I am guessing that this decision would not pass through today's Elder and Rabbi boards.

The reason for this law? If the woman discovered a gray hair, she might yank it out; and yanking out hair was considered working, which was forbidden on the Sabbath. Can you imagine a church today trying to enforce such a law? They would most likely sustain a mass evacuation. Maybe that was just one of the reasons for the exodus of the children of Israel!

OLDER WOMEN LIKEWISE ARE TO BE REVERENT IN THEIR BEHAVIOR, not malicious gossips nor enslaved to much wine, teaching what is good, so that they may encourage the young women to love their husbands, to love their children, to be sensible, pure, workers at home, kind, being subject to their own husbands, so that the word of God will not be dishonored. (Titus 2:3-5 NASB)

DESIDERIUS ERASMUS
Women, can't live with them; can't live without them.[191]

---

[191] Desiderius Erasmus, All the Familiar Colloquies of Desiderius Erasmus (Whitefish: Kessinger Publishing, 2010), 254.

THEN THE LORD GOD SAID, "IT IS NOT GOOD FOR THE MAN TO BE ALONE; I will make him a helper suitable for him." And out of the ground the Lord God formed every animal of the field and every bird of the sky, and brought them to the man to see what he would call them; and whatever the man called a living creature, that was its name. The man gave names to all the livestock, and to the birds of the sky, and to every animal of the field, but for Adam there was not found a helper suitable for him. So the Lord God caused a deep sleep to fall upon the man, and he slept; then He took one of his ribs and closed up the flesh at that place. And the Lord God fashioned into a woman the rib which He had taken from the man, and brought her to the man. Then the man said,

> "At last this is bone of my bones,
> And flesh of my flesh;
> She shall be called 'woman,'
> Because she was taken out of man."

For this reason a man shall leave his father and his mother, and be joined to his wife; and they shall become one flesh. And the man and his wife were both naked, but they were not ashamed. (Genesis 2:18-25 NASB)

DICK VAN DYKE
Women will never be as successful as men because they have no wives to advise them.[192]

---

[192] Ashton Applewhite, Tripp Evans, and Andrew Frothingham quoting Dick VanDyke, And I Quote, Revised Edition (New York City: Thomas Dunne Books, 2003), 451.

"THE LORD BLESS YOU, MY DAUGHTER," HE REPLIED. "This kindness is greater than that which you showed earlier: You have not run after the younger men, whether rich or poor. And now, my daughter, don't be afraid. I will do for you all you ask. All the people of my town know that you are a woman of noble character. Although it is true that I am a guardian-redeemer of our family, there is another who is more closely related than I. Stay here for the night, and in the morning if he wants to do his duty as your guardian-redeemer, good; let him redeem you. But if he is not willing, as surely as the LORD lives I will do it. Lie here until morning." (Ruth 3:10-13 NIV)

THERE WAS A CERTAIN MAN FROM RAMATHAIM, a Zuphite from the hill country of Ephraim, whose name was Elkanah son of Jeroham, the son of Elihu, the son of Tohu, the son of Zuph, an Ephraimite. He had two wives; one was called Hannah and the other Peninnah. Peninnah had children, but Hannah had none.

Year after year this man went up from his town to worship and sacrifice to the LORD Almighty at Shiloh, where Hophni and Phinehas, the two sons of Eli, were priests of the LORD. Whenever the day came for Elkanah to sacrifice, he would give portions of the meat to his wife Peninnah and to all her sons and daughters. But to Hannah he gave a double portion because he loved her, and the LORD had closed her womb. Because the LORD had closed Hannah's womb, her rival kept provoking her in order to irritate her. This went on year after year. Whenever Hannah went up to the house of the LORD, her rival provoked her till she wept and would not eat. Her husband Elkanah would say to her, "Hannah, why are you weeping? Why don't you eat? Why are you downhearted? Don't I mean more to you than ten sons?"

Once when they had finished eating and drinking in Shiloh, Hannah stood up. Now Eli the priest was sitting on his chair by the doorpost of the LORD's house. In her deep anguish Hannah prayed to the LORD, weeping bitterly. And she made a vow, saying, "LORD Almighty, if you will only look on your servant's misery and remember me, and not forget your servant but give her a son, then I will give him to the Lord for all the days of his life, and no razor will ever be used on his head."

As she kept on praying to the Lord, Eli observed her mouth. Hannah was praying in her heart, and her lips were moving but her voice was not heard. Eli thought she was drunk and said to her, "How long are you going to stay drunk? Put away your wine."

"Not so, my lord," Hannah replied, "I am a woman who is deeply troubled. I have not been drinking wine or beer; I was pouring out my soul to the Lord. Do not take your servant for a wicked woman; I have been praying here out of my great anguish and grief."

Eli answered, "Go in peace, and may the God of Israel grant you what you have asked of Him."

She said, "May your servant find favor in your eyes." Then she went her way and ate something, and her face was no longer downcast.

Early the next morning they arose and worshiped before the Lord and then went back to their home at Ramah. Elkanah made love to his wife Hannah, and the Lord remembered her. So in the course of time Hannah became pregnant and gave birth to a son. She named him Samuel, saying, "Because I asked the Lord for him."

When her husband Elkanah went up with all his family to offer the annual sacrifice to the Lord and to fulfill his vow, Hannah did not go. She said to her husband, "After the boy is weaned, I will take him and present him before the Lord, and he will live there always."

"Do what seems best to you," her husband Elkanah told her. "Stay here until you have weaned him; only may the Lord make good His word." So the woman stayed at home and nursed her son until she had weaned him.

After he was weaned, she took the boy with her, young as he was, along with a three-year-old bull, an ephah of flour and a skin of wine, and brought him to the house of the Lord at Shiloh. When the bull had been sacrificed, they brought the boy to Eli, and she said to him, "Pardon me, my lord. As surely as you live, I am the woman who stood here beside you praying to the Lord. I prayed for this child, and the

Lord has granted me what I asked of Him. So now I give him to the Lord. For his whole life he will be given over to the Lord." And he worshiped the Lord there (I Samuel 1:1-28 NIV).

THE ONE FLAW IN WOMEN, DONNA HENES

Women have strengths that amaze men…
They bear hardships and they carry burdens,
but they hold happiness, love and joy.
They smile when they want to scream.
They sing when they want to cry.
They cry when they are happy
And laugh when they are nervous.
They fight for what they believe in.
They stand up to injustice.
They don't take "no" for an answer
when they believe there is a better solution.
They go without so their family can have.
They go to the doctor with a frightened friend.
They love unconditionally.
They cry when their children excel
and cheer when their friends get awards.
They are happy when they hear about
a birth or a wedding.
Their hearts break when a friend dies.
They grieve at the loss of a family member,
Yet they are strong when they
Think there is no strength left.
They know that a hug and a kiss
can heal a broken heart.
Women come in all shapes, sizes and colors.
They'll drive, fly, walk, run or e-mail you
to show how much they care about you.
The heart of a woman is what

makes the world keep turning.
They bring joy, hope and love.
They have compassion and ideas.
They give moral support to their family and friends.
Women have vital things to say and everything to give.
However, if there is one flaw in women, it is that they forget their worth.[193]

HE WHO FINDS A WIFE FINDS A GOOD THING
And obtains favor from the Lord. (Proverbs 18:22 NASB)

---

[193] Donna Henes, The Queen of My Self, The One Flaw of Women (Holderness: Monarch Press, 2004).

Chapter 30

THE KINGDOM OF HEAVEN IS LIKE ...

"THE KINGDOM OF HEAVEN IS LIKE a treasure hidden in the field, which a man found and hid again; and from joy over it he goes and sells everything that he has and buys that field. (Matthew 13:44 NASB)

PARABLES OF JESUS, PATTI BURNETT

The Good Samaritan—A question was asked of Jesus by an "expert of Moses' law." This religious man did not have pure motives; he was trying to put Christ to the test. He asked how a person could be assured of a heavenly inheritance. The question must have been rhetorical since the man already knew the answer. "You shall love the Lord your God with all your heart, and with all your soul, and with all your strength, and with all your mind; and your neighbor as yourself" (Luke 10:27 NASB). The man became immediately aware that there were certain elements of society to whom he had been less than loving. In an attempt to justify his behavior, the man asked Christ to identify his neighbor.

Jesus answered the scribe with a story, also known as a parable. A Jewish man was on a trip when highway bandits attacked and robbed him. As the victim lay dying in a ditch, two very "religious" men walked by. Both the Priest and the Levite did more than just ignore the poor man; they actually crossed to the other side of the road. They feared touching a man who might have been dead and then having to undergo the weeklong purification process. Jesus used an example of men who were similar in status to the scribe in order to illustrate their hypocrisy and to hit a raw nerve with His audience. I am immediately struck by the contrast between these hypocrites and Mother Teresa, who touched the faces of the lepers and kneeled down at their level, treating their wounds and speaking of Christ's love for them.

The next person to enter the crime scene was a "despised Samaritan." Though regional neighbors, the Jews hated Samaritans because they were half-breeds – part Jewish and part Assyrian. The two groups disagreed on how to follow the Law of Moses. No Jew would have ever considered a Samaritan "Good." This enemy of the Jews felt uncharacteristic compassion for the victim and treated his injuries, transported him with his donkey, and nursed his wounds through the evening at a lodge. If this was not neighborly enough, he then left enough money

The Kingdom Of Heaven Is Like …

with the innkeeper to pay for the injured man's room and any further expenses he might incur.

I can more easily relate to this parable now after having been injured while hiking in the Rockies near our home. I twisted my ankle; and in trying to keep from falling, my hiking pole lodged itself between some rocks. I fell onto the handle of my pole, which broke several ribs and collapsed my lung. I was surprised how many hikers walked right by me and intentionally diverted their eyes so as not to see the pain in mine. I think those people were afraid to take responsibility for treating me like a fellow human being. Having been a search and rescue member and a ski patroller, I was in shock – emotionally and physically.

Years ago, when I was in middle school, I remember being told the story of Catherine "Kitty" Genevese. In Manhattan, New York, on March 13, 1964, Kitty, a 28-year-old bartender, was raped and stabbed 14 times by a man named Winston Moseley. There were 38 witnesses present, who stood back and did nothing as the young woman died. I remember being struck by the reality that people did not want to get involved. Perhaps it has to do with the litigious nature of our country or perhaps they feared for their own lives. You would think that out of 38 people, one would have been a brave neighbor. Today at least a handful of witnesses would have captured the video on their cell phones instead of actually helping the victim.

In our parable, the true neighbor was obviously the Samaritan, who showed kindness to the victim. Christ's intention was to show the scribes, the disciples, and believers today that His commandment to love our neighbors extends to strangers, and even enemies. That is exactly what Christ did when He died on the cross to pay for our sins. The Samaritan was certainly a Christ-like person.

This parable convicts me that every person within my scope of influence deserves Christ's love. It is not enough to love when it is convenient. Heaven forbid that someone should upset or disrupt my Google calendar. Christ's call is to be a neighbor to the unlovely, the unappreciative, and the unworthy—even when it's inconvenient. Dare I say, "especially when it's inconvenient" and we are forced to cross over to the other side of the road? Sometimes that road looks way too wide – too much traffic – too many potholes – cars traveling too fast. But perhaps it's time to let my navigational system recalculate.

People need to hear of a Savior who cares when they have been robbed of all dignity and respect—who cares when they have been stripped of all they hold dear—who cares that the world has wounded them and left them dying in one of life's many ditches. We must walk our talk and be ambassadors of hope.

The Prodigal Son—The religious leaders had been complaining that Jesus was spending an inordinate amount of time with tax collectors and sinners. Jesus decided to illustrate to them how much God cares about even the most notorious sinners.

One of the two sons approached his wealthy father, demanding his allotment of the inheritance, so he could set off on his own. Typically, the handing down of estates occurred after the father's death, and yet this particular father had no problem complying with the son's request. Perhaps he had a premonition that this might lead to a life learning experience that would benefit his son. Sure enough, in no time at all, the son wasted every denarius and was forced to take a job feeding pigs. He sank to such depths that he would have eaten pig food, but no one gave him anything.

The account indicates that he came to his senses. He grasped how foolish he had been and rehearsed a reunion speech to convince his dad that he was repentant and would become his hired servant. I have to believe that the father was expectantly watching for his son, because he saw the son coming from a long ways off. The father ran and embraced his youngest as the son began his prepared confessional address. The father would hear nothing of the son's proposal – interrupting him and having the servants set a celebration dinner. "For this son of mine was dead and is alive again; he was lost and is found. So, they began to celebrate" (Luke 15:24 NIV).

The older brother was indignant that his father had gone to such lengths to welcome the wayward son. He was jealous and hurt that his dad had never prepared such a feast for him although he had faithfully served and obeyed since his youth. The father explained that the older brother always had access to any of the family riches he desired. All that he had to do was ask.

Jesus is still in the job of search and rescue. His business is my business. If we allow sin to run its natural course, many people will eventually "come to their senses." God often allows us to reach the depths of despair and hopelessness before He intervenes. These are the times when believing friends must be available. Christ has called us to assist people in the transition from death to life – from lost to found. If we are not where the sinners are, but instead sanctimoniously clinging together in a holy huddle, we will never be available to tell them of the hope that Jesus offers. Our assignment is the apparent paradox of "being in the world but not of the world."

"AGAIN, THE KINGDOM OF HEAVEN IS LIKE a merchant seeking fine pearls, and upon finding one pearl of great value, he went and sold everything that he had and bought it.

"Again, the kingdom of heaven is like a dragnet that was cast into the sea and gathered fish of every kind; and when it was filled, they pulled it up on the beach; and they sat down and gathered the good fish into containers, but the bad they threw away. So it will be at the end of the age: the angels will come forth and remove the wicked from among the righteous, and they will throw them into the furnace of fire; in that place there will be weeping and gnashing of teeth.

"Have you understood all these things?" They said to Him, "Yes." And Jesus said to them, "Therefore every scribe who has become a disciple of the kingdom of heaven is like a head of a household, who brings out of his treasure new things and old. (Matthew 13:45-52 NASB)

> **MALCOLM MUGGERIDGE**
> Every happening, great and small,
> is a parable whereby God speaks to us,
> and the art of life is to get the message.[194]

AND AGAIN HE BEGAN TO TEACH BY THE SEA. And a great multitude was gathered to Him, so that He got into a boat and sat in it on the sea; and the whole multitude was on the land facing the sea. Then He taught them many things by parables, and said to them in His teaching:

"Listen! Behold, a sower went out to sow. And it happened, as he sowed, that some seed fell by the wayside; and the birds of the air came and devoured it. Some fell on stony ground, where it did not have much earth; and immediately it sprang up because it had no depth of earth. But when the sun was up it was scorched, and because it had no root it withered away. And some seed fell among thorns; and the thorns grew up and choked it, and it yielded no crop. But other seed fell on good ground and yielded a crop that sprang up, increased and produced: some thirtyfold, some sixty, and some a hundred."

And He said to them, "He who has ears to hear, let him hear!"

But when He was alone, those around Him with the twelve asked Him about the parable. And He said to them, "To you it has been given to know the mystery of the kingdom of God; but to those who are outside, all things come in parables, so that

'Seeing they may see and not perceive,
And hearing they may hear and not understand;
Lest they should turn,
And their sins be forgiven them.'"

---

[194] Malcolm Muggeridge, *Christ and the Media* (London: Regent College Publishing, 2003), 25.

And He said to them, "Do you not understand this parable? How then will you understand all the parables? The sower sows the word. And these are the ones by the wayside where the word is sown. When they hear, Satan comes immediately and takes away the word that was sown in their hearts. These likewise are the ones sown on stony ground who, when they hear the word, immediately receive it with gladness; and they have no root in themselves, and so endure only for a time. Afterward, when tribulation or persecution arises for the word's sake, immediately they stumble. Now these are the ones sown among thorns; they are the ones who hear the word, and the cares of this world, the deceitfulness of riches, and the desires for other things entering in choke the word, and it becomes unfruitful. But these are the ones sown on good ground, those who hear the word, accept it, and bear fruit: some thirtyfold, some sixty, and some a hundred."

Also, He said to them, "Is a lamp brought to be put under a basket or under a bed? Is it not to be set on a lampstand? For there is nothing hidden which will not be revealed, nor has anything been kept secret but that it should come to light. If anyone has ears to hear, let him hear."

Then He said to them, "Take heed what you hear. With the same measure you use, it will be measured to you; and to you who hear, more will be given. For whoever has, to him more will be given; but whoever does not have, even what he has will be taken away from him."

And He said, "The kingdom of God is as if a man should scatter seed on the ground, and should sleep by night and rise by day, and the seed should sprout and grow, he himself does not know how. For the earth yields crops by itself: first the blade, then the head, after that the full grain in the head. But when the grain ripens, immediately he puts in the sickle, because the harvest has come."

Then He said, "To what shall we liken the kingdom of God? Or with what parable shall we picture it? It is like a mustard seed which, when it is sown on the ground, is smaller than all the seeds on earth; but when it is sown, it grows up and becomes greater than all herbs, and shoots out large branches, so that the birds of the air may nest under its shade."

And with many such parables He spoke the word to them as they were able to hear it. But without a parable He did not speak to them. And when they were alone, He explained all things to His disciples. (Mark 4:1-34 NKJV)

> ### BRIAN D. MCLAREN
> Jesus was short on sermons, long on conversations; short on answers, long on questions; short on abstraction and propositions, long on stories and parables; short on telling you what to think, long on challenging you to think for yourself.[195]

NOW HE TOLD A PARABLE TO THOSE WHO WERE INVITED, when he noticed how they chose the places of honor, saying to them, "When you are invited by someone to a wedding feast, do not sit down in a place of honor, lest someone more distinguished than you be invited by him, and he who invited you both will come and say to you, 'Give your place to this person,' and then you will begin with shame to take the lowest place. But when you are invited, go and sit in the lowest place, so that when your host comes he may say to you, 'Friend, move up higher.' Then you will be honored in the presence of all who sit at table with you. For everyone who exalts himself will be humbled, and he who humbles himself will be exalted."

He said also to the man who had invited him, "When you give a dinner or a banquet, do not invite your friends or your brothers or your relatives or rich neighbors, lest they also invite you in return and you be repaid. But when you give a feast, invite the poor, the crippled, the lame, the blind, and you will be blessed, because they cannot repay you. For you will be repaid at the resurrection of the just."

---

[195] Brian D. McLaren, The Secret Message of Jesus: A Book Review (Nashville: W Publishing Group, 2006).

When one of those who reclined at table with him heard these things, he said to him, "Blessed is everyone who will eat bread in the kingdom of God!" (Luke 14:7-15 ESV)

NOW ALL THE TAX-COLLECTORS AND "OUTSIDERS" were crowding around to hear what He had to say. The Pharisees and the scribes complained of this, remarking, "This man accepts sinners and even eats his meals with them."

So Jesus spoke to them, using this parable: "Wouldn't any man among you who owned a hundred sheep, and lost one of them, leave the ninety-nine to themselves in the open, and go after the one which is lost until he finds it? And when he has found it, he will put it on his shoulders with great joy, and as soon as he gets home, he will call his friends and neighbors together. 'Come and celebrate with me,' he will say, 'for I have found that sheep of mine which was lost.' I tell you that it is the same in Heaven—there is more joy over one sinner whose heart is changed than over ninety-nine righteous people who have no need for repentance.

"Or if there is a woman who has ten silver coins, if she should lose one, won't she take a lamp and sweep and search the house from top to bottom until she finds it? And when she has found it, she calls her friends and neighbors together. 'Come and celebrate with me', she says, 'for I have found that coin I lost.' I tell you, it is the same in Heaven—there is rejoicing among the angels of God over one sinner whose heart is changed." (Luke 15:1-18 PHILLIPS)

> **MARK BATTERSON**
> I think you often say more by saying less.
> And interestingly enough, Jesus really set the standard.
> I mean, he could say more with fewer words than anybody.
> Most of the parables were less than 250 words. And, boy,
> did he have some one-liners just packed with truth.[196]

"**FOR THE KINGDOM OF HEAVEN IS LIKE THE OWNER OF AN ESTATE,** who went out in the morning at dawn to hire workmen for his vineyard. When he had agreed with laborers for a denarius for the day, he sent them into his vineyard. And he went out about the third hour (9:00 a.m.) and saw others standing idle in the marketplace; and he said to them, 'You also go into the vineyard, and I will pay you whatever is right (an appropriate wage).' And they went. He went out about the sixth hour (noon) and the ninth hour (3:00 p.m.), and did the same thing. And about the eleventh hour (5:00 p.m.) he went out and found others standing around, and he said to them, 'Why have you been standing here idle all day?' They answered him, 'Because no one hired us.' He told them, 'You go into the vineyard also.'

"When evening came, the owner of the vineyard said to his manager, 'Call the workers and pay them their wages, beginning with the last [to be hired] and ending with the first [to be hired].' Those who had been hired at the eleventh hour (5:00 p.m.) came and received a denarius each [a day's wage]. Now when the first [to be hired] came, they thought they would get more; but each of them also received a denarius. When they received it, they protested and grumbled at the owner of the estate, saying, 'These men who came last worked [only] one hour, and yet you have made them equal [in wages] to us who have carried [most of] the burden and [worked in] the scorching heat of the day.' But the owner of

---

[196] Mark Batterson, Draw the Circle: The 40 Day Prayer Challenge (Grand Rapids: Zondervan, 2012).

the estate replied to one of them, 'Friend, I am doing you no injustice. Did you not agree with me for a denarius? Take what belongs to you and go, but I choose to give to this last man [hired] the same as I give to you. Am I not lawfully permitted to do what I choose with what is mine? Or is your eye envious because I am generous?' So those who are last [in this world] shall be first [in the world to come], and those who are first, last." (Matthew 10:1-16 AMP)

Chapter 31

LEAD ON

AND YOU SHALL REMEMBER all the ways which the Lord your God has led you in the wilderness these forty years, in order to humble you, putting you to the test, to know what was in your heart, whether you would keep His commandments or not. (Deuteronomy 8:2 NASB)

PATTI BURNETT

IT HAS BEEN SAID that young Jewish men would follow so closely behind their assigned rabbi leaders that they would get covered in their dust. They so fervently desired to learn from these teachers that the young disciples would sit for hours at their feet absorbing the truths of God's Word and the wisdom of their elders.

Learning from a rabbi was not at all similar to today's educational system. The rabbi's student lived with him, ate with him – basically shared every aspect of the spiritual advisor's life (i.e., debating in the synagogues, performing weddings and funerals, caring for and giving to the poor, translating scripture, etc.). More than just the words of scripture, the student had a bird's eye view of what it meant to live out the scriptures.

Interesting that Jesus would choose someone like Peter and me to be His disciples. I'm far from perfect and so was Peter. But Jesus was and is looking for people who are teachable and willing to change.

Whose dust are we covered in?

JESUS CALLING, JANUARY 18th, SARAH YOUNG

I am leading you along the high road, but there are descents as well as ascents. In the distance you see snow-covered peaks glistening in brilliant sunlight. Your longing to reach those peaks is good, but you must not take shortcuts. Your assignment is to follow Me, allowing Me to direct your path. Let the heights beckon you onward, but stay close to Me.

Learn to trust Me when things go "wrong." Disruptions to your routine highlight your dependence on Me. Trusting acceptance of trials brings blessings that far outweigh them all. Walk hand in hand with Me through this day. I have lovingly planned every inch of the way. Trust does not falter when the path becomes rocky and steep. Breathe deep draughts of My Presence, and hold tightly to My hand. Together we can make it![197]

---

[197] Young, Jesus Calling, 19.

THE LORD SPOKE TO MOSES, saying, "sanctify to Me [that is, set apart for My purpose], every firstborn, the first offspring of every womb among the children of Israel, both of man and of animal; it is Mine."

Moses said to the people, "Remember [solemnly observe and commemorate] this day on which you came out of Egypt, out of the house of bondage and slavery; for by a strong and powerful hand the Lord brought you out of this place. And nothing leavened shall be eaten. On this day in the month Abib, you are about to go onward. And it shall be when the Lord brings you into the land of the Canaanite, the Hittite, the Amorite, the Hivite, and the Jebusite, which He swore to your fathers to give you, a land [of abundance] flowing with milk and honey, that you shall keep and observe this rite (service) in this month. For seven days you shall eat unleavened bread, and on the seventh day there shall be a feast to the Lord. Unleavened bread shall be eaten throughout the seven days; no leavened bread shall be seen with you, nor shall there be leaven within the borders of your territory. You shall explain this to your son on that day, saying, 'It is because of what the Lord did for me when I came out of Egypt.' It shall serve as a sign to you on your hand (arm), and as a reminder on your forehead, so that the instruction (law) of the Lord may be in your mouth; for with a strong and powerful hand the Lord brought you out of Egypt. Therefore, you shall keep this ordinance at this time from year to year.

"Now it shall be when the Lord brings you into the land of the Canaanite, as He swore to you and your fathers, and gives it to you, you shall set apart and dedicate to the Lord all that first opens the womb. All the firstborn males of your livestock shall be the Lord's. Every firstborn of a donkey you shall redeem by [substituting] a lamb [as a sacrifice for it], but if you do not [wish to] redeem it, then you shall break its neck; and every firstborn among your sons you shall redeem [that is, "buy back" from God with a suitable sacrifice]. And it shall be when your son asks you in time to come, saying, 'What does this mean?' you shall say to him, 'With a strong and powerful hand the Lord brought us out of Egypt, from the house of bondage and slavery. For it happened, when Pharaoh stubbornly refused to let us go, that the Lord struck every firstborn in the land of Egypt, both the firstborn of man and the firstborn of animal. Therefore, I sacrifice to the Lord all the males, the first [to be born] of every womb, but every firstborn of my sons I redeem.' So it shall serve as a sign and a reminder on your [left] hand (arm) and as frontlets between your eyes, for by a strong and powerful hand the Lord brought us out of Egypt."

So it happened, when Pharaoh let the people go, God did not lead them by way of the land of the Philistines, even though it was nearer; for God said, "The people might change their minds when they see war [that is, that there will be war], and return to Egypt." But God led the people around by the way of the wilderness toward the Red Sea; the sons of Israel went up in battle array (orderly ranks, marching formation) out of the land of Egypt. Moses took the bones of Joseph with him, for Joseph had solemnly ordered (placed under an oath) the Israelites, saying, "God will assuredly take care of you, and you must carry my bones away from here with you." They journeyed from Succoth [in Goshen] and camped at Etham on the edge of the wilderness. The [presence of the] Lord was going before them by day in a pillar (column) of cloud to lead them along the way, and in a pillar of fire by night to give them light, so that they could travel by day and by night. He did not withdraw the pillar of cloud by day, nor the pillar of fire by night, from going before the people. (Exodus 13:1-22 AMP)

ALL THE WAY MY SAVIOR LEADS ME, FANNY CROSBY

All the way my Savior leads me,
Cheers each winding path I tread,
Gives me grace for every trial,
Feeds me with the living bread.
Though my weary steps may falter,
And my soul athirst may be,
Gushing from the Rock before me,
Lo! a spring of joy I see,

Lead On

> Gushing from the Rock before me,
> Lo! a spring of joy I see.[198]

THE LORD SAID TO MOSES, "Get going, you and the people you brought up from the land of Egypt. Go up to the land I swore to give to Abraham, Isaac, and Jacob. I told them, 'I will give this land to your descendants.' And I will send an angel before you to drive out the Canaanites, Amorites, Hittites, Perizzites, Hivites, and Jebusites. Go up to this land that flows with milk and honey…

It was Moses' practice to take the Tent of Meeting and set it up some distance from the camp. Everyone who wanted to make a request of the Lord would go to the Tent of Meeting outside the camp.

Whenever Moses went out to the Tent of Meeting, all the people would get up and stand in the entrances of their own tents. They would all watch Moses until he disappeared inside. As he went into the tent, the pillar of cloud would come down and hover at its entrance while the **Lord** spoke with Moses. When the people saw the cloud standing at the entrance of the tent, they would stand and bow down in front of their own tents. Inside the tent of meeting, the **Lord** would speak to Moses face to face, as one speaks to a friend. Afterward Moses would return to the camp, but the young man who assisted him, Joshua son of Nun, would remain behind in the Tent of Meeting.

One day Moses said to the Lord, "You have been telling me, 'Take these people up to the Promised Land.' But You haven't told me whom You will send with me. You have told me, 'I know you by name, and I look favorably on you.' If it is true that You look favorably on me, let me know Your ways so I may understand You more fully and continue to enjoy Your favor. And remember that this nation is Your very own people."

The Lord replied, "I will personally go with you, Moses, and I will give you rest—everything will be fine for you."

---

[198] R. Mullins (performer), "All The Way My Savior Leads Me," Fanny Crosby (writer), distributed by Brightest and Best, 1875.

Then Moses said, "If You don't personally go with us, don't make us leave this place. How will anyone know that You look favorably on me—on me and on Your people—if You don't go with us? For Your presence among us sets Your people and me apart from all other people on the earth."

The L‍ord replied to Moses, "I will indeed do what You have asked, for I look favorably on You, and I know You by name."

Moses responded, "Then show me Your glorious presence."

The L‍ord replied, "I will make all My goodness pass before you, and I will call out my name, Yahweh, before you. For I will show mercy to anyone I choose, and I will show compassion to anyone I choose. But you may not look directly at My face, for no one may see Me and live." The L‍ord continued, "Look, stand near Me on this rock. As My glorious presence passes by, I will hide you in the crevice of the rock and cover you with My hand until I have passed by. Then I will remove my hand and let you see Me from behind. But My face will not be seen. (Exodus 33:1, 7-23 NLT)

STREAMS IN THE DESERT, DECEMBER 31ˢᵗ, L.B. COWMAN

The shepherds of the Alps have a beautiful custom of ending the day by singing an evening farewell to one another. The air is so pure that the songs can be heard for very long distances. As the sun begins to set, they gather their flocks and begin to lead them down the mountain paths while they sing, "'Thus far has the Lord helped us,' Let us praise His name!"…

Let us also call out to one another through the darkness until the night becomes alive with the sound of many voices, encouraging God's weary travelers. And may the echoes grow into a storm of hallelujahs that will break in thundering waves around His sapphire throne. Then as the morning dawns, we will find ourselves on the shore of the "sea of glass" (Revelations 4:6), crying out with the redeemed hosts of heaven,

"To Him who sits on the throne and to the Lamb be praise and honor and glory and power, for ever and ever" (Rev. 5:13 NIV)!

> This my song through endless ages,
> Jesus led me all the way.
> And again, they shouted: "Hallelujah!"[199]

DO YOU THUS DEAL WITH THE LORD,
O foolish and unwise people?
Is He not your Father, who bought you?
Has He not made you and established you?
"Remember the days of old,
Consider the years of many generations.
Ask your father, and he will show you;
Your elders, and they will tell you:
When the Most High divided their inheritance to the nations,
When He separated the sons of Adam,
He set the boundaries of the peoples
According to the number of the children of Israel.
For the LORD's portion is His people;
Jacob is the place of His inheritance.
"He found him in a desert land
And in the wasteland, a howling wilderness;
He encircled him, He instructed him,
He kept him as the apple of His eye.
As an eagle stirs up its nest,
Hovers over its young,
Spreading out its wings, taking them up,
Carrying them on its wings,
So the LORD alone led him,
And there was no foreign god with him.

---

[199] Cowman, Streams in the Desert, 486.

"He made him ride in the heights of the earth,
That he might eat the produce of the fields;
He made him draw honey from the rock,
And oil from the flinty rock;
Curds from the cattle, and milk of the flock,
With fat of lambs;
And rams of the breed of Bashan, and goats,
With the choicest wheat;
And you drank wine, the blood of the grapes. (Deuteronomy 32:6-14 NKJV)

> **LEE STROBEL**
> If Jesus is the Son of God, His teachings are more than just good ideas from a wise teacher, they are divine insights on which I can confidently build my life.[200]

---

[200] Lee Stroebel, The Case for Christ (Grand Rapids: Zondervan, 1998) 266.

Chapter 32

AND DEATH SHALL BE NO MORE

THEN I HEARD AGAIN what sounded like the shout of a vast crowd or the roar of mighty ocean waves or the crash of loud thunder:

"Praise the Lord!
 For the Lord our God, the
 Almighty, reigns.
Let us be glad and rejoice,
 and let us give honor to Him.
For the time has come for the wedding feast of the Lamb,
 and His bride has prepared herself.
She has been given the finest of pure white
 linen to wear."
For the fine linen represents the good
 deeds of God's holy people.

And the angel said to me, "Write this: Blessed are those who are invited to the wedding feast of the Lamb." And he added, "These are true words that come from God." (Revelation 19:6-9 NLT)

PATTI BURNETT

IF YOU ARE ANYTHING LIKE ME, the concept of eternal life is "inconceivable." I sometimes ponder what it will be like as we approach the pearly gates of heaven. I doubt it will at all be like the following jokes, but maybe you need a little chuckle right now:

- A taxi driver and a priest died. Upon arrival at heaven's gate, St. Peter asks which one of the two is the driver, and the driver replies "Me!" "Alright, come on into heaven." The priest asks, "How about me?" "Well, the reason why I'm not letting you in is that when you're preaching, all your followers are asleep, whereas when the driver's driving, all the passengers are praying."

- Three men die and head to the gates of heaven. One is a mathematician. One is a philosopher. One is a lawyer. St. Peter is there to determine if he will let them in. He tells all three men he is going to ask them a question and that if they get it correct, they will enter heaven. He pulls the mathematician into a room and asks him: "What is 2+2?" The mathematician answers, "Assuming all number values are accounted for and there are no variables to solve, the answer would be 4." St. Peter lets the mathematician into heaven. He pulls the philosopher into the room and asks him the same question. The philosopher answers, "Assuming you're assigning the arbitrary values to these symbols that we created on earth, and assuming that you and I agree to accept those values, then the answer would be 4." St. Peter lets the philosopher into heaven. Finally he calls the lawyer into the room and asks him, "What is 2+2?" The lawyer walks to the door, shuts it, draws the shades on the windows of the room, leans in close to St. Peter looks around and answers: "What do you want it to be?"

- A lawyer dies and appears in front of the golden gates of heaven. He finds himself at the back of a long queue of Popes. Suddenly, St. Peter grabs him and takes him straight through the pearly gates. "I don't understand," the lawyer said, puzzled. "There's hundreds of Popes waiting in line and you've let me in before them. Why?" "Sir," said St. Peter. "We've had lots of Popes here. But, you are our FIRST lawyer."

- Why are the gates of Heaven guarded? Because everybody's dying to get in.

- St. Peter was standing at the pearly gates of Heaven when a group of New Yorkers walked up. "Hey St. Petey, may we come into heaven?" St. Peter replies, "Well, we have never had New Yorkers in heaven before; let me ask God." He leaves the pearly gates and goes to see God. "God, there is a group of New Yorkers at the pearly gates. Should I let them in?" God thinks for a moment and says, "We have never had New Yorkers in heaven before. Let's see how it goes. Let them in." St. Peter leaves God, only to come running back a few minutes later. "THEY'RE GONE!" He said. "The New Yorkers?" "NO, THE PEARLY GATES."

- When men go to heaven there are two gates which they can choose from. The first is labeled "Men Who Are Controlled by Their Wives" and the other labeled "Men Who Control Their Wives." The first gate had thousands of men waiting to enter, while the second gate only had one man in line. When God came to check on the lines, he approached the one individual standing in the "Men Who Control Their Wives" line and asked, "Why are you the only man standing here?" The man replied: "I don't know. My wife told me to stand here."

- A wealthy businessman dies and is standing in front of the gates of heaven. St. Peter meets him there and congratulates him on his success on earth. He says "You know, it's a shame that you have done so much and can't take it with you. I'm going to do something special just for you." He hands the man a briefcase, saying, "You have one day to go back to earth. You can gather up anything you want, and whatever you can fit in this briefcase you can bring with you into heaven. As the man is walking around on earth, he takes a moment to think about what he wants to fit into the briefcase. He's drawn to the hundreds of millions of dollars he earned over his lifetime, but he knows there's no way it will all fit. As he's thinking, he passes a store with a huge sign saying, "WE BUY GOLD," and he has an idea. If they buy gold, they probably sell it too. "A briefcase full of gold will be far more valuable than a briefcase full of cash." First, he goes to his bank and withdraws all his money. He then goes to the store and buys out all of the gold they have. As the sun begins to set on his last day on earth, the man finds one last store and buys $8 million more of gold bars, completely filling his briefcase. He sits down on the curb to rest, proud of how smart he is, thinking to fill his briefcase with gold. As the last rays of the sun slip below the horizon, he is transported back to the gates of heaven where St. Peter meets him and asks to see what he brought. Beaming with pride, the man opens his briefcase, showing Peter the rows of gold bars. St. Peter looks at the bars for a moment, then stares at the man incredulously and asks, "Paving stones?"

- A young lawyer died and stood before the gates of heaven. Lawyer: "St. Peter, what happened? I was as healthy as an ox, and I'd barely passed my 48th birthday!" St. Peter: "48? According to your billable hours you were 172."

- A cat died and went to heaven. God met the animal at the pearly gates and said, "You have been a good cat all these years. Anything you want is yours for the asking." The cat thought for a moment and then said, "All my life I lived on a farm and slept on hard, wooden floors ... I would like a real fluffy pillow to sleep on." God said, "Say no more." Instantly, the cat had a HUGE fluffy pillow. A few days later, 12 mice were all simultaneously killed in an accident, and they all went to heaven. God met the mice at the gates of heaven, with the exact same offer that He made to the cat. The mice said, "Well, we have had to run all of our lives ... from cats, dogs, and even from people with brooms. If we could have some roller skates, we would never have to run again." God answered, "It is done." All the mice had beautiful little roller skates. About a week later, God decided to check on the cat ... He found her sound asleep on her fluffy pillow. God gently awakened the cat and asked, "Is everything okay? How have you been doing? Are you happy?" The cat replied, "Oh, everything's just WONDERFUL ... I've never been so happy in my life! My pillow is always fluffy and those little "Meals-on-Wheels" that you have been sending over are delicious."

In all seriousness, I am sure that my mom and dad will be right there at the pearly gates when I get to heaven. And they won't just be there to greet me, but also all of their dozens of children, grandchildren, and great grandchildren. Great, great grandchildren?

I have lots of questions about heaven. How huge were the pearls that comprise the twelve pearly gates? How wonderful to exist in a world where every person is filled with the Spirit of God and exhibits all of the fruit of the Spirit all the time. There will be no war - just peace. Sounds heavenly!

The Bible says that "He (God) has made everything beautiful in its time. He has also set eternity in the human heart; yet no one can fathom what God has done from beginning to end" (Ecclesiastes 3:11

NIV). Every human being (Christian and Non-Christian) from birth has a God-given awareness that there is something beyond this earthly existence.

When we buried my mom and dad's ashes, my siblings and I all found comfort and joy in knowing that our parents would finally receive their heavenly rewards. I wish I could watch a You Tube of their first day in Heaven.

Thank You, Heavenly Father, that when You created heaven, You had me in mind. How humbling to know that You, the very Creator of all things, would care enough to send Your one and only Son to die and be resurrected so that I could spend eternity in the *"Happiest Place in The Universe"*.

THIS IS A REVELATION FROM JESUS CHRIST, which God gave Him to show His servants the events that must soon take place. He sent an angel to present this revelation to His servant John, who faithfully reported everything he saw. This is his report of the word of God and the testimony of Jesus Christ.

God blesses the one who reads the words of this prophecy to the church, and He blesses all who listen to its message and obey what it says, for the time is near.

This letter is from John to the seven churches in the province of Asia.

Grace and peace to you from the One who is, who always was, and who is still to come; from the sevenfold Spirit before His throne; and from Jesus Christ. He is the faithful witness to these things, the first to rise from the dead, and the ruler of all the kings of the world.

All glory to Him who loves us and has freed us from our sins by shedding His blood for us. He has made us a kingdom of priests for God His Father. All glory and power to Him forever and ever! Amen.

Look! He comes with the clouds of heaven.
And everyone will see Him—

even those who pierced Him.
And all the nations of the world
will mourn for Him.

Yes! Amen!

"I am the Alpha and the Omega—the beginning and the end," says the Lord God. "I am the one who is, who always was, and who is still to come—the Almighty One."

I, John, am your brother and your partner in suffering and in God's Kingdom and in the patient endurance to which Jesus calls us. I was exiled to the island of Patmos for preaching the word of God and for my testimony about Jesus. It was the Lord's Day, and I was worshiping in the Spirit. Suddenly, I heard behind me a loud voice like a trumpet blast. It said, "Write in a book everything you see, and send it to the seven churches in the cities of Ephesus, Smyrna, Pergamum, Thyatira, Sardis, Philadelphia, and Laodicea."

When I turned to see who was speaking to me, I saw seven gold lampstands. And standing in the middle of the lampstands was someone like the Son of Man. He was wearing a long robe with a gold sash across His chest. His head and his hair were white like wool, as white as snow. And His eyes were like flames of fire. His feet were like polished bronze refined in a furnace, and His voice thundered like mighty ocean waves. He held seven stars in His right hand, and a sharp two-edged sword came from His mouth. And his face was like the sun in all its brilliance.

When I saw Him, I fell at His feet as if I were dead. But He laid His right hand on me and said, "Don't be afraid! I am the First and the Last. I am the living one. I died, but look—I am alive forever and ever! And I hold the keys of death and the grave.

"Write down what you have seen—both the things that are now happening and the things that will happen. This is the meaning of the mystery of the seven stars you saw in my right hand and the seven gold lampstands: The seven stars are the angels of the seven churches, and the seven lampstands are the seven churches. (Revelation 1:1-20 NLT)

THE HOLY CITY, MICHAEL CRAWFORD

Last night I lay a sleeping there came a dream so fair
I stood in old Jerusalem, beside the temple there
I heard the children singing and ever as they sang
I thought the voice of Angels from Heaven in answer rang
I thought the voice of Angels from Heaven in answer rang

Jerusalem, Jerusalem
Lift up your gates and sing
Hosanna in the highest
Hosanna to your King

And once again the scene was changed, new earth there seemed to be
I saw the Holy City beside the tideless sea
The light of God was on its streets, the gates were open wide
And all who would might enter and no one was denied
No need of moon or stars by night or sun to shine by day
It was the new Jerusalem that would not pass away
It was the new Jerusalem that would not pass away

Jerusalem, Jerusalem
Sing for the night is o'er
Hosanna in the highest
Hosanna for evermore[201]

H.G. WELLS
The doctrine of the Kingdom of Heaven, which was the main teaching of Jesus, is certainly one of the most revolutionary doctrines that ever stirred and changed human thought.[202]

---

[201] Michael Crawford (performer), "The Holy City," distributed by OCP Publications, track 9 on On Eagle's Wings, 1998, cassette.

[202] H.G. Wells, A Short History of the World (London: Cassell & Company, 1922), 215.

AFTER THIS, I HEARD WHAT SOUNDED LIKE A VAST CROWD IN HEAVEN SHOUTING,

"Praise the LORD!
Salvation and glory and power belong to our God.
His judgments are true and just.
He has punished the great prostitute
　　who corrupted the earth with her immorality.
He has avenged the murder of His servants."
And again their voices rang out:
"Praise the LORD!
The smoke from that city ascends forever and ever!"
Then the twenty-four elders and the four living beings fell down and worshiped God, who was sitting on the throne. They cried out, "Amen! Praise the LORD!"
And from the throne came a voice that said,
"Praise our God,
　　all His servants,
　　all who fear Him,
　　from the least to the greatest." (Revelation 19:1-5 NLT)

GEORGE WASHINGTON

No people can be bound to acknowledge and adore the invisible hand which conducts the affairs of men more than the people of the United States. Every step by which they have advanced to the character of an independent nation seems to have been distinguished by some token of providential agency... We ought to be no less persuaded that the propitious smiles of heaven cannot be expected on a nation that disregards the eternal rules of order and right, which heaven itself has ordained.[203]

---

[203] Michael Waldman quoting George Washington, My Fellow Americans (Naperville: Sourcebooks, 2010), 6.

Chapter 33

IT WILL BE WORTH IT ALL WHEN WE SEE JESUS

THEN I SAW A NEW HEAVEN AND A NEW EARTH; for the first heaven and the first earth passed away, and there is no longer any sea. And I saw the holy city, new Jerusalem, coming down out of heaven from God, prepared as a bride adorned for her husband ...

And I heard a loud voice from the throne, saying, "Behold, the tabernacle of God is among the people, and He will dwell among them, and they shall be His people, and God Himself will be among them, and He will wipe away every tear from their eyes; and there will no longer be any death; there will no longer be any mourning, or crying, or pain; the first things have passed away." And He who sits on the throne said, "Behold, I am making all things new." And He said, "Write, for these words are faithful and true." Then He said to me, "It is done. I am the Alpha and the Omega, the beginning and the end. I will give water to the one who thirsts from the spring of the water of life, without cost. The one who overcomes will inherit these things, and I will be his God and he will be My Son. (Revelation 21:1-7 NASB)

PATTI BURNETT

I PARTICIPATED IN A VIDEO CONFERENCE CALL in which about 26 participants discussed grief and loss. There were many suggestions about ways to better assist those in our Parkinson's support groups who were rapidly approaching the end of their life's journey. There were opportunities for our cohort to openly grieve and cry over the losses that we had all experienced over the last few years, especially with the Covid pandemic.

Every time I considered speaking, there were at least two or three others with their hands up. I wanted to make sure that every person who needed to share had that opportunity. Some interjected even two or three times—this was a topic that weighed heavily on all our hearts.

As we approached our designated time of conclusion, I realized that I would not have a chance to add my two cents. So I typed out a chat and wrote: "Please don't think I'm preaching, but this is what I believe. The Bible says that God has placed eternity in the hearts of people. Jesus said that He was going to prepare a place for us. If we believe in heaven then death can be a time of celebration, not of fear. This is what I believe."

Since I submitted this just before the meeting ended, not many had opportunities to respond. One person said, "Thank you" and another answered that she was an agnostic.

I know that at least one or two others participating in the meeting were Christians who believe in heaven. I wish that in this day and age people would not be afraid to talk about God and heaven. Instead we can expect derision, jabs, and criticism in response to even the mention of God. Makes me think that the days are short. Maranatha Lord Jesus!

BUT YOU HAVE COME TO MOUNT ZION and to the city of the living God, the heavenly Jerusalem, and to myriads of angels [in festive gathering], and to the general assembly and assembly of the firstborn who are registered [as citizens] in heaven, and to God, who is Judge of all, and to the spirits of the righteous (the redeemed in heaven) who have been made perfect [bringing them to their final glory], and to Jesus, the Mediator of a new covenant [uniting God and man], and to the sprinkled blood, which speaks [of mercy], a better and nobler and more gracious message than the blood of Abel [which cried out for vengeance].

See to it that you do not refuse [to listen to] Him who is speaking [to you now]. For if those [sons of Israel] did not escape when they refused [to listen to] Him who warned them on earth [revealing God's will], how much less will we escape if we turn our backs on Him who warns from heaven? His voice shook the earth [at Mount Sinai] then, but now He has given a promise, saying, "Yet once more I will shake not only the earth, but also the [starry] heaven." Now this [expression], "Yet once more," indicates the removal and final transformation of all those things which can be shaken—that is, of that which has been created—so that those things which cannot be shaken may remain. Therefore, since we receive a kingdom which cannot be shaken, let us show gratitude, and offer to God pleasing service and acceptable worship with reverence and awe; for our God is [indeed] a consuming fire. (Hebrews 12:22-29 AMP)

WELL DONE, THE AFTERS, SONGWRITERS: JASON INGRAM, MATT FUQUA, JOSH HAVENS

What will it be like when my pain is gone
And all the worries of this world just fade away?
What will it be like when You call my name
And that moment when I see You face to face?
I'm waiting my whole life to hear You say
Well done, well done
My good and faithful one
Welcome to the place where you belong
Well done, well done

> My beloved child
> You have run the race and now you're home
> Welcome to the place where you belong[204]

THEN THE RIGHTEOUS WILL SHINE forth like the sun in the kingdom of their Father. The one who has ears, let him hear. (Matthew 13:43 NASB)

> ### JOHN CALVIN
> Although believers are now pilgrims on earth, yet by their confidence they surmount the heavens so that they cherish their future inheritance in their bosoms with tranquility.[205]

"DO NOT LET YOUR HEART BE TROUBLED; believe in God, believe also in Me. In My Father's house are many dwelling places; if it were not so, I would have told you; for I go to prepare a place for you. If I go and prepare a place for you, I will come again and receive you to Myself, that where I am, there you may be also. And you know the way where I am going." Thomas said to Him, "Lord, we do not know where You are going, how do we know the way?" Jesus said to him, "I am the way, and the truth, and the life; no one comes to the Father but through Me. (John 14:1-7 NASB)

HOME WHERE I BELONG, B.J. THOMAS
> They say that heaven's pretty, and living here is too.
> But if they said that I would have to choose between the two.
> I'd go home; Going home, Where I belong.

---

[204]The Afters (performers), "Well Done," Joshua Havens and Matt Fuqua (writers), distributed by Fellow Ships Music, track one on The Beginning & Everything After, 2018, album.

[205]John Calvin, Calvin's commentary on 1 Peter 1:1 and 1 Peter 2:11.

And sometimes when I'm dreaming, it comes as no surprise.
That if you look and see the homesick feeling in my eyes.
I'm going home; Going home, Where I belong.
While I'm here, I'll serve Him gladly, and sing Him all my songs.
I'm here, But not for long.[206]

LISTEN, I TELL YOU A MYSTERY: we will not all sleep, but we will all be changed—in a flash, in the twinkling of an eye, at the last trumpet. For the trumpet will sound, the dead will be raised imperishable, and we will be changed. For the perishable must clothe itself with the imperishable, and the mortal with immortality. (1 Corinthians 15:41-43 Message)

DAILY WITH THE KING, THE LORD OF WHAT IS TO COME, JANUARY 2ⁿᵈ, W. GLYN EVANS

I am a planned-for-the-future man. I am destined for God's eternal drama. The eyes of the all-seeing Sculptor have scanned me and set me aside for developing. Lord, now I see what you meant when You said, "He has … set eternity in their heart" (Ecclesiastes 3:11 NASB). We are being made for tomorrow, for the future, for eternity. To look within ourselves now and be discouraged is to miss it all. God, You look at us in Your tomorrow and rejoice over us as one finding great spoil.[207]

THEREFORE, IF YOU HAVE BEEN RAISED WITH CHRIST, keep seeking the things that are above, where Christ is, seated at the right hand of God. Set your minds on the things that are above, not on the things that are on earth. For you have died, and your life is hidden with

---

[206] B.J. Thomas, "Home Where I Belong," Pat Terry (writer), Chris Christian (producer), distributed by Label Myrrh Records, Live by The Downings album by a Secular Artist, 1977, cassette.

[207] W.G. Evans, Daily with the King, The Lord of What is to Come (Chicago: Moody, 1979), 2

Christ in God. When Christ, who is our life, is revealed, then you also will be revealed with Him in glory. (Colossians 3:1-4 NASB)

WHEN WE SEE CHRIST, ESTHER KERR RUSTHOI

Oft times the day seems long, our trials hard to bear,
We're tempted to complain, to murmur and despair;
But Christ will soon appear to catch His Bride away,
All tears forever over in God's eternal day.
It will be worth it all when we see Jesus,
Life's trials will seem so small when we see Christ;
One glimpse of His dear face all sorrow will erase,
So bravely run the race till we see Christ.[208]

FINAL JOURNEY, CHARLES SPURGEON

The hour is approaching when the message will come to us, as it comes to all, "Arise, and leave the home in which you lived, from the city in which you have done your business, from your family, from your friends. Arise, and take your final journey."

And what do we know of the journey? And what do we know of the country to which we are going? We have read a little about it, and part has been revealed to us by the Spirit; but how little do we know of the realms of the future! We know that there is a black and stormy river called Death. God bids us cross it, promising to be with us.

And after death, what comes? What wonder-world will open upon our astonished sight? What scene of glory will be unfolded to our view? No traveler has ever returned to tell. But we know enough of the heavenly land to make us welcome our summons there with joy and gladness.

The journey of death may be dark, but we may face it fearlessly, knowing that God is with us as we walk through the gloomy valley, and therefore we need fear no evil. We shall be departing from all we have known and loved here, but we shall be going to our Father's house—to

---

[208] E.K. Rusthoi, "When We See Jesus," in Dr. Croly's 1854 Psalms and Hymns for Public Worship (1909).

our Father's home, where Jesus is–to that royal "city that has foundations, whose designer and builder is God." This will be our last relocation, to live forever with Him we love, in the midst of His people, in the presence of God.

Christian, meditate much on heaven; it will help you to press on and to forget the difficulty of the journey. This vale of tears is but the pathway to the better country: This world of woe is but the stepping-stone to a world of bliss.[209]

JEANNE LEONARD
We walk by faith, you walk by sight.
We walk in shadows, you walk in Light.
We are still running, you've finished the race.
We know in part, you know the whole.
We are still striving, you've reached the goal.
We see the glass darkly...you see face-to-face.
"How could we ever try to hold you here?
How could we keep you bound?
When everything we long for, everything we hope for,
You have finally found.
"In the twinkling of an eye, you have been changed.
Freed from this body, loosed from earth's chains.
Standing with the Father...clothed in robes of white.[210]

---

[209] Charles Spurgeon, Devotional Classics of C.H. Spurgeon (Shallotte: Sovereign Grace Publishers, Inc., 2000), 7.

[210] Jeanne Leonard

AFTER THESE THINGS I LOOKED, AND BEHOLD, a great multitude which no one could count, from every nation and all the tribes, peoples, and languages, standing before the throne and before the Lamb, clothed in white robes, and palm branches were in their hands; and they cried out with a loud voice, saying,

"Salvation belongs to our God who sits on the throne, and to the Lamb."

And all the angels were standing around the throne and around the elders and the four living creatures; and they fell on their faces before the throne and worshiped God, saying,

"Amen, blessing, glory, wisdom, thanksgiving, honor, power, and might belong to our God forever and ever. Amen."

Then one of the elders responded, saying to me, "These who are clothed in the white robes, who are they, and where have they come from?" I said to him, "My lord, you know." And he said to me, "These are the ones who come out of the great tribulation, and they have washed their robes and made them white in the blood of the Lamb. For this reason they are before the throne of God, and they serve Him day and night in His temple; and He who sits on the throne will spread His tabernacle over them. They will no longer hunger nor thirst, nor will the sun beat down on them, nor any scorching heat; for the Lamb in the center of the throne will be their shepherd, and will guide them to springs of the water of life; and God will wipe every tear from their eyes. (Revelation 7:9-17 NASB)

> ### HEAVEN ... YOUR REAL HOME,
> ### JONI EARECKSON TADA
>
> Hardships are God's way of helping me get my mind on the hereafter. And I don't mean hereafter as a death wish or an escape from reality; I mean hereafter as the true reality. And nothing beats rehearsing a few time-honored Scriptures if you want to put reality into a heavenly perspective. Like, every time my corset digs in my side, or I'm faced with a 4-week stint in bed, I look beyond the negatives and see the positives: I recall that pilgrims aren't supposed to feel at home on earth; I set my heart and mind on things above and dream of the day I'll see my Bridegroom; I remember the promise of a new body, a new heart and mind. And I think about the crowns I'll be able to cast at Jesus' feet. These things make up the soon and coming reality, so today, get your mind on the hereafter. The soul that mounts up to heaven's kingdom cannot fail to triumph.[211]

AND HE SAID TO ME, "It is done! I am the Alpha and the Omega, the beginning and the end. I will give of the fountain of the water of life freely to him who thirsts. He who overcomes shall inherit all things, and I will be his God and he shall be My son. But the cowardly, unbelieving, abominable, murderers, sexually immoral, sorcerers, idolaters, and all liars shall have their part in the lake which burns with fire and brimstone, which is the second death."

Then one of the seven angels who had the seven bowls filled with the seven last plagues came to me and talked with me, saying, "Come, I will show you the bride, the Lamb's wife." And he carried me away in the Spirit to a great and high mountain, and showed me the great

---

[211] Joni Eareckson Tada, Heaven ... Your Real Home (Grand Rapids: Zondervan, 2010), 249.

city, the holy Jerusalem, descending out of heaven from God, having the glory of God. Her light was like a most precious stone, like a jasper stone, clear as crystal. Also she had a great and high wall with twelve gates, and twelve angels at the gates, and names written on them, which are the names of the twelve tribes of the children of Israel: three gates on the east, three gates on the north, three gates on the south, and three gates on the west.

Now the wall of the city had twelve foundations, and on them were the names of the twelve apostles of the Lamb. And he who talked with me had a gold reed to measure the city, its gates, and its wall. The city is laid out as a square; its length is as great as its breadth. And he measured the city with the reed: twelve thousand furlongs. Its length, breadth, and height are equal. Then he measured its wall: one hundred and forty-four cubits, according to the measure of a man, that is, of an angel. The construction of its wall was of jasper; and the city was pure gold, like clear glass. The foundations of the wall of the city were adorned with all kinds of precious stones: the first foundation was jasper, the second sapphire, the third chalcedony, the fourth emerald, the fifth sardonyx, the sixth sardius, the seventh chrysolite, the eighth beryl, the ninth topaz, the tenth chrysoprase, the eleventh jacinth, and the twelfth amethyst. The twelve gates were twelve pearls: each individual gate was of one pearl. And the street of the city was pure gold, like transparent glass.

But I saw no temple in it, for the Lord God Almighty and the Lamb are its temple. The city had no need of the sun or of the moon to shine in it, for the glory of God illuminated it. The Lamb is its light. And the nations of those who are saved shall walk in its light, and the kings of the earth bring their glory and honor into it. Its gates shall not be shut at all by day (there shall be no night there). And they shall bring the glory and the honor of the nations into it. But there shall by no means enter it any that defiles, or causes an abomination or a lie, but only those who are written in the Lamb's Book of Life. (Revelations 21:6-26 NKJV)

THE DIVINE EMBRACE, KEN GIRE

Jesus has gone ahead of us to prepare a place for us, but if we don't show up there will be no honeymoon. A wedding feast has been prepared for us too, but if we don't love Him back, His joy is not made full. And in that sense, He needs our love. One resplendent day His love for us and ours for Him will be celebrated in heaven. A feast, we are told, awaits us there. Meanwhile, here on earth, Jesus shares with us a table set for two.

When I imagine what it would be like sitting across the table from the Lord Jesus Himself, another scene from the film Les Misérables comes to mind. Jean Valjean visits the recovering Fantine, who has been bathed and dressed by an attending nun. When the nun brings her a bowl of soup, Fantine smiles at Valjean and says, "What about you? Don't you eat?"

The next scene is outside in the fresh air, where Valjean has set a table for two. On the table is wine, bread, fruit, cheese, and meat. After carrying Fantine to her chair, Valjean drapes a quilt around her shoulders. His hand brushes across hers as he takes a knife and slices off a wedge of cheese for her. The look in Fantine's eyes as she gazes into his, brimming at the awareness of her unworthiness for his love, is such a holy moment that you can't help but sigh.

Jesus longs for times like that with us. To drape a quilt around our shoulders. To brush His hand against ours. To gaze into our eyes. And to have us gaze into His. There are words He longs to say to you and to me. And words He longs to hear from us. This is our food and our drink, our daily bread and cup of wine.

It is also His. Our words of love are his daily bread. Our brimming eyes, his cup of wine.

But He longs for more than that. He longs not just to dine but to dance.

He wants us to be more than a companion. He wants us to be His partner.

That is why he moves our chair, and with the offer of His hand, draws us into the divine embrace.[212]

---

[212] Gire, The Divine Embrace, 219-221.

AND HE SHOWED ME A PURE RIVER OF WATER OF LIFE, clear as crystal, proceeding from the throne of God and of the Lamb. In the middle of its street, and on either side of the river, was the tree of life, which bore twelve fruits, each tree yielding its fruit every month. The leaves of the tree were for the healing of the nations. And there shall be no more curse, but the throne of God and of the Lamb shall be in it, and His servants shall serve Him. They shall see His face, and His name shall be on their foreheads. There shall be no night there: They need no lamp nor light of the sun, for the Lord God gives them light. And they shall reign forever and ever.

Then he said to me, "These words are faithful and true." And the Lord God of the holy prophets sent His angel to show His servants the things which must shortly take place.

"Behold, I am coming quickly! Blessed is he who keeps the words of the prophecy of this book."

Now I, John, saw and heard these things. And when I heard and saw, I fell down to worship before the feet of the angel who showed me these things.

Then he said to me, "See that you do not do that. For I am your fellow servant, and of your brethren the prophets, and of those who keep the words of this book. Worship God." And he said to me, "Do not seal the words of the prophecy of this book, for the time is at hand. He who is unjust, let him be unjust still; he who is filthy, let him be filthy still; he who is righteous, let him be righteous still; he who is holy, let him be holy still."

"And behold, I am coming quickly, and My reward is with Me, to give to every one according to his work. I am the Alpha and the Omega, the Beginning and the End, the First and the Last."

Blessed are those who do His commandments, that they may have the right to the tree of life, and may enter through the gates into the city. But outside are dogs and sorcerers and sexually immoral and murderers and idolaters, and whoever loves and practices a lie.

"I, Jesus, have sent My angel to testify to you these things in the churches. I am the Root and the Offspring of David, the Bright and Morning Star."

And the Spirit and the bride say, "Come!" And let him who hears say, "Come!" And let him who thirsts come. Whoever desires, let him take the water of life freely. (Revelations 22: 1-17 NKJV)

SOME DAY MY PRINCE WILL COME, LARRY MOREYS

Once there was a princess
Was the princess you?
And she fell in love
Was it hard to do?
It was very easy
Anyone could see that the prince was charming
The only one for me
Was he strong and handsome?
Was he big and tall?
There's nobody like him
Anywhere at all
Did he say he loved you?
Did he steal a kiss?
He was so romantic
I could not resist
Someday my prince will come
Someday we'll meet again
And away to his castle we'll go
To be happy forever I know
Someday when spring is here
We'll find our love anew
And the birds will sing

And wedding bells will ring
Someday when my dreams come true[213]

I KEPT LOOKING UNTIL THRONES WERE SET UP,
And the Ancient of Days took His seat;
His garment was white as snow,
And the hair of His head like pure wool.
His throne was ablaze with flames,
Its wheels were a burning fire.
A river of fire was flowing
And coming out from before Him;
Thousands upon thousands were serving Him,
And myriads upon myriads were standing before Him;
The court convened,
And the books were opened.
(Daniel 7:9-10 NASB)

THOMAS MOORE
Earth has no sorrow that heaven cannot heal.[214]

O LORD, I WILL HONOR AND PRAISE YOUR NAME,
    for You are my God.
You do such wonderful things!
You planned them long ago,
    and now You have accomplished them.
You turn mighty cities into heaps of ruins.
Cities with strong walls are turned to rubble.

---

[213] Larry Morey (lyricist) and Frank Churchill (music), "Some Day My Prince Will Come," Adriana Caselotti (performer), Walt Disney's Snow White and the Seven Dwarves (1937).

[214] Thomas Moore, Amazing Grace: 366 Inspiring Hymns for Daily Devotions (Grand Rapids: Kregel Publications, 2002), 199.

Beautiful palaces in distant lands disappear
    and will never be rebuilt.
Therefore, strong nations will declare Your glory;
    ruthless nations will fear You.
But You are a tower of refuge to the poor, O Lord,
    a tower of refuge to the needy in distress.
You are a refuge from the storm
    and a shelter from the heat.
For the oppressive acts of ruthless people
    are like a storm beating against a wall,
    or like the relentless heat of the desert.
But You silence the roar of foreign nations.
As the shade of a cloud cools relentless heat,
    so the boastful songs of ruthless people are stilled.
In Jerusalem, the Lord of Heaven's Armies
    will spread a wonderful feast
    for all the people of the world.
It will be a delicious banquet
    with clear, well-aged wine and choice meat.
There He will remove the cloud of gloom,
    the shadow of death that hangs over the earth.
He will swallow up death forever!
The Sovereign Lord will wipe away all tears.
He will remove forever all insults and mockery
    against His land and people.
The Lord has spoken!
In that day the people will proclaim,
    "This is our God!
We trusted in Him, and He saved us!
This is the Lord, in whom we trusted.
Let us rejoice in the salvation He brings!" (Isaiah 25:1-9 NLT)

Chapter 34

FROM HERE TO ETERNITY

"THIS IS HOW MUCH GOD LOVED THE WORLD: He gave His son, His one and only son. And this is why: so that no one need be destroyed; by believing in Him, anyone can have a whole and lasting life. God didn't go to all the trouble of sending His son merely to point an accusing finger, telling the world how bad it was. He came to help, to put the world right again. Anyone who trusts in Him is acquitted; anyone who refuses to trust Him has long since been under the death sentence without knowing it. And why? Because of that person's failure to believe in the one-of-a-kind Son of God when introduced to Him. (John 3:16-18 message)

PATTI BURNETT

I LOVE CHAPTER ONE OF PAUL'S LETTER TO THE PHILIPPIANS.
It is rich in lessons about attitudes of thankfulness and rejoicing. How amazing to get insight into Paul's supernatural ability to graciously accept His status while in prison, recognizing that his "circumstances have turned out for the greater progress of the gospel" (Philippians 1:12 AMP). I so desire to have that same attitude. Unfortunately, when I feel the pain that radiates down my leg, or burns in my entire mouth, or paralyzes my gut, I become consumed by the emotional duress of knowing Dan has all this to deal with – that's when I have difficulty writing in my journal the things for which I'm thankful. Yet, Paul in much worse circumstances said, "For to me, to live is Christ, and to die is gain" (Philippians 1:21 KJV). Paul was "hard-pressed from both directions" – to be with Christ, while at the same time recognizing that God might still have work for Him here on planet earth.

Dan and I were sick after returning from my Dad's Celebration of Life. I went into Summit Medical Center, thinking I might have pneumonia again; my left lung has been a problem child for a while now. As happens before most of my Parkinson's appointments, I was asked questions like "Have you ever thought of harming yourself or trying to take your own life?" I wonder if that's a question for everybody or just people with neurodegenerative diseases.

All my life I've been a risk taker, but I have never thought or attempted anything close to suicide. However, I can say that, like Paul, there are times when I think it would be better to be at home with the Lord. Eternal life is very appealing. Life here on this earth is hard in many ways. Our country, might I say the world, is antagonistic, even hateful, toward Christians, which makes me think the end is near. As we, hopefully, near the conclusion of a pandemic of biblical proportions, one wonders whether this will become the norm. The weather patterns produce unprecedented storm events with increasing death and destruction each coming year. Also, after having just watched my parents go through the end-stages of life, I do not relish the possibility of a hospital bed and cognition issues, especially being a person with Parkinson's.

However, like Paul I can echo that where You want me Lord is where I want to be. "What then? Only that in every way, whether in pretense or in truth, Christ is proclaimed, and in this I rejoice. But not only that, I also will rejoice, for I know that this will turn out for my deliverance through your prayers and the provision of the Spirit of Jesus Christ, according to my eager expectation and hope, that I will not be put to shame in anything, but that with all boldness, Christ will even now, as always, be exalted in my body, whether by life or death" (Philippians 1:18-20 NASB).

> ### SAINT IGNASIUS
> Among the many signs of a lively faith and hope we have in eternal life, one of the surest is not being overly sad at the death of those whom we dearly love in our Lord.[215]

ONCE A RELIGIOUS LEADER ASKED JESUS THIS QUESTION: "Good teacher, what should I do to inherit eternal life?"

"Why do you call me good?" Jesus asked him. "Only God is truly good. But to answer your question, you know the commandments: 'You must not commit adultery. You must not murder. You must not steal. You must not testify falsely. Honor your father and mother.'"

The man replied, "I've obeyed all these commandments since I was young."

When Jesus heard his answer, he said, "There is still one thing you haven't done. Sell all your possessions and give the money to the poor, and you will have treasure in heaven. Then come, follow me."

---

[215] Saint Ignatius. from https://www.allgreatquotes.com/authors/saint-ignatius/

But when the man heard this he became very sad, for he was very rich.

When Jesus saw this, he said, "How hard it is for the rich to enter the Kingdom of God! In fact, it is easier for a camel to go through the eye of a needle than for a rich person to enter the Kingdom of God!"

Those who heard this said, "Then who in the world can be saved?"

He replied, "What is impossible for people is possible with God."

Peter said, "We've left our homes to follow You."

"Yes," Jesus replied, "and I assure you that everyone who has given up house or wife or brothers or parents or children, for the sake of the Kingdom of God, will be repaid many times over in this life, and will have eternal life in the world to come." (Luke 18:18-30 NLT)

> **CORRIE TEN BOOM**
> You know, eternal life does not start when we go to heaven. It starts the moment you reach out to Jesus. He never turns His back on anyone. And He is waiting for you.[216]

NOW THERE WAS A MAN OF THE PHARISEES, named Nicodemus, a ruler of the Jews; this man came to Jesus at night and said to Him, "Rabbi, we know that You have come from God as a teacher; for no one can do these signs that You do unless God is with him." Jesus responded and said to him, "Truly, truly, I say to you, unless someone is born again he cannot see the kingdom of God."

Nicodemus said to Him, "How can a person be born when he is old? He cannot enter his mother's womb a second time and be born, can he?" Jesus answered, "Truly, truly, I say to you, unless someone is born of water and the Spirit, he cannot enter the kingdom of God. That which has been born of the flesh is flesh, and that which has been born of the

---

[216] Corrie ten Boom, from https://quotefancy.com/quote/786990/Corrie-ten-Boom-You-know-eternal-life-does-not-start-when-we-go-to-heaven-It-starts-the

Spirit is spirit. Do not be amazed that I said to you, 'You must be born again.' The wind blows where it wishes, and you hear the sound of it, but you do not know where it is coming from and where it is going; so is everyone who has been born of the Spirit."

Nicodemus responded and said to Him, "How can these things be?" Jesus answered and said to him, "You are the teacher of Israel, and yet you do not understand these things? Truly, truly, I say to you, we speak of what we know and testify of what we have seen, and you people do not accept our testimony. If I told you earthly things and you do not believe, how will you believe if I tell you heavenly things? No one has ascended into heaven, except He who descended from heaven: the Son of Man. And just as Moses lifted up the serpent in the wilderness, so must the Son of Man be lifted up, so that everyone who believes will have eternal life in Him. (John 3:1-15 NASB)

OSWALD CHAMBERS
Eternal life is not a gift from God; eternal life is the gift of God.[217]

SOON ANOTHER FEAST CAME AROUND and Jesus was back in Jerusalem. Near the Sheep Gate in Jerusalem there was a pool, in Hebrew called Bethesda, with five alcoves. Hundreds of sick people—blind, crippled, paralyzed—were in these alcoves. One man had been an invalid there for thirty-eight years. When Jesus saw him stretched out by the pool and knew how long he had been there, he said, "Do you want to get well?"

The sick man said, "Sir, when the water is stirred, I don't have anybody to put me in the pool. By the time I get there, somebody else is already in."

---
[217]Chambers, *My Utmost for His Highest*. April 12.

Jesus said, "Get up, take your bedroll, start walking." The man was healed on the spot. He picked up his bedroll and walked off.

That day happened to be the Sabbath. The Jews stopped the healed man and said, "It's the Sabbath. You can't carry your bedroll around. It's against the rules."

But he told them, "The man who made me well told me to. He said, 'Take your bedroll and start walking.'"

They asked, "Who gave you the order to take it up and start walking?" But the healed man didn't know, for Jesus had slipped away into the crowd.

A little later Jesus found him in the Temple and said, "You look wonderful! You're well! Don't return to a sinning life or something worse might happen."

The man went back and told the Jews that it was Jesus who had made him well. That is why the Jews were out to get Jesus—because He did this kind of thing on the Sabbath.

But Jesus defended Himself. "My Father is working straight through, even on the Sabbath. So am I."

That really set them off. The Jews were now not only out to expose Him; they were out to kill Him. Not only was He breaking the Sabbath, but He was calling God his own Father, putting Himself on a level with God.

So Jesus explained Himself at length. "I'm telling you this straight. The Son can't independently do a thing, only what He sees the Father doing. What the Father does, the Son does. The Father loves the Son and includes Him in everything He is doing.

"But you haven't seen the half of it yet, for in the same way that the Father raises the dead and creates life, so does the Son. The Son gives life to anyone He chooses. Neither He nor the Father shuts anyone out. The Father handed all authority to judge over to the Son so that the Son will be honored equally with the Father. Anyone who dishonors the Son, dishonors the Father, for it was the Father's decision to put the Son in the place of honor.

"It's urgent that you listen carefully to this: Anyone here who believes what I am saying right now and aligns himself with the Father, who has in fact put me in charge, has at this very moment the real, lasting life and is no longer condemned to be an outsider. This person has taken a giant step from the world of the dead to the world of the living.

"It's urgent that you get this right: The time has arrived—I mean right now!—when dead men and women will hear the voice of the Son of God and, hearing, will come alive. Just as the Father has life in Himself, he has conferred on the Son life in Himself. And He has given Him the authority, simply because He is the Son of Man, to decide and carry out matters of Judgment.

"Don't act so surprised at all this. The time is coming when everyone dead and buried will hear His voice. Those who have lived the right way will walk out into a resurrection Life; those who have lived the wrong way, into a resurrection Judgment.

"I can't do a solitary thing on my own: I listen, then I decide. You can trust my decision because I'm not out to get my own way but only to carry out orders. If I were simply speaking on my own account, it would be an empty, self-serving witness. But an independent witness confirms me, the most reliable Witness of all. Furthermore, you all saw and heard John, and he gave expert and reliable testimony about Me, didn't he?

"But My purpose is not to get your vote, and not to appeal to mere human testimony. I'm speaking to you this way so that you will be saved. John was a torch, blazing and bright, and you were glad enough to dance for an hour or so in his bright light. But the witness that really confirms me far exceeds John's witness. It's the work the Father gave Me to complete. These very tasks, as I go about completing them, confirm that the Father, in fact, sent Me. The Father who sent Me, confirmed Me. And you missed it. You never heard His voice, you never saw His appearance. There is nothing left in your memory of His Message because you do not take his Messenger seriously.

"You have your heads in your Bibles constantly because you think you'll find eternal life there. But you miss the forest for the trees. These

Scriptures are all about Me! And here I am, standing right before you, and you aren't willing to receive from Me the life you say you want.

"I'm not interested in crowd approval. And do you know why? Because I know you and your crowds. I know that love, especially God's love, is not on your working agenda. I came with the authority of My Father, and you either dismiss Me or avoid Me. If another came, acting self-important, you would welcome him with open arms. How do you expect to get anywhere with God when you spend all your time jockeying for position with each other, ranking your rivals and ignoring God?

"But don't think I'm going to accuse you before my Father. Moses, in whom you put so much stock, is your accuser. If you believed, really believed, what Moses said, you would believe me. He wrote of me. If you won't take seriously what he wrote, how can I expect you to take seriously what I speak?" (John 5:1-47 Message)

J.I. PACKER
What were we made for? To know God. What aim should we have in life? To know God. What is the eternal life that Jesus gives? To know God. What is the best thing in life? To know God. What in humans gives God most pleasure? Knowledge of Himself.[218]

JESUS ANSWERED THEM AND SAID, "Most assuredly, I say to you, you seek Me, not because you saw the signs, but because you ate of the loaves and were filled. Do not labor for the food which perishes, but for the food which endures to everlasting life, which the Son of Man will give you, because God the Father has set His seal on Him."

---

[218] J.I. Packer, Knowing God (Downers Grove: Intervarsity Press, 2021), 33.

Then they said to Him, "What shall we do, that we may work the works of God?"

Jesus answered and said to them, "This is the work of God, that you believe in Him whom He sent."

Therefore they said to Him, "What sign will You perform then, that we may see it and believe You? What work will You do? Our fathers ate the manna in the desert; as it is written, 'He gave them bread from heaven to eat.' "

Then Jesus said to them, "Most assuredly, I say to you, Moses did not give you the bread from heaven, but My Father gives you the true bread from heaven. For the bread of God is He who comes down from heaven and gives life to the world."

Then they said to Him, "Lord, give us this bread always."

And Jesus said to them, "I am the bread of life. He who comes to Me shall never hunger, and he who believes in Me shall never thirst. But I said to you that you have seen Me and yet do not believe. All that the Father gives Me will come to Me, and the one who comes to Me I will by no means cast out. For I have come down from heaven, not to do My own will, but the will of Him who sent Me. This is the will of the Father who sent Me, that of all He has given Me I should lose nothing, but should raise it up at the last day. And this is the will of Him who sent Me, that everyone who sees the Son and believes in Him may have everlasting life; and I will raise him up at the last day." (John 6:26-40 NKJV)

WHAT SHALL WE SAY, THEN? Shall we go on sinning so that grace may increase? By no means! We are those who have died to sin; how can we live in it any longer? Or don't you know that all of us who were baptized into Christ Jesus were baptized into His death? We were therefore buried with Him through baptism into death in order that, just as Christ was raised from the dead through the glory of the Father, we too may live a new life.

For if we have been united with Him in a death like His, we will certainly also be united with Him in a resurrection like His. For we know that our old self was crucified with Him so that the body ruled by sin might be done away with, that we should no longer be slaves to sin—because anyone who has died has been set free from sin.

Now if we died with Christ, we believe that we will also live with Him. For we know that since Christ was raised from the dead, He cannot die again; death no longer has mastery over Him. The death He died, He died to sin once for all; but the life He lives, He lives to God.

In the same way, count yourselves dead to sin but alive to God in Christ Jesus. Therefore do not let sin reign in your mortal body so that you obey its evil desires. Do not offer any part of yourself to sin as an instrument of wickedness, but rather offer yourselves to God as those who have been brought from death to life; and offer every part of yourself to Him as an instrument of righteousness. For sin shall no longer be your master, because you are not under the law, but under grace.

What then? Shall we sin because we are not under the law but under grace? By no means! Don't you know that when you offer yourselves to someone as obedient slaves, you are slaves of the one you obey—whether you are slaves to sin, which leads to death, or to obedience, which leads to righteousness? But thanks be to God that, though you used to be slaves to sin, you have come to obey from your heart the pattern of teaching that has now claimed your allegiance. You have been set free from sin and have become slaves to righteousness.

I am using an example from everyday life because of your human limitations. Just as you used to offer yourselves as slaves to impurity and to ever-increasing wickedness, so now offer yourselves as slaves to righteousness leading to holiness. When you were slaves to sin, you were free from the control of righteousness. What benefit did you reap at that time from the things you are now ashamed of? Those things result in death! But now that you have been set free from sin and have become slaves of God, the benefit you reap leads to holiness, and the result is eternal life. For the wages of sin is death, but the gift of God is eternal life in Christ Jesus our Lord. (Romans 6:1-23 NIV)

> ### *ADRIAN ROGERS*
> My salvation does not hinge on my emotions. I have an official record. I have the Word of God: "These things have I written unto you that believe on the name of the Son of God, that ye may know that ye have eternal life."[219]

I, PETER, AM AN APOSTLE ON ASSIGNMENT BY JESUS, the Messiah, writing to exiles scattered to the four winds. Not one is missing, not one forgotten. God the Father has His eye on each of you and has determined by the work of the Spirit to keep you obedient through the sacrifice of Jesus. May everything good from God be yours!

What a God we have! And how fortunate we are to have Him, this Father of our Master Jesus! Because Jesus was raised from the dead, we've been given a brand-new life and have everything to live for, including a future in heaven—and the future starts now! God is keeping careful watch over us and the future. The Day is coming when you'll have it all—life healed and whole.

I know how great this makes you feel, even though you have to put up with every kind of aggravation in the meantime. Pure gold put in the fire comes out of it proved pure; genuine faith put through this suffering comes out proved genuine. When Jesus wraps this all up, it's your faith, not your gold, that God will have on display as evidence of His victory.

You never saw Him, yet you love Him. You still don't see Him, yet you trust Him—with laughter and singing. Because you kept on believing, you'll get what you're looking forward to: total salvation.

The prophets who told us this was coming asked a lot of questions about this gift of life God was preparing. The Messiah's Spirit let them in

---

[219] Adrian Rogers, from https://quotefancy.com/quote/1528171/Adrian-Rogers-My-salvation-does-not-hinge-on-my-emotions-I-have-an-official-record-I-have, Amerian Southern Baptist pastor and conservative author, president of the Southern Baptist Convention.

on some of it—that the Messiah would experience suffering, followed by glory. They clamored to know who and when. All they were told was that they were serving you, you who by orders from heaven have now heard for yourselves—through the Holy Spirit—the Message of those prophecies fulfilled. Do you realize how fortunate you are? Angels would have given anything to be in on this!

So roll up your sleeves, put your mind in gear, be totally ready to receive the gift that's coming when Jesus arrives. Don't lazily slip back into those old grooves of evil, doing just what you feel like doing. You didn't know any better then; you do now. As obedient children, let yourselves be pulled into a way of life shaped by God's life, a life energetic and blazing with holiness. God said, "I am holy; you be holy."

You call out to God for help and He helps—He's a good Father that way. But don't forget, He's also a responsible Father, and won't let you get by with sloppy living.

Your life is a journey you must travel with a deep consciousness of God. It cost God plenty to get you out of that dead-end, empty-headed life you grew up in. He paid with Christ's sacred blood, you know. He died like an unblemished, sacrificial lamb. And this was no afterthought. Even though it has only lately—at the end of the ages—become public knowledge, God always knew He was going to do this for you. It's because of this sacrificed Messiah, whom God then raised from the dead and glorified, that you trust God, that you know you have a future in God.

Now that you've cleaned up your lives by following the truth, love one another as if your lives depended on it. Your new life is not like your old life. Your old birth came from mortal sperm; your new birth comes from God's living Word. Just think: a life conceived by God Himself! That's why the prophet said,

> The old life is a grass life,
> its beauty as short-lived as wildflowers;
> Grass dries up, flowers droop,
> God's Word goes on and on forever.

This is the Word that conceived the new life in you. (1 Peter 1:1-25 MSG)

> ### *FRANCIS OF ASSISI*
> O divine Master, grant that I may not so much seek to be consoled as to console; to be understood as to understand; to be loved as to love. For it is in giving that we receive; it is in pardoning that we are pardoned; and it is in dying that we are born to eternal life.[220]

EVERYONE WHO BELIEVES that Jesus is the Christ has become a child of God. And everyone who loves the Father loves His children, too. We know we love God's children if we love God and obey His commandments. Loving God means keeping His commandments, and His commandments are not burdensome. For every child of God defeats this evil world, and we achieve this victory through our faith. And who can win this battle against the world? Only those who believe that Jesus is the Son of God.

And Jesus Christ was revealed as God's Son by His baptism in water and by shedding His blood on the cross—not by water only, but by water and blood. And the Spirit, who is truth, confirms it with His testimony. So we have these three witnesses - the Spirit, the water, and the blood—and all three agree. Since we believe human testimony, surely we can believe the greater testimony that comes from God. And God has testified about His Son. All who believe in the Son of God know in their hearts that this testimony is true. Those who don't believe this are actually calling God a liar because they don't believe what God has testified about His Son.

---

[220]Suzanne Castle and Andra Moran quoting Francis of Assisi, Brim: Creative Overflow in Worship Design (Des Peres: Chalice Press, 2013) 130.

And this is what God has testified: He has given us eternal life, and this life is in His Son. Whoever has the Son has life; whoever does not have God's Son does not have life.

I have written this to you who believe in the name of the Son of God, so that you may know you have eternal life. And we are confident that He hears us whenever we ask for anything that pleases Him. And since we know He hears us when we make our requests, we also know that He will give us what we ask for.

If you see a fellow believer sinning in a way that does not lead to death, you should pray, and God will give that person life. But there is a sin that leads to death, and I am not saying you should pray for those who commit it. All wicked actions are sin, but not every sin leads to death.

We know that God's children do not make a practice of sinning, for God's Son holds them securely, and the evil one cannot touch them. We know that we are children of God and that the world around us is under the control of the evil one.

And we know that the Son of God has come, and He has given us understanding so that we can know the true God. And now we live in fellowship with the true God because we live in fellowship with His Son, Jesus Christ. He is the only true God, and He is eternal life.

Dear children, keep away from anything that might take God's place in your hearts. (I John 5:1-21 NLT)

FREDERICK BUECHNER

In other words to live Eternal Life in the full and final sense is to be with God as Christ is with Him, and with each other as Christ is with us.[221]

---

[221] Frederick Buechner, Beyond Words: Daily Readings in the ABC's of Faith (New York City: HarperCollins Publishers, 2009), 99.

I COUNSEL YOU to buy from me gold that has been heated red hot and refined by fire, so that you may become truly rich and white clothes [representing righteousness] to clothe yourself so that the shame of your nakedness will not be seen; and healing salve to put on your eyes so that you may see. Those whom I [dearly and tenderly] love, I rebuke and discipline [showing them their faults and instructing them]; so be enthusiastic and repent [change your inner self—your old way of thinking, your sinful behavior—seek God's will]. Behold, I stand at the door [of the church] and continually knock. If anyone hears my voice and opens the door, I will come in and eat with him (restore him), and he with Me. He who overcomes [the world through believing that Jesus is the Son of God], I will grant to him [the privilege] to sit beside Me on My throne, as I also overcame and sat down beside My Father on His throne. He who has an ear, let him hear and heed what the Spirit says to the churches.'" (Revelations 3:18-22 AMP)

LEE STROBEL

Believing the right things about Jesus isn't enough. You're not adopted as God's child until you confess and turn away from your wrongdoing and receive the freely offered gift of forgiveness and eternal life that Jesus purchased with His death on the cross. Until you do that, you'll always be on the outside looking in.[222]

"*I KEPT LOOKING IN THE NIGHT VISIONS,*
And behold, with the clouds of heaven
One like a son of man was coming,
And He came up to the Ancient of Days
And was presented before Him.
And to Him was given dominion,
Honor, and a kingdom,
So that all the peoples, nations, and populations of all languages

---

[222]Lee Stroebel, Atheist-turned-Christian, former editor of Chicago Tribune, best-selling author, from https://www. azquotes.com/quote/694730

Might serve Him.
His dominion is an everlasting dominion
Which will not pass away;
And His kingdom is one
Which will not be destroyed. (Daniel 7:13-14 NASB)

JOEL C. ROSENBERG

Lord Jesus, I need You. Thank You for dying on the cross for my sins. Thank You for rising from the dead. I believe You are the Way, the Truth, and the Life. I believe You are the only way to heaven, the only way to the Father. And right now, as an act of the will, by faith, I open the door of my life and receive You as my Savior and Lord. Thank You for forgiving my sins. Thank You for giving me eternal life. Have mercy on me, Lord. Show me Your will. Teach me Your Word. Guide me by Your Holy Spirit. Take the throne of my life, Lord Jesus, and make me the kind of person You want me to be. In Your holy and precious name I pray, amen.[223]

---

[223] Joel C. Rosenberg, Dead Heat (Carol Stream: Tyndale House, 2012), 310.

Chapter 35

I WILL BE THEIR GOD AND THEY WILL BE MY PEOPLE

"THE DAYS ARE COMING," declares the Lord, "When I will make a new covenant with the people of Israel and with the people of Judah.

It will not be like the covenant I made with their ancestors when I took them by the hand to lead them out of Egypt, because they broke my covenant, though I was a husband to them," declares the Lord.

"This is the covenant I will make with the people of Israel after that time," declares the Lord.

"I will put My law in their minds and write it on their hearts. I will be their God, and they will be My people.

No longer will they teach their neighbor, or say to one another, 'Know the Lord,' because they will all know Me, from the least of them to the greatest," declares the Lord.

"For I will forgive their wickedness and will remember their sins no more." (Jeremiah 31:31-34 NIV)

PATTI BURNETT

GROWING UP IN A STRICT, LEGALISTIC CHURCH, my first impressions of becoming a Christian looked a lot like this: God told you all the things you couldn't do. You agreed with what He said, and you were saved. Sound like the Old Testament's Old Covenant?

Today, my understanding of becoming a Christian looks more like this:

- You learn about a God who became a Man.
- This Man loved you and gave His life on a cross in order to pay the penalty for all of the sins you ever did and ever will do.
- Not only did He pay the price; He then came back to life so that you could have a new life. He conquered death.

You might ask, "What do I have to do to activate this New Covenant?" Believe in your heart that Jesus is God and that the sacrifice He made on Calvary's cross He made for you specifically. God actually gives us a new heart and inscribes on that heart the message "Saved by the blood of Jesus. Covered by God's grace."

The new covenant looks like this: God gives everything. All you have to give in return are your ugly sins, surrendered from a repentant heart and a genuine desire to live as His disciple. He no longer remembers your sins; in fact, He separates them from you as far as the east is from the west. He died; and because He lives, you live. It's the great exchange: your sins for His life; and if that isn't enough, He gives you a new heart.

THE GREAT EXCHANGE

NEW COVENANT	OLD COVENANT
• Grace	• Law
• Jesus' death on the cross	• The continuous sacrifice of animals
• A heart of flesh	• A heart of stone
• The gift of salvation	• A continual attempt to obey the law
• Direct access to God	• The ritual of going through the high priest
• A forgiven conscience	• A guilty conscience
• His life	• Your death

With the New Covenant, God's grace is overwhelming, all-consuming, and more than enough.

NOW THIS IS THE MAIN POINT OF THE THINGS WE ARE SAYING: we have such a high priest, who is seated at the right hand of the throne of the Majesty in the heavens, a Minister of the sanctuary and of the true tabernacle which the Lord erected, and not man.

For every high priest is appointed to offer both gifts and sacrifices. Therefore it is necessary that this One also have something to offer. For if He were on earth, He would not be a priest, since there are priests who offer the gifts according to the law; who serve the copy and shadow of the heavenly things, as Moses was divinely instructed when he was about to make the tabernacle. For He said, "See that you make all things according to the pattern shown you on the mountain." But now He has obtained a more excellent ministry, inasmuch as He is also Mediator of a better covenant, which was established on better promises.

For if that first covenant had been faultless, then no place would have been sought for a second. Because finding fault with them, He says: "Behold, the days are coming, says the Lord, when I will make a new covenant with the house of Israel and with the house of Judah—not according to the covenant that I made with their fathers in the day when I took them by the hand to lead them out of the land of Egypt; because they did not continue in My covenant, and I disregarded them, says the Lord. For this is the covenant that I will make with the house of Israel after those days, says the Lord: I will put my laws in their mind and write them on their hearts; and I will be their God, and they shall be my people. None of them shall teach his neighbor, and none his brother, saying, 'Know the **Lord**,' for all shall know Me, from the least of them to the greatest of them. For I will be merciful to their unrighteousness, and their sins and their lawless deeds I will remember no more."

In that He says, "A new covenant," He has made the first obsolete. Now what is becoming obsolete and growing old is ready to vanish away. (Hebrews 8:1-13 NKJV)

> ## JOHN CHISUM
> In the Old Testament, God dealt with His people as a nation … Their relationship was completely external. But in the New Covenant, the presence of God moved out of the temple and into our hearts.[224]

THE OLD SYSTEM UNDER THE LAW OF MOSES WAS ONLY A SHADOW, a dim preview of the good things to come, not the good things themselves. The sacrifices under that system were repeated again and again, year after year, but they were never able to provide perfect cleansing for those who came to worship. If they could have provided

---
[224]John Chisum, songwriter and singer, from https://www.azquotes.com/quote/1178288

perfect cleansing, the sacrifices would have stopped, for the worshipers would have been purified once for all time, and their feelings of guilt would have disappeared.

But instead, those sacrifices actually reminded them of their sins year after year. For it is not possible for the blood of bulls and goats to take away sins. That is why, when Christ came into the world, He said to God,

> "You did not want animal sacrifices or sin offerings.
> But You have given me a body to offer.
> You were not pleased with burnt offerings
> or other offerings for sin.
> Then I said, 'Look, I have come to do Your will, O God—
> as is written about Me in the Scriptures.'"

First, Christ said, "You did not want animal sacrifices or sin offerings or burnt offerings or other offerings for sin, nor were You pleased with them" (though they are required by the law of Moses). Then He said, "Look, I have come to do your will." He cancels the first covenant in order to put the second into effect. For God's will was for us to be made holy by the sacrifice of the body of Jesus Christ, once for all time.

Under the old covenant, the priest stands and ministers before the altar day after day, offering the same sacrifices again and again, which can never take away sins. But our High Priest offered Himself to God as a single sacrifice for sins, good for all time. Then He sat down in the place of honor at God's right hand. There He waits until His enemies are humbled and made a footstool under His feet. For by that one offering He forever made perfect those who are being made holy.

And the Holy Spirit also testifies that this is so. For He says,

> "This is the new covenant I will make
> with My people on that day, says the LORD:
> I will put My laws in their hearts,

and I will write them on their minds."
Then He says,
"I will never again remember
their sins and lawless deeds."

And when sins have been forgiven, there is no need to offer any more sacrifices.

And so, dear brothers and sisters, we can boldly enter heaven's Most Holy Place because of the blood of Jesus. By His death, Jesus opened a new and life-giving way through the curtain into the Most Holy Place. And since we have a great High Priest who rules over God's house, let us go right into the presence of God with sincere hearts fully trusting Him. For our guilty consciences have been sprinkled with Christ's blood to make us clean, and our bodies have been washed with pure water.

Let us hold tightly without wavering to the hope we affirm, for God can be trusted to keep His promise. Let us think of ways to motivate one another to acts of love and good works. And let us not neglect our meeting together, as some people do, but encourage one another, especially now that the day of His return is drawing near.

Dear friends, if we deliberately continue sinning after we have received knowledge of the truth, there is no longer any sacrifice that will cover these sins. There is only the terrible expectation of God's judgment and the raging fire that will consume His enemies. For anyone who refused to obey the law of Moses was put to death without mercy on the testimony of two or three witnesses. Just think how much worse the punishment will be for those who have trampled on the Son of God, and have treated the blood of the covenant, which made us holy, as if it were common and unholy, and have insulted and disdained the Holy Spirit who brings God's mercy to us. For we know the One who said,

"I will take revenge.
I will pay them back."

He also said,

> "The LORD will judge His own people. It is a terrible thing to fall into the hands of the living God.

Think back on those early days when you first learned about Christ. Remember how you remained faithful even though it meant terrible suffering. Sometimes you were exposed to public ridicule and were beaten, and sometimes you helped others who were suffering the same things. You suffered along with those who were thrown into jail, and when all you owned was taken from you, you accepted it with joy. You knew there were better things waiting for you that will last forever.

So do not throw away this confident trust in the Lord. Remember the great reward it brings you! Patient endurance is what you need now, so that you will continue to do God's will. Then you will receive all that He has promised.

> "For in just a little while,
> the Coming One will come and not delay.
> And my righteous ones will live by faith.
> But I will take no pleasure in anyone who turns away."

But we are not like those who turn away from God to their own destruction. We are the faithful ones, whose souls will be saved. (Hebrews 10:1-39 NLT)

CHARLES SPURGEON

Because God is the living God, He can hear; because He is a loving God, He will hear; because He is our covenant God, He has bound Himself to hear.[225]

---

[225] Charles Spurgeon, The Promises of God: A New Edition of the Classic Devotional (Wheaton: Crossway, 2019), 31.

SURROUNDED THEN AS WE ARE BY THESE SERRIED RANKS OF WITNESSES, let us strip off everything that hinders us, as well as the sin which dogs our feet, and let us run the race that we have to run with patience, our eyes fixed on Jesus the source and the goal of our faith. For He Himself endured a cross and thought nothing of its shame because of the joy He knew would follow His suffering; and He is now seated at the right hand of God's throne. Think constantly of Him enduring all that sinful men could say against Him and you will not lose your purpose or your courage.

After all, your fight against sin has not yet meant the shedding of blood, and you have perhaps lost sight of that piece of advice which reminds you of our sonship in God: 'My son, do not despise the chastening of the Lord, nor be discouraged when you are rebuked by Him; for whom the Lord loves He chastens, and scourges every son whom He receives'.

Bear what you have to bear as "chastening"—as God's dealing with you as sons. No true son ever grows up uncorrected by his father. For if you had no experience of the correction which all sons have to bear you might well doubt the legitimacy of your sonship. After all, when we were children we had fathers who corrected us, and we respected them for it. Can we not much more readily submit to a heavenly Father's discipline, and learn how to live?

For our fathers used to correct us according to their own ideas during the brief days of childhood. But God corrects us all our days for our own benefit, to teach us His holiness. Now obviously no "chastening" seems pleasant at the time: it is in fact most unpleasant. Yet when it is all over we can see that it has quietly produced the fruit of real goodness in the characters of those who have accepted it in the right spirit. So take a fresh grip on life and brace your trembling limbs. Don't wander away from the path but forge steadily onward. On the right path the limping foot recovers strength and does not collapse.

Let it be your ambition to live at peace with all men and to achieve holiness "without which no man shall see the Lord". Be careful that none of you fails to respond to the grace which God gives, for if he does there can very easily spring up in him a bitter spirit which is not only bad in itself but can also poison the lives of many others. Be careful too, that none of you falls into impurity or loses his reverence for the things of God and then, like Esau, is ready to sell his birthright to satisfy the momentary hunger of his body. Remember how afterwards, when he wanted to have the blessing which was his birthright, he was refused. He never afterwards found the way of repentance though he sought it desperately and with tears.

You have not had to approach things which your senses could experience as they did in the old days—flaming fire, black darkness, rushing wind and out of it a trumpet-blast, a voice speaking human words. So terrible was that voice that those who heard it begged and prayed that it might stop speaking, for what it had already commanded was more than they could bear—'And if so much as a beast touches the mountain, it shall be stoned or thrust through with an arrow'. So fearful was the spectacle that Moses cried out, 'I am exceedingly afraid and trembling'.

No, you have been allowed to approach the true Mount Zion, the city of the living God, the heavenly Jerusalem. You have drawn near to the countless angelic army, the great assembly of Heaven and the Church of the first-born whose names are written above. You have drawn near to God, the judge of all, to the souls of good men made perfect, and to Jesus, mediator of a new agreement, to the cleansing of blood which tells a better story than the age-old sacrifice of Abel.

So be sure you do not refuse to hear the voice of God! For if they who refused to hear those who spoke to them on earth did not escape, how little chance of escape is there for us if we refuse to hear the one who speaks from Heaven. Then His voice shook the earth, but now He promises: 'Yet once more I shake not only the earth, but also heaven'.

This means that in this final "shaking" all that is impermanent will be removed, that is, everything that is merely "made", and only the unshakeable things will remain. Since then we have been given a kingdom that is "unshakeable", let us serve God with thankfulness in the ways which please Him, but always with reverence and holy fear. For it is perfectly true that our 'God is a burning fire'. (Hebrews 12:1-29 PHILLIPS)

> **CHARLES SPURGEON**
> Settle this in your heart. Whether I am up or down, the Lord Jesus is the same. Whether I sing or sigh, the promise is true and the Promiser is faithful. Whether I stand on the summit or am hidden in the vale, the covenant stands fast and everlasting love abides.[226]

"COME, EVERYONE WHO THIRSTS,
    come to the waters;
and he who has no money,
    come, buy and eat!
Come, buy wine and milk
    without money and without price.
Why do you spend your money for that which is not bread,
    and your labor for that which does not satisfy?
Listen diligently to Me, and eat what is good,
    and delight yourselves in rich food.
Incline your ear, and come to Me;
    Hear, that your soul may live;
And I will make with you an everlasting covenant,
    My steadfast, sure love for David.
Behold, I made him a witness to the peoples,
    a leader and commander for the peoples.
Behold, you shall call a nation that you do not know,

---

[226]Charles Spurgeon, The Best Strengthening Medicine: Metropolitan Tabernacle Pulpit Volume 37, The Spurgeon Center, June 21, 2019, https://www.spurgeon.org/resource-library/sermons/the-best-strengthening-medicine/#flipbook/.

and a nation that did not know you shall run to you,
because of the L ORD your God, and of the Holy One of Israel,
    for He has glorified you.

"Seek the Lord while He may be found;
    Call upon Him while he is near;
Let the wicked forsake his way,
    And the unrighteous man his thoughts;
Let him return to the Lord, that He may have compassion on him,
    And to our God, for He will abundantly pardon.
For My thoughts are not your thoughts,
    Neither are your ways my ways, declares the **Lord**.
For as the heavens are higher than the earth,
    So are My ways higher than your ways
And My thoughts than your thoughts.

"For as the rain and the snow come down from heaven
    And do not return there but water the earth,
Making it bring forth and sprout,
    Giving seed to the sower and bread to the eater,
So shall My word be that goes out from My mouth;
    It shall not return to Me empty,
But it shall accomplish that which I purpose,
    And shall succeed in the thing for which I sent it.
"For you shall go out in joy
    And be led forth in peace;
The mountains and the hills before you
    Shall break forth into singing,
And all the trees of the field shall clap their hands.
Instead of the thorn shall come up the cypress;
    instead of the brier shall come up the myrtle;
and it shall make a name for the L ORD,
    an everlasting sign that shall not be cut off. (Isaiah
    55:1-13 ESV)

> ### KAY ARTHUR
> So many times we say that we can't serve God because we aren't whatever is needed. We're not talented enough or smart enough or whatever. But if you are in covenant with Jesus Christ, He is responsible for covering your weaknesses, for being your strength. He will give you His abilities for your disabilities.[227]

YES, TRUTH IS GONE,
    and anyone who renounces evil is attacked.
The Lord looked and was displeased
    to find there was no justice.
He was amazed to see that no one intervened to help
    the oppressed.
So He Himself stepped in to save them with
    His strong arm,
    and His justice sustained Him.
He put on righteousness as
    His body armor
    and placed the helmet of salvation on His head.
He clothed Himself with a robe of vengeance
    and wrapped Himself in a cloak of divine passion.
He will repay His enemies for their evil deeds.
His fury will fall on His foes.
He will pay them back even to the ends of the earth.
In the west, people will respect the name of the Lord;
    in the east, they will glorify Him.
For He will come like a raging flood tide
    driven by the breath of the Lord.
"The Redeemer will come to Jerusalem
    to buy back those in Israel
    who have turned from their sins,"
    says the Lord.

---

[227] Kay Arthur, Beloved: From God's Heart to Yours: A Daily Devotional (Eugene: Harvest House Publishing, 1994), 6.

"And this is My covenant with them," says the LORD. "My Spirit will not leave them, and neither will these words I have given you. They will be on your lips and on the lips of your children and your children's children forever. I, the LORD, have spoken! (Isaiah 59:15-21 NLT)

> ### JOHN ELDREDGE
> Most Christians are still living with an Old Testament view of their heart. Jeremiah 17:9 says, "My heart is deceitfully wicked." No, it's not. Not after the work of Christ, because the promise of the new covenant is a new heart.[228]

---

[228] Dick Staub and John Eldredge, Wild at Heart, Christianity Today, The Dick Staub Interview, November 1, 2003, https://www.christianitytoday.com/ct/2003/novemberweb-only/11-10-21.0.html.

Chapter 36

OUR GOD IS AN AWESOME GOD

REJOICE AND SHOUT FOR JOY, you inhabitant of Zion, for great in your midst is the Holy One of Israel. (Isaiah 12:6 NASB)

PATTI BURNETT

NO PERSON WILL EVER BE ABLE to fully comprehend the greatness of our God, at least not while we are here on this earth. Consider the act of making a dry path through the Red Sea to aid the Israelites' escape from the Egyptians. Then ponder the collapse of this channel, drowning all of Pharoah's army.

Humans are constantly trying to discount God's greatness. Dr. Bruce Parker, former chief scientist of the National Oceanic and Atmospheric Administration's National Ocean Service, believes that Moses understood the moon and tides so that he could schedule their crossing of the Red Sea during low tide. Consequently, as high tide rushed in, the Egyptians were drowned. However, this explanation has been debunked because the waters only drawback for up to 20 minutes, hardly enough time for the Children of Israel to pass through.

Others would argue that a tsunami caused the seas to part.

But my favorite explanation comes from the story of a little boy who had been sent to Sunday School. His parents asked him what he had learned. He told them that God had sent Moses as a General to deliver the Israelites from Egypt. He organized the people into an army that was led up to the edge of the Red Sea. Moses then had them build a pontoon bridge over the Sea. After the Israelites crossed over on the bridge, the Egyptians tried to follow them, but the Israelites exploded the bridge when the Egyptian army was in the middle of it, and they all drowned. The parents were a bit shocked until the little boy explained that the teacher had told the story differently, but the boy said that if he told them the story the way the teacher told it they'd never believe it.

In the same way people try to explain away God, but God's rebuke is quite poignant. Read what He told Job:

"And now, finally, God answered Job from the eye of a violent storm. He said:

'Why do you confuse the issue?
    Why do you talk without knowing what you're talking about?
Pull yourself together, Job!
    Up on your feet! Stand tall!
I have some questions for you,
    and I want some straight answers.
Where were you when I created the earth?
    Tell me, since you know so much!
Who decided on its size? Certainly you'll know that!
    Who came up with the blueprints and measurements?
How was its foundation poured,
    and who set the cornerstone,
While the morning stars sang in chorus
    and all the angels shouted praise?
And who took charge of the ocean
    when it gushed forth like a baby from the womb?
That was me! I wrapped it in soft clouds,
    and tucked it in safely at night.
Then I made a playpen for it,
    a strong playpen so it couldn't run loose,
And said, 'Stay here, this is your place.
    Your wild tantrums are confined to this place.'
"And have you ever ordered Morning, 'Get up!'
    told Dawn, 'Get to work!'
So you could seize Earth like a blanket
    and shake out the wicked like cockroaches?
As the sun brings everything to light,
    brings out all the colors and shapes,
The cover of darkness is snatched from the wicked—
    they're caught in the very act!

CHRONIC HOPE

"Have you ever gotten to the true bottom of things,
    explored the labyrinthine caves of deep ocean?
Do you know the first thing about death?
    Do you have one clue regarding death's dark mysteries?
And do you have any idea how large this earth is?
    Speak up if you have even the beginning of an answer.

"Do you know where Light comes from
    and where Darkness lives
So you can take them by the hand
    and lead them home when they get lost?
Why, of course you know that.
You've known them all your life,
    grown up in the same neighborhood with them!

"Have you ever traveled to where snow is made,
    Seen the vault where hail is stockpiled,
    The arsenals of hail and snow that I keep in readiness
    For times of trouble and battle and war?
Can you find your way to where lightning is launched,
    or to the place from which the wind blows?
Who do you suppose carves canyons
    for the downpours of rain, and charts
    the route of thunderstorms
That bring water to unvisited fields,
    deserts no one ever lays eyes on,
Drenching the useless wastelands
    so they're carpeted with wildflowers and grass?
And who do you think is the father of rain and dew,
    the mother of ice and frost?
You don't for a minute imagine
    these marvels of weather just happen, do you?

"Can you catch the eye of the beautiful Pleiades sisters,
    or distract Orion from his hunt?
Can you get Venus to look your way,
    or get the Great Bear and her cubs to come out and play?
Do you know the first thing about the sky's constellations
    and how they affect things on Earth?

"Can you get the attention of the clouds,
    and commission a shower of rain?
Can you take charge of the lightning bolts
    And have them report to you for orders?

"Who do you think gave weather-wisdom to the ibis,
    and storm-savvy to the rooster?
Does anyone know enough to number all the clouds
    or tip over the rain barrels of heaven
When the earth is cracked and dry,
    the ground baked hard as a brick?

"Can you teach the lioness to stalk her prey
    and satisfy the appetite of her cubs
As they crouch in their den,
    waiting hungrily in their cave?
And who sets out food for the ravens
    when their young cry to God,
        fluttering about because they have no food?" (Job 38:1-51 MSG)

This is the God who knows my name. Who saw me in my mother's womb? He's the One who knows my heart and He alone is worthy of my praise.

> ### ROY LESSIN
> God is bigger than time, dates, and appointments. He wants you to move through this day with a quiet heart, an inward assurance that He is in control, a peaceful certainty that your life is in His hands, a deep trust in His plan and purposes, and a thankful disposition, toward all that He allows. He wants you to put your faith in Him, not in a timetable. He wants you to wait on Him and wait for Him. In His perfect way He will put everything together, see to every detail… arrange every circumstance… and order every step to bring to pass what He has for you.[229]

OH, THE DEPTH OF THE RICHES both of the wisdom and knowledge of God! How unsearchable are His judgments and unfathomable His ways! For who has known the mind of the Lord, or who became His counselor? Or who has first given to Him that it might be paid back to him again? For from Him and through Him and to Him are all things. To Him be the glory forever. Amen. (Romans 11:33-36 NASB)

RICK WARREN
If you give it to God, He transforms your test into a testimony, your mess into a message, and your misery into a ministry.[230]

"LISTEN, YOU HEAVENS, AND I WILL SPEAK;
And let the earth hear the words of my mouth!
May my teaching drip as the rain,
My speech trickle as the dew,

---

[229] Roy Lessin, from https://www.azquotes.com/quote/1200856, Co-founded DaySpring Cards in 1971, author and minister.

[230] Rick Warren, from https://www.quotemaster.org/qa40149a6e273eb60bc09799917 4815f8.

As droplets on the fresh grass,
And as the showers on the vegetation.

For I proclaim the name of the Lord;
Ascribe greatness to our God!
The rock! His work is perfect,
For all His ways are just;
A God of faithfulness and without injustice,
Righteous and just is He. (Deuteronomy 32:1-4 NASB)

> **OUT OF THE SALTSHAKER, BECKY PIPPERT**
> For Jesus, greatness was seen not in the degree to which He was elevated, but the degree to which He came down and identified.[231]

HONOR THE LORD, YOU HEAVENLY BEINGS;
    honor the LORD for
His glory and strength.
Honor the LORD for the glory of His name.
Worship the LORD in the splendor of His holiness.
The voice of the LORD echoes above the sea.
The God of glory thunders.
The LORD thunders over the mighty sea.
The voice of the LORD is powerful;
the voice of the LORD is majestic.
The voice of the LORD splits the mighty cedars;
    the LORD shatters the cedars of Lebanon.
He makes Lebanon's mountains skip like a calf;
He makes Mount Hermon leap like a young wild ox.
The voice of the LORD strikes
    with bolts of lightning.

---
[231] Pippert, Out of the Saltshaker, 31.

The voice of the LORD makes the barren wilderness quake;
    the LORD shakes the wilderness of Kadesh.
The voice of the LORD twists mighty oaks
    and strips the forests bare.
In His Temple everyone shouts, "Glory!"
The Lord rules over the floodwaters.
The Lord reigns as king forever.
The Lord gives His people strength.
The Lord blesses them with peace. (Psalm 29:1-11 NLT)

> **CORRIE TEN BOOM**
> Never be afraid to trust an unknown future to a known God.[232]

WHOM HAVE I IN HEAVEN BUT YOU?
And besides You, I desire nothing on earth.
My flesh and my heart may fail,
But God is the strength of my heart and My portion forever.
For, behold, those who are far from You will perish;
You have destroyed all those who are unfaithful to You.
But as for me, the nearness of God is my good;
I have made the Lord God my refuge,
That I may tell of all Your works. (Psalm 73:25-28 NASB)

A.W. TOZER
The goodness of God is infinitely more wonderful than
we will ever be able to comprehend.[233]

---

[232] Carole A. Wageman quoting Corrie ten Boom, The Light Shines Through: Our Stories are God's Story (New York: Church Publishing, Inc., 2017), 116.

[233] Tozer, The Pursuit of God, 44.

JEHOVAH IS KING! HE IS ROBED IN MAJESTY AND STRENGTH. THE WORLD IS HIS THRONE.
O Lord, You have reigned from prehistoric times, from the everlasting past. The mighty oceans thunder Your praise. You are mightier than all the breakers pounding on the seashores of the world! Your royal decrees cannot be changed. Holiness is forever the keynote of Your reign. (Psalm 93:1-5 TLB)

A.W. TOZER
God is looking for those with whom He can do the impossible – what a pity that we plan only the things that we can do by ourselves.[234]

I KNOW THAT THE LORD WILL MAINTAIN THE CAUSE OF THE AFFLICTED,
And justice for the poor.
Certainly the righteous will give thanks to Your name;
The upright will dwell in Your presence. (Psalm 140:12-13 NASB)

MAX LUCADO

God is able to place stars in their sockets and suspend the sky like a curtain; surely He is mighty enough to light your path.[235]

"COMFORT, O COMFORT MY PEOPLE," SAYS YOUR GOD.
"Speak tenderly to Jerusalem,
And call out to her, that her time of compulsory service in warfare is finished,

---

[234] John Maxwell quoting A.W. Tozer, The 21 Most Powerful Minutes in a Leader's Day (Nashville: Thomas Nelson, 2007), 27.

[235] Max Lucado, from https://www.azquotes.com/quote/1400532.

That her wickedness has been taken away [since
    her punishment is sufficient],
That she has received from the Lord's hand
    Double [punishment] for all her sins."

A voice of one is calling out,
    "Clear the way for the **Lord** in the wilderness [remove
    the obstacles];
Make straight and smooth in the desert a highway for our God.
    "Every valley shall be raised,
And every mountain and hill be made low;
    And let the rough ground become a plain,
And the rugged places a broad valley.
    "And the glory and majesty and splendor of the Lord will
    be revealed,
And all humanity shall see it together;
    For the mouth of the Lord has spoken it."
A voice says, "Call out [prophesy]."
    Then he answered, "What shall I call out?"
[The voice answered:] All humanity is [as frail as] grass,
    and all that makes it attractive [its charm,
    its loveliness] is [momentary] like the flower of the field.
The grass withers, the flower fades,
    When the breath of the **Lord** blows upon it;
Most certainly [all] the people are [like] grass.
    The grass withers, the flower fades,
But the word of our God stands forever.
    O Zion, herald of good news,
Get up on a high mountain.
    O Jerusalem, herald of good news,
Lift up your voice with strength,
    Lift it up, do not fear;
Say to the cities of Judah,

"Here is your God!"
Listen carefully, the Lord G<small>OD</small> will come with might,
    And His arm will rule for Him.
Most certainly His reward is with Him,
    And His restitution accompanies Him.
He will protect His flock like a shepherd.
    He will gather the lambs in His arm,
He will carry them in His bosom;
    He will gently and carefully lead those nursing their young.
(Isaiah 40:1-11 AMP)

TONY EVANS
Sometimes God lets you be in a situation that only He can fix so that you can see that He is the One who fixes it. Rest. He's got it.[236]

---

[236]Tony Evans, from https://quotefancy.com/quote/1724194/Tony-Evans-Sometimes-God-lets-you-be-in-a-situation-that-only-He-can-fix-so-that-you-can

Epilogue

AS I WROTE this final chapter of CHRONIC HOPE, the last few days had been especially tough, and my resilience was pretty much exhausted. It is thought that Burning Mouth Syndrome (BMS) affects about 1% of the population; but the medical community is stumped as to its cause and treatment. One of my theories was that it was a result of my hiatal hernia and acid backing up from my stomach through the esophagus and into my mouth. Symptoms usually include a burning or scalding feeling and a bitter or metallic taste. My swollen gums get stuck on my teeth which then cause me to continually lick my lips. Because of the accumulation of phlegm and saliva in my throat, my speech is often slurred and my throat irritated; I sound drunk. There is a deep, productive cough that is spasmodic in nature and very difficult to stop. BMS appears to be with me almost nonstop during my waking hours and there is usually some relief while I sleep.

BMS' inopportune timing is not especially helpful. The symptoms also tend to worsen over the course of the day. One blessing is that eating and sometimes drinking tend to alleviate the pain.

The cause could be a vitamin and mineral deficiency. Most people who have BMS also have gastrointestinal issues, which explains why a disproportionate number of people with Parkinson's have it, according to the research.

I had recently memorized 2 Timothy 2:20-21 (NIV). "In a large house there are articles not only of gold and silver, but also of wood and clay; some are for special purposes and some for common use. Those who cleanse themselves from the latter will be instruments for special purposes, made holy, useful to the Master and prepared to do any good work." I pray that God will cleanse me so I can be a moldable, useful golden vessel that has gone through the purifying fire and is ready to be used by the Potter.

I often wonder where I would be today had I not gone through all the pain, disappointments, and doubts of the last ten years. I believe that our God is able to do anything – nothing is too difficult or impossible for Him.

Healed of Parkinson's I could still be patrolling. I could still be running marathons. I could still be leading women's Bible studies. I could still be training and handling search and rescue dogs. Being the over-achiever that I am, the list goes on and on and on. But ... maybe it was the Father's plan that I not be so obsessed with completely filling my schedule, trying to please all of the people all of the time, pretending to be Wonder Woman. I would not have been able to spend as much time with Jaxson, Noah, Maverick, and Emerson Hope if God had not put a hitch in my giddy up. I love that we live within minutes of our daughters' families, and I think it has a lot to do with our availability to the grandkids. Would I be able to mentor women who are newly diagnosed with Parkinson's if I were traveling all over the world skiing Haute Routes and teaching avalanche dog schools?

Nothing that has happened to my body and mind over the last few years surprises the Lord God. In fact, there's little doubt that each pothole was especially placed in my path for a specific purpose. God has shown me that, left to my own devices, I can be an inordinately self-centered and egotistical woman. God had to slow me down and show me that He had a higher calling for my life.

Jesus came for one purpose: to die. His death has drawn millions to our Father God. He alone can take on that responsibility since He is the only perfect sacrifice who can meet the requirements of a Righteous God. There are people out there who God has been preparing to meet you. But it's probably not the proud you; He probably made the appointment with the humble you.

Epilogue

We can kick against the spurs and handicap the Lord's purpose in our lives, or we can get on board and see Him work miracles. Through you? Definitely! Even through me!

Oh, I forgot to mention. I just had my first of the three Deep Brain Stimulation surgeries. It's quite lovely. They place you in a head frame that makes a person look like the Bride of Frankenstein. Realize that you are most likely conscious all of the time. Then they drill a nickel-sized hole through your skull on one side to implant electrodes and electrical stimulation to control abnormal brain activity. A week later they will drill a hole on the other side of my skull. A week later another surgery involves implanting a pacemaker-like device under the skin in my upper chest. After some computer programming this should control the amount of stimulation that goes to various locations in my brain. The success rate for this procedure is pretty high but of course there are risks. Thanks for your prayers.

There is **CHRONIC HOPE: God's Redeeming Presence in the Midst of Pain** for you and for me.

THE POTTER'S HAND, DARLENE ZSCHECH

Beautiful Lord, wonderful Savior
I know for sure all of my days are held in Your hand
And crafted into Your perfect plan
You gently called me into Your presence
Guiding me by Your Holy Spirit
Teach me dear Lord, to live all of my life
Through Your eyes
And I'm captured by Your Holy calling
Set me apart, I know You're drawing me to Yourself
Lead me Lord, I pray
Take me and mold me, use me, fill me
I give my life to the Potter's hand
Call me, You guide me, lead me, walk beside me
I give my life to the Potter's hand
You gently call me into Your presence
Guiding me by Your Holy Spirit
Teach me dear Lord, to live all of my life
Through Your eyes
I'm captured by Your Holy calling
Set me apart, I know You're drawing me to Yourself
Lead me Lord, I pray[237]

---

[237]Hillsong Worship, The Potter's Hand, Darlene Joyce Zschech (composer and performer), 1998.